Marquis Los Cabos Beach Resort & Spa, Baja California Sur, Mexico – p45

Welcome to the 2009 edition
Guide to The Americas, Caribbean, Atlantic & Pacific.

Each year we are able to bring you a more diverse and comprehensive portfolio of places to stay thanks to the concerted effort of our experienced inspection team.

We pride ourselves on understanding the vacation expectations of our discerning readership and in anticipating your needs, not only for relaxation, but for adventure too!

Whether you are looking for a peaceful ocean front resort, a sophisticated city hotel, a luxury inn, spa, remote eco lodge or even a catered private villa, we have found the place for you!

Few guides offer such a rich geographic diversity or the extent of accommodation options which makes your search for that extra special vacation easier and more rewarding.

Our Guide is designed to help you make the right choice and to lead you to our website www.johansens.com. Here you can "check availability" and communicate directly with the hotels of your choice. This edition includes many of our longtime favorites as well as more than 80 new hotels in exciting destinations from Ecuador to Nova Scotia!

Our portfolio comprises 6 published Guides, featuring more than 1,100 annually inspected and recommended hotels, resorts, inns, spas and venues across more than 60 countries. See them all at www.johansens.com. Each hotel entry page invites you to 'Tell us about you stay' so we look forward to your comments when you return from your vacation!

Wishing you safe and rewarding travels in 2009!

Andrew Warren
Managing Director

Hudson Bay
Labrador Sea
Canada p13
Atlantic Ocean
United States p70
Bermuda p354
Mexico p43
The Bahamas p352
Turks & Caicos p409
Cuba
Jamaica p386
Haiti
Dominican Republic p378
Belize p270
Puerto Rico p390
Guatemala p283
Honduras P287
Curaçao p376
El Salvador
Nicaragua
Costa Rica p275
Panama
Venezuela
Guyana
French Guiana
Surinam
Colombia
Pacific Ocean
Ecuador p342
Peru p348
Brazil p302
Bolivia
Paraguay
Chile p334
Argentina p291
Uruguay p350
Atlantic Ocean
Pacific Ocean
Fiji Islands p417
British Virgin Islands p372
Anguilla p358
St. Martin p404
US Virgin Islands
Saint-Barthélemy p393
St Kitts & Nevis p396
Antigua & Barbuda p361
Montserrat
Guadeloupe
Dominica
Caribbean Sea
Martinique
Saint Lucia p398
Saint Vincent & The Grenadines p406
Barbados p368
Grenada p384

Hotel Healdsburg, California, U.S.A. – p90

Contents

Las Ventanas al Paraíso, A Rosewood Resort, Baja California Sur, Mexico – p48

Making a Reservation

Making a Reservation at one of our Recommended Properties.

Selecting a Property by Location:

- Using the map at the front of the Guide, identify the country you wish to visit.
- Turn to the relevant page and search alphabetically by state or region and then by property.
- Or, turn to the map at the beginning of each section and locate a property by location, where it is marked by the corresponding page number.

You may also find a property by name or name of a town/village in the indexes, starting on page 454.

Once you have chosen a property, visit **johansens.com** where you will be able to check availability and in many cases make an instant reservation! You may also call or email our hotels directly using the contact information on each page. The prices listed should only be used as a guide, exact prices should be confirmed with the property once the dates for travel have been selected. Please note: most rates are listed as "room" rates, not "per person" rates and include taxes, some are all-inclusive and may be subject to state taxes. **Whichever way you make your reservation, please mention Condé Nast Johansens as your source of reference.**

Readers should be aware that when making a reservation at a property they are entering into a legal contract. A hotelier, under certain circumstances, is entitled to make a charge when guests fail to arrive, even if notice of the cancellation is given. Please be aware of this when making hotel reservations.

All Guides are available from bookstores or by calling Freephone Toll Free 1 800 564 7518 (U.S.) or 0800 269379 (U.K.)

Key to Symbols

- 23 Total number of rooms
- Quiet location
- Access for wheelchairs to at least 1 bedroom and public rooms
- 24-hour room service
- M 23 Meeting/conference facilities with maximum number of delegates
- 8 Children welcome, with minimum age where applicable
- Dogs accommodated in rooms or kennels
- Fireplaces in rooms
- Cable/satellite TV in all bedrooms
- DVD DVD player in all bedrooms
- CD player in all bedrooms
- ISDN/modem point in all bedrooms
- WiFi Wireless Internet connection available in part or all rooms
- At least 1 non-smoking bedroom
- Air conditioning
- Elevator available for guests' use
- Jacuzzi/whirlpool
- Gym/fitness facilties on-site
- SPA A dedicated spa offering extensive health and beauty treatments
- Indoor swimming pool
- Outdoor swimming pool
- Tennis court on-site
- Fishing on-site
- Fishing can be arranged
- Golf course on-site
- Golf course nearby
- Horse riding can be arranged
- Scuba diving on-site managed/owned by the property
- Scuba diving nearby (no direct association with property)
- Water sports on site, 2 or more water sports managed/owned by the property e.g. sailing/boarding/jet-skiing
- Water sport activities nearby – 2 or more water sports can take place nearby (no direct association with the property)
- Located in a ski resort
- Skiing nearby
- H Property has a helicopter landing pad
- Licensed for wedding ceremonies
- NR HP National Register of Historic Places

Post Ranch Inn, California, U.S.A. – p81

/italie Taittinger, who works for the family Champagne house

Blue Waters, Antigua – p365

Condé Nast Johansens

Condé Nast Johansens Ltd, 6-8 Old Bond Street, London W1S 4PH, U.K.
Tel: +44 207 499 9080 Fax: +44 207 152 3565
E-mail: info@johansens.com
www.johansens.com

Vice President & Publishing Director:	Lesley J. O'Malley-Keyes
Assistants to Publishing Director:	Jennifer Power
	Hannah Shimko
Hotel Inspectors:	Terri Bisignano
	Brooke Burns
	Felipe Candiota
	Mollie Christenson
	Griselda Contreras
	Tiffany Dowd
	Ana Lucia Fernandez
	Dana Halliday
	Kass Hanson
	Susan Hendrickson Henry
	Michael Kelly
	Kerry Kerr
	Nancy McLachlan
	Renata Medeiros
	Cheryl Murphy
	Christiane Potts
	Roberto Prata
	Pablo Pries
	Joanne Priestly
	Arianna Rossell
	Freda Rothermel
Production Manager:	Kevin Bradbrook
Production Editor:	Laura Kerry
Senior Designer:	Michael Tompsett
Copywriters:	Tiffany Dowd
	Hannah Shimko
Client Services Director:	Fiona Patrick
PA to Managing Director:	Lucy Mankaryous
Managing Director:	Andrew Warren

Whilst every care has been taken in the compilation of this Guide, the publishers cannot accept responsibility for any inaccuracies or for changes since going to press, or for consequential loss arising from such changes or other inaccuracies, or for any other loss direct or consequential arising in connection with information describing establishments in this publication.

Recommended establishments, if accepted for inclusion by our Inspectors, pay an annual subscription to cover the costs of inspection, the distribution and production of copies placed in hotel bedrooms and other services.

The publishers request readers not to cut, tear or otherwise mark this Guide except Guest Survey Reports and Order Forms. No other cuttings may be taken without the written permission of the publishers.

Condé Nast Johansens Ltd. is part of The Condé Nast Publications Ltd.
ISBN 978-1-903665-42-8
Printed in England by St. Ives plc
Distributed in the U.K. and Europe by Portfolio, Brentford (bookstores).
In North America by Casemate Publishing, Pennsylvania (bookstores).

Awards for Excellence

The Condé Nast Johansens 2008 Americas Awards for Excellence were held in February and March 2008. Awards were presented to hotels throughout the Americas that represented the finest quality and service. An important source of information for these awards was the feedback provided by guests who completed Condé Nast Johansens Guest Comment Cards and who voted online. Go to www.johansens.com to make your guest comments and vote for our 2009 Awards for Excellence.

2008 Winners appearing in this Guide:

Mexico & Central America:

Most Excellent Resort

• ESPERANZA, AN AUBERGE RESORT
– Cabo San Lucas, Mexico, p44

Most Excellent Hotel

• HOTEL PUNTA ISLITA – Islita, Costa Rica, p278

Most Excellent Spa Hotel

• GRAND VELAS ALL SUITES & SPA RESORT
– Nuevo Vallarta, Mexico, p62

South America:

Most Excellent Beach Hotel

• POUSADA DO TOQUE – São Miguel dos Milagres, Brazil, p303

Most Excellent Hotel

• PONTA DOS GANCHOS – Governador Celso Ramos, Brazil, p326

Most Excellent Romantic Hideaway

• CORRENTOSO LAKE & RIVER HOTEL
– Villa La Angostura, Argentina, p299

Most Excellent Spa Hotel

• KUROTEL – Gramado, Brazil, p324

Most Excellent Lodge

• POUSADA DO ENGENHO – São Francisco de Paula, Brazil, p325

Image from Ponta dos Ganchos, Santa Catarina, Brazil, p326

Image from Ponta dos Ganchos, Santa Catarina, Brazil, p326

Awards for Excellence

Canada and the United States of America:

Most Excellent Resort
• LAPLAYA BEACH & GOLF RESORT – Florida, U.S.A., p141

Most Excellent Inn
• OLD EDWARDS INN AND SPA – North Carolina, U.S.A., p214

Most Excellent Spa Hotel
• SANCTUARY ON CAMELBACK MOUNTAIN – Arizona, U.S.A., p74

Most Excellent Hotel
• HOTEL BEL-AIR – California, U.S.A., p94

Most Excellent Ranch
• HIDDEN MEADOW RANCH – Arizona, U.S.A., p73

Most Excellent Small Hotel
• HOTEL QUINTESSENCE – Quebec , Canada, p38

Most Excellent Golf Resort
• BALLANTYNE RESORT – North Carolina, U.S.A., p210

Most Excellent Romantic Hideaway
• WICKANINNISH INN – British Columbia, Canada, p18

Most Excellent Country House Hotel
• BLANTYRE – Massachusetts, U.S.A., p175

Atlantic, Caribbean and Pacific:

Most Excellent Resort
• GRACE BAY CLUB – Turks and Caicos Islands, p411

Most Excellent Hotel
• BIRAS CREEK RESORT – Virgin Gorda, British Virgin Islands, p373

Most Excellent Romantic Hideaway
• ROYAL DAVUI ISLAND RESORT – Ugaga Island, Fiji Islands, p423

Most Excellent Spa Hotel
• PARROT CAY – Turks and Caicos Islands, p414

The Americas, Atlantic, Caribbean and Pacific:

Most Excellent Service
• THE HAY-ADAMS – Washington, DC, U.S.A., p129

Most Excellent Business Partner
• HOTEL PLAZA ATHENEE – New York City, U.S.A., p198

Canada - British Columbia

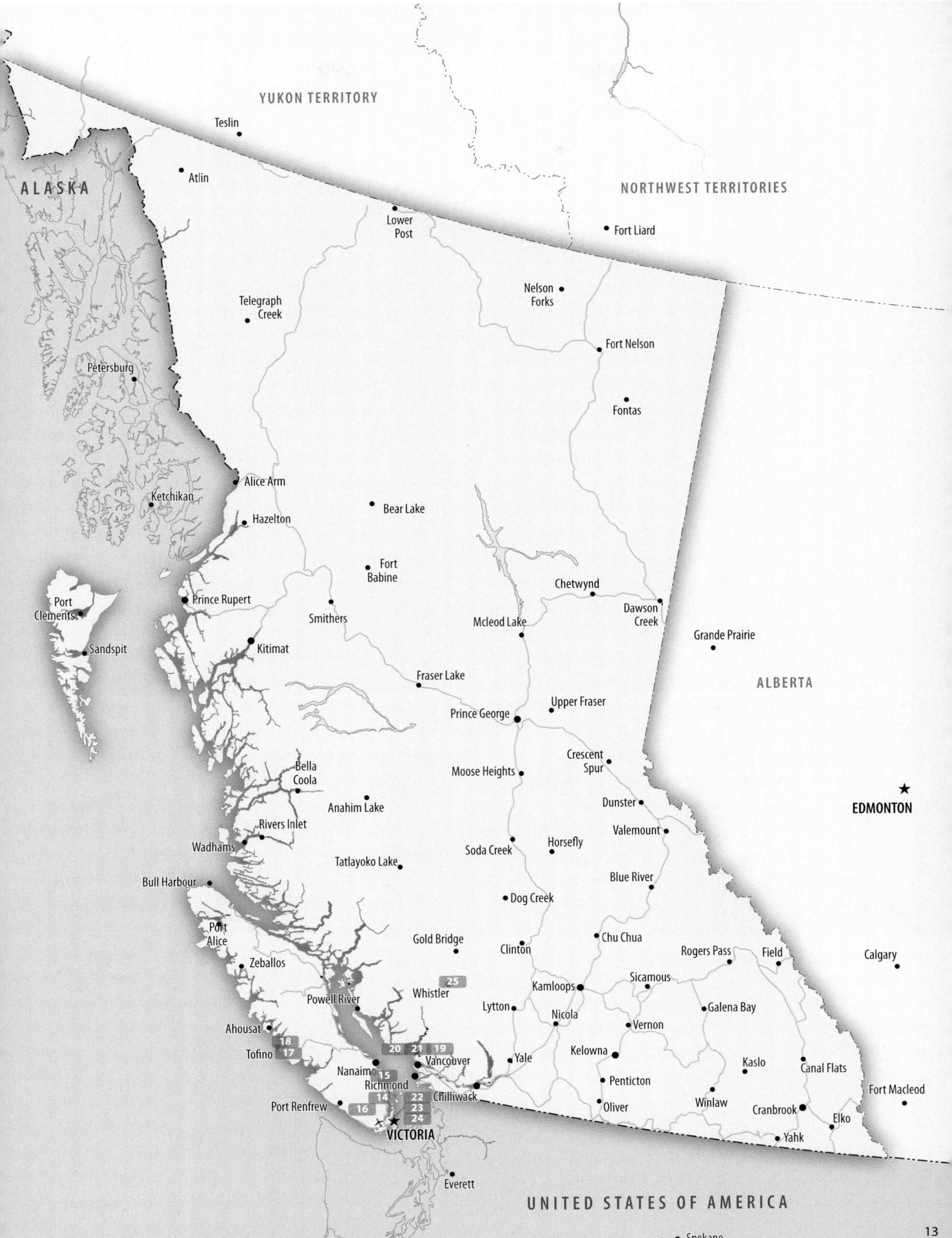

CANADA - BRITISH COLUMBIA (MALAHAT)

The Aerie Resort & Spa

P.O. BOX 108, 600 EBEDORA LANE, MALAHAT, VICTORIA, BRITISH COLUMBIA V0R 2L0
Tel: +1 250 743 7115 **Fax:** +1 250 743 4766 **U.S./Canada Toll Free:** 1 800 518 1933
Web: www.johansens.com/aeriebc **E-mail:** resort@aerie.bc.ca

Set on a mountainside high above the Pacific Ocean with spectacular 180° views, this secluded resort, voted the No. 1 Hotel in North America 2006 by Travel & Leisure magazine, exudes relaxation and rest. There are 3 different buildings for your stay, each with its own special charm and incredible views. Villa Cielo, at the resort's highest point, is a spectacular location for groups and families. You will enjoy fine wine and gourmet cuisine with creative menus influenced by the freshest local ingredients available. Savor an exclusive vintage on the outdoor Bonelli Lounge with a cozy fireplace while taking in the breathtaking vistas. Guided tours of local farms and British Columbia wineries are popular, as well as cooking classes led by the resort's own celebrated chef. The Aerie Spa and Wellness Centre will leave you rejuvenated and inspired.

Our inspector loved: *The truly romantic hideaway setting with the most spectacular views.*

Price Guide:
rooms C$139-C$900

35 M 24 WiFi SPA

Awards/Ratings: Wine Spectator Award of Excellence 2008

Attractions: Cowichan Bay, 12 miles; Bear Mountain Golf, 12 miles; Butchart Gardens, 25 miles
Towns/Cities: Victoria, 22 miles; Nanaimo, 44 miles
Airports: Victoria International Airport, 28 miles; Victoria Harbour (Sea Planes), 22 miles

Affiliations: Relais & Châteaux

Hastings House Country Estate

160 UPPER GANGES ROAD, SALT SPRING ISLAND, BRITISH COLUMBIA V8K 2S2
Tel: +1 250 537 2362 **Fax:** +1 250 537 5333 **U.S./Canada Toll Free:** 1 800 661 9255
Web: www.johansens.com/hastingshouse **E-mail:** info@hastingshouse.com

Our inspector loved: *The gourmet Pacific Northwest cuisine served nightly in the Dining Room.*

Price Guide: (double occupancy, including morning hamper, excluding taxes)
rooms C$310
suites C$410
deluxe hillside C$510

Attractions: Sidney Marine Safarai, 500 yards; Stoneridge Pottery, 2 miles; Salt Spring Vineyard and Garry Oaks Winery, 7 miles; Salt Spring Island Cheese Co., 10 miles
Towns/Cities: Duncan, 20 miles; Victoria, 30 miles; Vancouver, 50 miles
Airports: Victoria International Airport, 15 miles; Vancouver International Airport, 40 miles

Affiliations: Small Luxury Hotels of the World

This graceful and intimate resort is set along 22 acres of rolling lawns, gardens and forests overlooking Ganges Harbour. The stately 11th-century, Sussex-style Manor House is central to the Estate and was built in 1940 from natural stone and native woods. The 18 suites are situated in 6 buildings. Each is filled with English country antiques, sumptuous fabrics and local artwork. The cuisine, created by European-trained Chef Marcel Kauer, includes Salt Spring Island lamb, local seafood and the freshest produce and herbs from the Estate's gardens and orchards. His daily menus are complemented by an exceptional wine cellar offering the best of British Columbia and worldwide wines.

CANADA - BRITISH COLUMBIA (SOOKE)

SOOKE HARBOUR HOUSE

1528 WHIFFEN SPIT ROAD, SOOKE, BRITISH COLUMBIA V9Z 0T4
Tel: +1 250 642 3421 **Fax:** +1 250 642 6988
Web: www.johansens.com/sookeharbour **E-mail:** info@sookeharbourhouse.com

Considered One of Canada's Top Five Hotels by Travel and Leisure Magazine 2008, Sooke Harbour House was once a migratory camping ground of the T'sou-ke First Nations. Today, it is a charming small hotel that celebrates food, art and wine offering individually decorated rooms that are cozy and brimming with original West Coast artwork and sculptures, unique hand-painted pillows and beautiful ocean views. Wine Director and owner, Sinclair Philip, his wife Frederique and their team of chefs take great pride in their wine cellar and the produce grown in their garden that is used alongside fresh local ingredients. The gourmet restaurant won Vancouver Magazine's Best Vancouver Island Restaurant Award 2008. In addition to such accolades this is also a certified organic property with flower-filled gardens containing more than 200 edible herbs, flowers and vegetables. The Sea-renity Spa combines elements of stone, herbs and the sea in their relaxing therapies.

Our inspector loved: *The exceptional gourmet cuisine that is prepared from the freshest local ingredients, and the award-winning wine cellar.*

Price Guide: (including breakfast)
rooms C$305-C$650

28 150 SPA

Awards/Ratings: Wine Spectator Award of Excellence 2007; DiRoNA

Attractions: Wine Cellar Tours, on-site; Fishing Charters and Whale-Watching, 5-min drive; Butchart Gardens, 28 miles
Towns/Cities: Victoria, 45-min drive
Airports: Victoria International Airport, 1-hour drive; Vancouver International Airport, 1-hour drive and ferry crossing

Clayoquot Wilderness Resort

BEDWELL RIVER OUTPOST, BOX 130, TOFINO, BRITISH COLUMBIA V0R 2Z0
Tel: +1 250 726 8235 **Fax:** +1 250 726 8558 **U.S./Canada Toll Free:** 1 888 333 5405
Web: www.johansens.com/clayoquot **E-mail:** info@wildretreat.com

Our inspector loved: *The exceptionally warm hospitality, and the outstanding gourmet dining experience.*

Price Guide: (all inclusive)
luxury outpost accommodations from C$4,750

20 40
SPA

Attractions: Clayoquot Sound Biosphere, 1 mile; Downtown Tofino, 20-min boat ride; Pacific Rim National Park, 20-min boat ride
Towns/Cities: Tofino, 20-min boat ride; Vancouver, 1-hour seaplane flight
Airports: Tofino Airport, 40-min water taxi ride

Clayoquot Wilderness Resort, located in the Clayoquot Sound Biosphere Reserve close to the seaside village of Tofino, offers a truly exclusive and unique vacation. This ultra-luxurious eco-destination features 4-star accommodations, world-class coastal cuisine, extraordinary adventure and breathtaking wilderness. After a day of guided activities, relax at the Healing Grounds, an eco-safari style massage and therapeutic treatment center with 4 massage and treatment tents, 3 wood-fired cedar hot tubs, a wood-fired cedar sauna, outdoor showers, seawater baths and wraparound sun decks. Alternately, chill out in a lounge tent where you can sit back and enjoy a good book, play a game of chess or browse the Internet. Rest easy in your extremely cozy outpost deluxe guest accommodation tent; spacious white canvas retreats built on raised wooden platforms. Meals created by Chef Timothy May make sure you have energy all day long with his fresh gourmet cuisine.

Wickaninnish Inn

OSPREY LANE AT CHESTERMAN BEACH, TOFINO, BRITISH COLUMBIA V0R 2Z0
Tel: +1 250 725 3100 **Fax:** +1 250 725 3110 **U.S./Canada Toll Free:** 1 800 333 4604
Web: www.johansens.com/wickaninnish **E-mail:** info@wickinn.com

Located on Vancouver Island's picturesque rugged West Coast, this rustic retreat sits on nature's edge overlooking expansive Chesterman Beach. Luxurious rooms and suites are highlighted with floor-to-ceiling picture windows, cozy fireplaces, double-soaker tubs and magnificent pieces of local art. Step out onto your balcony to breathe the fresh salt air and watch the Tofino surfers or perhaps a bald eagle soaring by. Beautiful all year-round, and the home of winter storm watching, the setting will inspire you to explore the rainforest and beaches with rain slickers and boots provided for you by the inn. The West Coast Canadian gourmet cuisine at The Pointe Restaurant, with its incredible 240° views of the open Pacific Ocean, is not to be missed!

***Our inspector loved:** Watching a winter storm from a candle-lit soaker tub.*

Price Guide:
rooms C$280-C$680
suites C$400-C$1,500

75 50 DVD WiFi SPA

Awards/Ratings: Condé Nast Johansens Most Excellent Romantic Hideaway 2008; Condé Nast Johansens Most Excellent Lodge 2007; Condé Nast Traveler Gold List 2007

Attractions: Clayoquot Sound UNESCO Biosphere Reserve, on-site; Pacific Rim National Park Reserve, 3 miles
Towns/Cities: Ucluelet, 25 miles; Nanaimo, 124 miles; Victoria, 196 miles
Airports: Tofino, 5 miles; Victoria Intl., 196 miles

Affiliations: Relais & Châteaux

Wedgewood Hotel & Spa

845 HORNBY STREET, VANCOUVER, BRITISH COLUMBIA V6Z 1V1
Tel: +1 604 689 7777 **Fax:** +1 604 608 5348 **U.S./Canada Toll Free:** 1 800 663 0666
Web: www.johansens.com/wedgewoodbc **E-mail:** info@wedgewoodhotel.com

Our inspector loved: *Relaxing in the Bacchus Restaurant & Piano Lounge, and the exceptional cuisine in the dining room.*

Price Guide:
rooms C$280-C$600
suites C$380-C$1,500

83 100 SPA

Awards/Ratings: Condé Nast Traveler Gold List 2007 and 2008

Attractions: Robson Street, close by; Stanley Park, 2 miles; Vancouver Aquarium, 3 miles; Capilano Suspension Bridge and Park, 6 miles
Towns/Cities: North Vancouver, 7 miles; Burnaby, 9 miles; Victoria, 61 miles; Whistler, 76 miles
Airports: Vancouver International Airport, 9 miles; Victoria International Airport, 35 miles

Affiliations: Relais & Châteaux

This world-class boutique hotel has long been Vancouver's best kept secret. Located in chic downtown, this intimate and romantic hotel exudes elegance and charm. Beautiful personal touches by the hands-on owner, Eleni Skalbania, can be seen throughout, from the fresh flowers to the rich upholstered furniture and Murano Venetian crystal fixtures. Exceptional service levels, discreetly presented, ensure the perfect romantic getaway. The beautiful rooms have balconies, fine linens and duvets and the expansive Penthouse Suites are unrivaled with fireplaces, wet-bars, Jacuzzi tubs in luxurious spa bathrooms and scenic garden terraces - frequented by celebrities! Executive Chef Lee Parsons creates delectable French cuisine at the popular Bacchus Restaurant & Piano Lounge, with its inviting fireplace, bar and lounge.

PAN PACIFIC VANCOUVER

300-999 CANADA PLACE, VANCOUVER, BRITISH COLUMBIA V6C 3B5
Tel: +1 604 662 8111 **Fax:** +1 604 685 8690 **U.S./Canada Toll Free:** 1 800 937 1515
Web: www.johansens.com/panpacific **E-mail:** reservations.yvr@panpacific.com

Our inspector loved: *The stunning views of the harbor, city and mountains from the rooms.*

Price Guide: (room only)
rooms C$239-C$610
suites C$610-C$4,000

504 700 SPA

Awards/Ratings: Condé Nast Traveler Gold List 2007 and 2008

Attractions: Robson Street, 1 mile; Stanley Park, 1.5 miles; Vancouver Aquarium, 1.5 miles; Capilano Suspension Bridge, 5.5 miles
Towns/Cities: Burnaby, 8.5 miles; Whistler, 76 miles; Seattle, 143 miles
Airports: Vancouver International Airport, 12 miles

A grand waterfront hotel, the Pan Pacific Vancouver is one of the area's larger architecturally unique hotels. The splendid glass lobby provides breathtaking panoramic views of the harbor, majestic mountains, Stanley Park and the city skyline. Beyond the showcase lobby, the hotel hallways and rooms have a more intimate feel. Each room is luxuriously appointed with modern hotel amenities including Frette linens, marble baths and flat-screen televisions. Watch the sea planes land in Coal Harbour from the comfort of your room. The waterfront restaurants and lounge provide award-winning selections of West Coast Cuisine, including the Five Sails Restaurant. In the summer, enjoy lunch on the patio terrace overlooking the sea. The spa will pamper you with customized treatments.

The Sutton Place Hotel Vancouver

845 BURRARD STREET, VANCOUVER, BRITISH COLUMBIA V6Z 2K6
Tel: +1 604 682 5511 **Fax:** +1 604 682 5513 **U.S./Canada Toll Free:** 1 866 378 8866
Web: www.johansens.com/suttonplacebc **E-mail:** res_vancouver@suttonplace.com

Our inspector loved: *The wine tastings in the Private Tasting Room in the hotel's very own Sutton Place Wine Merchant.*

Price Guide: (excluding taxes)
rooms C$331-C$496
executive suites C$421-C$586
grand suites C$451-C$616

397 300 SPA

Awards/Ratings: AAA 5 Diamond 1989-2008; Condé Nast Traveler Gold List 2008

Attractions: Robson Street, close by; Stanley Park, 1 mile; Orpheum Theater, 1 mile; Granville Island, 3 miles
Towns/Cities: Victoria, 70 miles; Whistler, 77 miles
Airports: Vancouver International Airport, 8 miles

This grand hotel brings a touch of Europe to Vancouver with its luxurious and elegant setting. Rated AAA 5 Diamonds 19 years in a row, the level of service and attention to detail is evident. In addition to comfortable and well-appointed modern guest rooms, the hotel also offers extended stays at La Grande Résidence. Fleuri Restaurant showcases exceptional French cuisine by Executive Chef Raman Anand, and chocolate lovers can indulge in chocolate fondue or exotic fruit drizzled with chocolate at the all-you-can-eat chocolate buffet. For spiritual health, try the Vida Signature Ayurvedic treatment at the Vida Wellness Spa. A favorite for entertainment industry professionals, the popular Gerard Lounge is reminiscent of an English club with leather chairs and tapestries. Sit by the cozy fireplace for cocktails and bistro fare. The Sutton Place Wine Merchant is a popular new addition.

CANADA - BRITISH COLUMBIA (VICTORIA)

BRENTWOOD BAY LODGE & SPA

849 VERDIER AVENUE, VICTORIA, BRITISH COLUMBIA V8M 1C5

Tel: +1 250 544 2079 **Fax:** +1 250 544 2069 **U.S./Canada Toll Free:** 1 888 544 2079

Web: www.johansens.com/brentwood **E-mail:** info@brentwoodbaylodge.com

Our inspector loved: *The Sushi & Saki Bar where sushi is made from fresh ingredients flown in daily from Japan.*

Price Guide: (including breakfast)
oceansuites C$179-C$699

Located on pristine Brentwood Bay, in the heart of the wine country, close to the charming city of Victoria, this boutique hotel is a 5-star luxury lodge with a contemporary flair. Each elegant oceansuite has beautiful handcrafted furnishings, fine Italian linens, spa bathrooms and romantic fireside seating areas, perfect for savoring a glass of British Columbia wine from the Lodge's very own award-winning wine cellar. Dine seaside at the acclaimed SeaGrille where you can find the freshest in west-coast cuisine. The wood-burning fireplaces, dramatic artwork, and cozy wine bar complete the romantic ambience. A variety of sports are available at the Eco-Adventure Centre located dockside at the Lodge's 50-slip marina, and don't forget to indulge in a treatment at the ocean-front Essence of Life Spa!

Attractions: Butchart Gardens, 2 miles; Royal B.C. Museum, 14 miles; Parliament Buildings, 14 miles; Craigdarroch Castle, 15 miles

Towns/Cities: Sidney, 8 miles; Victoria, 14 miles; Malahat, 23 miles

Airports: Victoria International Airport, 20 miles; B.C. Ferries, 90-min ferry ride from Vancouver to Victoria (Tsawwassen to Swartz Bay)

Fairholme Manor

638 ROCKLAND PLACE, VICTORIA, BRITISH COLUMBIA V8S 3R2

Tel: +1 250 598 3240 **Fax:** +1 250 598 3299 **U.S./Canada Toll Free:** 1 877 511 3322

Web: www.johansens.com/fairholme **E-mail:** info@fairholmemanor.com

Our inspector loved: *The owner's own "Fabulous Fairholme" cookbook featuring her favorite breakfast and brunch recipes.*

Price Guide: (including breakfast, excluding taxes) rooms C$125-C$325

Attractions: Royal B.C. Museum, 2 miles; Victoria Symphony 2 miles; Swartz Bay, 13 miles; Butchart Gardens, 13 miles
Towns/Cities: Victoria Inner Harbour, 1 mile
Airports: Victoria International Airport, 16 miles

This pleasantly restored Victorian mansion is nestled in a quiet area of Victoria's Rockland area, near Victoria's Inner Harbour, bordering the gardens of Government House. European in style, and extremely private, the inn showcases beautiful original artwork and Viennese antiques. Popular with honeymooners and couples, the inn's suites are spacious in size and most have a king bed, fireplace and lovely views. The Olympic Grand Suite features an elegant chandelier and private ocean-view deck. The 2-bedroom Rose Garden Suite has a kitchen and a private deck. Sumptuous breakfasts are served daily in the sunlit dining room or on the common porch overlooking the gardens. Lemon ricotta pancakes are a favorite among guests, in addition to the home-made granola and mouth-watering baked goods.

Villa Marco Polo Inn

1524 SHASTA PLACE, VICTORIA, BRITISH COLUMBIA V8S 1X9
Tel: +1 250 370 1524 **Fax:** +1 250 370 1624 **U.S./Canada Toll Free:** 1 877 601 1524
Web: www.johansens.com/villamarcopolo **E-mail:** enquire@villamarcopolo.com

__Our inspector loved:__ The incredibly warm welcome to this immaculate and tucked away gem of an inn.

Price Guide: (including breakfast)
suites C$190–C$325

4 25 12 SPA

Attractions: Art Gallery of Greater Victoria, 0.5 miles; Royal British Columbia Museum, 1 mile; Inner Harbour, 2 miles; Butchart Gardens, 14 miles
Towns/Cities: Salt Spring Island, 28.4 miles; Vancouver, 68 miles; Tofino, 197 miles; Seattle, WA, 30-min flight
Airports: Victoria International Airport, 17.6 miles

This elegant inn, located in Victoria's historic Rockland quarter, is designed in the style of an Italianate Renaissance mansion. Built in 1923 as a gift to a young bride, and now a popular venue for destination weddings, it features 4 beautifully appointed suites, elegant interiors and an Italianate garden with reflecting pool and fountains. Suites feature double soaker tubs, fine linens, hardwood floors with Persian carpets, antiques and fine arts from the owner's family collections. Gourmet breakfasts are served in the dining room or the Italian Orangerie; special diets such as vegan, gluten-free or vegetarian meals are prepared on request. In the afternoon, enjoy tea and sherry in the garden or by the fire in the wood-paneled library. Activities such as whale-watching, sailing, kayaking and wine country tours can be arranged. And a variety of luxurious treatments and esthetic services at the Villa's recently opened Penthouse Spa Hammam is also available.

ADARA HOTEL

4122 VILLAGE GREEN, WHISTLER, BRITISH COLUMBIA V0N 1B4
Tel: +1 604 905 4009 **Fax:** +1 604 905 4665 **U.S./Canada Toll Free:** 1 866 502 3272
Web: www.johansens.com/adara **E-mail:** info@adarahotel.com

Our inspector loved: *The inspirational urban lodge décor and prime location in Whistler Village.*

Price Guide:
rooms C$279-C$869

41

Attractions: All a short walk away: Whistler Golf Club; A.T.V. Tours; Heli Tours
Towns/Cities: Squamish, 60 miles; Vancouver, 75 miles
Airports: Vancouver International Airport, 70 miles

Affiliations: Small Luxury Hotels of the World

Adara Hotel is the first boutique urban lodge-style hotel to open in the celebrated ski resort Whistler, home of the 2010 Olympic Winter Games and a short walk away from Whistler and Blackcomb Mountains. Small, sophisticated and rustic, this contemporary hotel is comfortable yet stylish, with each of its rooms rich in color and playful in décor. Innovative minimalist furniture and touches of faux mink throws put a playful spin on the typical lodge experience with spa-like bathrooms, luxurious beds, "floating" fireplaces and artful design details. With an outdoor summer pool and hot tub to take a dip while enjoying the spectacular mountain views, this luxury hotel will accommodate you all year round. You are steps away from the village's best restaurants and night-life and surrounded by a plethora of activities to enjoy including zip trekking, mountain biking, canoeing, kayaking, white-water rafting and bungee jumping!

Canada - Nova Scotia

CANADA - NOVA SCOTIA (EAST KEMPTVILLE)

Trout Point Lodge of Nova Scotia

189 TROUT POINT ROAD, OFF THE EAST BRANCH ROAD AND HIGHWAY 203, EAST KEMPTVILLE, NOVA SCOTIA B0W 1Y0
Tel: +1 902 761 2142 **Fax:** +1 800 980 0713 **U.S./Canada Toll Free:** 1 877 812 0112
Web: www.johansens.com/troutpoint **E-mail:** troutpoint@foodvacation.com

Our inspector loved: *Relaxing in the wood-fired hot tub overlooking the Tusket River.*

Price Guide: (double occupancy)
rooms C$205-C$350
cottages C$280-C$350

13 M 24 WiFi

Attractions: Tobeatic Wilderness Area, on-site; Shelburne Historic District, 34 miles; Mavilette Beach, 45-min drive; Kejimkujik Seaside Park, 64 miles
Towns/Cities: Kemptville, 15-min drive; Yarmouth, 25 miles; Shelburne, 34 miles; Halifax, 167 miles
Airports: Halifax Airport, 175 miles

Nestled next to the Tusket River, adjacent to the Tobeatic Wilderness Area of southern Nova Scotia, this civilized outpost offers a secluded and relaxed vacation with excellent food and a host of outdoor activities. Days begin with a hearty breakfast followed by the possibilities of fishing, hiking, kayaking, swimming or even a whale-watching trip! Later in the day, relax in the outdoor sauna and wood-fired hot tub before dinner, and enjoy drinks around the fire pit or in the cozy lounge while swapping stories of the day's adventures. The friendly and attentive staff is multilingual and includes an on-site naturalist. Rooms are elegantly rustic with comfortable beds, handcrafted furniture and Bvlgari amenities. Everything in the lodge is designed with eco-friendliness in mind, earning the property the coveted Parks Canada Sustainable Tourism Award. The food is creative and delicious, and you can even book one of Trout Point's "Cooking Classes and Culinary Vacations."

FOX HARB'R

1337 FOX HARBOUR ROAD, WALLACE, NOVA SCOTIA B0K 1Y0
Tel: +1 902 257 1801 **Fax:** +1 902 257 1852 **U.S./Canada Toll Free:** 1 866 257 1801
Web: www.johansens.com/foxharbr **E-mail:** mail@foxharbr.com

Our inspector loved: *All the great amenities in such a rural and beautiful location.*

Price Guide: (excluding tax and gratuities)
studio suites C$300-C$325
executive suites C$300-C$400

72 ... 165 ... SPA

Attractions: Jost Vineyards, 9 miles; Wild Blueberry and Maple Center, Oxford, 20 miles; Springhill Miners' Museum, 39 miles; Anne Murray Centre, Springhill, 40 miles
Towns/Cities: Springhill, 40 miles; Moncton, NB, 90 miles; Halifax, 100 miles; Yarmouth, 290 miles
Airports: Private Airport, on site; Halifax International Airport, 84 miles; Moncton International Airport, NB, 85 miles

Nestled along 4 miles of secluded seacoast on the Northumberland Strait in Nova Scotia, is Fox Harb'r resort. This 1,000-acre private oasis of breathtaking scenery and warm maritime hospitality boasts a 4885-ft. private runway and a marina. The 72 luxuriously-appointed guest suites have private balconies and terraces, granite floors, the finest of linens and individual wet bars. Spend your day on the Graham Cooke designed championship golf course, a magnificent blend of Scottish links and parkland golf. Indulge yourself in the soothing calm and lavish care of the European spa and wellness center or take in a host of recreational activities available on-site. Fine dining, with fresh seasonal ingredients, an award-winning wine cellar and uncompromising attention to detail will ensure your stay is nothing short of spectacular.

HUDSON BAY
NUNAVUT
MANITOBA
Weir River
Winisk
Sachigo Lake
JAMES BAY
QUÉBEC
Balmertown
Falls
Moosonee
Kenora
Vermilion Bay
Armstrong
Chibougamau
Hearst
Mine Centre
Terrace Bay
Thunder Bay
White River
Timmins
Rouyn-Noranda
Val-d'or
Kirkland Lake
La Tuque
LAKE SUPERIOR
Sault Ste. Marie
Elliot Lake
Sudbury
North Bay
Joliette
Montréal
30
OTTAWA
Minneapolis
Midland
LAKE HURON
Owen Sound
Barrie
Peterborough
Kingston
Belleville
Oshawa
LAKE ONTARIO
Brampton
35
Toronto
Kitchener
Niagara-on-the-Lake
Syracuse
Hamilton
Madison
Milwaukee
Port Huron
London
Buffalo
31
32
33
34
LAKE MICHIGAN
Detroit
Chatham
Windsor
LAKE ERIE
Erie
Chicago
Moines
Toledo
Davenport
Cleveland
Newark
UNITED STATES OF AMERICA

Inn at Manitou

81 INN ROAD, MCKELLAR, ONTARIO POG 1C0
Tel: +1 705 389 2171 **Fax:** +1 705 389 3818 **U.S./Canada Toll Free:** 1 800 571 8818
Web: www.johansens.com/manitou **E-mail:** inn@manitou-online.com

Beautifully located on one of Ontario's most pristine lakes, just north of Toronto, this intimate luxury golf, tennis and spa resort is exceptional for its accommodations and cuisine. Each of the charming rooms is spacious and well-appointed, many bordering the lake below. Luxury suites feature high cedar cathedral ceilings, step-down living rooms, antique marble mantles and wood-burning fireplaces. The Spa at Manitou provides personal fitness, health and beauty spa programs, while The Manitou Golf Academy challenges the most experienced of players. But let's not forget the tennis facilities comprising 11 courts - 4 clay, 6 outdoor hard and 1 indoor hard - and the international tennis professionals on-hand to help improve your game. Dining is a 5-star experience: a kitchen of 12 French chefs makes the restaurant one of the best in Canada offering fresh local cuisine. Don't miss the weekly wine tasting led by the sommelier in the gazebo overlooking the lake.

***Our inspector loved:** The complete peace at this beautiful and remote inn located on the edge of a pristine lake surrounded by trees.*

Price Guide: (all inclusive, closed from October 20th - May 10th)
standard to deluxe C$285-C$375
luxury C$450-C$485

35 M 70 SPA

Awards/Ratings: DiRoNA 2001-2008; Wine Spectator Award of Excellence 2000-2008

Attractions: Georgian Bay 30,000 Island Cruise, 25 miles
Towns/Cities: Parry Sound, 25 miles; Barrie, 81 miles; Toronto, 155 miles
Airports: Parry Sound (Private Aircrafts Only), 28 miles; Pearson International Airport, 155 miles

Affiliations: Relais & Châteaux

THE CHARLES INN

209 QUEEN STREET, BOX 642, NIAGARA-ON-THE-LAKE, ONTARIO L0S 1J0
Tel: +1 905 468 4588 **Fax:** +1 905 468 2194 **U.S./Canada Toll Free:** 1 866 556 8883
Web: www.johansens.com/charlesinnca **E-mail:** inquire@charlesinn.ca

Our inspector loved: *The beautiful gardens overlooking the oldest golf course in North America, and the friendly staff.*

Price Guide: (including breakfast)
rooms C$99-C$299
suites C$245-C$374

Attractions: Shaw Festival Theaters, 0.5 miles; Award-Winning Wineries, 1 mile; Niagara Falls, 10 miles; World-Class Golf, 10 miles
Towns/Cities: Niagara Falls, 15-min drive; Toronto, 80-min drive; Buffalo, NY, 45-min drive
Airports: Niagara District Airport (private aircrafts only), 5 miles; Buffalo International Airport, 35 miles; Toronto International Airport, 60 miles

This 1832 luxurious manor house offers an elegant and romantic setting located on the main street of Niagara-on-the-Lake. Recently refurbished, each of the beautiful and comfortable guest rooms is unique in décor, many with cozy wood burning or gas fireplaces and large private verandas to enjoy a view of the golf course or Lake Ontario. Relaxing spa services are available at the inn's sister property Shaw Spa where you can indulge in an array of rejuvenating treatments including the very popular vinotherapy. Enjoy the Chef's lounge and patio's menus and for dinner, savor the inn's gourmet tasting menu featuring delectable Ontario lamb, Atlantic salmon and other local delicacies. The inn is ideally located in Niagara-on-the-Lake where you can enjoy world-class theater, exceptional golf courses, fine dining, wineries and historical sites.

HARBOUR HOUSE

85 MELVILLE STREET, BOX 760, NIAGARA-ON-THE-LAKE, ONTARIO
Tel: +1 905 468 4683 **Fax:** +1 905 468 0366 **U.S./Canada Toll Free:** 1 866 277 6677
Web: www.johansens.com/harbourhouseca **E-mail:** inquire@harbourhousehotel.ca

Our inspector loved: *The daily complimentary wine and cheese reception that gives guests a chance to mingle.*

Price Guide: (including breakfast)
rooms C$199-C$355
suites C$310-C$445

31 30 SPA

Harbour House is a welcoming and romantic retreat ideally located in the heart of Niagara-on-the-Lake. Comfortable and tastefully decorated rooms and suites have luxurious king-sized feather-top beds and down duvets, fireplaces, whirlpool baths and entertainment centers, as well as beautiful views of the Niagara River. Sumptuous breakfasts in the Conservatory are the perfect way to start the day with home-made Harbour House granola, fresh-baked croissants, breads and scones accompanied by their very own specially blended coffee. In the late afternoon, you are invited to sample the region's most celebrated vintage wines in the Library Lobby. The Niagara River Recreation Trail nearby is perfect for cycling and walking. Enjoy a popular rejuvenation treatment at the sister property's Shaw Spa.

Attractions: Shaw Festival Theaters, 0.5 miles; Award-Winning Wineries, 1 mile; Niagara Falls, 10 miles; World-Class Golf Courses, 10 miles
Towns/Cities: Niagara Falls, 15-min drive; Buffalo, NY, 45-min drive; Toronto, 80-min drive
Airports: Niagara District Airport (private aircrafts only), 5 miles; Buffalo International Airport, 35 miles; Toronto International Airport, 60 miles

RIVERBEND INN & VINEYARD

16104 NIAGARA RIVER PARKWAY, NIAGARA-ON-THE-LAKE, ONTARIO L0S 1J0
Tel: +1 905 468 8866 **Fax:** +1 905 468 8829 **U.S./Canada Toll Free:** 1 888 955 5553
Web: www.johansens.com/riverbend **E-mail:** fd@riverbendinn.ca

Our inspector loved: *Looking through the bedroom window out to the beautiful vineyard and gardens.*

Price Guide: (room only)
rooms C$160-C$325
suites C$260-C$370

21 42

Attractions: Reif Estates Winery, 3-min drive; Shaw Festival, 3-min drive; Niagara Falls, 30-min drive
Towns/Cities: Niagara-on-the-Lake, 5-min drive; Buffalo, 45-min drive
Airports: Niagara District Airport, 6.5 miles; Welland-Port Colborne Airport, 23 miles; Buffalo Niagara International Airport, 27 miles

This historic 1860s Georgian mansion was carefully restored in 2002 by the Wiens family to create a beautiful country inn with Old World charm. Set within its own working chardonnay and merlot vineyards overlooking the Niagara River, the atmosphere is quiet and casual. Each of the classically elegant rooms and suites is decorated with rich colors, antique furnishings, fireplaces and original hardwood flooring. The 1890s salon bar, with its marble pillars and roaring fireplace, is a popular place to meet. Enjoy the creative country cuisine in the 26-seat dining room or relax in the 40-seat vineyard patio with a bottle of the estate's wine. Explore the manicured lawns and gardens, 17 acres of vineyards and take in the breathtaking views.

Shaw Club Hotel & Spa

P.O. BOX 642, 92 PICTON STREET, NIAGARA-ON-THE-LAKE, ONTARIO L0S 1J0
Tel: +1 905 468 5711 **Fax:** +1 905 468 4988 **U.S./Canada Toll Free:** 1 800 511 7070
Web: www.johansens.com/shawclub **E-mail:** inquire@shawclub.com

Our inspector loved: *The contemporary, bright and lively atmosphere. You'll feel like a member of an exclusive club.*

Price Guide: (including breakfast)
rooms C$155-C$345
suites C$285-C$475

30 24 DVD WiFi SPA

Located across from the Shaw Festival Theatre on Main Street, this hotel is ideally situated to explore the cultural, scenic and historical activities that the area offers all year round. Minimalist and modern in design, the hotel is designed to feel more like a private club than a hotel. Each of the beautifully appointed guest rooms is adorned with original photography by local artists, Egyptian cotton linens, cozy down pillows and duvets and the latest in modern technology. Before heading to the theater, enjoy cocktails on the patio of Zees, Niagara's hottest new restaurant where you can experience innovative and whimsical cuisine in an ultra-chic setting. The Shaw Spa will renew you with its extensive array of treatments including the popular chocotherapy and vinotherapy.

Attractions: Whirlpool Jet Boat, 0.5 miles; Shaw Festival Theatre, 1-min walk; World-Class Wineries, 1 mile; Niagara Falls, 10 miles
Towns/Cities: Niagara Falls, 15-min drive; Buffalo, NY, 45-min drive; Toronto, 80-min drive
Airports: Niagara District Airport (private aircrafts only), 5 miles; Buffalo International Airport, 35 miles; Toronto International Airport, 60 miles

WINDSOR ARMS

18 ST. THOMAS STREET, TORONTO, ONTARIO M5S 3E7
Tel: +1 416 971 9666 **Fax:** +1 416 921 9121 **U.S./Canada Toll Free:** 1 877 999 2767
Web: www.johansens.com/windsorarms **E-mail:** reserve@windsorarmshotel.com

Our inspector loved: *The prime location in Yorkville, Toronto's most fashionable shopping, entertainment and dining area.*

Price Guide: (including Continental breakfast, excluding taxes)
rooms C$275-C$295
suites C$325-C$2,000

28 500 SPA

Awards/Ratings: Wine Spectator Award of Excellence 2008

Attractions: Exclusive Boutique Shopping, 1-min walk; Royal Ontario Museum, 5-min walk; Royal Conservatory of Music, 5-min walk; CN Tower, 10-min drive
Towns/Cities: Ottawa, 250 miles
Airports: Pearson International Airport, 15 miles

Affiliations: Small Luxury Hotels of the World

Originally constructed in 1927 to mirror the University of Toronto's signature Victorian buildings, the Windsor Arms underwent an extensive renovation to preserve the historical characteristics and update its facilities. The result combined in Old World charm alongside modern luxury earning the property the title of No. 1 Hotel in Toronto 2007 by Condé Nast Traveler. The 3-story Courtyard Café serves excellent cuisine in one of the city's most impressive dining rooms with dramatic David Bierk paintings, huge chandeliers and a grand piano. The addition of "Prime," a modern steakhouse open 7 days a week for dinner, adds yet another feather to the cap of this fine hotel. Afternoon and high tea can be savored in the Tea Room by the original 1927 fireplace. The 2-floor spa's philosophy of "intimate privacy" aims to provide the ultimate pampering experience.

Canada - Québec

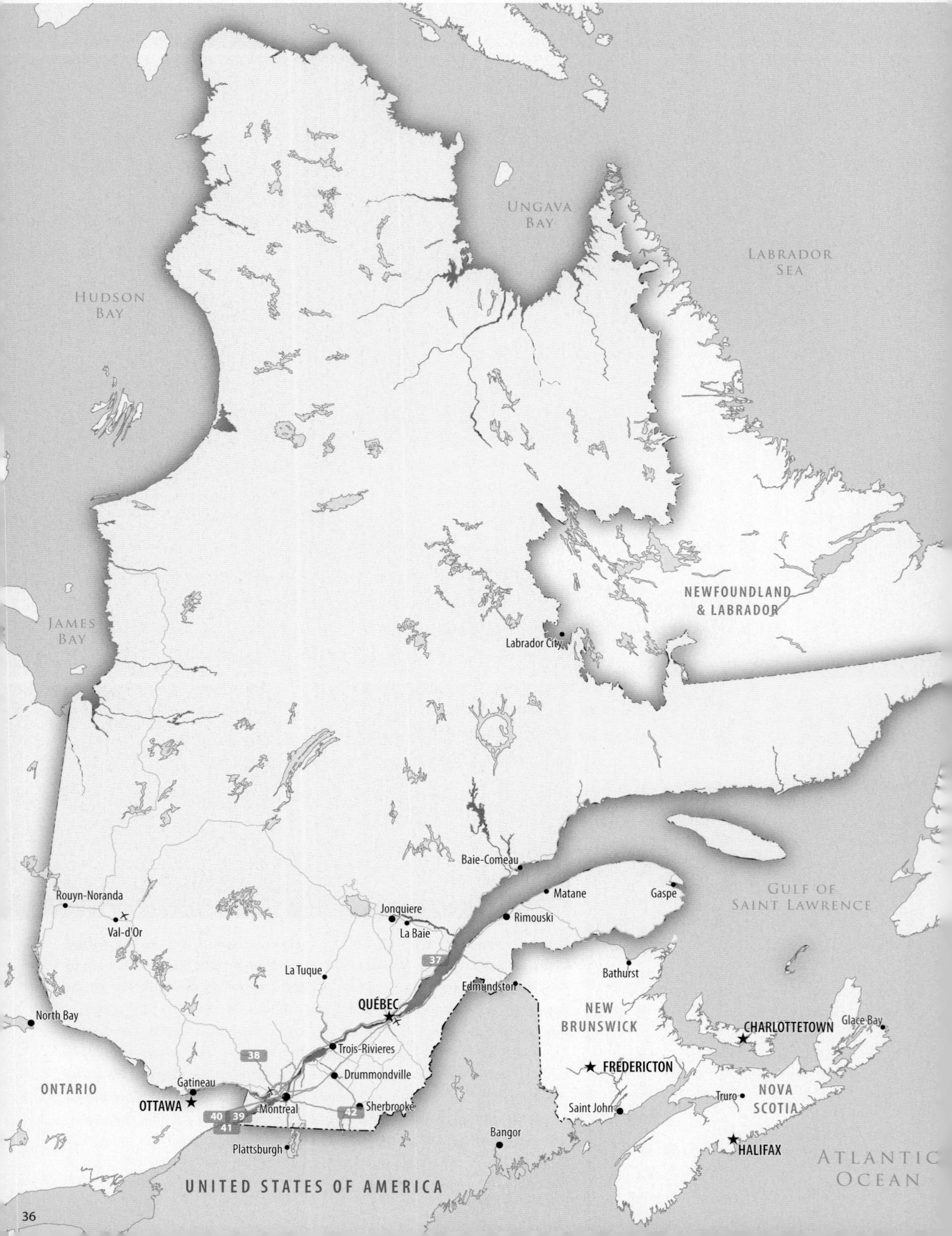

La Pinsonnière

124 SAINT-RAPHAËL, CAP-À L'AIGLE, LA MALBAIE, QUÉBEC G5A 1X9
Tel: +1 418 665 4431 **Fax:** +1 418 665 7156 **U.S./Canada Toll Free:** 1 800 387 4431
Web: www.johansens.com/lapinsonniere **E-mail:** pinsonniere@relaischateaux.com

Our inspector loved: *The spectacular view, the tranquility and the warm Canadian hospitality.*

Price Guide: (excluding tax)
rooms C$295-C$345
suites C$345-C$495

18 50 SPA

Attractions: Casino, 7 miles; Golf, 7 miles; Whale Watching Cruises, 20 miles; Parc des Hautes Gorges de la Riviere Malbaie, 40 miles
Towns/Cities: Québec City, 90 miles; Montréal, 250 miles
Airports: Jean Lesage International Airport, 90 miles; Trudeau Airport, Montréal, 250 miles

Affiliations: Relais & Châteaux

Celebrating its 30th anniversary, the 5-star La Pinsonnière blends naturally into the beauty of the Charlevoix region of Québec, perched on a hill in the charming village of Cap-à-l'Aigle overlooking stunning views of the St. Lawrence River. Formerly the home of Senator Marc Drouin, this family-run inn offers luxurious guest rooms with spa bathrooms, fireplaces, down bedding and frette robes and slippers. The terrace is the perfect setting to enjoy a light lunch or dinner overlooking the colorful gardens, and the noteworthy restaurant offers delectable and creative cuisine prepared from many local produce. Take a tour of the multiple award-winning wine cellar with its impressive 12,000 bottles and 750 labels, and make sure you visit the art gallery, walk the nature trails, and relax on the private beach.

HÔTEL QUINTESSENCE

3004 CHEMIN DE LA CHAPELLE, MONT-TREMBLANT, QUÉBEC J8E 1E1
Tel: +1 819 425 3400 **Fax:** +1 819 425 3480 **U.S./Canada Toll Free:** 1 866 425 3400
Web: www.johansens.com/quintessence **E-mail:** info@hotelquintessence.com

"The quintessential things of life" are what this boutique hotel strives to provide, allowing you to experience a lasting sense of well-being. This unique area is a year-round destination with luxuriously decorated suites featuring oversized bathrooms, wood-burning fireplaces and stunning lake views. The multitude of outdoor activities include down-hill and cross-country skiing, sledding and mountain biking, but there are also many places to relax in the 3-acre landscaped grounds, boardwalk by the lake, and lake-facing infinity pool and hot tubs. Q Restaurant and Wine Bar is a great dining experience where traditional specialties are complemented by fresh organic herbs grown in the hotel gardens. And let's not forget the 5,000 bottle capacity wine cellar located in a secluded turret with tasting rooms where connoisseurs can experience some of the world's finest wines.

Our inspector loved: *The infinity pool overlooking the lake and mountains.*

Price Guide:
Q and executive suites C$299-C$649
deluxe and presidential suites C$599-C$1,549

Awards/Ratings: Condé Nast Johansens Most Excellent Small Hotel, U.S.A. & Canada 2008

Attractions: Tremblant Resort, on-site; Golf Le Maitre, 8 miles; Mont-Tremblant National Park, 20 miles; Le Ranch Mont-Tremblant, 30 miles
Towns/Cities: Montréal, 85 miles; Ottawa, ON, 100 miles; Boston, MA, 520 miles; New York City, NY, 680 miles
Airports: Mont-Tremblant International Airport, La Macaza, 15 miles; Pierre-Elliott-Trudeau Airport, Montréal, 85 miles; Ottawa International Airport, ON, 110 miles

Auberge du Vieux-Port

97 DE LA COMMUNE EST, MONTRÉAL, QUÉBEC H2Y 1J1
Tel: +1 514 876 0081 **Fax:** +1 514 876 8923 **U.S./Canada Toll Free:** 1 888 660 7678
Web: www.johansens.com/aubergeduvieuxport **E-mail:** info@aubergeduvieuxport.com

***Our inspector loved:** The European charm and the perfect location in the heart of Old Montréal.*

Price Guide: (including full breakfast and 1 glass of wine with cheese selection between 5pm-7pm each evening)
rooms C$230-C$265
suites C$285

27

Attractions: Palais des Congrès, 0.5 miles; Casino de Montréal, 1 mile; Montréal Museum of Fine Arts, 1 mile; Biodome de Montréal, 3 miles
Towns/Cities: Mont-Tremblant, 85 miles; Ottawa, ON, 125 miles; Québec City, 160 miles
Airports: Montréal-Pierre Elliott Trudeau International Airport, 13 miles; St. Hubert Airport, 30 miles; Montréal-Mirabel International Airport, 37 miles

Located in the romantic and timeless area of Montréal's Old Port, Auberge du Vieux-Port is a cozy and elegant boutique hotel overlooking the St. Lawrence River. The hotel offers 27 luxury rooms with queen, king or 2 double beds, and an elaborate full breakfast each morning. In the evening, enjoy a glass of wine and cheese selection while relaxing on the terrace with stunning views of the Old Port and the River. Dining at Narcisse Bistro & Bar à Vin is a treat, serving seasonal French bistro cuisine and a wide range of wines, all while the soothing sounds of live jazz fills the air. Or dine on the rooftop terrace with spectacular views, especially during the International Fireworks Festival. Close to boutiques, galleries and historic sites, this hotel is the perfect base to explore Old Montréal.

Hôtel Nelligan

106 RUE SAINT-PAUL OUEST, MONTRÉAL, QUÉBEC H2Y 1Z3
Tel: +1 514 788 2040 **Fax:** +1 514 788 2041 **U.S./Canada Toll Free:** 1 877 788 2040
Web: www.johansens.com/nelligan **E-mail:** info@hotelnelligan.com

This boutique hotel mingles modern décor with the charm of Old Montréal. Rooms are furnished with high quality custom linens and drapery, dark wood furniture and many have fireplaces; suites are spacious with luxurious bathrooms. Passages of Emile Nelligan's beautiful poems are transcribed on the walls, immersing guests in Québec culture. The elegant ground floor consists of an efficient check-in and full concierge service, a library, garden atrium serving both breakfast and afternoon tea, and a bar-salon with welcoming leather and rattan furniture. Enjoy a pre-dinner drink in Verses Bar - martinis are their specialty - before heading to Verses Restaurant where modern French cuisine is underscored by Québec's finest fresh produce. Or dine in the new Méchant Boeuf Bar-Brasserie, a chic pub with a British flavor and French accents. Its friendly atmosphere is enhanced by the D.J. who plays the best classic rock all night long! Try the Méchant Burger, hailed as the best in town.

Our inspector loved: *The loft suites with large bathrooms and Jacuzzis.*

Price Guide: (including Continental breakfast and a glass of wine with cheese platter)
rooms C$235-C$260
suites C$300-C$1,450

Attractions: Casino de Montréal, 1 mile; Montréal Museum of Fine Arts, 1 mile; Old Port of Montréal, 3 miles; Montréal Olympic Park, 5 miles
Towns/Cities: Mont-Tremblant, 85 miles; Ottawa, ON, 125 miles; Québec City, 160 miles
Airports: Montréal-Pierre Elliott Trudeau International Airport, 13 miles; St. Hubert Airport, 30 miles; Montréal-Mirabel International Airport, 36 miles

CANADA - QUÉBEC (MONTRÉAL)

LE PLACE D'ARMES HÔTEL & SUITES

55 RUE SAINT-JACQUES OUEST, MONTRÉAL, QUÉBEC H2Y 3X2
Tel: +1 514 842 1887 **Fax:** +1 514 842 6469 **U.S./Canada Toll Free:** 1 888 450 1887
Web: www.johansens.com/hotelplacedarmes **E-mail:** reservation@hotelplacedarmes.com

***Our inspector loved:** The beautifully designed bathrooms with their large rain showers and luxuriously deep tubs.*

Price Guide: (including Continental breakfast and a glass of wine with cheese platter)
rooms C$230-C$285
suites C$325-C$1,200

135 M 350 SPA

Attractions: Old Montréal; Casino de Montréal, 1 mile; Montréal Museum of Fine Arts, 1 mile; Biodôme de Montréal, 3 miles
Towns/Cities: Mont-Tremblant, 85 miles; Ottawa, ON, 125 miles; Québec City, 160 miles
Airports: Pierre Elliott Trudeau International Airport, 13 miles; St. Hubert Airport, 30 miles; Mirabel International Airport, 37 miles

Old Montréal's first boutique hotel combines classic urban chic with the 19th-century architecture of the 3 historic buildings that comprise Le Place d'Armes. Rooms have high ceilings, exposed brickwork and a contemporary, comfortable feel. The bathrooms are large and luxurious with rain showers and deep soaking tubs. Guests are offered several dining options: Restaurant Aix Cuisine du Terroir, devoted to the enjoyment of local Québec cooking with an elaborate seasonal menu; Suite 701, which serves great martinis and creative cuisine in a chic gourmet bar/lounge setting; and there is also a rooftop terrace offering lunch, dinner and cocktails during the summer. Rainspa, featuring Montréal's only hammam, is a must! The traditional Middle Eastern steam bath, along with many body and facial treatments, is a great experience.

CANADA - QUÉBEC (NORTH HATLEY)

MANOIR HOVEY

575 HOVEY ROAD, NORTH HATLEY, QUÉBEC J0B 2CO
Tel: +1 819 842 2421 **Fax:** +1 819 842 2248 **U.S./Canada Toll Free:** 1 800 661 2421
Web: www.johansens.com/manoirhovey **E-mail:** manhovey@manoirhovey.com

This romantic and charming historic countryside inn is an ideal getaway all year round. Set alongside picturesque Lake Massawippi, luxurious rooms range from cozy to spacious, with fireplaces, bright bathrooms and whirlpool baths, beautiful canopy beds and private lakeside balconies. The award-winning restaurant features innovative haute cuisine using the finest local and regional products from Québec. The extensive wine list boasts over 900 labels. There is plenty to do in the winter including snow shoeing, dog sledding and ice skating on the inn's very own rink. And in the summer, relax on the small sandy beach or take a canoe off the private dock. English cream teas should be savored on the terrace and to complete the pampering, don't forget to schedule a Swedish massage.

Our inspector loved: *The peaceful setting.*

Price Guide: (per person)
superiors C$170-C$220
deluxes C$195-C$260
treetops and vista suites C$265-C$460

Awards/Ratings: Wine Spectator Award of Excellence 2008

Attractions: Lake Cruises on Mahogany Boat, 5-min walk; Private Skating Rink, 5-min walk; Louis St. Laurent Museum, 5 miles; Cross-Country and Downhill Skiing, 30 miles
Towns/Cities: Montréal, 90 miles; Québec, 150 miles; Ottawa ON, 220 miles; Boston MA, 275 miles
Airports: Air Sherbrooke, 30 miles; Pierre Trudeau Intl., 110 miles; Burlington Intl., VT, 120 miles

Affiliations: Relais & Châteaux

UNITED STATES OF AMERICA
Mexicali
Baja California Norte
Sonara
Hermosillo
Baja California Sur
Chihuahua
Chihuahua
Coahuila
Sinaloa
La Paz
Culiacan
Durango
Nuevo Leon
47
46
44
45
Cabo San Lucas
48
Durango
Monterrey
Mazatlán
Zacatecas
Tamaulipas
Zacatecas
Nayarit
San Luis Potosi
Ciudad Victoria
Tepic
Aguascalientes
62
San Luis Potosi
Puerto Vallarta
57
55
50
CARIBBEAN SEA
56
Leon
54
Jalisco
Guadalajara
Guanajuato
53
52
Querétaro
58
59
60
Hidalgo
Colima
Morelia
Michoacán
49
MEXICO CITY
61
Toluca
51
Yucatan
69
Zihuatanejo
Puebla
Merida
Guerrero
Campeche
Cancun
Chilpancingo
66
67
Acapulco
68
Villahermosa
Veracruz
65
64
Quintana Roo
63
Oaxaca
Tabasco
Campeche
PACIFIC OCEAN
Chetumal
Oaxaca
Chiapas
BELIZE
GUATEMALA
HONDURAS
EL SALVADOR

ESPERANZA, AN AUBERGE RESORT

KM. 7 CARRETERA TRANSPENINSULAR, PUNTA BALLENA, CABO SAN LUCAS, BAJA CALIFORNIA SUR 23410
Tel: +52 624 145 6400 **Fax:** +52 624 145 6499 **U.S./Canada Toll Free:** 1 866 311 2226
Web: www.johansens.com/esperanza **E-mail:** info@esperanzaresort.com

Situated atop the bluffs of Punta Ballena, overlooking 2 private beach coves on the Sea of Cortez, this modern Cabo San Lucas resort combines luxurious amenities with traditional Baja style. All ocean-view rooms have outdoor terraces, original handcrafted furnishings and beautiful local artwork. Your stay in a Luxury Suite is complete with private butler services. The regional cuisine at El Restaurante, with its expansive wine and tequila menus, is not to be missed, carved into the ocean bluffs with multi-level stone terraces that flow down to the ocean's edge. After a day at the private beach, pamper yourself at the spa, or enjoy a rejuvenating hand and foot massage by the pool.

***Our inspector loved:** The whale-watching.*

Price Guide: (excluding tax and service fee)
casitas U.S.$608-U.S.$2,080
suites U.S.$1,728-U.S.$8,960
villas U.S.$1,600-U.S.$6,400

57 90 SPA

Awards/Ratings: Condé Nast Johansens Most Excellent Resort, Mexico & Central America 2008; Condé Nast Traveler Gold List 2007

Attractions: La Galeria, 2-min walk; Night-life and Shops, 10-min walk; Kayaking and Sailing,10-min drive; Whale-Watching and Sport Fishing, 5 miles
Towns/Cities: Cabo San Lucas, 2 miles; San José del Cabo, 14 miles; Todos Santos, 42 miles
Airports: San José del Cabo (S.J.D.), 15 miles

Affiliations: The Leading Hotels of the World

Marquis Los Cabos Beach Resort & Spa

LOTE 74, KM. 21.5 CARRETERA TRANSPENINSULAR, FRACCIONAMIENTO CABO REAL, LOS CABOS, BAJA CALIFORNIA SUR 23400
Tel: +52 624 144 2000 **Fax:** +52 624 144 2001 **U.S./Canada Toll Free:** 1 877 238 9399
Web: www.johansens.com/marquisloscabos **E-mail:** info@marquisloscabos.com

Our inspector loved: *The stunning view of the Sea of Cortez from the lobby with its dramatic waterfall.*

Price Guide: (including wake up coffee)
rooms U.S.$465-U.S.$550
suites U.S.$825-U.S.$1,100

237 500 SPA

Attractions: Whale-Watching and Kayaking, 1 mile; Cabo San Lucas Night-life and Restaurants, 4 miles; Sport Fishing, 5 miles; Sailing, 5 miles
Towns/Cities: San José del Cabo, 4 miles; Cabo San Lucas, 12 miles; Todos Santos, 42 miles; La Paz, 100 miles
Airports: Los Cabos International Airport, 10 miles

Affiliations: The Leading Hotels of the World

This family-owned resort, set in lush landscaping and looking out to incredible views, offers the ultimate in luxury and service. Upon entering the lobby, the stunning infinity pool appears to fall into the Sea of Cortez with its water cascading dramatically down 36 feet to a spectacular pool. Each of the resort suites has lovely ocean views from private balconies or terraces and is adorned with original oil paintings. Those of you who prefer to hear the waves while you sleep can stay in one of 28 beach-side casitas, each with private pool. Lounge on the pristine, white sand beach or relax in the resort's full-service spa, one of the largest in Latin America. There are 3 outstanding restaurants including the highly-acclaimed Canto del Mar.

MEXICO - BAJA CALIFORNIA SUR (SAN JOSÉ DEL CABO)

Casa del Mar Suites Golf & Spa Resort

KM 19.5 CARRETERA TRANSPENINSULAR, SAN JOSÉ DEL CABO, BAJA CALIFORNIA SUR 23400
Tel: +52 624 145 7700 **Fax:** +52 624 144 0034 **U.S./Canada Toll Free:** 1 888 227 9621
Web: www.johansens.com/casadelmar **E-mail:** reservations@casadelmarmexico.com

Our inspector loved: *The Old World charm of the lobby, and dining on the beach.*

Price Guide: (excluding 10% service charge)
junior suites U.S.$395-U.S.$683
master suite U.S.$435-U.S.$886

31 60 SPA

Casa Del Mar is wonderfully located on a long stretch of beach where blue skies meet turquoise ocean. The charming lobby is decorated in traditional Mexican style and the surrounding grounds are tropical lush gardens. With several pools and dining areas to choose from you can go wherever your mood takes you and find relaxation and serenity. The suites feature the classic design of old Mexican haciendas with rich dark woods and soft colors that blend effectively with hand-crafted antique furniture from the fine craftsmen of Guadalajara. Recently voted Mexico's Leading Golf Resort, Cabo Real Golf Course provides a variety of hazards and is considered the toughest front-nine in Los Cabos! A relaxing day should be spent at the spa, Sueños del Mar. Spoil yourself with a sensorial experience like no other with the Mexican Hot Stone Massage Ceremony. The Spa has 7 indoor cabins and beautiful ocean-front "on the sand palapas."

Attractions: Whale Watching, 2-min walk; Golf, 5-min drive; Sport Fishing, 5 miles; Sailing, 5 miles
Towns/Cities: Cabo San Lucas, 5 miles; San José del Cabo, 10 miles; Todos Santos, 35 miles; La Paz, 110 miles
Airports: Los Cabos International Airport, 15 miles; San José International Airport (S.J.D.), 20 miles

Affiliations: Small Luxury Hotels of the World

Casa Natalia

BLVD. MIJARES 4, SAN JOSÉ DEL CABO, BAJA CALIFORNIA SUR 23400
Tel: +52 624 146 7100 **Fax:** +52 624 142 5110 **U.S./Canada Toll Free:** 1 888 277 3814
Web: www.johansens.com/casanatalia **E-mail:** casa.natalia@casanatalia.com

Our inspector loved: *Relaxing in my private hammock overlooking the pool.*

Price Guide: (excluding 13% tax and 15% service charge per room per night)
deluxe rooms U.S.$250-U.S.$425
spa suites U.S.$375-U.S.$575

16 13

Attractions: Art District, 1-min walk; 17th-Century San José del Cabo Historic Town, 5-min walk; Boutique Shopping, 5-min walk; Sport Fishing, 2 miles
Towns/Cities: San José del Cabo, on the doorstep; Cabo San Lucas, 20 miles; Todos Santos, 50 miles; La Paz, 186 miles
Airports: San José del Cabo International Airport, 9 miles

Affiliations: Mexico Boutique Hotels; Small Luxury Hotels of the World

This European-style boutique hotel nestles amidst palm trees and tropical bougainvillea in the heart of historic San José del Cabo. The owners, Nathalie and Loïc Tenoux, were inspired by the natural beauty of the region and worked with a famed Mexican architect to create an environment that reflected the spectacular landscape by creating hand-plastered walls, wood beams, tropical flowers and waterfalls. Each guest room is individually decorated combining local artwork, striking contemporary furnishings and earthy colors. Step out onto your private balcony where breakfast is served daily and relax in a hammock overlooking the courtyard, pool or neighboring tropical estuary. Alternatively, take advantage of the shuttle service to the nearby beach club. At night, open flame braziers light up the outdoors where you can enjoy dinner and cocktails alfresco. Owner Loïc Tenoux, serves innovative Mexican-Euro cuisine at Mi Cocina restaurant.

MEXICO - BAJA CALIFORNIA SUR (SAN JOSÉ DEL CABO)

LAS VENTANAS AL PARAÍSO, A ROSEWOOD RESORT

KM 19.5 CARRETERA TRANSPENINSULAR, SAN JOSÉ DEL CABO, BAJA CALIFORNIA SUR 23400
Tel: +52 624 144 2800 **Fax:** +52 624 144 2801 **U.S./Canada Toll Free:** 1 888 767 3966
Web: www.johansens.com/lasventanas **E-mail:** lasventanas@rosewoodhotels.com

Las Ventanas al Paraíso, meaning "Windows to Paradise," is an idyllic desert luxury boutique resort built on the beautiful southern tip of Cabo San Lucas, Baja Peninsula. Visually serene with Mediterranean-Mexican architecture, the resort features intricate swimming pools and lovely patios overlooking the Sea of Cortez. Marble showers, limestone floors and cozy fireplaces adorn each of the expansive suites. Savor inspired cuisine at "The Restaurant" while dining alfresco with its incredible views. For more casual fare, the ocean's edge Sea Grill serves contemporary Mexican cuisine. The perfect place to unwind is at the Tequila & Ceviche Bar to enjoy fresh seafood and exclusive Mexican tequilas. The separate 2,400-bottle wine cellar, La Cava, features weekly A Taste of Baja dinners. The world-class Spa offers personalized treatments for the ultimate relaxation.

Our inspector loved: *The tranquil setting overlooking the beach and sparkling waters.*

Price Guide: (excluding 13% tax and 15% service charge)
suites U.S.$525-U.S.$6,000
residence suites U.S.$1,425-U.S.$4,400

71 50 SPA

Attractions: Whale-Watching, 2-min walk; Golf, 5-min drive; Sailing, 5 miles; Sport Fishing, 5 miles
Towns/Cities: Cabo San Lucas, 20 miles; San José del Cabo, 20 miles; Todos Santos, 60 miles; La Paz, 110 miles
Airports: San José del Cabo International Airport, 20 miles

Hotel Boutique Casa Vieja Mexico

EUGENIO SUE 45 (COLONIA POLANCO), MEXICO DISTRITO FEDERAL 11560
Tel: +52 55 52 82 0067 **Fax:** +52 55 52 81 3780
Web: www.johansens.com/casavieja **E-mail:** sales@casavieja.com

Our inspector loved: *The great location for exploring the city.*

Price Guide:
suites U.S.$325-U.S.$950

10 M 30 DVD

Attractions: Chapultepec Park, 1 mile; Anthropological Museum, 1 mile; Teotihuacan Archeological Site, 30 miles
Towns/Cities: Cuernavaca, 53 miles; Puebla, 78 miles; Taxco, 94 miles
Airports: Mexico City International Airport, 9 miles

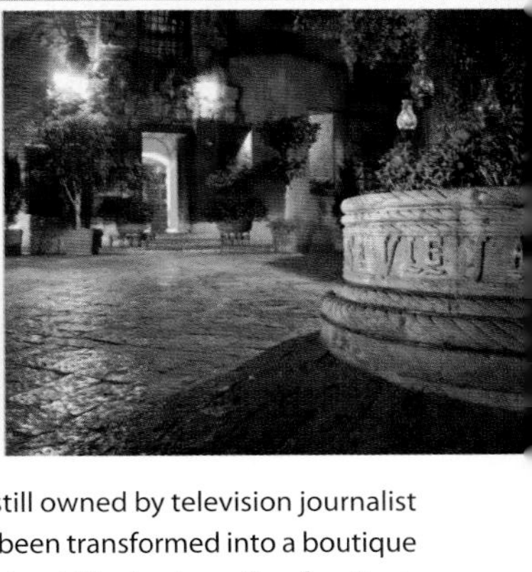

This exquisite mansion, once home to and still owned by television journalist and broadcaster Lolita Ayala, Casa Vieja has been transformed into a boutique hotel. The interior designer traveled throughout Mexico to gather furniture, textiles, paintings, statuary, chandeliers and rugs reflecting vibrant aspects of Mexican culture. Walls are vividly hand-painted by artisans, and treasures from the proprietor's personal art collection are on display for you to enjoy. The 10 suites include a 2-bedroom, 2-bathroom presidential suite, master suites with living room and 1-bedroom junior suites. There is a casual roof terrace restaurant bar, and an adjoining formal salon that serves traditional and modern cuisine by award-winning Chef Fernando Guadalupe, who is happy to prepare special requests according to your wishes.

QUINTA LAS ACACIAS

PASEO DE LA PRESA 168, GUANAJUATO, GUANAJUATO 36000
Tel: +52 473 731 1517 **Fax:** +52 473 731 1862 **U.S./Canada Toll Free:** 1 888 497 4129
Web: www.johansens.com/acacias **E-mail:** quintalasacacias@prodigy.net.mx

Our inspector loved: *The home-from-home ambience.*

Price Guide: (double occupancy)
standard rooms U.S.$220-U.S.$275
suite with Jacuzzi U.S.$340-U.S.$362
master suite U.S.$368-U.S.$398

17 M 25

Attractions: Diego Rivera Museum, 20-min walk; Juarez Theater, 20-min walk; Mummies Museum, 10-min drive; Valenciana Mine, 10-min drive
Towns/Cities: Leon, 45-min drive; San Miguel Allende, 90-min drive; Queretaro, 2.5-hour drive
Airports: B.J.X. International Airport (Bajio o Leon), 30-min drive

Affiliations: Mexico Boutique Hotels

Evoking the atmosphere of former times in Mexico, the striking façade of Quinta Las Acacias is a testament to the French architecture that once dominated the city of Guanajuato. The interior has retained the characteristics of the original building and is filled with wood and marble floors, period furniture and Oriental rugs. Standard suites are individually appointed with brass, wicker and wooden furnishings and the Mexican suites have Jacuzzis, and are bedecked with Mexican arts and curio from the country as well as terraces covered in flowers and verdant plants. The balcony by the opulent European-styled Master Suite affords magnificent views across Florencio Antillon Park. Master Chef, Pedro Garcia, has combined authentic family recipes with international favorites and the result is a gourmet menu that appeals to all palates.

Loma Del Mar

FRAGATAS LOTE F17 SEC. HOTELERA II, IXTAPA - ZIHUATANEJO, GUERRERO 40884
Tel: +52 755 555 04 60 **Fax:** +52 755 555 04 61 **U.S./Canada Toll Free:** 1 866 496 1082
Web: www.johansens.com/lomadelmar **E-mail:** erios@lomadelmar.com

Our inspector loved: *The gourmet restaurant, La Luna de Shiva, that serves delectable modern, Mexican cuisine.*

Price Guide:
rooms U.S.$591-U.S.$650
suites U.S.$716-U.S.$896

16 SPA

Attractions: Arts and Crafts Market, 6 miles; Marina, 8 miles
Towns/Cities: Petatlan, 19 miles
Airports: Ixtapa-Zihuatanejo Airport, 9 miles

Affiliations: Small Luxury Hotels of the World

This Mediterranean and contemporary Mexican-style resort, beautifully located across from the prestigious Palm Real Golf Course in Ixtapa, is a truly relaxing retreat. 16 Luxury Suites and Penthouses are set amid the palms, lakes and lush tropical vegetation with breathtaking golf course views. Each of the 1 and 2-bedroom air-conditioned suites are Mexican contemporary in décor with exquisite details and natural tones, and include fully-fitted kitchens, dining areas and spacious terraces with superb views. The main restaurant, La Luna de Shiva, will tempt your palate with delightful modern Mexican cuisine or try La Pampa Steak House, a traditional Argentinean steak house overlooking Ixtapa Bay. For ultimate relaxation, take a Pilates or yoga class followed by a calming treatment at the spa or at the recently opened thalasso.

El Tamarindo Beach & Golf Resort

KM 7.5 HIGHWAY 200, CARRETERA BARRA DE NAVIDAD - PUERTO VALLARTA, CIHUATLAN, JALISCO 48970
Tel: +52 315 351 5031 **Fax:** +52 315 351 5070
Web: www.johansens.com/eltamarindo **E-mail:** reserve@eltamarindoresort.com

***Our inspector loved:** The amazing ocean-front casitas.*

Price Guide:
ocean-front casitas U.S.$1,125-U.S.$1,300
garden casitas U.S.$875-U.S.$1, 095
luxurious 4-bedroom ocean-front residences U.S.$3,600-U.S.$10,000

32 M 40 DVD WiFi SPA

Attractions: Jungle Tour, 19 miles; Deep-Sea Fishing/Scuba Diving, 31 miles; Polo, 31 miles
Towns/Cities: Barra de Navidad, 6 miles; Manzanillo, 28 miles; Puerto Vallarta, 137 miles
Airports: Manzanillo Airport, 22 miles; Puerto Vallarta Airport, 137 miles

Affiliations: Mexico Boutique Hotels

Costalegre on the Mexican Pacific Coast covers 124 miles of undeveloped, unspoiled, eco-friendly resorts. Chic décor and casual elegance are what you will find at El Tamarindo. This intimate resort features 29 spacious, open casitas and 3 private 4-bedroom ocean-front residences surrounded by lush palm trees and gardens. Each accommodation has a marble bathroom, teak flooring, a private garden and plunge pool. Encompassed by 2,040 acres, the resort is located alongside 2 miles of private beach that looks out to magnificent views of the Pacific Ocean and Sierra Madre. At the end of the day choose your location for dinner: in the main restaurant, at your casita, on the private pier or on the beach! The signature 18-hole golf course by David Fleming is set against spectacular views of the Pacific, and of course a great variety of water sports are available to all.

El Careyes Beach Resort

KM 53.5, CARRETERA BARRA DE NAVIDAD-PUERTO VALLARTA, COSTA CAREYES, JALISCO 48970
Tel: +52 315 351 0000 **Fax:** +52 315 351 0100 **Mexico Toll Free:** 1 800 433 3989
Web: www.johansens.com/elcareyes **E-mail:** careyes@careyeshotel.com

Our inspector loved: *The private, small and quiet bay in the middle of nowhere.*

Price Guide:
pool view suites U.S.$355-U.S.$435
suites U.S.$449-U.S.$889
2/3bedroom villas U.S.$795-U.S.$1,005

53 120 DVD WiFi SPA

Awards/Ratings: AAA 5 Diamond 2007 and 2008

Attractions: Deep-Sea Fishing, 30-min boat ride
Towns/Cities: Careyitos, 1.9 miles; Chamela, 6 miles; Perula, 16 miles; Puerto Vallarta, 99 miles
Airports: Manzanillo Airport, 47 miles; Puerto Vallarta Airport, 99 miles

Affiliations: Mexico Boutique Hotels

Nestled in a secluded cove on the Pacific Ocean, this Mediterranean-style resort is an elegant Mexican retreat. Suites and casitas look out to breathtaking views of the Pacific and are designed in the artistic Costa Careyes (the turtle coast) style, each with whitewashed walls, splashes of color on the painted alcoves and original crafts and artwork. The rich terracotta tones blend beautifully with the surrounding lush green tropical rainforest. La Lantana restaurant serves fine Mexican and international cuisine, perfect for a romantic alfresco candle-lit dinner, while the bar and the beach-front sitting areas are romantic places to capture the sunset or watch the moonlight fall onto the sea. Relax by the eye-catching and central free-form pool that winds throughout the grounds or visit the Spa at El Careyes to ensure total well-being for your mind, body and soul.

Hotelito Desconocido

PLAYON DE MISMALOYA S/N,MUNICIPIO DE TOMATLÁN, LA CRUZ DE LORETO, JALISCO 48460
Tel: +52 322 281 4010 **Fax:** +52 322 281 4178 **U.S./Canada Toll Free:** 1 800 013 1313
Web: www.johansens.com/hotelito **E-mail:** reservaciones@hotelito.com

This eco-luxury resort is a unique retreat designed by Italian fashion designer, Marcello Murzilli (Charro). Charming, romantic and rustic, it is built in the style of a Mexican village with palafito bungalows atop stilts. Each overlooks either the crystal clear water of the lagoon or beach or is found nestled in the sand dunes. The most private are only accessible by row boat. The full service El Mundo de la Salud Spa exudes harmony and balance enhanced by its peaceful location amongst the birds and nature. Take part in the traditional body cleansing ceremony in the Temazcal ancient sweat lodge for an unforgettable experience. The resort's 2 restaurants, Nopalito and El Cantarito, are also set on stilts over the blue water with a view of the estuary. The authentic Mexican cuisine with fresh daily menus will blow your mind!

Our inspector loved: *The enchanting natural surroundings.*

Price Guide: (including breakfast)
rooms U.S.$460-U.S.$830
suites U.S.$610-U.S.$1,230

24 SPA

Attractions: Bird-Watching, on-site
Towns/Cities: La Cruz de Loreto, 3 miles; Tomatlán, 25 miles; Puerto Vallarta, 56 miles
Airports: Puerto Vallarta Airport, 56 miles; Manzanillo Airport, 75 miles;

Affiliations: Small Luxury Hotels of the World; Mexico Boutique Hotels

Las Alamandas Resort

CARRETERA BARRA DE NAVIDAD - PUERTO VALLARTA KM 83.5, COL. QUEMARO, JALISCO 48850
Tel: +52 322 285 5500 **Fax:** +52 322 285 5027 **U.S./Canada Toll Free:** 1 888 882 9616
Web: www.johansens.com/alamandas **E-mail:** info@alamandas.com

Our inspector loved: *The private beach, lake and river where you can enjoy peace and quiet contemplation.*

Price Guide: (excluding taxes and service charge)
luxury rooms U.S.$371-U.S.$2,070

Attractions: Bird Island Tour, on-site; 4 Secluded Beaches, on-site
Towns/Cities: Perula, 6 miles; Barra de Navidad, 51 miles; Manzanillo, 68 miles; Puerto Vallarta, 74.5 miles
Airports: Manzanillo Airport, 68 miles; Puerto Vallarta Airport, 74.5 miles

Affiliations: Mexico Boutique Hotels; Preferred Boutique

A perfect paradise for those seeking beauty, romance and privacy, Las Alamandas is surrounded by 1,500 acres of tropical gardens, breathtaking blue lagoons and endless white sandy beaches. Colorful décor is in a traditional Mexican style with stunning fabrics and elegant design complemented by hand-painted artefacts and Mexican folk art. Pale yellow paths with stone mosaics wind through fragrant flowers to the bedrooms, which have oversized bathrooms with private outdoor showers and spacious terraces overlooking the Pacific Ocean. The 2 excellent restaurants serve unique dishes featuring freshly-caught fish, free-range chicken and organic meats, fruits and vegetables from the hotel's orchards. Owner, Isabel Goldsmith-Patiño, has spearheaded many projects to preserve the Mexican coastline and bird lovers will appreciate the bird sanctuary within the grounds.

MEXICO - JALISCO (GUADALAJARA)

CLARUM 101

PARQUE JUAN DIEGO 101, COL. CHAPALITA, C.P. 45050, GUADALAJARA, JALISCO
Tel: +52 33 1201 7507 **Fax:** +52 33 1201 7508
Web: www.johansens.com/clarum101 **E-mail:** info@clarum101.com

Hidden away on one of the most beautiful streets in Guadalajara, this chic and hip hotel is perfect for the sophisticated traveler. The hotel boasts 6 unique private rooms and 3 stunning suites, each stylishly decorated in white with bursts of vibrant color by local artists. The open-air design of the rooms creates a feeling of comfort, while providing every cutting-edge amenity. The smartly dressed staff, all in black, are extremely service-oriented and will cater to your every whim. Tapas and Asian fusion-inspired entrées are perfectly paired with an extensive selection of wines, cool martinis or exquisite herbal teas. The panoramic rooftop terrace is the ideal place for star-gazing and enjoying a savory glass of red wine.

Our inspector loved: *The spectacular modern, minimalist concept.*

Price Guide: (including Continental breakfast)
rooms U.S.$230-U.S.$295

9 DVD WiFi

Attractions: Gallerias Shopping Mall, 3-min drive; Downtown, 20-min drive; Tlaquepaque 30-min drive
Towns/Cities: Chapala, 40-min drive; Tequila, 1-hour drive;
Airports: Miguel Hidalgo International Airport, 16 miles

Affiliations: Mexico Boutique Hotels

Casa Velas Hotel Boutique

PELICANOS 311, FRACC. MARINA VALLARTA, PUERTO VALLARTA, JALISCO 48354
Tel: +52 322 226 6688 **Fax:** +52 322 226 6699 **U.S./Canada Toll Free:** 1 866 529 8813.
Web: www.johansens.com/casavelas **E-mail:** reservaciones@hotelcasavelas.com

Our inspector loved: *The magnificent personalized service and friendly staff.*

Price Guide: (including all à la carte meals, snacks, and unlimited premium beverages, per person) suites U.S.$270-U.S.$3,000

SPA

Attractions: El Malecon (Boardwalk), 7 miles; Canopy Tour, 15 miles; Sport Fishing, 50 miles; Las Caletas, 50 miles
Towns/Cities: Puerto Vallarta, 5 miles; Nuevo Vallarta, 7 miles; Punta de Mita, 40 miles; San Sebastian Silver Town, 70 miles
Airports: Puerto Vallarta Airport, 2 miles

Affiliations: The Leading Small Hotels of the World; Preferred Hotels & Resorts

This hotel is well-known for its secluded location and sense of intimacy. The traditional Mexican-style textures and colors are stunning and enhance the luxurious accommodations. The hotel is surrounded by Marina Vallarta Golf Course, and has a state-of-the-art gym. At the heart of the resort is SPA Casa Velas, a world-class spa and wellness retreat designed to revitalize and rejuvenate both body and soul. Personalized treatments and pampering services are enhanced by the tranquil, tropical atmosphere. A private ocean-front beach club has a comfortable lounge area and a superb restaurant, which serves Oriental specialties. For gourmet dining, enjoy the elegant Emiliano restaurant in the main hotel.

CANTERA DIEZ

CALLE BENITO JUÁREZ 63, CENTRO, MORELIA, MICHOACÁN
Tel: +52 443 312 54 19
Web: www.johansens.com/canteradiez **E-mail:** contact@canteradiezhotel.com

Our inspector loved: *The sophisticated rooms with large glass doors that allow you to see the Jacuzzi.*

Price Guide:
standard suites U.S.$253
junior suites U.S.$333.50
master suites U.S.$374
cantera suite U.S.$431.50

11

This charming luxury boutique hotel, set in one of Mexico's most beautiful Colonial cities, has been recently restored to preserve its original architectural details that are over 300 years old. Upon entering the welcoming and striking lobby, with its impressive fire pit and chic décor, you will be led to your elegant and comfortable suite that has been thoughtfully designed by renowned engineer, Juan Carlos Doce. Each features stunning furnishings dressed in rich colors that harmoniously blend modern and historic design. Exquisite paintings and designs by noted Mexican artists Irma Obegón and Rodrigo Traviño can be found throughout the hotel. Discriminating travelers will enjoy the high level of service and attention to detail. With spectacular views of the Cathedral, the hotel's location is ideal for exploring the secret history of the Purepecha culture.

Attractions: Morelia Center, on-site; Cathedral, 2-min walk
Towns/Cities: Patzcuaro, 24 miles
Airports: Morelia International Airport, 12 miles

Hotel Virrey de Mendoza

AV. MADERO PTE. 310, CENTRO HISTÓRICO, MORELIA, MICHOACÁN 58000
Tel: +52 44 33 12 06 33 **Fax:** +52 44 33 12 67 19 **U.S./Canada Toll Free:** 1 877 88 92 161
Web: www.johansens.com/hvirrey **E-mail:** hvirrey@prodigy.net.mx

Our inspector loved: *The individually decorated guest rooms, and the centuries-old castle.*

Price Guide: (including breakfast)
rooms MXN$2,100-MXN$2,700
suites MXN$2,900-MXN$4,100

55 100 3 DVD WiFi

Attractions: Convention Center, 0.6 miles; Historical Center, 1 mile
Towns/Cities: Patzcuaro, 33 miles
Airports: Michoacán Airport, 53 miles

Housed in a building that since 1595 has witnessed many memorable events in Mexican history, this hotel has a reputation of being one of the most beautiful in the country, dating back to its opening in 1938. Retaining the magnificence of its former Colonial atmosphere, the patio, with its exquisite features and majestic glass window, provides a stunning and singular touch. The comfortable and elegant rooms, suites and Virreynal Suite are distinctively decorated with priceless antiques. Some have balconies overlooking either the Main Square, Cathedral or Avenida Madero. The Del Virrey Restaurant serves breakfast, lunch and dinner, and offers traditional Michoacán food and international haute cuisine.

Villa Montaña Hotel & Spa

PATZIMBA 201, VISTA BELLA, MORELIA, MICHOACÁN 58090
Tel: +52 443 314 02 31 **Fax:** +52 443 315 14 23
Web: www.johansens.com/montana **E-mail:** res@villamontana.com.mx

Nestled in the Santa Maria Hills, with stunning views over the city of Morelia, Villa Montaña offers a serene and tranquil private retreat. Each cottage-like room and suite enjoys a secluded setting amongst sub-tropical gardens interconnected by paths and patios adorned with statues and exotic plants. In the bedrooms, exquisite Colonial antiques combine with traditional Michoacán crafts; even the fireplaces are works of art. The elegant yet casual dining area serves an innovative menu of contemporary international and Mexican cuisine. The restaurant's specialty is roasted Cornish rock hen with black truffle, and there is an extensive wine list to complement every dish. Business clients will benefit from the full-service conference center and smaller meeting rooms, while the enchanting hilltop setting provides a wonderful backdrop for weddings.

Our inspector loved: *The elegant spa that is simply amazing.*

Price Guide:
rooms U.S.$210-U.S.$290
suites U.S.$355-U.S.$490

36 100 SPA

Attractions: Convention Center, 0.6 miles; Historical Center, 1.9 miles; The Cathedral, 1.9 miles
Towns/Cities: Cuitzeo, 20 miles; Patzcuaro, 33 miles
Airports: Francisco J. Mujica Airport, 16 miles

Affiliations: Mexico Boutique Hotels

Las Mañanitas

RICARDO LINARES 107, CENTRO 62000, CUERNAVACA, MORELOS
Tel: +52 777 362 00 00 **Fax:** +52 777 318 36 72 **U.S./Canada Toll Free:** 1 888 413 9199
Web: www.johansens.com/lasmananitas **E-mail:** reservaciones@lasmananitas.com.mx

Our inspector loved: *Having a delicious dinner in the romantically lit garden at night.*

Price Guide: (including breakfast)
suites U.S.$260-U.S.$501

25 M 350 12 SPA

Awards/Ratings: DiRoNA 2008

Attractions: Cortez Palace, 2 miles; Borda Gardens, 2 miles; Archeological Site of Xochicalco, 19 miles
Towns/Cities: Tepoztlan, 16 miles; Mexico City, 59 miles; Taxco, 62 miles
Airports: Mexico City International Airport, 68 miles

Affiliations: Relais & Châteaux

This idyllic retreat is a welcoming sanctuary, located in the charming mountain town of Cuernavaca, Mexico, known as the "city of eternal spring." The Spanish Colonial style suites are beautifully decorated, surrounded by splendid gardens of flowers and sculptures by renowned artists. Enjoy the peacefulness of this sophisticated property while relaxing by the beautiful open-air pool set within the private gardens of the hotel. At Las Mañanitas Restaurant, savor award-winning Mexican and international cuisine in the dining room or on the open-air terraces where you will be surrounded by exotic birds and eye-catching artwork. Traditional Mexican desserts are a delectable treat. Cuernavaca enjoys a spring-like climate all year round and is the ideal base for exploring Mexico's ancient ruins, museums and nearby towns.

Grand Velas All Suites & Spa Resort

AV. COCOTEROS 98 SUR, NUEVO VALLARTA, RIVIERA NAYARIT 63735
Tel: +52 322 226 8000 **Fax:** +52 322 297 2005 **U.S./Canada Toll Free:** +1 877 398 2784
Web: www.johansens.com/grandvelas **E-mail:** reservas@grandvelas.com

Artfully constructed in a crescent shape allowing every suite an ocean view, this beach-front resort is a blend of the traditional and contemporary. The décor expresses a new take on original Mexican design, utilizing indigenous materials from native villages and the Asian tropics. Hand-made carvings and engravings adorn the walls and the use of rich, natural hues creates an inviting ambience. There are a wealth of activities to choose from including water sports, golf and tennis, and the spa has an extensive range of therapies and indoor treatment area. The entertainment continues into the evening with shows by the resident magician and performances in the outdoor theater. There are no less than 5 restaurants serving snacks, international, Mexican, Italian and French cuisine.

Our inspector loved: *The pool area, including the infinity pool, and wide range of outdoor activities.*

Price Guide: (all inclusive)
rooms U.S.$460-U.S.$4,500
suites U.S.$1.056-U.S.$10,000

267 M 600 SPA

Awards/Ratings: Condé Nast Johansens Most Excellent Spa Hotel, Mexico & Central America 2006-2008; AAA 5 Diamond

Attractions: Malecon Puerto Vallarta, 16 miles; Marietas Islands, 124 miles; Whale-Watching, 124 miles
Towns/Cities: Puerto Vallarta, 16 miles
Airports: Puerto Vallarta Airport, 9 miles

Affiliations: The Leading Hotels of the World

Casa Cid de Leon

AV. MORELOS 602, CENTRO, OAXACA, OAXACA 68000
Tel: +52 951 51 47013/60414 **Fax:** +52 951 51 47 013
Web: www.johansens.com/leon **E-mail:** casaciddeleon@prodigy.net.mx

Our inspector loved: *The welcoming setting that makes you feel right at home.*

Price Guide: (including breakfast, excluding 18% tax)
suites U.S.$200-U.S.$230

SPA

Attractions: City Attractions, The Zócalo and Santo Domingo Church, close by
Towns/Cities: Etla, 10 miles; Monte Albán, 20-min drive; Mitla, 45-min drive
Airports: Oaxaca Airport, 15-min drive

Affiliations: Mexico Boutique Hotels

Once over the threshold of this unpretentious, quaint and inviting hotel you will immediately revel in the warmth, comfort and harmony of its atmosphere and ambience. The charming, attentive staff provide superb service which includes a daily delivery of fresh flowers and a delicious Oaxacan breakfast to your very own suite or if you prefer, to the beautiful terrace. During the evening the chef will suggest Mexican traditional dishes for dinner but is happy to prepare an array of meals and will even create specially requested meals with prior arrangement. Comprising 4 suites, this is a truly private retreat with each suite being a unique and stylish haven. The one which attracts most attention is La Bella Eopca, which has 3 balconies overlooking the street. The 2-story, 2-bathroom El Mio Cid Suite is ideal for a family, while the suites located downstairs, La Dominica and Aranjuez, are popular for their spaciousness, peaceful air and warm, home-from-home character.

Casa Oaxaca

CALLE GARCÍA VIGIL 407, CENTRO, OAXACA, OAXACA 68000
Tel: +52 951 514 4173 **Fax:** +52 951516 4412
Web: www.johansens.com/oaxaca **E-mail:** reservaciones@casaoaxaca.com.mx

Our inspector loved: *The individual Mexican décor in each room, and the personal service.*

Price Guide: (including Continental breakfast, welcome drink and cocktail, Internet access and parking)
rooms U.S.$$177-U.S.$253
suites U.S.$277-U.S.$354

7 DVD WiFi

Attractions: Archeology Zones, Dainzu, 12 miles; Monte Alban, 32 miles
Towns/Cities: Noxhitlan, 53 miles
Airports: Oaxaca Airport, 9 miles

Located in the center of the beautiful ancient city of Oaxaca, declared part of the world's cultural heritage by UNESCO, Casa Oaxaca is a traditional Colonial house that perfectly combines Old World charm with the convenience of modern living. Open spiral staircases are stunning against white and earth tone walls, complemented by designer armchairs and amazing Mexican pieces of art. A picturesque garden has a heavenly "Temazcal" steam bath, where herbs, used for centuries by the indigenous Mexican people, cure and balance the mind, body and spirit. Aromatherapy massages, facials, yoga and pedicures and manicures with reflexology can be arranged. Tempting classic, seasonal Oaxacan dishes are lovingly created, by appointment only, in the superb restaurant, which has a quiet, intimate ambience. Tour guides of Oaxaca and transportation can be organized.

La Casona de Tita

GARCÍA VIGIL 805, CENTRO, C.P. 68000 OAXACA, OAXACA
Tel: +52 951 5 16 1400 **Fax:** +52 951 5 16 1402
Web: www.johansens.com/lacasonadetita **E-mail:** lacasonadetita@yahoo.com.mx

Our inspector loved: *The minimalist style, and the hospitality.*

Price Guide: (including breakfast)
rooms MXN$1,800-MXN$3,000

Attractions: Museum of Santo Domingo, 5-min walk; Contemporary Art Museum, 5-min walk; Zocalo, 10-min walk; Traditional Markets, 12-min walk
Towns/Cities: El Tule, 25-min drive; Santa María Coyotepec, 25-min drive; Mitla, 35-min drive; Ocotlan, 40-min drive
Airports: Oaxaca Airport, 25-min drive

This beautifully restored 19th-century mansion, set in the heart of Oaxaca, the colonial capital of Southern Mexico, is an elegant and private hideaway. Tranquil and luxurious, 6 spacious guest rooms and suites maintain the property's historical ambience and are decorated in calming brown tones. Each has soaring beamed ceilings, antique furniture, exquisite contemporary Mexican art, and fine Oaxacan hand-woven linens. Modern conveniences will ensure a comfortable stay. All rooms face onto the lovely central courtyard with trickling patio fountain. The sunny terrace and dining room are a charming setting to enjoy the complimentary traditional Mexican breakfast, make conversation or simply read a favorite book. The concierge can arrange visits to the beautiful beaches, archeological ruins, and nearby colonial buildings and Cathedral.

Ceiba del Mar Beach & Spa Resort

COSTERA NORTE LTE. 1, S.M. 10, MZ. 26, PUERTO MORELOS, QUINTANA ROO 77580
Tel: +52 998 872 8060 **Fax:** +52 998 872 8061 **U.S./Canada Toll Free:** 1 877 545 6221
Web: www.johansens.com/ceibademar **E-mail:** reserve@ceibadelmar.com

Set on a stretch of pristine beach along the Caribbean coast of Mexico's Yucatan Peninsula, Ceiba del Mar Beach & Spa Resort is secluded, yet only a walk away from the charming seaport town of Puerto Morelos. The 88 guest rooms include spacious master suites and terrace-topped penthouses with dazzling views of the sea, whose interiors are quietly exquisite with a soothing sensation of space and innovative touches. The vast swimming pool features a congenial swim-up bar and there are 2 restaurants. One is located on the beach with a rooftop bar and serves a variety of Mexican and international cuisine, while the palapa-topped pagoda at the end of a long wooden pier is a lovely choice for candle-lit dinners and even weddings. The Spa at Ceiba del Mar is famous for its holistic treatments and revitalizing aromatherapy with indigenous Maya elements.

Our inspector loved: *The incredible terrace-topped penthouses and the privacy and tranquility of the location.*

Price Guide: (all inclusive and bed and breakfast rates available, excluding 17% tax and service charge)
rooms U.S.$390-U.S.$480
suites U.S.$440-U.S.$1,315

88 140 SPA

Attractions: Xcaret Park, 25 miles; Xelha Eco Park, 62 miles; Tulum Archeological Site, 68 miles
Towns/Cities: Cancun, 12 miles; Playa Del Carmen, 19 miles; Cozumel, 50 miles
Airports: Cancun Airport, 14 miles

Affiliations: Preferred Boutique

Grand Velas All Suites & Spa Resort, Riviera Maya

CARRETERA CANCÚN-TULUM KM. 62, PLAYA DEL CARMEN, MUNICIPIO DEL SOLIDARIDAD, QUINTANA ROO 77710
Tel: +52 984 109 5600 **Fax:** +52 984 109 5602 **U.S./Canada Toll Free:** 1 866 657 1404
Web: www.johansens.com/rivieramaya **E-mail:** reservationsrm@grandvelas.com

Our inspector loved: *This latest edition to the Grand Velas family resorts.*

Price Guide: (all inclusive, double occupancy)
master U.S.$760-U.S.$900
ambassador U.S.$880-U.S.$1,100
ambassador grand class U.S.$1,280-U.S.$1,600

497 1400 SPA

Attractions: Xcaret Ecological Park, 10 miles; Xel-ha Ecological Park, 40 miles; Coba, 72 miles; Chichen-Itza Archeological Site, 176 miles
Towns/Cities: Playa del Carmen, 7 miles; Cancun, 35 miles; Tulum, 46 miles; Cozumel, 45-min ferry ride from Playa del Carmen
Airports: Cancun International Airport, 40-min drive

The recently completed Grand Velas is in the heart of the stunning Riviera Maya. Close to beaches, ecological parks and archeological sites, this is a wonderful base from which to explore the Yucatan Peninsula. An all-inclusive resort with perfect ambiances and accommodations for couples, families and business travelers, there are 92 suites within the adults-only ambiance with a separate pool, restaurants and bars. 2 more ambiances comprise 405 suites ideal for any traveler, located in lush vegetation or facing the beach. The resort's suite accommodations embody luxury living with amenities such as dedicated butler service, outdoor plunge pool, indoor whirlpool bathtub and 24-hour room service. Experience a Culinary Tour with the resort's variety of specialty, gourmet restaurants that includes light fare by the pool and formal dining. There is also a Convention Center able to host large company retreats and small conferences, the spa and state-of-the-art fitness center.

Casa Nalum

SIAN KA'AN BIOSPHERE RESERVE, QUINTANA ROO
Tel: +52 19991 639 510
Web: www.johansens.com/casanalum **E-mail:** info@nalum.com

Casa Nalum is a private villa located inside the biosphere reserve of Sian Ka'an. The house combines eco-design with all the modern comforts of home and has only 4 rooms, including a master bedroom. This all-inclusive villa has a beautiful open-air common area that expands into a deck with gorgeous views of the Mexican Caribbean waters, and a scenic lagoon located behind the main house where a private boat can take you to explore ancient Mayan canals. The location offers complete peace and relaxation, and the welcoming staff includes a full-time private concierge, maid, cook, butler and gardener to accommodate your every need. Dining is a wonderful experience with its exciting fusion of Mexican and European flavors that can be experienced in the formal dining room or alfresco on one of the terraces.

Our inspector loved: *The exclusive and spectacular natural surroundings.*

Price Guide: (per week, all inclusive, 4-night minimum stay)
house U.S.$10,500-U.S.$21,000

Awards/Ratings: Condé Nast Johansens Most Excellent Romantic Hideaway, Mexico & Central America 2007

Attractions: Mayan Canals, close by; Fly-Fishing, close by; Tulum Archeological Site, 12 miles
Towns/Cities: Tulum, 9 miles; Playa del Carmen, 50 miles; Coba, 34 miles; Cancun, 87 miles
Airports: Cancun International Airport, 75 miles

Hacienda Xcanatún - Casa de Piedra

CALLE 20 S/N, COMISARÍA XCANATÚN, KM. 12 CARRETERA MÉRIDA - PROGRESO, MÉRIDA, YUCATÁN 97302
Tel: +52 999 941 0273 **Fax:** +52 999 941 0319 **U.S./Canada Toll Free:** 1 888 883 3633
Web: www.johansens.com/xcanatun **E-mail:** hacienda@xcanatun.com

Our inspector loved: *Having a massage on the terrace looking out to the amazing garden while listening to the birds.*

Price Guide: (including breakfast)
suites U.S.$245-U.S.$345

18 80
SPA

Awards/Ratings: Condé Nast Johansens Most Excellent Boutique Hotel, Mexico & Central America 2006

Attractions: Dzibilchaltun, 3 miles; Uxmal Archeological Site, 50 miles; Chichen Itza Archeological Site, 75 miles
Towns/Cities: Downtown Mérida, 8 miles; Progreso, 12 miles; Cancun, 202 miles
Airports: Mérida Airport, 16 miles; Cancun Airport, 199 miles

Affiliations: Mexico Boutique Hotels

Recipient of The American Academy of Hospitality Sciences Star Diamond Award for 6 consecutive years and rated AAA 4 Diamonds, this former 18th-century sisal plantation offers privacy, 5-star cuisine and attentive service. Set in 9 acres of gardens, all of the spacious, romantic suites feature carved cedar doors, Caribbean Colonial furnishings and original oil paintings. Each has a veranda or balcony strung with hammocks and sky-lit marble-wrapped bathrooms fitted with a hydrotherapy tub/shower or hand-crafted stone tub filled by a waterfall. Start the day by taking breakfast on the dining terrace or in your own suite, and savor international-Caribbean cuisine and Yucatecan specialties in Casa de Piedra. Stress-reducing massages, body-wraps and Mayan healing treatments are available in the spa. Private meetings, weddings and parties are accommodated in the family chapel with on-site planners. The hotel has a children's policy, so please call for information.

Alabama

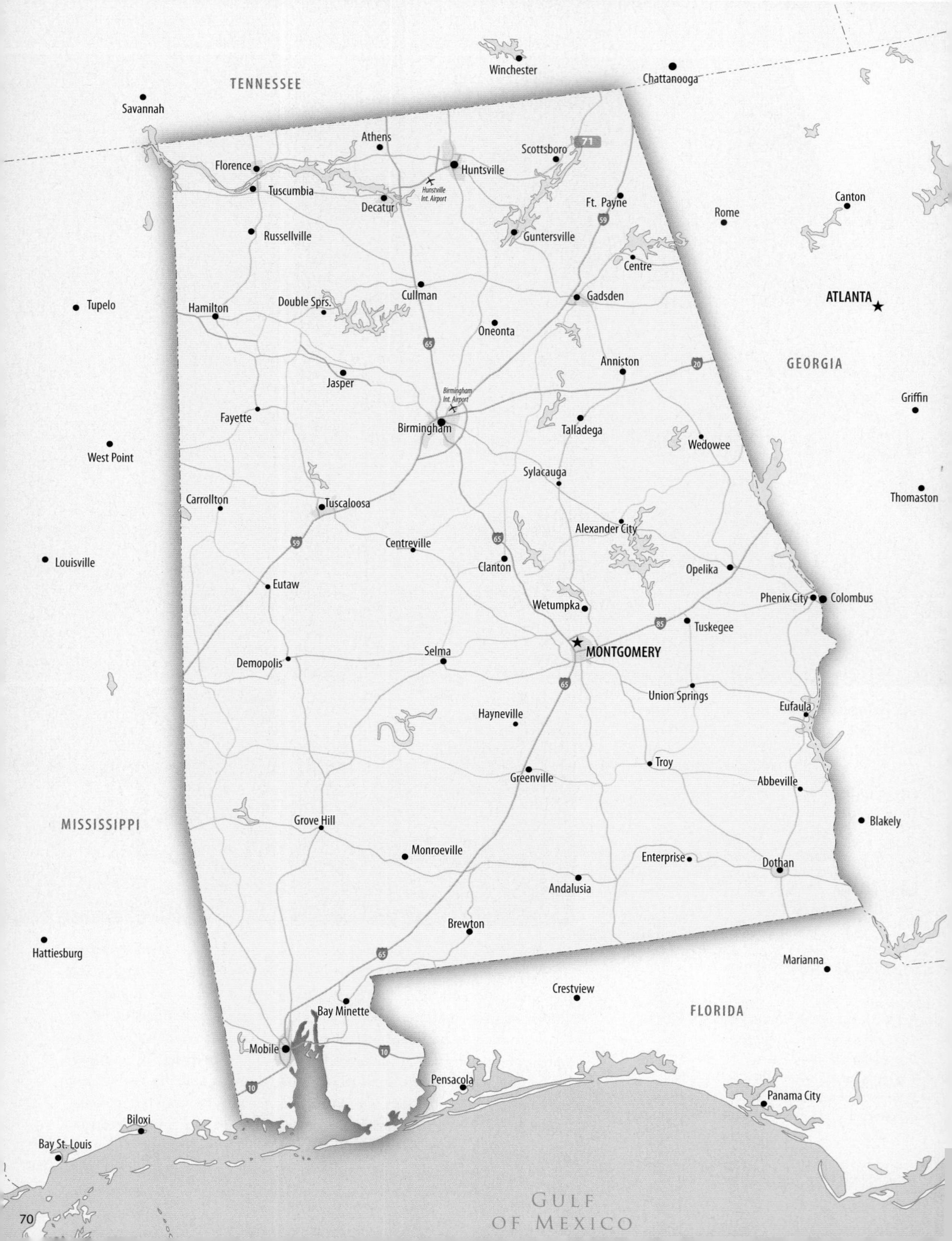
TENNESSEE
Savannah
Winchester
Chattanooga
Athens
Scottsboro
71
Florence
Huntsville
Tuscumbia
Hunstville Int. Airport
Decatur
Ft. Payne
Rome
Canton
59
Russellville
Guntersville
Centre
Cullman
Gadsden
ATLANTA
Tupelo
Hamilton
Double Sprs.
Oneonta
65
Anniston
20
GEORGIA
Jasper
Birmingham Int. Airport
Griffin
Fayette
Birmingham
Talladega
Wedowee
West Point
Sylacauga
Thomaston
Carrollton
Tuscaloosa
Alexander City
59
Centreville
65
Louisville
Clanton
Opelika
Eutaw
Phenix City
Columbus
Wetumpka
85
Tuskegee
MONTGOMERY
Demopolis
Selma
65
Union Springs
Eufaula
Hayneville
Troy
Greenville
Abbeville
MISSISSIPPI
Grove Hill
Blakely
Monroeville
Enterprise
Dothan
Andalusia
Brewton
Hattiesburg
65
Marianna
Crestview
FLORIDA
Bay Minette
Mobile
10
Pensacola
10
Panama City
Biloxi
Bay St. Louis
GULF
OF MEXICO

Lodge on Gorham's Bluff

101 GORHAM DRIVE, PISGAH, ALABAMA 35765
Tel: +1 256 451 8439 **Fax:** +1 256 451 3510
Web: www.johansens.com/gorhamsbluff **E-mail:** reservations@gorhamsbluff.com

Our inspector loved: *The stunning view, relaxing ambience, and sensational cuisine.*

Price Guide: (full or modified American plan available)
lodge rooms $190-$295
cottages $190-$295

Attractions: Unclaimed Baggage Center, Scottsboro, 20 miles; Russell Cave National Monument, Bridgeport, 35 miles; Tennessee Aquarium, Chattanooga, TN, 45 miles; U.S. Space & Rocket Center, Huntsville, 60 miles
Towns/Cities: Chattanooga, TN, 48 miles; Huntsville, 60 miles; Birmingham, 128 miles; Atlanta, GA, 132 miles
Airports: Huntsville Airport, 73 miles; Birmingham Airport, 122 miles; Atlanta, GA, Airport, 144 miles

Situated high above the stunning Tennessee River Valley on a bluff in the foothills of the Appalachian Mountains, with 6 rooms featuring beautiful stone fireplaces, soft down bedding and whirlpools, the Lodge on Gorham's Bluff offers complete relaxation in a picturesque setting. Each of the rooms is individually appointed with charming accents such as Oriental rugs, rich wood wardrobes and bookshelves, four-poster beds, and floor-to-ceiling windows, creating an elegant yet homey atmosphere. Soak up the incredible views of the river, fields of flowers, and rolling hills, take a dip in the swimming pool, or explore the town of Gorham's Bluff, a start-up community with a special dedication to the arts. End the day with a delicious, gourmet Southern-style meal served by candlelight in the Lodge's restaurant.

Arizona

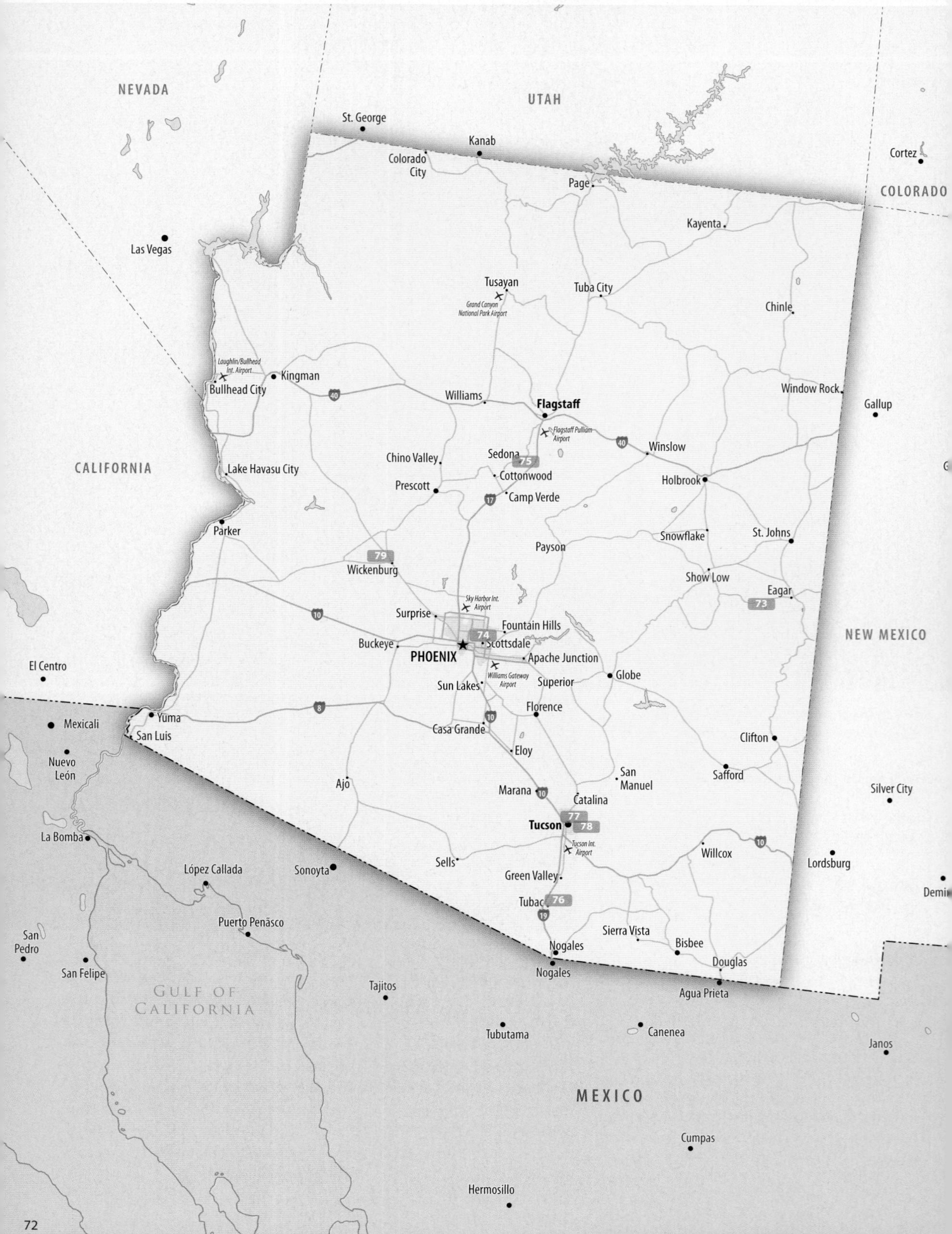

NEVADA
UTAH
COLORADO
CALIFORNIA
NEW MEXICO
MEXICO
GULF OF CALIFORNIA
St. George
Kanab
Colorado City
Page
Cortez
Kayenta
Las Vegas
Tusayan
Grand Canyon National Park Airport
Tuba City
Chinle
Laughlin/Bullhead Int. Airport
Kingman
Bullhead City
Williams
Flagstaff
Flagstaff Pulliam Airport
Window Rock
Gallup
Winslow
Sedona
Chino Valley
Cottonwood
Lake Havasu City
Prescott
Camp Verde
Holbrook
Parker
Snowflake
St. Johns
Payson
Wickenburg
Show Low
Sky Harbor Int. Airport
Eagar
Surprise
Fountain Hills
Buckeye
Scottsdale
PHOENIX
Apache Junction
Globe
Williams Gateway Airport
Sun Lakes
Superior
El Centro
Florence
Mexicali
Yuma
San Luis
Casa Grande
Clifton
Nuevo León
Eloy
Ajo
San Manuel
Safford
Marana
Catalina
Silver City
Tucson
La Bomba
Tucson Int. Airport
Sells
Willcox
Lordsburg
López Callada
Sonoyta
Green Valley
Deming
Tubac
Puerto Penãsco
San Pedro
Sierra Vista
Bisbee
Nogales
Douglas
San Felipe
Agua Prieta
Tajitos
Tubutama
Canenea
Janos
Cumpas
Hermosillo

Hidden Meadow Ranch

620 COUNTRY ROAD 1325, GREER, ARIZONA 85927
Tel: +1 928 333 1000 **Fax:** +1 928 333 1010 **U.S./Canada Toll Free:** 1 866 333 4080
Web: www.johansens.com/hiddenmeadow **E-mail:** info@hiddenmeadow.com

Our inspector loved: *Enjoying amazing meals at the Ranch House beneath the beautiful timber framed roof and in front of a roaring fire.*

Price Guide: (all inclusive, double occupancy)
private cabin from $500-$600

Awards/Ratings: Condé Nast Johansens Most Excellent Ranch, U.S.A. & Canada 2008

Attractions: Apache-Sitgreaves National Forest, 0.1 miles; Antique Tours, 20 miles; Historical Museum Tours, 20 miles
Towns/Cities: Greer, 5 miles; Sunrise Ski Area, 15 miles; Show Low, 30 miles; Phoenix, 225 miles
Airports: Springerville Municipal Alrport, 15 miles; Show Low Airport, 30 miles; Phoenix International Sky Harbor Airport, 225 miles

Embraced by 2 million acres of spectacular Apache-Sitgreaves National Forest and shaded by towering aspen and ponderosa pine trees, this acclaimed retreat within Arizona's White Mountains is a luxurious and peaceful getaway. The rhythms of the ranch are governed by the seasons: cool summers, falls framed by golden leaf glows, snowy, sunshine-filled winters and spring fields of purple iris. The well-appointed log cabins have cozy wood-burning fireplaces and living areas, and if you travel with your pet, there are even cabins available with attached dog runs. Enjoy decadent full mountain breakfasts, picnic lunches and 4-course gourmet dinners in the casually elegant Ranch House. Cookout breakfasts, margarita wagon rides, barbecues and campfire picnics are regularly arranged. Children enjoy participating in the specifically-designed Ranch Roundup program.

U.S.A. - ARIZONA (PARADISE VALLEY - SCOTTSDALE)

SANCTUARY ON CAMELBACK MOUNTAIN

5700 EAST MCDONALD DRIVE, SCOTTSDALE, ARIZONA 85253
Tel: +1 480 948 2100 **Fax:** +1 480 483 7314 **U.S./Canada Toll Free:** 1 800 245 2051
Web: www.johansens.com/sanctuarycamelback **E-mail:** info@sanctuaryaz.com

Perched atop Camelback Mountain, everything about the Sanctuary complements its spectacular setting. Luxurious Mountain Casitas feature modern furnishings, spacious bathrooms with oversized tubs. Some have wood-burning fireplaces and outdoor terraces. Stylish Spa Casitas are set around the infinity-edge pool and intimate spa. Sanctuary offers distinctive homes terraced high on Camelback Mountain, each unique in style with patios, secluded pools and views of Paradise Valley. The Sanctuary Spa practises Asian-inspired treatments in 14 indoor and outdoor treatment rooms, a meditation garden, reflecting pond and Watsu pool. There is also a state-of-the-art fitness center and movement studio. "elements" restaurant overlooks the Valley and offers fine American cuisine with Asian accents, while cocktails are served inside and outside at "jade bar" and "edge," an ultra-chic outdoor deck.

Our inspector loved: *The view of Camelback Mountain from the pool.*

Price Guide:
casita and spa rooms $235-$725
casita and spa suites $340-$855
luxurious homes $1,500-$4,000

Awards/Ratings: Condé Nast Johansens Most Excellent Spa Hotel, U.S.A. & Canada 2007 and 2008

Attractions: Hiking and Biking, 5-min walk; Golf, 5-min drive; Shopping, 5-min drive; Desert Lakes and Fishing, 35-min drive
Towns/Cities: Sedona, 100 miles; Tucson, 120 miles; Flagstaff, 130 miles
Airports: Phoenix International Airport, 8 miles; Scottsdale Airport, 15 miles

Affiliations: Small Luxury Hotels of the World

Sedona Rouge Hotel & Spa

2250 WEST HIGHWAY 89A, SEDONA, ARIZONA 86336
Tel: +1 928 203 4111 **Fax:** +1 928 203 9094 **U.S./Canada Toll Free:** 1 866 312 4111
Web: www.johansens.com/sedonarouge **E-mail:** info@sedonarouge.com

***Our inspector loved:** Sitting on the rooftop terrace and enjoying the view of Sedona's Red Rock country.*

Price Guide:
rooms $185-$300
suites $240-$400

77 · 120 · SPA

Awards/Ratings: Wine Spectator Award of Excellence 2007

Attractions: Indian Ruins and Vortexs, 10 miles; Out of Africa Wildlife Park, 20 miles; Verde Valley Railroad, 30 miles; The Grand Canyon, 120 miles
Towns/Cities: Flagstaff, 30 miles; Phoenix, 100 miles; Scottsdale, 110 miles; Las Vegas, 290 miles
Airports: Sedona Airport, 2 miles; Flagstaff Airport, 30 miles; Phoenix International Sky Harbor Airport, 100 miles

Surrounded by landscaped gardens, secluded courtyards and the stunning Red Rock country vistas of Arizona, this city boutique hotel has gained a reputation as a relaxing and stylish retreat with an exotic ambience. The opulent, modern décor features intricate and rich textures reminiscent of Andalucía, while cascading fountains and delicate ironwork balconies enhance the welcoming exterior. Each of the cool, attractive guest rooms has an individual and tranquil charm with fine linens, a spacious bathroom and imported furniture. The rooftop terrace enjoys a 360° panoramic view and is the perfect spot to lounge in the shade or chat over a cool drink. The Spa at Sedona Rouge offers seasonal custom treatments, yoga classes, a spa boutique, a tranquility room and gardens. Reds restaurant serves an imaginative menu of American cuisine.

U.S.A. - ARIZONA (TUBAC)

TUBAC GOLF RESORT & SPA

ONE OTERO ROAD, TUBAC, ARIZONA 85646
Tel: +1 520 398 2211 **Fax:** +1 520 395 3523 **U.S./Canada Toll Free:** 1 800 848 7893
Web: www.johansens.com/tubac **E-mail:** info@tubacgolfresort.com

Our inspector loved: *Dining at the Stables Grille while enjoying the sunset across the golf course and mountains.*

Price Guide:
posadas $129-$239
casita suites $149-$269
hacienda suites $179-$299

98 300 SPA NR HP

Set within the historic 500-acre Otero Ranch, this 200-year-old property has undergone a $40 million expansion and renovation to become an ideal romantic escape. Warmly decorated guest rooms are set within 4 beautifully landscaped acres of winding brick pathways, lovely fountains and views of the majestic mountain ranges. Beehive fireplaces, red tile roofs and brick archways maintain its historic charm while providing you with all the modern amenities required. There are no less than 3 restaurants at the resort serving indigenous cuisine, and a new 27-hole championship golf course nestled within the cottonwood trees alongside the Santa Cruz River. Visit the spa to relax and enjoy being pampered with the assortment of treatments that feature Southwestern flair.

Attractions: Tumacacori Mission, De Anza Trail, 10-min drive; Whipple Observatory, 25-min drive; Arizona-Sonora Desert Museum, 30-min drive; Kartchner Caverns, 1-hour drive
Towns/Cities: Patagonia, 15 miles; Nogales, Mexico, 20 miles; Tucson, 40 miles; Tombstone, 75 miles
Airports: Tucson International Airport, 36 miles

Arizona Inn

2200 EAST ELM STREET, TUCSON, ARIZONA 85719
Tel: +1 520 325 1541 **Fax:** +1 520 881 5830 **U.S./Canada Toll Free:** 1 800 933 1093
Web: www.johansens.com/arizonainn **E-mail:** reservations@arizonainn.com

Our inspector loved: *Relaxing in the beautiful gardens and enjoying the Arizona sun.*

Price Guide: (excluding tax)
rooms $170-$400
suites $290-$800

95 180 DVD NR HP

Awards/Ratings: Condé Nast Traveler Gold List 2008

Attractions: Major League Baseball Spring Training, 15-min drive; Pima Air & Space Museum, 20-min drive; Sabino Canyon, 25-min drive; Arizona-Sonaran Desert Museum, 25-min drive
Towns/Cities: Tombstone, 60 miles; Phoenix, 120 miles; Bisbee, 120 miles
Airports: Tucson International Airport, 10 miles; Phoenix International Airport, 120 miles

With more than 75 years of family ownership, this beautiful Mediterranean-style inn is situated in a residential area close to the city center. Surrounded by 14 acres of immaculate lawns, mature trees, flowerbeds, hedged private patios and water features, the inn combines modern comfort with antique charm, and is as eclectic in décor as it is cosmopolitan in service and clientele. Little has changed since opening in the 1930s when owner and Arizona Congresswoman Isabella Greenway welcomed guests such as Eleanor Roosevelt and John D. Rockefeller Jr. Today's men and women of distinction and of the entertainment world return time and again to enjoy their favorite rooms or private villas.

TANQUE VERDE RANCH

14301 EAST SPEEDWAY BOULEVARD, TUCSON, ARIZONA 85748
Tel: +1 520 296 6275 **Fax:** +1 520 721 9427 **U.S./Canada Toll Free:** 1 800 234 3833
Web: www.johansens.com/tanqueverde **E-mail:** dude@tvgr.com

Our inspector loved: *Relaxing after a full day of horseback riding in the beautiful swimming pool with an amazing view of the Rincon Mountains.*

Price Guide: (including 3 meals per day and scheduled activities. Double occupancy, excluding tax and service charge.)
rooms $325-$560
suites $390-$640

74 150 SPA

The magic of the American West is waiting for you here. Established in 1868, this quality resort is recognized as the last luxurious outpost of the Old West. Located on 640 acres in the spectacular, lush desert foothills of the Rincon Mountains, surrounded by the Saguaro National Park and adjacent to Coronado National Forest, Tanque Verde offers breathtaking mountain and desert views. Rates are fully inclusive of all the scheduled ranch activities such as hiking, mountain biking, nature programs, a children's program and more. 3 sparkling pools, 2 whirlpool spas and 2 saunas provide the perfect way to relax after a long day in the saddle, while soothing massages and luxurious body treatments may be arranged on-site in La Sonora Spa.

Attractions: Pima Air & Space Museum, 20-min drive; Major League Baseball Spring Training, 25-min drive; Old Tucson, 35-min drive; Arizona Sonoran Desert Museum, 35-min drive
Towns/Cities: Tombstone, 60 miles; Bisbee, 120 miles; Phoenix, 135 miles
Airports: Tucson International Airport, 25 miles; Phoenix International Airport, 135 miles

RANCHO DE LOS CABALLEROS

1551 SOUTH VULTURE MINE ROAD, WICKENBURG, ARIZONA 85390
Tel: +1 928 684 5484 **Fax:** +1 928 684 9565 **U.S./Canada Toll Free:** 1 800 684 5030
Web: www.johansens.com/caballeros **E-mail:** home@sunc.com

Our inspector loved: *The horseback trails in the high desert and "team penning," a must try horseback riding experience.*

Price Guide: (including breakfast, lunch and dinner)
rooms $405-$545
suites $520-$625

79 175 SPA NR HP

Attractions: Trap and Skeet Shooting, 5-min walk; Hot-Air Ballooning, 10-min drive; Hassayampa River Preserve, 10-min drive; Ghost Towns and Abandoned Mines, 20-min drive
Towns/Cities: Wickenburg, 5-min drive; Prescott, 50 miles; Jerome, 75 miles; Sedona, 100 miles
Airports: Phoenix Skyharbor International Airport, 50 miles

This full-service ranch is enveloped in 20,000 acres of desert cactus plants and blooming flowers; the epitome of South Western allure. Inside, each of the rooms and suites of this family-owned property has been carefully decorated with handcrafted furniture and Mexican tiling and fabrics, while outside there is an abundance of activities to enjoy. Admire the awe-inspiring flora and fauna of Arizona, and the 300 species of birds in the area. At dusk, head down to the South Yucca Flats for a cookout and enjoy a barbecue over an open mesquite fire. But make sure to take time out to visit Los Caballeros Spa where the menu includes a variety of massages, nourishing body wraps and luxurious spa manicures and pedicures by the fire. Events can be organized at the 4,500 sq. ft. Palo Verde conference center.

California

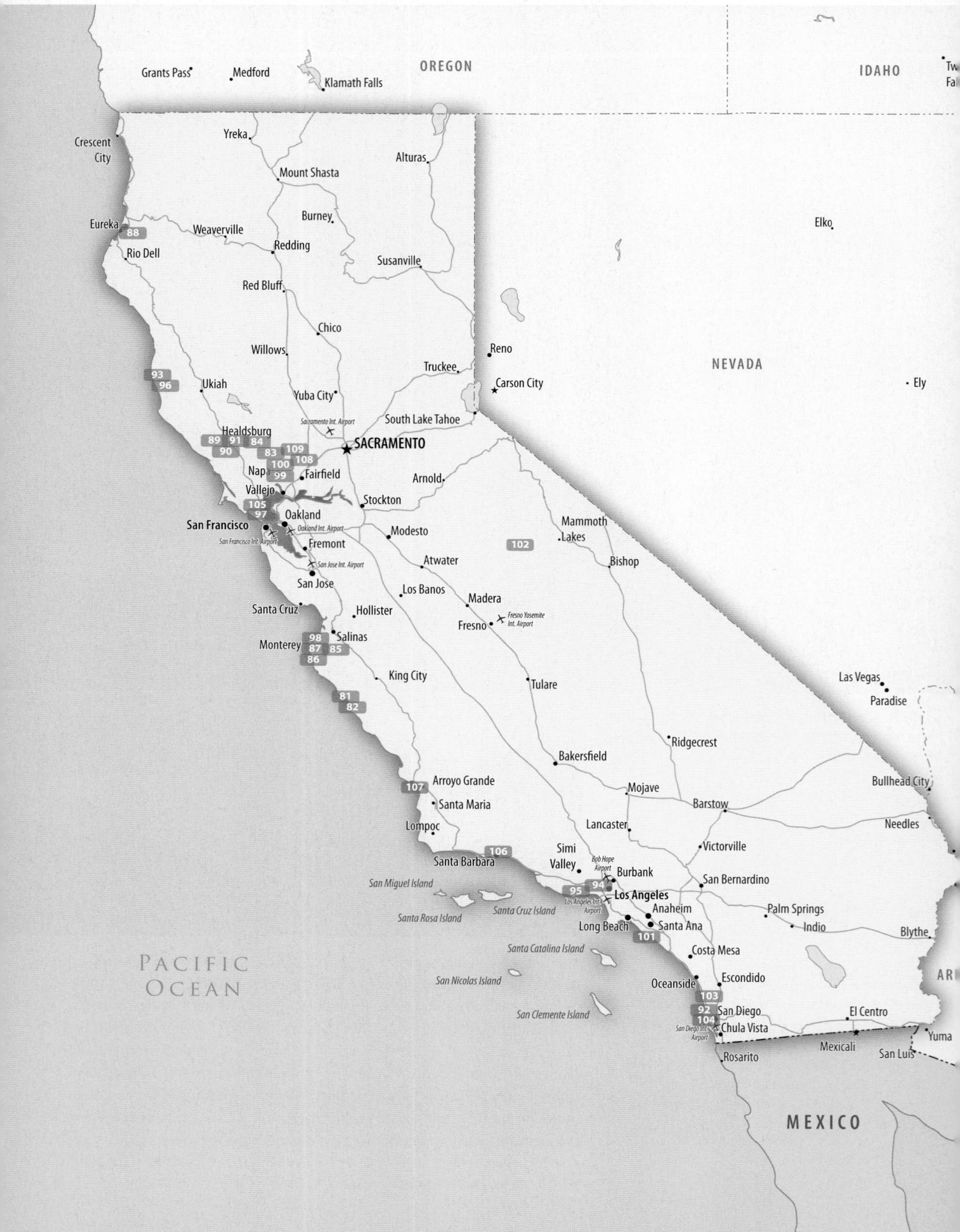

Grants Pass
Medford
Klamath Falls
OREGON
IDAHO
Crescent City
Yreka
Alturas
Mount Shasta
Burney
Eureka
88
Weaverville
Redding
Rio Dell
Susanville
Elko
Red Bluff
Chico
Willows
Reno
NEVADA
Truckee
93
96
Ukiah
Carson City
Ely
Yuba City
Sacramento Int. Airport
South Lake Tahoe
Healdsburg
89
91
84
90
83
109
108
SACRAMENTO
100
99
Napa
Fairfield
Arnold
Vallejo
Stockton
105
97
Oakland
San Francisco
Oakland Int. Airport
San Francisco Int. Airport
Modesto
Mammoth Lakes
102
Fremont
Bishop
San Jose Int. Airport
Atwater
San Jose
Los Banos
Madera
Santa Cruz
Hollister
Fresno Yosemite Int. Airport
Fresno
Salinas
98
Monterey
87
85
86
King City
Las Vegas
Tulare
Paradise
81
82
Ridgecrest
Bakersfield
Arroyo Grande
107
Bullhead City
Mojave
Santa Maria
Barstow
Lompoc
Lancaster
Needles
106
Simi Valley
Victorville
Santa Barbara
Bob Hope Airport
Burbank
San Miguel Island
San Bernardino
95
94
Los Angeles
Los Angeles Int. Airport
Santa Cruz Island
Santa Rosa Island
Anaheim
Palm Springs
Long Beach
Santa Ana
Indio
101
Blythe
Santa Catalina Island
Costa Mesa
PACIFIC OCEAN
San Nicolas Island
Oceanside
Escondido
103
92
San Diego
San Clemente Island
104
El Centro
Chula Vista
San Diego Int. Airport
Yuma
Mexicali
San Luis
Rosarito
MEXICO

Post Ranch Inn

HIGHWAY 1, P.O. BOX 219, BIG SUR, CALIFORNIA 93920
Tel: +1 831 667 2200 **Fax:** +1 831 667 2512 **U.S./Canada Toll Free:** 1 800 527 2200
Web: www.johansens.com/postranchinn **E-mail:** reservations@postranchinn.com

Our inspector loved: *The incredible beauty, rustic elegance and secluded peacefulness. The in-room spa treatments are heavenly.*

Price Guide: (including breakfast)
rooms $550-$2,185
suites and villas $1,785-$3,000

40

SPA

Awards/Ratings: Condé Nast Johansens Most Excellent Inn 2006; Condé Nast Traveler Gold List 1998-2008

Attractions: Hawthorne Gallery, 1 mile; Henry Miller Library, 1.5 miles; Point Sur Lighthouse, 9 miles
Towns/Cities: Carmel-by-the-Sea, 30 miles; Monterey, 35 miles
Airports: Monterey Peninsula, 35 miles; San José Intl., 106 miles; San Francisco Intl., 150 miles

Affiliations: Small Luxury Hotels of the World

Like a jewel in its setting, Post Ranch Inn sits amid the unparalleled beauty of Big Sur's rugged coastline, rolling mountains and towering redwoods. Luxurious redwood and stone accommodations provide stunning panoramas of the Pacific while stilted tree houses enjoy mountain vistas. Each room has a wood-burning fireplace, spa tub, organic-cotton linens and private terrace. Some rooms feature private deck hot tubs. Post Ranch Inn offers a world-class amenity package attuned to natural surroundings. Bask in the infinity pools or heated lap pool, take a guided nature walk or yoga class, or harmonize the body and soul with luxurious spa treatments. The Inn's Lexus Hybrid S.U.V.s provide guest shuttles for local sightseeing adventures. Dining is a distinct pleasure: Sierra Mar offers breathtaking views, award-winning cuisine and an extensive wine list.

U.S.A. - CALIFORNIA (BIG SUR)

VENTANA INN AND SPA

HIGHWAY 1, BIG SUR, CALIFORNIA 93920
Tel: +1 831 667 2331 **Fax:** +1 831 667 2419 **U.S./Canada Toll Free:** 1 800 628 6500
Web: www.johansens.com/ventanainn **E-mail:** reservations@ventanainn.com

Snuggly nestled on a gently sloping wooded hillside overlooking Big Sur's rugged coastline, the enchanting Ventana Inn provides unforgettable luxury, unique architecture, world-class dining and spectacular spa treatments. Newly decorated rooms are stunning with wood paneling, open fireplaces and plenty of space. Many rooms have their own balconies with sweeping vistas of the Pacific Ocean and the green and gold flowered hills of the surrounding countryside. Some rooms benefit from private decks with Jacuzzi tubs and hammocks. Each meal in the restaurant is outstandingly fresh, simple and delicious. The fantastic spa offers complimentary yoga as well as a large variety of holistic treatments, and the hotel is situated in 243 acres of meadows and hills, ideal for those who enjoy the outdoors.

Our inspector loved: *The spacious yet cozy rooms and decks overlooking the beautiful natural grounds.*

Price Guide:
rooms \$500-\$700
suites \$700-\$1,500

60 20 SPA

Awards/Ratings: Condé Nast Traveler Gold List 2008; Wine Spectator Award of Excellence 1992-2007

Attractions: Hiking, 1-min walk; Ventana Discovery Walk, 5-min walk; Cielo Restaurant, 10-min walk
Towns/Cities: Big Sur, 1 mile; Carmel, 28 miles
Airports: Monterey Airport, 45 miles; San José International Airport, 106 miles; San Francisco International Airport, 150 miles

Calistoga Ranch

580 LOMMEL ROAD, CALISTOGA, CALIFORNIA 94515
Tel: +1 707 254 2800 **Fax:** +1 707 254 2992 **U.S./Canada Toll Free:** 1 800 942 4220
Web: www.johansens.com/calistogaranch **E-mail:** reservations@calistogaranch.com

Our inspector loved: *The serene surroundings and the perfectly appointed rooms.*

Price Guide:
deluxe lodges $550-$945
1-bedroom lodges $750-$1,125
2-bedroom lodges $1,900-$3,850

46 350 SPA

Awards/Ratings: Condé Nast Traveler Gold List 08

Attractions: Hiking, 1-min walk; Wine Tasting, 5 miles; Horseback Riding, 5 miles; Hot Air Ballooning, 10 miles
Towns/Cities: Napa, 25 miles; Russian River, 35 miles; San Francisco, 75 miles; Mendocino, 100 miles
Airports: Sonoma Airport, 20 miles; San Francisco Airport, 80 miles; Oakland Airport, 90 miles

Affiliations: The Leading Hotels of the World

Hidden away on a private canyon in the renowned Napa Valley, this luxury and exclusive resort, set within 157 acres of nature, is the perfect getaway for good food, wine and relaxation. Free-standing guest lodges feature natural cedar exteriors, warm décor, beds with down duvets, cozy fireplaces and views of the serene forest and mountain. The Lakehouse restaurant highlights the region's finest American cuisine with organic ingredients bought from nearby farmers located in Napa Valley and Northern California complemented by wines from local vintners. The Bathhouse practises sophisticated spa treatments that take advantage of the region's natural healing mineral waters. However, for a more active pastime, enjoy the state-of-the-art fitness center, the yoga deck, the pool overlooking stunning views of the resort's private vineyard and oak groves and hiking in the surrounding area.

SOLAGE CALISTOGA

755 SILVERADO TRAIL, CALISTOGA, CALIFORNIA 94515
Tel: +1 707 226 0800 **Fax:** +1 707 226 0809 **U.S./Canada Toll Free:** 1 866 942 7442
Web: www.johansens.com/solagecalistoga **E-mail:** reservations@solagecalistoga.com

Our inspector loved: *The warm, indulgent suites and the fabulous spa.*

Price Guide:
studios $395-$755
suites $790-$980

89 300 SPA

This eco-friendly boutique resort beautifully blends rustic and organic design with a sophisticated, city flair. Loft-style studios and suites are designed with high ceilings, warm woods and natural stone. The calming and earthy color scheme enhances this airy and modern retreat, set within 22 acres of the renowned Napa Valley. The geothermal Spa Solage is the place to be pampered with a personalized full-body mud "cocktail" at the resort's unique Mud Bar. Solbar at Solage has a delectable and healthy menu of bistro fare and uses the freshest organic ingredients inspired by the Napa Valley region. Savor a local Napa Valley wine while sitting by the fire on the spacious terrace where you can take in the spectacular mountain views.

Attractions: Biking, on-site; Fine Dining, 1-min walk; Wine Tasting, 5 miles; Arts and Shopping, 5 miles
Towns/Cities: Calistoga, 5 miles; Napa, 25 miles; Russian River, 35 miles; San Francisco, 75 miles
Airports: Sacramento Airport, 60 miles; San Francisco Airport, 80 miles; Oakland Airport, 90 miles

Affiliations: Preferred Boutique

Bernardus Lodge

415 CARMEL VALLEY ROAD, CARMEL VALLEY, CALIFORNIA 93924
Tel: +1 831 658 3400 **Fax:** +1 831 658 3584 **U.S./Canada Toll Free:** 1 888 648 9463
Web: www.johansens.com/bernardus **E-mail:** reservations@bernardus.com

Our inspector loved: *The gorgeous views.*

Price Guide: (excluding 10.5% occupancy tax and a $20 per room, per night exclusive resort fee)
rooms $415-$825
1 and 2-bedroom suites $1,065-$1,990

57 228 SPA

Awards/Ratings: Wine Spectator Award of Excellence 2001-2008; Condé Nast Traveler Gold List 2007 and 2008

Attractions: Hiking, 2 miles; Monterey Bay Aquarium, 20 miles; 17-mile Beach, 20 miles
Towns/Cities: Carmel Valley, 5 miles; Carmel-by-the-Sea, 15 miles; Big Sur, 45 miles
Airports: Monterey, 15 miles; San José, 90 miles; San Francisco, 120 miles

Affiliations: The Leading Small Hotels of the World

Nestled within verdant acres of oak trees and pines, Bernardus Lodge was designed to complement and enhance the pristine beauty of the natural landscape. Both the exterior and interior convey Carmel Valley's signature welcoming charm and blend intimacy with sophistication. The sumptuous suites are located in adobe village-style buildings along a terraced hillside. All have French doors that open out to spacious balconies with stunning mountain or garden views. Dining options include the restaurant Marinus, which boasts 1,850 wine labels with over 35,000 bottles to choose from. Unwind and enjoy a game of croquet or bocce on the lawn or take time out to relax in the spa. All in all, the Lodge is the perfect place for those who wishing to immerse themselves in the beauty and lifestyle of California's Wine Country.

U.S.A. - CALIFORNIA (CARMEL-BY-THE-SEA)

L'AUBERGE CARMEL

MONTE VERDE AT SEVENTH, CARMEL-BY-THE-SEA, CALIFORNIA 93921

Tel: +1 831 624 8578 **Fax:** +1 831 626 1018

Web: www.johansens.com/laubergecarmel **E-mail:** reservations@laubergecarmel.com

This romantic European-style inn is the ideal getaway for the discerning gourmand. Built in 1929, the inn has undergone major renovation work, transforming the entrance, guest rooms and landscaped courtyard. Bedrooms are individually decorated and have every modern comfort including flat-screen T.V.s and generous bathrooms. Warm jewel tones and fine fabrics complement the charm of the architecture, and the floor heating is very welcoming and cozy. A truly memorable gastronomic experience awaits you: a sumptuous French country Continental breakfast is served each morning, and the 12-table restaurant, ruled by Executive Chef Christophe Grosjean, creates gastronomic delights that will please the most refined palate. The underground wine cellar houses a 4,500-bottle worldwide wine collection, notably from Monterey County, California and France.

Our inspector loved: *The gorgeous courtyard and private wine cellar.*

Price Guide: (including full country breakfast, excluding tax and $20 service charge)
rooms $350-$605

20

Awards/Ratings: Condé Nast Johansens Most Excellent Small Hotel, U.S.A. & Canada 2007; Condé Nast Traveler Gold List 2008

Attractions: Carmel-by-the-Sea Shops and Restaurants, 1 mile; Hiking, 5 miles; 17-mile Scenic Drive and Pebble Beach, 10 miles; Monterey Bay Aquarium, 15 miles

Towns/Cities: Carmel Valley, 5 miles; Monterey, 15 miles; Big Sur, 40 miles; San Francisco, 110 miles

Airports: Monterey Airport, 15 miles; San José Airport, 90 miles

Affiliations: Relais & Châteaux

TRADEWINDS CARMEL

MISSION STREET AT THIRD AVENUE, CARMEL-BY-THE-SEA, CALIFORNIA 93921
Tel: +1 831 624 2776 **Fax:** +1 831 624 0634 **U.S./Canada Toll Free:** 1 800 624 6665
Web: www.johansens.com/tradewinds **E-mail:** reservations@tradewindscarmel.com

Our inspector loved: *The beautiful Asian-style rooms and appointments as well as the peaceful Bhudda garden.*

Price Guide: (including breakfast)
rooms $295-$550

28 30

Attractions: Carmel Beach, 1 mile; 17-mile Scenic Drive and Pebble Beach, 3 miles; Carmel-by-the-Sea Shops and Restaurants, 3-min walk; Monterey Bay Aquarium, 6 miles
Towns/Cities: Carmel Valley, 5 miles; Monterey, 13 miles; Big Sur, 35 miles;
Airports: Monterey Airport, 7 miles; San José International Airport, 90 miles

Nestled on a quiet, tree-lined residential street, this luxury boutique hotel has a Zen-like quality that guarantees a tranquil, relaxing stay. Tradewinds' guest rooms provide ultimate comfort in opulent surroundings and most have been styled with an Asian influence complemented by authentic Balinese and Chinese wooden furnishings. Inspiring views of the lush courtyard, Point Lobos and Carmel Bay can be enjoyed from bedroom balconies. King and queen rooms have stylish, custom marble bathrooms and most king rooms boast spa jets in tubs. King suites offer the utmost privacy and are situated in the View Wing, which offers spectacular vistas across the Pacific Ocean. There are many art galleries in the area, in addition to great shopping, renowned wineries and world-class restaurants.

The Carter House Inns

301 L STREET, EUREKA, CALIFORNIA 95501
Tel: +1 707 444 8062 **Fax:** +1 707 444 8067 **U.S./Canada Toll Free:** 1 800 404 1390
Web: www.johansens.com/carterhouse **E-mail:** reserve@carterhouse.com

Comprised of 4 beautifully renovated buildings, Carter House Inns is the jewel of the crown that is the historic district of Eureka. The warmest of welcomes awaits you and the hospitable staff are attentive but never intrusive. Tasteful interior design incorporates sumptuous fabrics, original artwork and antique furnishings. In each one of the luxurious bedrooms, aspects of a bygone era meet contemporary in-room entertainment centers, and large windows bathe the room in natural sunlight. At Restaurant 301 dishes are created from local ingredients such as freshly caught Kumamoto oysters from Humboldt Bay and produce from the property's very own garden. In the grounds over 300 varieties of herbs, fruit and vegetables are grown and each afternoon you will be invited to collect ingredients for the evening's menu.

Our inspector loved: *The menu and wine list offered at Restaurant 301; a gastronomic delight.*

Price Guide: (including breakfast, wine and hors d'oeuvres, cookies, tea, turndown service and chocolate truffles, excluding 9% tax)
rooms $190-$233
suites $304-$612

9 12

Awards/Ratings: Wine Spectator Grand Award 1998-2007

Attractions: Hiking, 5-min walk; Horseback Riding, 10-min drive; Kayaking, 5 miles; Redwood National Park, 30 miles
Towns/Cities: Redding, 145 miles; Santa Rosa, 181 miles; Napa - Sonoma, 200 miles; San Francisco, 275 miles
Airports: Arcata Airport, 15 miles

THE GRAPE LEAF INN

539 JOHNSON STREET, HEALDSBURG, CALIFORNIA 95448
Tel: +1 707 433 8140 **Fax:** +1 707 433 3140 **U.S./Canada Toll Free:** 1 866 732 9131
Web: www.johansens.com/grapeleaf **E-mail:** info@grapeleafinn.com

Our inspector loved: *The delicious gourmet country breakfast.*

Price Guide: (including breakfast)
rooms $225-$395
vineyard cottages $425-$790

Attractions: Healdsburg Plaza and Fine Restaurants, 1 mile; Hiking and Hot-Air Balloon Rides, 1 mile; Wineries, 5 miles
Towns/Cities: Russian River, 5 miles; Calistoga, 30 miles; Napa, 45 miles
Airports: Sonoma Airport, 10 miles; Oakland Airport, 90-min drive; San Francisco Airport, 105-min drive

The 106-year-old Grape Leaf Inn has 12 distinct beautifully appointed rooms. Many accommodations feature 2-person spa tub/showers, king beds and fireplaces; one room boasts a 2-person steam shower and Japanese soaking tub. A 10-acre vineyard property with 3 charmingly renovated cottages has recently been added, affording the opportunity to experience authentic vineyard living. Surrounded by 80-year-old Zinfandel vines, each cottage has its own private outdoor hot tub, and one even has its own 100-year-old wine cellar. After a day of relaxation or wine-hopping among the more than 120 wineries within 20 minutes of the inn, you may step behind the secret bookcase and enjoy complimentary tastings of Sonoma County wines and cheeses in the "Speakeasy" cellar before dining out.

HOTEL HEALDSBURG

25 MATHESON STREET, HEALDSBURG, CALIFORNIA 95448
Tel: +1 707 431 2800 **Fax:** +1 707 431 0414 **U.S./Canada Toll Free:** 1 800 889 7188
Web: www.johansens.com/healdsburg **E-mail:** frontoffice@hotelhealdsburg.com

Situated in the picturesque Northern Sonoma Wine Country, Hotel Healdsburg captures the charm of its surroundings with its minimalist yet elegant accommodations. Each of the 55 rooms is spacious, and many feature French doors that lead onto balconies with views of the surrounding countryside, town plaza or hotel grounds. You may wish to take advantage of the many activities the Wine Country affords, including hiking, canoeing, and of course, exceptional vineyard tours! After the day's activities, return to enjoy fine dining at Hotel Healdsburg's signature restaurant, Charlie Palmer's Dry Creek Kitchen. With indoor and outdoor seating options, the Dry Creek kitchen draws upon local flavors to present a constantly-evolving menu and comprehensive wine list.

Our inspector loved: *The striking décor, open walkways and elegant furnishings.*

Price Guide: (including breakfast)
rooms $275-$595
suites $690-$790

55 80 SPA

Awards/Ratings: Condé Nast Traveler Gold List 2008

Attractions: Historic Healdsburg Plaza, close by; Vineyards, 1 mile; The Russian River, 1 mile; Lake Sonoma, 10 miles.
Towns/Cities: Santa Rosa, 12 miles; Sebastopol, 22 miles; Calistoga, 27 miles; Sonoma, 45 miles
Airports: Sonoma Airport, 11 miles; Oakland Airport, 75 miles; San Francisco Airport, 85 miles

Les Mars

27 NORTH, HEALDSBURG, CALIFORNIA 95448
Tel: +1 707 433 4211 **Fax:** +1 707 433 4611
Web: www.johansens.com/lesmarshotel **E-mail:** inquiries@lesmarshotel.com

Our inspector loved: *The elegant furnishings and beautifully appointed rooms.*

Price Guide: (including breakfast)
rooms $475-$1,050

16 16 DVD WiFi

Attractions: Fine Dining, 1-min walk; Wineries, 5 miles; Horseback Riding, 15 miles
Towns/Cities: Russian River, 3 miles; Napa, 25 miles; San Francisco, 70 miles; Mendocino, 90 miles
Airports: Sonoma Airport, 10 miles; Oakland Airport, 90 miles; San Francisco Airport, 90 miles

Affiliations: Relais & Châteaux

Les Mars is a gracious country house-style estate in the heart of Sonoma Wine Country that exudes Old World luxury and fine European style. Privately owned by the Mars family, you are welcomed as if you are visiting friends. Luxury guest rooms are elegant in design with beautiful canopied beds covered in exquisite linens and oversized European shams, Louis XV tables, and deep-soaking Bain Ultra bathtubs to indulge in. Unique 17th and 18th-century antiques are found throughout the hotel along with wonderful Belgian tapestries decorating the walls. Fresh cut flowers brighten each floor. After a day of exploring the region by bike, gather in the library for wine pairings with delicious local cheeses. The unobtrusive yet attentive service by the staff will make you feel particularly special.

Estancia La Jolla Hotel & Spa

9700 NORTH TORREY PINES ROAD, LA JOLLA, CALIFORNIA 92037
Tel: +1 858 550 1000 **Fax:** +1 858 550 1001 **U.S./Canada Toll Free:** 1 877 4 ESTANCIA
Web: www.johansens.com/estancialajolla **E-mail:** reservations@estancialajolla.com

Located just a "chip shot" from the renowned Torrey Pines Golf Course, Estancia La Jolla Hotel & Spa is an adobe-style luxury hotel, spa and executive learning retreat. The well-appointed rooms include one Presidential Suite and have attractive marble baths and lovely patios or balconies with views of lush courtyards. The surrounding fragrant gardens showcase many native California plantings and are enhanced by fountains, flamenco guitar music, outdoor fireplaces and picturesque pathways. The hotel's 2 restaurants offer traditional California and Spanish fusion cuisine in the casual-chic Adobe el Restaurante and the Mustangs & Burros where you can dine alfresco or indoors with live music. The Bodega Wine Bar serves some of California's finest wines. The Spa at Estancia La Jolla is a full-service spa with an array of organic treatments with 9 treatment rooms, and the state-of-the-art Learning Retreat is a certified I.A.C.C. conference center with 25,000 sq. ft. of meeting facilities.

Our inspector loved: *Relaxing in a poolside cabana in the California sun.*

Price Guide:
rooms $250-$360
suites $520-$1,500

210 250 WiFi SPA

Attractions: Torrey Pines Glider Port, 1 mile; Torrey Pines Golf Course and State Preserve, 1 mile; Birch Aquarium, 1 mile; University of California, San Diego, 1 mile
Towns/Cities: La Jolla, 3 miles; Del Mar, 5 miles; San Diego, 12 miles; Carlsbad, 20 miles
Airports: San Diego International Airport, 12 miles; Palomar Airport, 25 miles

Stevenswood Spa Resort

8211 NORTH HIGHWAY 1, LITTLE RIVER, MENDOCINO, CALIFORNIA 95456
Tel: +1 707 937 2810 **Fax:** +1 707 937 1237 **U.S./Canada Toll Free:** 1 800 421 2810
Web: www.johansens.com/stevenswood **E-mail:** stay@stevenswood.com

Our inspector loved: *The lovely property, and wonderful spa space.*

Price Guide:
rooms $249-$895

Attractions: Ocean/Bluff, on-site; Tennis and Spa Treatments, on-site; Golf, close by; Wineries, 20 miles
Towns/Cities: Mendocino, 2-min drive; San Francisco, 90 miles
Airports: Sonoma Airport, 45 miles; Oakland Airport (OAK), 3-hour drive; San Francisco Airport (SFO), 3-hour drive

Flanked by the Pacific Ocean and a forest of redwoods, Stevenswood Spa Resort takes full advantage of its scenic Northern California location. Each of the suites features imported furnishings, Tempur-pedic mattresses covered with 1,000-thread count Egyptian cotton linens, wood-burning fireplaces, and Northern Californian art. All offer stunning views of the ocean, meadows or the resort's private botanical garden and beautifully landscaped grounds. The Restaurant at Stevenswood serves innovative Wine Country cuisine, much of its ingredients coming directly from the Stevenswood Ranch, and provides lavish gourmet breakfasts each morning. Wellness is a top priority at Stevenswood, the home of "Indigo Eco/Spa," California's first eco-spa, as well as the Ocean View Fitness Room.

Hotel Bel-Air

701 STONE CANYON ROAD, LOS ANGELES, CALIFORNIA 90077
Tel: +1 310 472 1211 **Fax:** +1 310 909 1611 **U.S./Canada Toll Free:** 1 800 648 4097
Web: www.johansens.com/belair **E-mail:** sales@hotelbelair.com

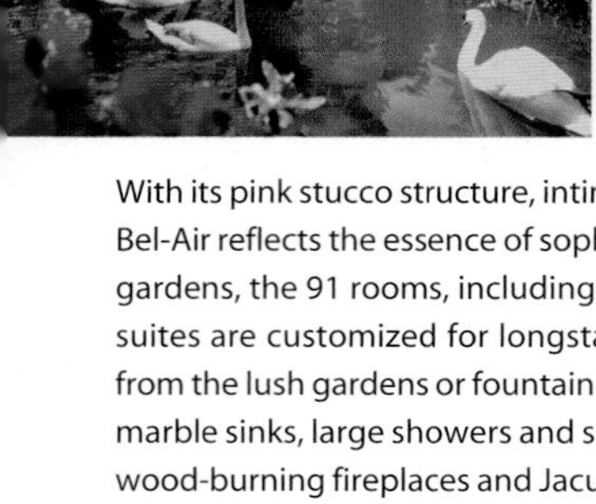

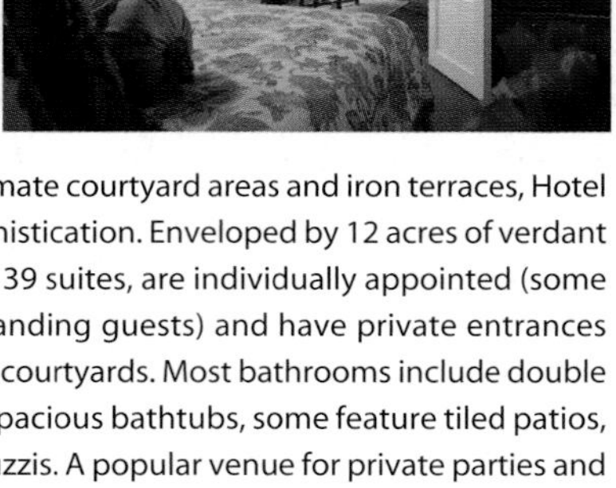

With its pink stucco structure, intimate courtyard areas and iron terraces, Hotel Bel-Air reflects the essence of sophistication. Enveloped by 12 acres of verdant gardens, the 91 rooms, including 39 suites, are individually appointed (some suites are customized for longstanding guests) and have private entrances from the lush gardens or fountain courtyards. Most bathrooms include double marble sinks, large showers and spacious bathtubs, some feature tiled patios, wood-burning fireplaces and Jacuzzis. A popular venue for private parties and weddings, the recently-opened Palm Room boasts a plasma monitor, pocket doors to create breakouts, 2 fireplaces and a private patio with fountain. Exquisite meals are served in the restaurant and alfresco on the terrace while the wood-paneled bar provides inviting surrounds.

Our inspector loved: *The sense of seclusion and superior service.*

Price Guide:
rooms $395-$650
suites $875-$4,500

91 24 M 45

Awards/Ratings: Condé Nast Johansens Most Excellent Hotel, U.S.A. & Canada 2008; Condé Nast Traveler Gold List 2008; Condé Nast Johansens Most Excellent Service, The Americas, Atlantic, Caribbean & Pacific Islands 2007; Mobil 5 Star 2007

Attractions: Getty Museum, 1 mile; Rodeo Drive, 5 miles; Universal Studios, 10 miles; Malibu Beach, 15 miles
Towns/Cities: Westwood, 1 mile; Brentwood, 2 miles; Century City, 2 miles; Beverly Hills, 5 miles
Airports: Los Angeles Airport, 13 miles; Burbank Airport, 19 miles

Affiliations: The Leading Hotels of the World

Malibu Beach Inn

22878 PACIFIC HIGHWAY, MALIBU, CALIFORNIA 90265

Tel: +1 310 456 6444 **Fax:** +1 310 456 1499 **U.S./Canada Toll Free:** 1 800 462 5428

Web: www.johansens.com/malibubeach **E-mail:** reservations@malibubeachinn.com

Our inspector loved: *The exceptional service, custom touches, and perfectly appointed guest rooms.*

Price Guide:
rooms $325-$1,025
suites $780-$1,650

Attractions: Beach, on-site; Malibu Country Mart, 1 mile; Hiking Trails and Nature Lagoon, 5-min walk; Shopping, Galleries and Theaters, 5-min walk
Towns/Cities: Santa Monica, 10 miles; Los Angeles, 14 miles; Burbank, 45 miles; Santa Barbara, 75 miles
Airports: Santa Monica Airport, 10 miles; Los Angeles International Airport, 30 miles; Burbank Airport, 45 miles

Situated on "Billionaire's Beach," in one of the wealthiest neighborhoods in America, Malibu Beach Inn captures the pristine beauty of the Malibu coastline with its landscaping, unique architecture and stylish décor. This intimate hotel's rooms boast breathtaking ocean views with private balconies, contemporary furnishings made from exotic dark wood, natural tile showers, Trina Turk robes, and several have warming fireplaces. Artwork by contemporary painter Glenn Ness is featured throughout. Savor the sun at the private beach club followed by dinner at the Carbon Beach Club featuring California coastal cuisine with its Pacific Rim flair. Wine enthusiasts will enjoy the extensive list of small-production wines from California's leading vintners. Dine indoors or outdoors taking in the incredible Pacific Ocean views. The European-trained staff will ensure an amazing stay.

U.S.A. - CALIFORNIA (MENDOCINO)

THE STANFORD INN BY THE SEA

COAST HIGHWAY ONE & COMPTCHE-UKIAH ROAD, MENDOCINO, CALIFORNIA 95460

Tel: +1 707 937 5615 **Fax:** +1 707 937 0305 **U.S./Canada Toll Free:** 1 800 331 8884

Web: www.johansens.com/stanfordinn **E-mail:** info@stanfordinn.com

This relaxing retreat on the rugged California coastline rests comfortably between lush forest and the majestic Pacific Ocean. The Eden-like grounds surrounding the property are stunning and consist of flower, herb and vegetable gardens. In fact, the inn is a family home and certified organic farm, the products of which are used to create fantastic gourmet vegetarian and vegan cuisine in the highly-acclaimed Ravens restaurant. You will not be disappointed with the exquisite overnight accommodation: all of the rooms and suites boast pine and redwood paneling, a roaring log fire, king or queen four-poster or sleigh bed and are embellished with plants, antiques and works of art. Enjoy a relaxing massage, private yoga session, the spa and sauna, or more energetic pursuits in nearby Mendocino.

Our inspector loved: *Ravens restaurant: a culinary treat even for non-vegetarians!*

Price Guide:
rooms $265-$325
suites $395-$810

38 M 80 SPA

Awards/Ratings: Wine Spectator Award of Excellence 2007

Attractions: Canoeing and Kayaking on Big River; Hiking and Biking, on-site

Towns/Cities: Mendocino, 1 mile; St. Helena, 115 miles

Airports: San Francisco Airport, 150 miles; Oakland Airport, 160 miles

U.S.A. - CALIFORNIA (MILL VALLEY)

MILL VALLEY INN

165 THROCKMORTON AVENUE, MILL VALLEY, CALIFORNIA 94941
Tel: +1 415 389 6608 **Fax:** +1 415 389 5051 **U.S./Canada Toll Free:** 1 800 595 2100
Web: www.johansens.com/millvalleyinn **E-mail:** millvalleyinn@jdvhospitality.com

Our inspector loved: *The tranquil creek view rooms and the location, just steps from the town center.*

Price Guide: (including breakfast)
rooms $169–$419

Attractions: Muir Woods National Park, 5 miles; Mount Tamalpais, 5 miles; San Francisco Bay, 15 miles
Towns/Cities: San Francisco, 15 miles; Wine Country, 45 miles
Airports: San Francisco Airport, 26 miles; Oakland Airport, 34 miles

30 minutes north of San Francisco, Mill Valley is set in a unique location at the foot of Mount Tamalpais, surrounded by redwood trees. This romantic hideaway combines the quaint charm of a historic Californian mill town with the sophisticated air of a contemporary European hotel. With a modern, Tuscan-style ambience, the 25 distinctive bedrooms, including 2 cottages built along a creek, offer an eclectic style and king or queen-size bed. All reflect a respect for nature and incorporate furnishings handcrafted in Northern California. Breakfast is served on the splendid flower-filled Sun Terrace and includes fresh fruit, local pastries and espresso drinks. A wine hour is also served on the Sun Terrace during the afternoon. The Terrace Room offers space for small meetings and presentations.

U.S.A. - CALIFORNIA (MONTEREY)

OLD MONTEREY INN

500 MARTIN STREET, MONTEREY, CALIFORNIA 93940

Tel: +1 831 375 8284 **Fax:** +1 831 375 6730 **U.S./Canada Toll Free:** 1 800 350 2344

Web: www.johansens.com/oldmontereyinn **E-mail:** omi@oldmontereyinn.com

Our inspector loved: *The spa suites, which boast garden views, fireplaces and a free-standing spa tub.*

Price Guide: (including breakfast)
rooms $300-$380
suites $415-$480

Steeped in the history and flavor of its surroundings, Old Monterey Inn is reminiscent of the days of pioneers and the infamous Californian Golf Rush. Much of the original stonework of the manor remains, and the interior has been lovingly restored to its former glory. The guest rooms evoke the romance of a bygone era and antiques adorn every pocket and corner of the public rooms. Breakfasts may be served in the garden, dining room or simply in bed, and tempting afternoon treats include freshly-baked cookies served with tea and coffee. Wine and hors d'oeuvres tease the palate in the evenings, while there is a splendid choice of restaurants nearby.

Attractions: Monterey Aquarium and Boardwalk, 2 miles; Pebble Beach Golf Courses, 5 miles; 17-mile Scenic Drive, 5 miles; Wineries, 5 miles
Towns/Cities: Carmel-by-the-Sea, 5 miles; Big Sur, 30 miles; Santa Cruz, 45 miles
Airports: Monterey Peninsula Airport, 15-min drive

1801 First Inn

1801 FIRST STREET, NAPA, CALIFORNIA 94559
Tel: +1 707 224 3739 **Fax:** +1 707 224 3932 **U.S./Canada Toll Free:** 1 800 518 0146
Web: www.johansens.com/1801first **E-mail:** info@1801first.com

Our inspector loved: *The beautiful guest rooms and sun-drenched dining room.*

Price Guide: (excluding tax)
rooms $325-$525

Attractions: Copia, 1 mile; Wine Tasting and Touring, 1 mile; Napa Boutiques and Restaurants, 1 mile; Ballooning, 10 miles
Towns/Cities: Sonoma, 15 miles; Calistoga, 15 miles; Russian River, 30 miles; San Francisco, 60 miles
Airports: Oakland Airport, 65 miles; Sacramento Airport, 70 miles; San Francisco Airport, 75 miles

Built in 1903 by architect William Corlett, 1801 First Inn is an elegant boutique bed and breakfast property in the heart of downtown Napa. Stylish décor with natural colors will relax you immediately. With only 5 spacious suites, 2 cozy cottages and the Carriage House, your comfortable guest room offers a luxurious bed with sateen linens, bath with large soaking tub or Jacuzzi, plush bathrobes and romantic fireplace. After a restful night's sleep, treat yourself to a gourmet 3-course breakfast prepared by the inn's private chef! In the evening, wine, and often tastings from local wineries, and hors d'oeuvres are perfect ways to indulge before dinner. An invigorating morning massage or a late night therapy with candles, music and wine - all given in the privacy of your guest room - will complete your stay.

U.S.A. - CALIFORNIA (NAPA)

MILLIKEN CREEK INN & SPA

1815 SILVERADO TRAIL, NAPA, CALIFORNIA 94558
Tel: +1 707 255 1197 **Fax:** +1 707 255 3112 **U.S./Canada Toll Free:** 1 800 809 2986
Web: www.johansens.com/milliken **E-mail:** info@millikencreekinn.com

Our inspector loved: *The luxurious rooms with patios overlooking the peaceful garden and Napa River.*

Price Guide: (including breakfast)
rooms $325-$800

12 SPA

Awards/Ratings: Condé Nast Traveler Gold List 2008

Attractions: Napa River and Wine Train, 1 mile; Vineyards and Wine Tasting, 1 mile; Napa Fine Dining, 1 mile; Fishing, Golfing, Hiking, 5 miles
Towns/Cities: Yountville, 9 miles; Sonoma, 15 miles; St. Helena, 17 miles; Calistoga, 27 miles
Airports: Sonoma Airport, 48 miles; Oakland Airport, 51 miles; San Francisco Airport, 58 miles

On the banks of the Napa River, this intimate and elegant inn is nothing short of magical. The estate has a lively history dating back to 1857 when the main building served as a stagecoach stop during the days of the California Gold Rush. One of its most notable attributes is the attention to detail. Drawing from exotic Indian and Thai influences, the décor of the rooms enhances the placid beauty of the property. Everything from the gentle music and dimmed lighting that welcomes you to your room, to the linens, towels and French spa, has been impeccably chosen. This a special destination with special touches such as Magic Hour, a wine and gourmet cheese reception with local vintners pouring their favorite selections, complimentary breakfast served wherever you wish within the property, and an exclusive luxury spa.

Balboa Bay Club & Resort

1221 WEST COAST HIGHWAY, NEWPORT BEACH, CALIFORNIA 92663
Tel: +1 949 645 5000 **Fax:** +1 949 630 4315 **U.S./Canada Toll Free:** 1 888 445 7153
Web: www.johansens.com/balboabayclub **E-mail:** sales@balboabayclub.com

Our inspector loved: *The elegant rooms with magnificent views overlooking the bay.*

Price Guide:
rooms $270-$595
suites $600-$3,500

160 750 SPA

Attractions: Newport Harbor, 2-min walk; Fashion Island Shopping, 2 miles; Disneyland, 14 miles
Towns/Cities: Laguna Beach, 10 miles; Los Angeles, 45 miles; Santa Monica/Malibu, 50 miles; San Diego, 80 miles
Airports: John Wayne Airport, 15-min drive; Long Beach Airport, 25-min drive; Los Angeles International Airport, 1-hour drive

Affiliations: Preferred Hotels & Resorts

This exquisite waterfront hotel is set in the heart of the California Riviera and is reminiscent of an Italian villa. Popular with the Hollywood elite, the casually elegant setting, gracious accommodations and hideaway atmosphere will make you feel right at home. Stylish guest rooms are calming with cozy feather-top beds, marble and granite baths with soaker tubs and beautiful plantation shutters that open out to spacious furnished patios with lovely waterfront or courtyard and neighborhood views. Chef Josef Lageder will tempt your palate with his inspired cuisine at the luxurious First Cabin restaurant. Some of the finest Californian wines and French champagne will complement your dinner perfectly. Duke's Place offers more casual fare with live entertainment and nightly dancing. The private Spa Environment, located harbor-side, is a peaceful escape.

Château du Sureau & Spa

48688 VICTORIA LANE, OAKHURST, CALIFORNIA 93644
Tel: +1 559 683 6860 **Fax:** +1 559 683 0800
Web: www.johansens.com/chateausureau **E-mail:** chateau@chateausureau.com

Situated in a nature lover's paradise, with a backdrop of Yosemite National Park, this romantic haven will immediately make you feel relaxed in its warm and luxurious ambience. There are only 12 guest rooms and each is immaculately designed and appointed to incorporate a sense of traditional luxury and style while providing every modern convenience. The carefully chosen soft furnishings complement beautiful antique pieces and encourage you to indulge in lazy days spent reading and enjoying the comfort of indoors. Over the kitchen door hangs a quotation from Oscar Wilde, "I have the simplest of tastes, I only want the best," and this is reflected in Erna's Elderberry House restaurant where a French country estate atmosphere has been created. 2 and 3-day cooking courses can be arranged.

Our inspector loved: *The great full-service spa.*

Price Guide:
rooms $385-$585
suites $2,950

12 SPA

Awards/Ratings: Mobil 5 Star; AAA 5 Diamond; Condé Nast Johansens Most Excellent Inn, U.S.A. & Canada 2007

Attractions: Bass Lake, 10 miles; Sierra National Forest, 20 miles; Yosemite National Park, 45 miles
Towns/Cities: Fresno, 55 miles; Merced, 65 miles
Airports: Fresno Airport, 55 miles

Affiliations: Relais & Châteaux

THE INN AT RANCHO SANTA FE

5951 LINEA DEL CIELO, RANCHO SANTA FE, CALIFORNIA 92067
Tel: +1 858 756 1131 **Fax:** +1 858 759 1604 **U.S./Canada Toll Free:** 1 800 843 4661
Web: www.johansens.com/ranchosantafe **E-mail:** reservations@theinnatrsf.com

Our inspector loved: *The romantic setting among California's golden foothills.*

Price Guide:
rooms $295-$420
suites $610-$1,500

87 150 SPA NR HP

Attractions: Del Mar Racetrack, 3 miles; Old Town San Diego, 20 miles; San Diego Zoo and Seaworld, 25 miles; Temecula Wine Country and Ballooning, 45-min drive
Towns/Cities: Del Mar, 6 miles; La Jolla, 15 miles; San Diego, 20 miles; San Clemente, 40 miles
Airports: Palomar Airport, 10 miles; Montgomery Field Airport, 15 miles; San Diego International Airport, 20 miles

This romantic inn is set amidst 23 acres of landscaped grounds in the center of the upscale residential area of Rancho Santa Fe. Designed in 1924 by Lillian Rice, one of the first female architects in California, this is a unique example of Spanish Colonial revival style. The beautiful guest rooms, including 14 suites and several Spanish-tiled cottages with up to 3 bedrooms, are dotted around the gardens surrounding the original main building. Many rooms offer private outdoor patios and romantic wood-burning fireplaces. The Innfusion Dining Room presents Rancho Cuisine of the Southern California traditions from the finest and freshest local ingredients, and "East Meets West" fine Asian cuisine. Expertly prepared by Executive Chef John Beriker, his countless awards include Winner of Best Dining Experience and Best New Chef of the Year by Gault Millau. Enjoy the croquet lawn and benefit from box seats and turf club passes during the thoroughbred racing season.

TOWER23 HOTEL

4551 OCEAN BLVD., SAN DIEGO, CALIFORNIA 92109
Tel: +1 858 270 2323 **Fax:** +1 858 274 2333 **U.S./Canada Toll Free:** 1 866 TOWER23
Web: www.johansens.com/tower23 **E-mail:** Reserve23@t23hotel.com

Our inspector loved: *Seeing and hearing the Pacific Ocean from the bedroom balcony.*

Price Guide:
spirit pads $199-$409
sky pads $219-$429
surf pads $279-$489

44 90

Attractions: Beach Cruising and Bike Trails, 1-min walk; Surfing and Fishing, 1-min walk; Jet Skiing and Windsurfing, 10-min walk; Golf, 15-min drive
Towns/Cities: La Jolla, 3 miles; Coronado, 10 miles; Del Mar, 10 miles; San Clemente, 55 miles
Airports: San Diego International Airport, 10 miles; Palomar Airport, 30 miles

Tower23 Hotel has a beautiful beach hotel atmosphere in both architecture and design. Its 44 sleek, modernist rooms are divided into 3 types: Spirit, Sky, and Surf Pads and 2 distinctive suite categories: Sanctuary and Sweet. Each features a signature Serenity bed, step-in rain shower, plush bathrobes by Boca Terry, Egyptian cotton bath towels and customized bar and nutrition centers. The fresh design schemes include private balconies or patios, high-end amenities and teak furnishings. Massage and spa services are available en suite. In the evenings, the Tower Deck is the ultimate place to watch spectacular sunsets while lounging on a teak chaise. The indoor/outdoor ocean-front restaurant, JRDN Surf:Sky:Spirit, features California fresh cuisine in a hip, contemporary environment.

Inn Above Tide

30 EL PORTAL, SAUSALITO, CALIFORNIA 94965
Tel: +1 415 332 9535 **Fax:** +1 415 332 6714 **U.S./Canada Toll Free:** 1 800 893 8433
Web: www.johansens.com/innabovetide **E-mail:** stay@innabovetide.com

Our inspector loved: *The stunning views of San Francisco Bay.*

Price Guide:
rooms $305-$1,050

Attractions: Coastal Bike Trails, on the doorstep; Golden Gate Bridge, 5 miles; Golden Gate National Recreation Area, 5 miles; Golden Gate Park, 10-min walk
Towns/Cities: Downtown San Francisco, 10 miles; Napa, 20 miles; Sonoma, 20 miles; Healdsburg 50 miles
Airports: San Francisco Airport, 30 miles; Oakland Airport, 35 miles

There can be few more spectacular settings than this relaxing retreat situated on the waters of San Francisco Bay. The inn claims, "there are hundreds of hotels around San Francisco Bay. There is, however, only one on it." Each room and suite is carefully and luxuriously designed with private decks on the bay where waves lap just below your feet. Many of the bedrooms have fireplaces, which in winter provide wonderful coziness while watching the otters play in the waters outside. Generous breakfasts can be served in your room, private deck or in the drawing room; during sunset, enjoy cheese and wine while taking in the panoramic City skyline and Bay or water views. The concierge will happily arrange dinner reservations and spa treatments.

HARBOR VIEW INN

28 WEST CABRILLO BOULEVARD, SANTA BARBARA, CALIFORNIA 93101
Tel: +1 805 963 0780 **Fax:** +1 805 963 7967 **U.S./Canada Toll Free:** 1 800 755 0222
Web: www.johansens.com/harborview **E-mail:** sylvie@harborviewinnsb.com

This ocean-front hotel lies across the white sands of West Beach and the historic Stearns Wharf, just a short stroll from Santa Barbara's downtown boutiques and attractions. Casually elegant and inviting, the spacious and well-appointed rooms and 13 luxury suites all have a private patio or balcony. Eladio's Restaurant & Bar serves California comfort food and looks out to gorgeous panoramic views. The heated fountain patio is an ideal place to relax, enjoy a great meal and people watch. Cocktails are also served and there is a bar with an extensive list of regional and international wines. The Harbor View Inn's impressive location is ideal for those of you interested in water sports such as kayaking and surfing.

***Our inspector loved:** The stunning ocean-view suites with beautiful mosaic bathrooms.*

Price Guide:
rooms $175-$425
suites $255-$795

115 SPA

Attractions: Stearns Wharf, 2-min walk; Santa Barbara Shopping and Dining, 1 mile
Towns/Cities: Santa Barbara, 1 mile; San Luis Obispo, 90 miles
Airports: Santa Barbara Airport, 11 miles; Los Angeles Airport, 95 miles

Dolphin Bay Resort & Spa

2727 SHELL BEACH ROAD, SHELL BEACH, CALIFORNIA 93449
Tel: +1 805 773 4300 **Fax:** +1 805 773 5200 **U.S./Canada Toll Free:** 1 800 516 0112
Web: www.johansens.com/thedolphinbay **E-mail:** info@thedolphinbay.com

Our inspector loved: *The large, lavish rooms.*

Price Guide:
1-bedroom suites $385-$785
2-bedroom suites $550-$920
2-bedroom penthouse suites $910-$1,325

70 50 DVD WiFi SPA

Awards/Ratings: Wine Spectator Award of Excellence 2008

Attractions: Fine Dining, 1-min walk; Biking, Hiking and Kayaking, 5 miles; Surfing and Sunbathing, 5-min walk; Wine Tasting, 15 miles
Towns/Cities: San Luis Obispo, 15 miles; Solvang, 35 miles; Los Angeles, 180 miles; San Francisco, 210 miles
Airports: San Luis Obispo County, 15 miles; Los Angeles, 180 miles; San Francisco, 210 miles

Affiliations: Small Luxury Hotels of the World

Set on the bluffs above the beautiful coastline of central California, Dolphin Bay Resort & Spa offers exclusive 1 and 2-bedroom suites designed for elegance and comfort. Each suite provides you with spacious living and dining rooms, gourmet kitchens, private balconies, fine Italian linens and all the amenities you would find in a luxury resort. The Lido Restaurant and Bar, with its dramatic Murano glass centerpiece and ocean views, features wonderful California Coastal Cuisine with an emphasis on locally-produced food and wine. Experience a signature treatment at the hotel's spa, La Bonne Vie, followed by a light meal from the Spa Esculent menu. The property boasts sweeping ocean views, and you will sometimes see playful local dolphins and migrating whales from the restaurant, terraces and the infinity-edge salt-water pool.

U.S.A. - CALIFORNIA (ST. HELENA)

The Inn at Southbridge

1020 MAIN STREET, ST. HELENA, CALIFORNIA 94574
Tel: +1 707 967 9400 **Fax:** +1 707 967 9486 **U.S./Canada Toll Free:** 1 800 520 6800
Web: www.johansens.com/southbridge **E-mail:** sbres@meadowood.com

This romantic 21-room inn is set at the entrance of the charming and historic town of St. Helena in the heart of famed Napa Valley. Spacious rooms are located on the second floor and feature beautiful French doors that open onto private balconies where you will enjoy lovely views of the courtyard, spa or hillside. Cozy fireplaces, vaulted ceilings and warming down comforters will ensure a comfortable stay. Begin your day with a lovely Continental breakfast of freshly-baked pastries and fresh-roasted coffee, all from local purveyors. And treat yourself to a soothing couples or Swedish massage at the Health Spa Napa Valley where you will also find the fitness center, calming eucalyptus steam rooms and lap pool. Wine tasting, fine dining, gourmet markets, galleries and boutiques are all nearby.

Our inspector loved: *The French doors that open out onto private balconies.*

Price Guide:
rooms $305-$630
suites $505-$740

21 000 SPA

Attractions: Spa, 1-min walk; Arts & Crafts Galleries, 1 mile; Wine Tasting, 5-min drive
Towns/Cities: Calistoga, 10 miles; Napa, 20 miles; San Francisco, 65 miles; Mendocino, 90 miles
Airports: Napa County Airport, 25 miles; Oakland Airport, 60 miles; San Francisco Airport, 80 miles

Affiliations: Small Luxury Hotels of the World

U.S.A. - CALIFORNIA (ST. HELENA)

MEADOWOOD NAPA VALLEY

900 MEADOWOOD LANE, ST. HELENA, CALIFORNIA 94574
Tel: +1 707 963 3646 **Fax:** +1 707 963 3532 **U.S./Canada Toll Free:** 1 800 458 8080
Web: www.johansens.com/meadowood **E-mail:** reservations@meadowood.com

Our inspector loved: *The quiet and serene environment, and well-appointed fitness center.*

Price Guide:
rooms $500-$920
suites $875-$6,775

85 SPA

Awards/Ratings: Condé Nast Traveler Gold List 2008

Attractions: Hiking, within the grounds; Wineries, 2 miles; World-Class Restaurants, 2 miles; Art Galleries and Antique Shopping, 2 miles
Towns/Cities: St. Helena, 2 miles; Rutherford, 5 miles; Oakville, 10 miles; Yountville, 15 miles
Airports: San Francisco Airport, 105-min drive; Oakland Airport, 105-min drive; Sacramento Airport, 105-min drive

Affiliations: Relais & Châteaux

Meadowood is an elegant private estate nestled in over 250 acres in the beautiful Napa Valley. It is a center for social, cultural and viticultural life, and as soon as you leave the highway, there is an overwhelming sense of tranquility and relaxation. The grounds are perfect for both relaxing weekend retreats and extravagant country parties, and the clubhouse commands a magnificent position overlooking the lawns. Most guests rooms have their own private decks from which to enjoy the surroundings, and you can choose where to take breakfast, whether in your room, on the deck or even as a picnic to take out into the countryside. The Restaurant, and the more informal Grill, serve a careful balance of fresh flavors with tempting colors and aromas.

Colorado

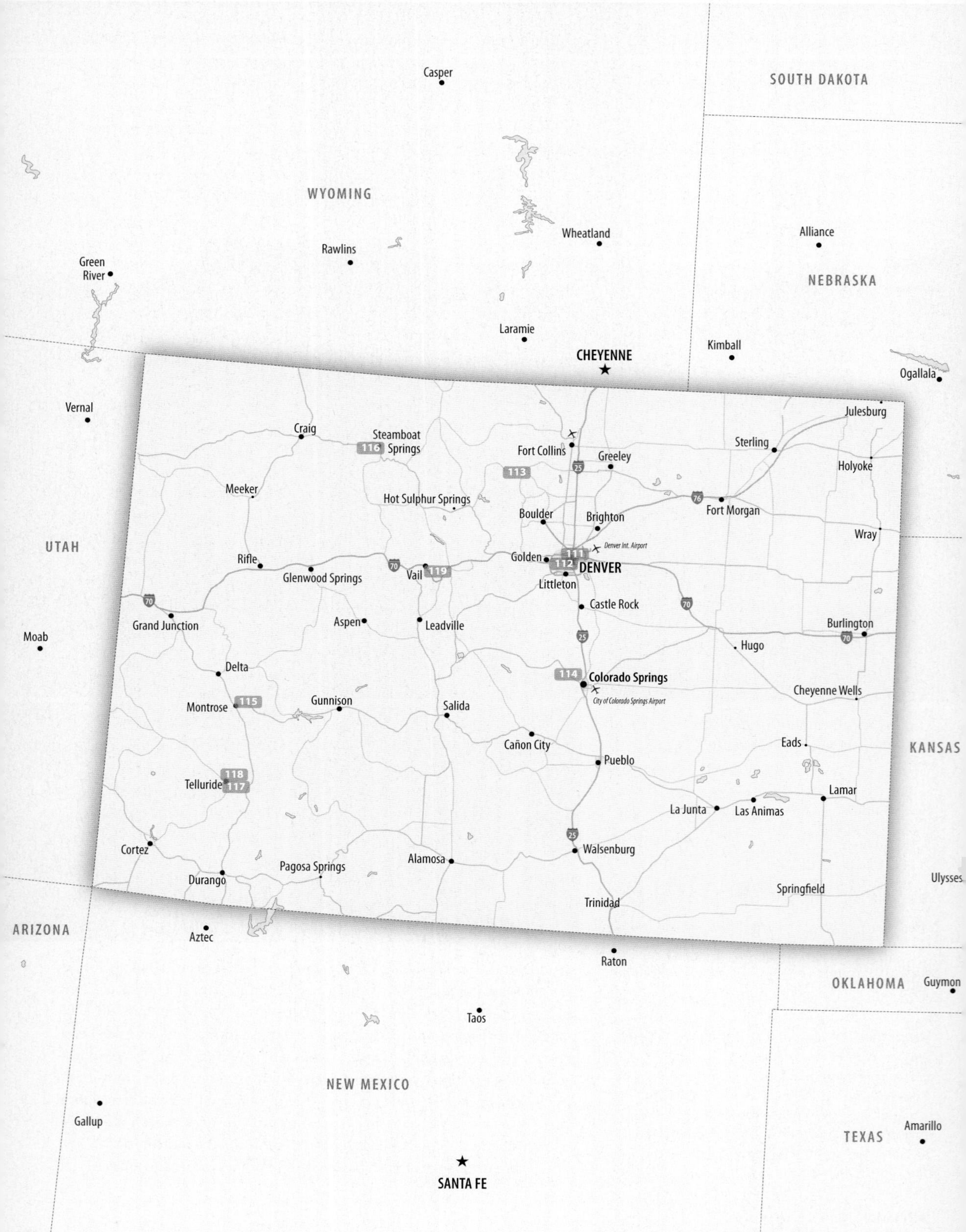

Casper
SOUTH DAKOTA
WYOMING
Wheatland
Alliance
Rawlins
Green River
NEBRASKA
Laramie
Kimball
CHEYENNE
Ogallala
Vernal
Julesburg
Craig
Steamboat Springs
116
Sterling
Fort Collins
Greeley
113
Holyoke
Meeker
Hot Sulphur Springs
76
Fort Morgan
Boulder
Brighton
UTAH
Wray
111
Denver Int. Airport
Rifle
Golden
112
DENVER
70
Vail
119
Glenwood Springs
Littleton
Castle Rock
25
Grand Junction
Aspen
Leadville
Burlington
Moab
Hugo
Delta
114
Colorado Springs
City of Colorado Springs Airport
Cheyenne Wells
Montrose
115
Gunnison
Salida
Cañon City
Eads
KANSAS
Pueblo
Telluride
118
117
Lamar
La Junta
Las Animas
Cortez
Walsenburg
Alamosa
Pagosa Springs
Durango
Ulysses
Springfield
Trinidad
ARIZONA
Aztec
Raton
OKLAHOMA
Guymon
Taos
NEW MEXICO
Gallup
Amarillo
TEXAS
SANTA FE

Castle Marne Bed & Breakfast Inn

1572 RACE STREET, DENVER, COLORADO 80206
Tel: +1 303 331 0621 **Fax:** +1 303 331 0623 **U.S./Canada Toll Free:** 1 800 926 2763
Web: www.johansens.com/castlemarne **E-mail:** info@castlemarne.com

Our inspector loved: *The private gourmet dinner for 2, elegantly served in the exquisitely restored Victorian dining room.*

Price Guide:
rooms $110-$240
suite $270

Attractions: Denver Botanic Gardens, 0.5 miles; Cherry Creek Shopping District, 1.5 miles; 16th Street Mall, 1.5 miles; Colorado Convention Center, 1.5 miles
Towns/Cities: Boulder, 25 miles; Colorado Springs, 60 miles
Airports: Denver International Airport, 12 miles

This Victorian home, now an elegant bed and breakfast inn, maintains many vestiges of the castle's past such as hand-rubbed woods, family heirlooms and ornate fireplaces. Following a careful restoration, original features dominate the interior, which is enhanced by Rococo gilt mirrors and fine antiques. The individually decorated bedrooms are stylish and display nuances of the period. Special private 6-course candle-lit dinners can be arranged and the daily delicious breakfasts and afternoon teas are delightful. House specialties include stuffed tomato with egg and spinach purée topped with parmesan and Jack cheeses, and the home-baked cakes and scones at teatime are to die for! The comfortable parlor is ideal for relaxing and reading a book beside the beautifully carved fireplace.

Hotel Monaco Denver - A Kimpton Hotel

1717 CHAMPA STREET AT 17TH, DENVER, COLORADO 80202
Tel: +1 303 296 1717 **Fax:** +1 303 296 1818 **U.S./Canada Toll Free:** 1 800 397 5380
Web: www.johansens.com/monaco **E-mail:** sales@monaco-denver.com

Our inspector loved: *The programs and amenities specially designed to pamper women business travelers.*

Price Guide:
rooms $200-$350
suites $300-$1,000

189 60 SPA

Situated in the midst of downtown Denver's attractions and sights, those of you seeking a sophisticated getaway will find that the AAA 4 Diamond awarded Hotel Monaco embodies the perfect blend of modernity and elegance. Each room boasts a bold and colorful décor that creates a stylish yet inviting atmosphere, and the variety of themed suites offer more luxurious options tailored to individual tastes and preferences. Panzano offers a dining experience not to be missed! Serving contemporary northern Italian cuisine prepared by Executive Chef Elise Wiggins, dishes include home-made pastas and pizzas, fresh seafood, and seasonal vegetables. Within walking distance of Denver Colorado's Convention Center, the 16th Street Mall, and a variety of shops, museums and restaurants, the hotel's convenient location enables you to fully enjoy all of the activities and sights Denver has to offer.

Attractions: Center for the Performing Arts and Convention Center, 5-min walk; Larimer Square, 5-min walk; Lower Downtown, 5-min walk; Coors Field, 10-min walk
Towns/Cities: Boulder, 28 miles; Colorado Springs, 60 miles; Fort Collins, 64 miles
Airports: Denver International Airport, 23 miles; Colorado Springs Airport, 80 miles

Taharaa Mountain Lodge

3110 SO. ST. VRAIN, ESTES PARK, COLORADO 80517
Tel: +1 970 577 0098 **Fax:** +1 970 577 0819 **U.S./Canada Toll Free:** 1 800 597 0098
Web: www.johansens.com/taharaa **E-mail:** info@taharaa.com

Our inspector loved: *The rugged mountain lodge, spectacular views, good food and great company!*

Price Guide: (including breakfast)
rooms $155-$185
suites $185-$345

18 100 13 DVD WiFi SPA

Attractions: Rocky Mountain National Park, 4 miles; Shopping, 4 miles; Art Galleries, 4 miles; Kayaking, 4 miles
Towns/Cities: Estes Park, 4 miles; Boulder, 35 miles
Airports: Denver Airport, 80 miles

Custom-built in 1997 out of log and stone on a high plateau in the Rocky Mountains, this luxurious hotel was created with comfort and enjoyment in mind and maximizes the impact of the mountains surrounding it. The hotel has stunning large windows, crackling fires and striking wood and stone work throughout. Each bedroom has its own unique theme and benefits from a fireplace and private deck. Breakfast is served in the Dining Room or on the adjacent deck where you can relax in the fresh, clean air surrounded by pine trees. The lodge is the perfect location for wildlife watching, fishing, biking, golf, horse riding, climbing, river rafting, hiking and a host of other exciting outdoor adventures. There is also an excellent solarium and outdoor spa with scenic views.

THE CLIFF HOUSE AT PIKES PEAK

306 CAÑON AVENUE, MANITOU SPRINGS, COLORADO 80829
Tel: +1 719 685 3000 **Fax:** +1 719 685 3913 **U.S./Canada Toll Free:** 1 888 212 7000
Web: www.johansens.com/thecliffhouse **E-mail:** info@thecliffhouse.com

Our inspector loved: *The gourmet dining experience with fine wine and dinner selections graciously recommended by the knowledgeable staff.*

Price Guide: (including breakfast)
rooms $145–$189
suites $199–$475

NR HP

Awards/Ratings: Wine Spectator Award of Excellence 2004-2007

Attractions: Garden of the Gods, 1 mile; Cliff Dwellings, 1 mile; Pikes Peak, 8 miles; Air Force Academy, 10 miles
Towns/Cities: Colorado Springs, 3 miles; Denver, 60 miles
Airports: Colorado Springs Airport, 8 miles; Denver Airport, 70 miles

Built in 1874 as a boarding house, The Cliff House is Colorado's second oldest operating hotel and was originally a key stop on the stagecoach trail. In the last couple of years it has been the subject of a $10-million refurbishment program and is now a hotel full of character that pays tribute to its heritage,while offering the very latest in modern comforts and luxury. Each room and suite is individually designed, and the wonderful "Celebrity" suites pay homage to their previous inhabitants that include Clark Gable, Teddy Roosevelt, Henry Ford and Buffalo Bill Cody. The hotel has gained wide renown for its gourmet dining and outstanding friendly service, and is a very romantic getaway. The menu is based on Colorado ingredients and traditional French cuisine, enhanced by modern international twists.

ELK MOUNTAIN RESORT

97 ELK WALK, MONTROSE, COLORADO 81401
Tel: +1 970 252 4900 **Fax:** +1 970 252 4913 **U.S./Canada Toll Free:** 1 877 355 9255
Web: www.johansens.com/elkmountain **E-mail:** reservations@elkmountainresort.com

Our inspector loved: *The total privacy of the mountain setting, attentive staff and the varied, challenging activities, especially the Valhalla Shooting Club.*

Price Guide:
deluxe lodge rooms $325-$600
3-bedroom cottages $600-$1,850

75 M 200 SPA

Awards/Ratings: Condé Nast Johansens Most Excellent Resort 2006

Attractions: National Forest, 1 mile; Shopping in Montrose, 15 miles; Shopping in Telluride, 35 miles; Skiing, 35 miles
Towns/Cities: Montrose, 15 miles; Telluride, 35 miles
Airports: Montrose, 19 miles; Telluride, 34 miles

Affiliations: Preferred Boutique

Part of the P.U.R.E. International portfolio, Elk Mountain Resort is simultaneously many things: a hidden romantic getaway, a gourmand's treasure, a spa retreat and a nature lover's paradise. The architecture blends into the natural surrounding environment, and the rustic exteriors of rough hewn log buildings conceal plush interiors. Whether you choose the main building or an independent cottage, all of the accommodations are impeccably appointed and furnished. Each fixture, piece of furniture, painting and linen has been carefully chosen; a philosophy that also extends to the staff. The service at the resort possesses an integrity that provides you with an exceptional experience. Dinner at the Tarragon restaurant is to be savored, as are selections from the impressive wine list. Elk Mountain Resort is a membership club and corporate retreat, and special booking conditions apply.

U.S.A. - COLORADO (STEAMBOAT SPRINGS)

Vista Verde Guest Ranch

P.O. BOX 770465, STEAMBOAT SPRINGS, COLORADO 80477
Tel: +1 970 879 3858 **Fax:** +1 970 879 6814 **U.S./Canada Toll Free:** 1 800 526 7433
Web: www.johansens.com/vistaverderanch **E-mail:** reservations@vistaverde.com

Nestled deep in the Rocky Mountains, Vista Verde is a truly unique ranch experience for all seasons. This 500-acre property provides accommodation in secluded, spacious log cabins or deluxe lodge rooms. In summer the crisp air and clear skies invite you to rise early, enjoy a hearty breakfast and try your hand at fishing, hot-air ballooning, hiking, white-water rafting and kayaking among many other activities on offer. Gourmet dinners are served in the main lodge; on some evenings there is an informal cookout. In fall, the rivers run lower, the elk move back in and the aspens prepare for a magical color extravaganza. A winter ranch experience is a must! You can sleigh ride, cross-country and downhill ski, dog sled, ice climb and horse ride.

Our inspector loved: *The fine dining in the rustic lodge followed by songs around a crackling outdoor fire topped off with a soak in a private hot tub under the starlit mountain sky.*

Price Guide: (per person, including activities and meals)
cabins $350-$500

20 40 6

Attractions: Ranch Activities, 1-min walk; Mountain Sports, 1-min walk; Skiing, 25 miles; Shopping, 25 miles
Towns/Cities: Steamboat Springs, 25 miles
Airports: Hayden Airport, 45 miles; Denver Airport, 175 miles

U.S.A. - COLORADO (TELLURIDE)

Fairmont Heritage Place, Franz Klammer Lodge

567 MOUNTAIN VILLAGE BOULEVARD, TELLURIDE, COLORADO 81435
Tel: +1 970 728 4239 **Fax:** +1 970 728 0788 **U.S./Canada Toll Free:** 1 888 728 0355
Web: www.johansens.com/fairmont **E-mail:** franzklammer@fairmont.com

Our inspector loved: *The spectacular view from the Himmel Spa Suite while awaiting an Aromatherapy Altitude Massage.*

Price Guide: (excluding tax; complimentary transportation from Telluride and Montrose Airports available)
2 and 3-bedroom luxury suites $350-$2,200

Attractions: Skiing, 3-min walk; Golf, 5-min walk; Hiking, 5-min walk; Shopping, 15-min gondola ride
Towns/Cities: Telluride, 15-min gondola ride or drive; Montrose, 67 miles
Airports: Telluride Airport (TEX), 15-min drive; Montrose Airport (MTJ), 67 miles; Denver Airport (DEN), 355 miles

Set in the idyllic pedestrian enclave of Mountain Village, accessible from Telluride by car or complimentary Gondola, the 2 and 3-bedroom luxury residences of the Fairmont Heritage Place, Franz Klammer Lodge offer stunning views of Colorado's magnificent San Juan Mountains. The Lodge, which features convenient access to skiing with slopeside ski valet, is decorated with stone, earthy tones, and high, open-beamed ceilings, creating a distinctively alpine atmosphere. Each residence includes a living room with a large, natural gas, stone fireplace, a gourmet kitchen with granite countertops, high, exposed beam or vaulted ceilings, spacious master bathrooms with jetted tubs, and a private balcony. The Lodge provides a private spa, gameroom, fitness center, outdoor heated swimming pool, and hot tubs.

U.S.A. - COLORADO (TELLURIDE)

The Hotel Telluride

199 NORTH CORNET STREET, TELLURIDE, COLORADO 81435
Tel: +1 970 369 1188 **Fax:** +1 970 369 1292 **U.S./Canada Toll Free:** 1 866 468 3501
Web: www.johansens.com/telluride **E-mail:** reservations@thehoteltelluride.com

Our inspector loved: *The walk-to-everything location in town, and the stunning beauty of the surrounding area.*

Price Guide: (including breakfast and complimentary shuttle to town center is available)
rooms $129-$529
suites $269-$999

59 DVD WiFi

The sense of understated luxury and alpine ambience at The Hotel Telluride is apparent from the moment you step into its impressive lobby, with its 2-story atrium, vaulted ceiling, massive stone fireplace, iron and antler chandelier, and 360° views of the magnificent San Juan Mountains. The air of mountain rusticity combined with European Old World elegance permeates through the entire hotel, and is reinforced by its heavy stone floors, warm wool rugs and leather furnishings. The luxuriously appointed guest rooms and suites include balconies offering breathtaking mountain views, custom furnishings and The Hotel Telluride's Incredible Beds, a welcome sight after a long day on the slopes. Wake up each morning to a hearty, complimentary breakfast buffet at the Bistro, which also serves drinks, tavern-style appetizers and light dinners.

Attractions: Shopping, 3-min walk; Hiking, 5-min walk; Skiing, 5-min walk; Lizardhead Wilderness Area, 15-min drive
Towns/Cities: Ridgway, 35 miles; Montrose, 62 miles
Airports: Telluride Airport, 15-min drive; Montrose Airport, 65 miles; Grand Junction Airport, 125 miles

VAIL MOUNTAIN LODGE & SPA

352 EAST MEADOW DRIVE, VAIL, COLORADO 81657
Tel: +1 970 476 0700 **Fax:** +1 970 476 6451 **U.S./Canada Toll Free:** 1 888 794 0413
Web: www.johansens.com/vailmountain **E-mail:** reservations@vailmountainlodge.com

Our inspector loved: *The state-of-the-art athletic club and spa, and soaking in the hot tub at sunset near the rushing waters of Gore Creek.*

Price Guide: (including breakfast)
rooms $159-$900
condos $315-$2,750

Awards/Ratings: DiRoNA; Condé Nast Traveler Gold List 2008

Attractions: Skiing, 3-min walk; Shopping, 3-min walk; Art Galleries, 3-min walk
Towns/Cities: Beaver Creek, 9 miles; Denver, 90 miles
Airports: Eagle Airport, 30 miles; Denver Airport, 115 miles

Beautifully situated on Gore Creek, Vail Mountain Lodge & Spa captures the charm of rustic camps of yesterday's Yellowstone. Its spacious rooms offer a comfortable and relaxing atmosphere after a long day on the slopes or at the popular Vail Athletic Club. Terra Bistro is a local favorite, whose primarily organic menu highlights seasonal ingredients influenced by Southwestern, Mediterranean, and Asian cultures. The Bistro also offers one of the most extensive wine lists in the area. The on-site Vail Athletic Club is an 18,000 sq. ft. fitness center with state-of-the-art functional training equipment, including Vail's only indoor climbing wall, and a wide variety of classes and private instruction such as yoga and Pilates. The Spa at Vail Mountain Lodge practises holistic treatments as well as massages and facials designed to be therapeutic as well as relaxing.

Connecticut

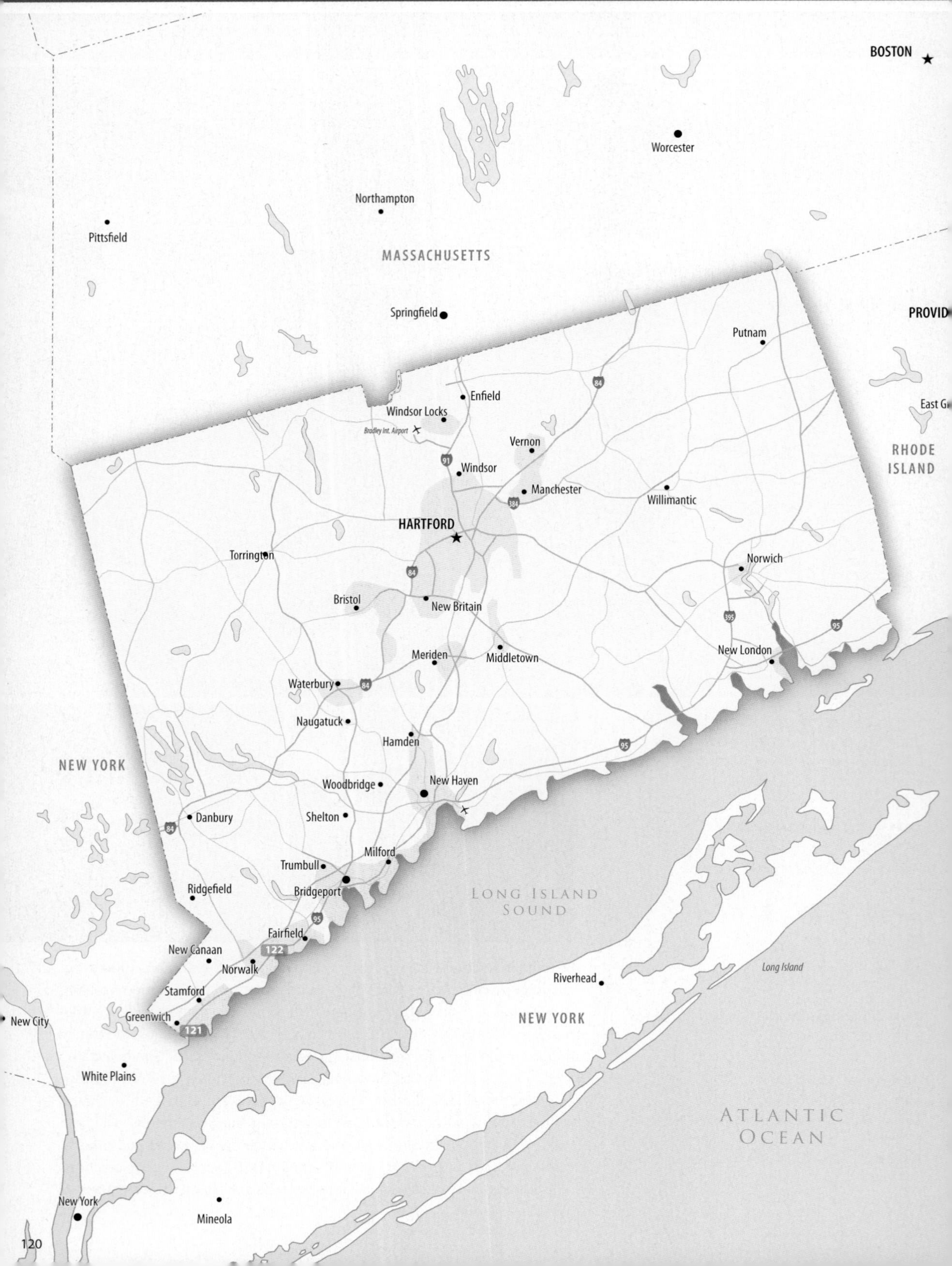

DELAMAR GREENWICH HARBOR

500 STEAMBOAT ROAD, GREENWICH, CONNECTICUT 06830
Tel: +1 203 661 9800 **Fax:** +1 203 661 2513 **U.S./Canada Toll Free:** 1 866 335 2627
Web: www.johansens.com/delamar **E-mail:** info@thedelamar.com

Our inspector loved: *The new Belvedere floor.*

Price Guide: (Belvedere floor guests receive Continental breakfast, afternoon wine and cheese and late night sandwiches and desserts, all rates exclude 12% tax)
rooms $369-$479
suites $600-$1,700

82 200 SPA

Attractions: Bruce Museum, 5-min walk; Todd's Point Beach, 10-min drive; Audubon Center, 15-min drive; Greenwich Polo Club, 8 miles
Towns/Cities: Old Greenwich, 5 miles; Stamford, 6 miles; White Plains, 14 miles; Manhattan, NY, 36 miles
Airports: White Plains Airport, 20-min drive; LaGuardia Airport, NY, 45-min drive; J.F.K. Airport, NY, 55-min drive

Affiliations: Small Luxury Hotels of the World

Situated in a spectacular waterfront location on Greenwich Harbor, this luxury hotel is built in the style of a beautiful Tuscan villa, with an authentic terracotta-tiled roof and soft yellow stucco walls. Inside, quality fabrics, subtle colors and distinctive Mediterranean furnishings abound, and the walls showcase original paintings and artworks, many from renowned private collection in Greenwich. Guest rooms are elegant with Italian linens, down duvets and spacious bathrooms with coral marble vanities and deep cast-iron tubs ideal for the business traveler or luxury weekend away. The new Belevedere floor provides concierge services, Continental breakfast and afternoon wine and cheese. The waterfront L'Escale Restaurant & Bar serves inventive Provençal cuisine. The hotel has its own private dock, which berths yachts up to 160 feet.

THE INN AT NATIONAL HALL

2 POST ROAD WEST, WESTPORT, CONNECTICUT 06880
Tel: +1 203 221 1351 **Fax:** +1 203 221 0276 **U.S./Canada Toll Free:** 1 800 628 4255
Web: www.johansens.com/nationalhall **E-mail:** info@innatnationalhall.com

Our inspector loved: *The unique and lavishly decorated suites with very spacious bathrooms.*

Price Guide: (including breakfast)
rooms $355-$395
suites $595-$895

This Italianate-style red brick building is idyllically set along a picturesque waterfront and is within a short stroll of fashionable Westport's shops, restaurants and galleries. Beautiful cherry woodwork and an eclectic mix of antiques and luscious fabrics combine to create the inspiring atmosphere of Old World opulence and sophistication. Each bedroom and suite is decorated to the highest possible standard of comfort and is filled with four-poster beds, hand-stencilled walls, lavish furnishings and meticulous attention to detail. Most rooms have scenic views over the Saugatuck River. Relax in the large yet cozy common room by the fireplace, or explore the surrounding neighborhood. During the summer, Westport comes alive with theater and musical productions held at the summer playhouse and outdoor riverside pavilion.

Attractions: Westport Country Playhouse, 5-min drive; Sherwood Island State Park, 10-min drive; Bruce Museum Greenwich, 15-min drive
Towns/Cities: Stamford, 14 miles; Greenwich, 19 miles; New York City, NY, 50 miles; Hartford, 50 miles
Airports: Westchester County Airport, 40-min drive; J.F.K./L.G.A. Airport, NY, 1-hour drive; Hartford Airport, 1-hour drive

Philadelphia
Camden
Media
West Chester
Woodbury
PENNSYLVANIA
Talleyville
Claymont
95
127
Wilmington
495
Elsmere
Newark
New Castle Airport
Brookside
95
Elkton
Salem
NEW JERSEY
Delaware City
Bridgeton
Middletown
Smyrna
DELAWARE BAY
DOVER
Camden
Harrington
Milford
ATLANTIC OCEAN
MARYLAND
Rehoboth Beach
126
124
125
Bridgeville
Georgetown
Easton
Seaford
Millsboro
Laurel
Cambridge
Salisbury

U.S.A. - DELAWARE (REHOBOTH BEACH)

THE BELLMOOR

SIX CHRISTIAN STREET, REHOBOTH BEACH, DELAWARE 19971
Tel: +1 302 227 5800 **Fax:** +1 302 227 0323 **U.S./Canada Toll Free:** 1 800 425 2355
Web: www.johansens.com/thebellmoor **E-mail:** info@thebellmoor.com

This warm and residential inn combines old-fashioned hospitality with first-class accommodations in the perfect seaside setting. The comfortable guest rooms range from garden and deluxe rooms to the generously sized Bellmoor Club Suites, accessible only by private elevator key. After a long day at the beach, cozy up next to the in-room fireplace, soak in the Ultra Masseur hydrotherapy tub or enjoy a drink from the wet bar. The Bellmoor Club Library serves snacks and drinks and is a wonderful place to read a book nestled by the fire. Start your day with the complimentary full American breakfast, and in the afternoon enjoy cookies and tea in the beautiful garden setting. The full-service Spa at The Bellmoor offers over 40 different services.

Our inspector loved: *The lovely rooms, tranquil garden area and full-service spa.*

Price Guide: (including breakfast)
rooms $125-$345
suites $195-$645

78 50 SPA

Attractions: Rehoboth Beach/Boardwalk, 0.5 miles
Towns/Cities: Dover, 45 miles; Wilmington, 85 miles
Airports: B.W.I. Airport, 110 miles; Philadelphia Airport, 110 miles

BOARDWALK PLAZA HOTEL

OLIVE AVENUE & THE BOARDWALK, REHOBOTH BEACH, DELAWARE 19971
Tel: +1 302 227 7169 **Fax:** +1 302 227 0561 **U.S./Canada Toll Free:** 1 800 332 3224
Web: www.johansens.com/boardwalkplaza **E-mail:** reservations@boardwalkplaza.com

Our inspector loved: *The smiling, attentive staff, and the prime beach-front location.*

Price Guide:
rooms $119-$479
suites $139-$529

84 100

Attractions: Rehoboth Beach and Boardwalk; Boutiques, Restaurants, Antiquing and Shopping, 5-min walk; Over 100 Outlet Stores, 5-min drive
Towns/Cities: Dewey Beach, 5-min drive; Historic Lewes, 10-min drive
Airports: Wilmington Airport, 90 miles; Philadelphia International Airport, 112 miles; Ronald Reagan Washington National Airport, 127 miles

Built in 1990, this Victorian-styled hotel, set in a premier resort town, will make you feel as if you have stepped into the past. The lively resident parrots welcome you to the lobby of this friendly hotel where the owners' collection of antiques and fine period reproductions enhances the recreated Victorian era elegance in each room. Soak in the spa pool after a jog on the beach or enjoy traditional afternoon tea in the elegant dining room. Victoria's Restaurant has beautiful views of the Atlantic from every table where you can sample an array of tasty dishes made with the freshest ingredients for breakfast, lunch and dinner. For drinks and lighter fare relax in the adjacent Plaza Pub. Enjoy the ultimate in pampering and inquire about the adults-only concierge floor, which offers upgraded amenities and access to the private rooftop sundeck and hot tub.

U.S.A. - DELAWARE (REHOBOTH BEACH)

HOTEL REHOBOTH

247 REHOBOTH AVENUE, REHOBOTH BEACH, DELAWARE 19971
Tel: +1 302 227 4300 **Fax:** +1 302 227 1200 **U.S./Canada Toll Free:** 1 877 247 7346
Web: www.johansens.com/hotelrehoboth **E-mail:** info@hotelrehoboth.com

Our inspector loved: *The spacious, well-appointed rooms, beautiful lobby and first-class Italian Restaurant.*

Price Guide: (including breakfast)
rooms $159-$359
suites $199-$459

52 40

The new for 2008 Hotel Rehoboth is located in the heart of Rehoboth Beach, a luxurious boutique hotel surrounded by all of Rehoboth's best restaurants, spas, salons, shops, beach and boardwalk. Hotel Rehoboth's warm friendly staff and the sounds of the baby grand piano will greet you as you enter the grand lobby with the eye-catching central staircase and welcoming fireplace. This beautiful first-class hotel offers all guests nightly turn-down service, wine and cheese in the afternoon, full breakfast each morning and a seasonal open-air beach shuttle daily. Guest rooms are luxurious and comfortable with all modern conveniences, spacious granite bathrooms, lavish linens, and many include private balconies for enjoying the fresh sea air and beach views. This luxury hotel is ideal for your next romantic getaway or family beach vacation in Rehoboth Beach: "The Nation's Summer Capital."

Attractions: Rehoboth Beach/Boardwalk, on-site; Restaurants, Shops, Convention Center and Tax Free Outlet Shopping, 2 miles
Towns/Cities: Wilmington, 90 miles; Baltimore, 110 miles; Philadelphia, 116 miles; Washington D.C., 127 miles
Airports: Baltimore/Washington International Thurgood Marshall Airport, 114 miles; Philadelphia Airport, 116 miles

Inn at Montchanin Village

ROUTE 100 & KIRK ROAD, MONTCHANIN, WILMINGTON, DELAWARE 19710
Tel: +1 302 888 2133 **Fax:** +1 302 888 0389 **U.S./Canada Toll Free:** 1 800 269 2473
Web: www.johansens.com/montchanin **E-mail:** inn@montchanin.com

Our inspector loved: *The beautiful gardens, large rooms and spa suites, and first-class restaurant.*

Price Guide: (excluding 8% tax)
rooms $192-$244
suites $290-$399

28 M 40 SPA NR HP

Attractions: Winterthur Museum, 1 mile; Hagley Museum, 2 miles; Longwood Gardens, 12 miles; Brandywine River Museum, 12 miles
Towns/Cities: Wilmington, 4 miles; Philadelphia, 28 miles; Washington D.C., 110 miles; New York City, 115 miles
Airports: Philadelphia Airport, 23 miles; Baltimore/Washington Airport, 80 miles; Newark/New Jersey Airport, 110 miles

Affiliations: Small Luxury Hotels of the World

Montchanin is a historical and charming 19th-century hamlet in the Brandywine Valley. This lovingly restored, family-run hotel retains a whimsical atmosphere of Colonial splendor that is quiet and romantic. Each of the immaculately decorated rooms is brimming with beautiful antiques and period reproductions, yet provide you with all the conveniences of a modern hotel. The spacious and exquisite bedrooms are individually decorated with an emphasis on luxury and comfort with beautiful frette linens and lovely fresh flowers. Most rooms have immaculately landscaped private courtyards and several have cozy fireplaces. The overall attention to detail creates a gracious and restful ambience. Krazy Kat's Restaurant, once the blacksmith's shop, has a fun and eclectic décor, and serves the most mouth-watering international cuisine. The Spa at Montchanin is now open with full-service treatments and offers room packages.

District of Columbia

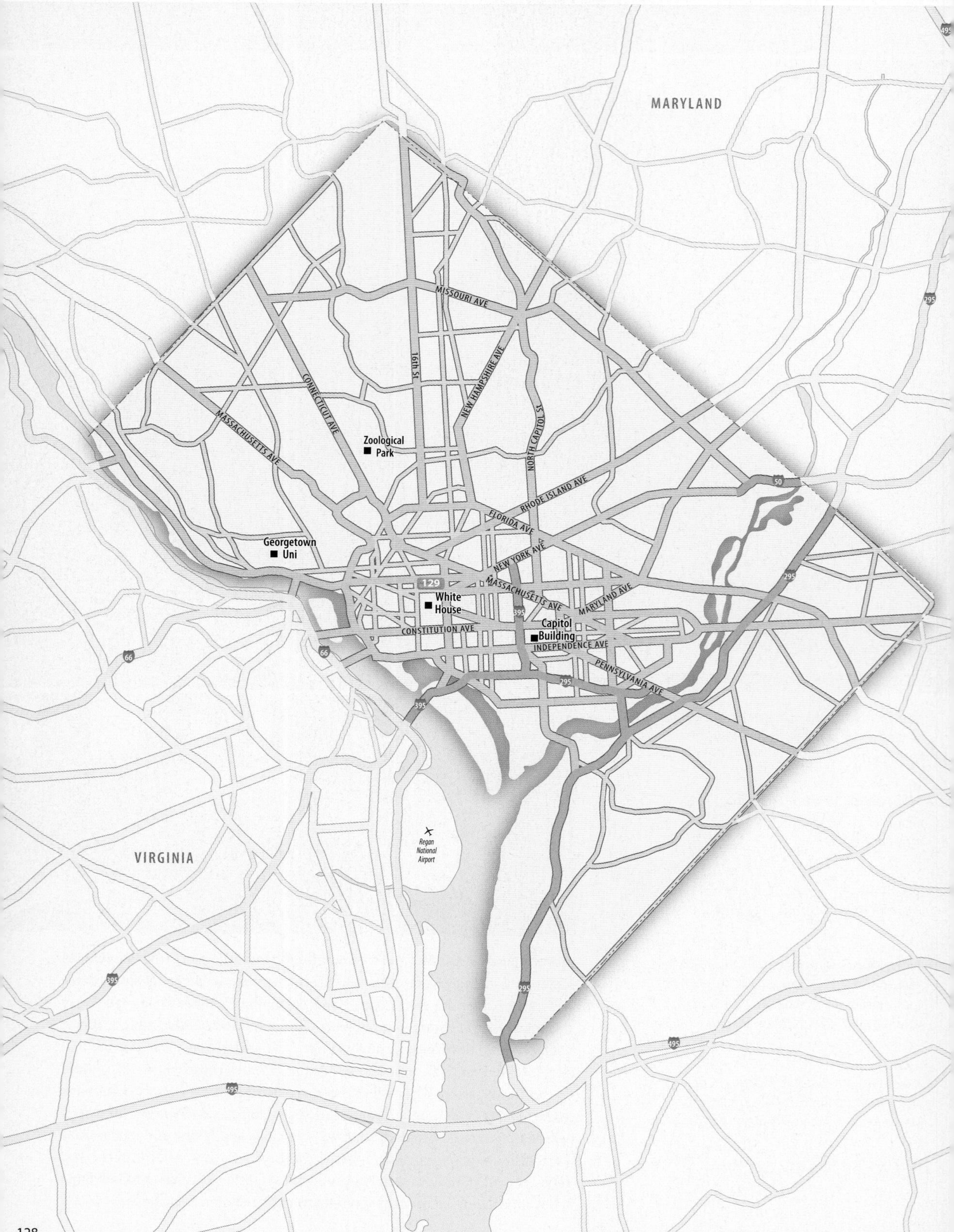

THE HAY-ADAMS

SIXTEENTH & H. STREETS N.W., WASHINGTON D.C., DISTRICT OF COLUMBIA 20006
Tel: +1 202 638 6600 **Fax:** +1 202 638 2716 **U.S./Canada Toll Free:** 1 800 424 5054
Web: www.johansens.com/hayadams **E-mail:** info@hayadams.com

Our inspector loved: *The spectacular service, and uninterrupted view of The White House.*

Price Guide:
rooms $425-$1,000
suites $1,300-$6,000

Awards/Ratings: Condé Nast Johansens Most Excellent Service, The Americas, Caribbean, Atlantic & Pacific Islands 2008; Condé Nast Johansens Most Excellent Hotel, U.S.A. & Canada 2007

Attractions: The White House, 0.1 miles; Smithsonian Museum, 0.3 miles; National Monuments, 0.3 miles; The Mint, 0.3 miles
Airports: Reagan National Airport, 5 miles; Dulles International Airport, 26 miles

Affiliations: The Leading Hotels of the World

Located across Lafayette Square from The White House, The Hay-Adams has retained its popularity and importance in the social life of Washington. Its Italian Renaissance architecture reflects the elegance of the interior with traditional furnishings and eye-catching antiques complemented by neutral tones and contemporary furniture. Upon entering, you will be amazed by the opulent lobby with its ornate ceiling, mahogany-colored paneling and European color schemes. Each bedroom is individually designed to an exceptionally high standard with plush sofas, canopied beds, uniquely detailed ceilings and remarkable views. The Lafayette restaurant is flooded with light and features Chippendale-style chairs and crystal chandeliers. Superb cuisine is served here together with an impressive selection of wines. For a light meal or delicious midnight snack, retreat to Off the Record bar.

Florida

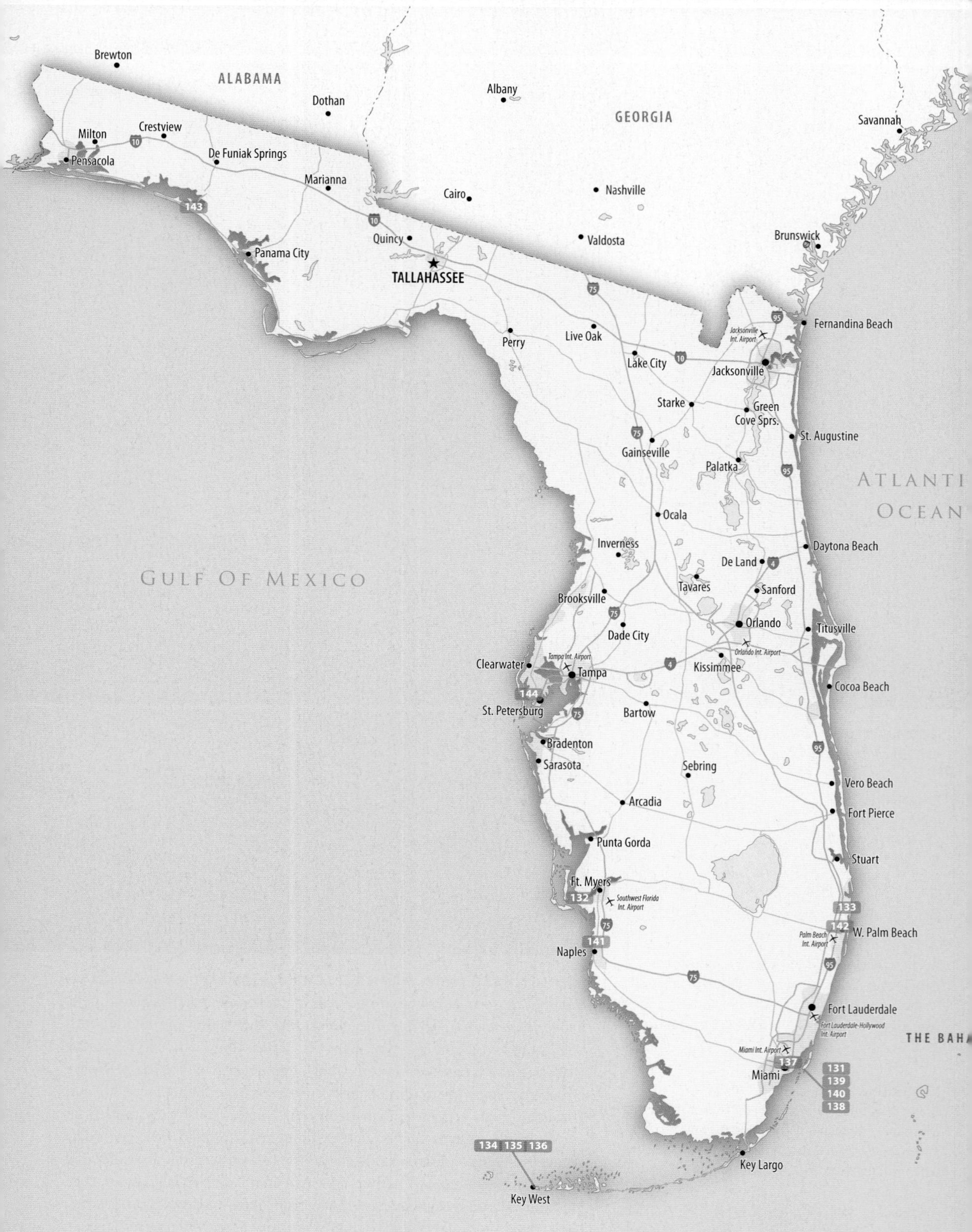

ALABAMA
GEORGIA
Brewton
Dothan
Albany
Savannah
Milton
Crestview
Pensacola
De Funiak Springs
Marianna
Cairo
Nashville
Quincy
Panama City
TALLAHASSEE
Valdosta
Brunswick
Fernandina Beach
Jacksonville Int. Airport
Perry
Live Oak
Lake City
Jacksonville
Starke
Green Cove Sprs.
St. Augustine
Gainseville
Palatka
ATLANTIC OCEAN
Ocala
Inverness
Daytona Beach
De Land
GULF OF MEXICO
Tavares
Sanford
Brooksville
Orlando
Titusville
Dade City
Orlando Int. Airport
Tampa Int. Airport
Clearwater
Tampa
Kissimmee
Cocoa Beach
St. Petersburg
Bartow
Bradenton
Sarasota
Sebring
Vero Beach
Arcadia
Fort Pierce
Punta Gorda
Stuart
Ft. Myers
Southwest Florida Int. Airport
W. Palm Beach
Palm Beach Int. Airport
Naples
Fort Lauderdale
Fort Lauderdale-Hollywood Int. Airport
THE BAH
Miami Int. Airport
Miami
Key Largo
Key West
10
75
95
4
143
144
132
141
133
142
137
131
139
140
138
134
135
136

Fisher Island Hotel & Resort

ONE FISHER ISLAND DRIVE, FISHER ISLAND, FLORIDA 33109
Tel: +1 305 535 6000 **Fax:** +1 305 535 6003 **U.S./Canada Toll Free:** 1 800 537 3708
Web: www.johansens.com/fisherisland **E-mail:** hotel@fisherislandclub.com

Our inspector loved: *The private location on the very exclusive Fisher Island.*

Price Guide: (including welcome drink of champagne or Fisher Island mimosa, full access to recreational amenities and golf cart for island transportation)
rooms $600-$1,100
suites $750-$3,600

62 200 SPA

Attractions: The Links at Fisher Island, 5-min drive; Miami Beach, 7-min drive; Miami Design District, 10-min drive
Towns/Cities: Miami, 11 miles; Coral Gables, 12 miles; Coconut Grove, 13 miles; Hollywood, 22 miles
Airports: Miami International Airport, 20-min drive

Affiliations: The Leading Hotels of the World

Originally built in the 1920s, this luxury resort hotel was once the Vanderbilt's impressive winter estate. Beautifully restored accommodations now include the Vanderbilt-era Cottages, luxurious 1-bedroom Villa Suites with private patios and hot tubs, and the Seaside Villas overlooking the Atlantic Ocean, adjacent to the private Beach Club. The Garwood Lounge, located inside the Vanderbilt mansion, is the perfect setting for cocktails at the piano bar before dinner at one of the several casual or fine dining restaurants. Complimentary golf carts are available to all guests who may wish to enjoy the on-site par 35 championship 9-hole golf course, and tennis is played at the Grand Slam tennis center. Spa Internazionale, with Fitness Center and Salon di Bellezza, offers world-class treatments in a tropical setting.

Sanibel Harbour Resort and Spa

17260 HARBOR POINTE DRIVE, FORT MYERS, FLORIDA 33908
Tel: +1 239 466 4000 **Fax:** +1 239 466 2150 **U.S./Canada Toll Free:** 1 888 237 4003
Web: www.johansens.com/sanibelresort **E-mail:** shrs@sanibel-resort.com

Nestled on a private peninsula overlooking Captiva and Sanibel Islands on the southwest Gulf Coast, this elegant and contemporary seaside resort is a perfect getaway for both couples and families. Rooms and suites in this grand hotel have elegant tropical décor and private balconies showcasing the beautiful island views. Relax on the beach in a seaside cabana or make a tee time at the nearby golf course. One of Condé Nast Traveler's Top Ten Spa Resorts in the U.S., the soothing Spa at Sanibel Harbour offers sea-inspired treatments. There are 6 dining options to choose from with wonderful menus of steak and seafood. Charley's Cabana Bar is the perfect spot to take in the breathtaking sunsets from its veranda before going on the dinner cruise. The resort is an ideal location for weddings and private events.

Our inspector loved: *Charley's Cabana Bar and the opportunity to enjoy a sunset dinner cruise aboard the hotel's luxury yacht, Sanibel Harbour Princess.*

Price Guide:
rooms $159-$499
suites $229-$799

386 960 SPA

Attractions: Shelling on the Islands of Sanibel and Captive, 9 miles; Bell Tower Shops, 9 miles; Edison Mall, 11 miles; Miromar Factory Outlet Mall, 20 miles
Towns/Cities: Sanibel Island, 9 miles; Fort Myers; Naples, 45-min drive
Airports: Southwest Florida International Airport, 19 miles

Affiliations: Preferred Hotels & Resorts

Jupiter Beach Resort & Spa

5 NORTH A1A, JUPITER, FLORIDA 33477-5190
Tel: +1 561 746 2511 **Fax:** +1 561 744 1741 **U.S./Canada Toll Free:** 1 800 228 8810
Web: www.johansens.com/jupiterbeachresort **E-mail:** reservations@jupiterbeachresort.com

Our inspector loved: *The spacious rooms, and incredible ocean views.*

Price Guide: (room only)
rooms $199-$399
suites $269-$1,500

159 100 SPA

Attractions: Jupiter Inlet Lighthouse, 2 miles; Abacoa Golf Club, 5 miles; The Gardens Mall, 8 miles; Kravis Center, 18 miles
Towns/Cities: West Palm Beach, 12 miles
Airports: Palm Beach International Airport, 21 miles; Fort Lauderdale International Airport, 68 miles; Miami International Airport, 89 miles

Jupiter Beach Resort & Spa is a 4 Star Diamond beach hotel located on the northern tip of Palm Beach County on the Atlantic Ocean. The intimate nature of this elegant boutique-style resort offers more of a private club feel than a hotel. The luxurious guest rooms are spacious with island-style décor and rich dark tropical woods. The Penthouse Suites have breathtaking views of the ocean and are beautifully decorated with designer furnishings. Visit the spa and indulge in an island wrap or sugar massage after a day on the expansive, secluded beach, and afterwards, enjoy a relaxing cup of tea or a warm Belgian chocolate shot at the Spa's Tea Bar. There are 3 on-site restaurants including the elegant Sinclairs Ocean Grill, the resort's signature Palm Beach restaurant, the Sandbar, which serves casual fare at the beach or by the pool, and Sinclairs Lounge, which provides weekend entertainment.

THE GARDENS HOTEL

526 ANGELA STREET, KEY WEST, FLORIDA 33040
Tel: +1 305 294 2661 **Fax:** +1 305 292 1007 **U.S./Canada Toll Free:** 1 800 526 2664
Web: www.johansens.com/gardenshotel **E-mail:** reservations@gardenshotel.com

Built as a Bahamian-style mansion in the 1800s, Gardens Hotel is surrounded by luscious flora. The botanical gardens, the vision and dream of Peggy Mills, flourished from 1930 to 1979, and today offer the same feeling of escape to hotel guests. The gardens even have 4 tinajones, used by Spanish colonials to catch water for drinking. The choice of rooms ranges from historic rooms in the original mansion and garden view rooms to rooms overlooking the courtyard. All feature fine European linens, crown molding and access to patios and verandas. The hotel also includes a heated pool, spa, and aviary for your enjoyment. This secluded hideaway is close to the infamous Duval Street and the excitement of Key West.

Our inspector loved: *Relaxing by the pool surrounded by beautiful gardens.*

Price Guide: (including breakfast)
rooms $200-$585
suites $415-$710

17 16 SPA

Attractions: Mallory Square, 5-min walk; Duval Street, 5-min walk; Mel Fisher Maritime Museum, 1 mile; Ernest Hemingway's Home, 2 miles
Towns/Cities: Miami, 150 miles
Airports: Key West Airport, 3.5 miles

Ocean Key Resort & Spa

ZERO DUVAL STREET, KEY WEST, FLORIDA 33040
Tel: +1 305 296 7701 **Fax:** +1 305 292 7685 **U.S./Canada Toll Free:** 1 800 328 9815
Web: www.johansens.com/oceankey **E-mail:** contactus@oceankey.com

Our inspector loved: *Dining with a view at Hot Tin Roof.*

Price Guide:
rooms $279-$749
suites $359-$1,729

100 M 250 SPA

Attractions: Key West Aquarium, 0.1 miles; Mel Fisher Maritime Heritage, 0.2 miles; Mallory Square, 1-min walk; Duvall Street, 1-min walk
Towns/Cities: Miami, 150 miles
Airports: Key West International Airport, 3 miles; Miami International Airport, 155 miles

Overlooking the Gulf of Mexico, adjacent to the famous Mallory Square, Ocean Key Resort & Spa radiates the tropical feel of Key West. Located in the premier wing of the resort are the ultra-luxurious suites that exude barefoot elegance. All suites are appointed with hand-crafted Dorado stone floors and have opulent bathrooms. Interiors embrace the style of the West Indies, while capturing the playfulness of the Florida Keys with shades of indigo, turquoise and lime that also reflect the unparalleled ocean front. The ocean-front Hot Tin Roof serves a creative and gourmet menu of Latin, Caribbean and South Florida flavors prepared by Executive Chef Miguel Blasini who is celebrated for his delectable "conch-fusion" cuisine. For more casual fare, you can choose to dine by the pool, at the Sunset Pier, or in the comfort of your very own room. Spa Terre is a relaxing retreat and specializes in exotic Balinese spa treatments and Thai body rituals.

Sunset Key Guest Cottages

245 FRONT STREET, KEY WEST, FLORIDA 33040
Tel: +1 305 292 5300 **Fax:** +1 305 292 5395 **U.S./Canada Toll Free:** 1 877 317 5800
Web: www.johansens.com/sunsetkey **E-mail:** rebecca.hysell@westinkeywestresort.com

Sunset Key is a 27-acre luxury island with a resort and a residential community located just 500 yards from historic "Old Town" Key West. Sunset Key Guest Cottages are accessible only by launch, which runs 24 hours a day from The Westin Key West Resort & Marina. This car-free island makes for the most tranquil vacation with its spectacular views of the Gulf of Mexico, fresh ocean air and colorful tropical blooms. Each of the luxurious 1, 2 and 3-bedroom cottages is nestled around tropical foliage and has either an ocean or garden view, wraparound veranda with Adirondack chairs, living room, dining area and a pre-stocked kitchen. Breakfast baskets are served to each cottage porch each morning, while meals are served in Latitudes Beach Cafe, an upscale yet casual dining experience in an alfresco beach-front setting. For a more intimate dinner you can request the Private Chef Service to prepare you dinner in your very own cottage.

Our inspector loved: *The privacy of this tropical island so close to the festivities of Key West.*

Price Guide:
1-bedroom cottages $664-$1,305
2-bedroom cottages $753-$2,080
3-bedroom cottages $1,132-$2,481

37 WiFi

Awards/Ratings: Condé Nast Traveler Gold List 2003-2007

Attractions: Mallory Square, 1 mile; Duval Street, 1 mile; Mel Fisher Maritime, 1 mile; Ernest Hemingway's Home, 2 miles
Towns/Cities: Miami, 160 miles
Airports: Key West International Airport, 4 miles; Miami International Airport, 160 miles

Grove Isle Hotel & Spa

FOUR GROVE ISLE DRIVE, COCONUT GROVE, FLORIDA 33133
Tel: +1 305 858 8300 **Fax:** +1 305 858 5908 **U.S./Canada Toll Free:** 1 800 884 7683
Web: www.johansens.com/groveisle **E-mail:** reservations@groveisle.com

Our inspector loved: *The spectacular views while dining by the water.*

Price Guide:
rooms $259-$689
suites $429-$859

49 250 SPA

Attractions: Grand Slam - Legends of Tennis Center, on-site; Vizcaya Museum and Gardens, 0.8 miles; CocoWalk, 1.5 miles; South Beach, 5 miles
Towns/Cities: Miami, 5 miles
Airports: Miami International Airport, 10 miles

This private 20-acre gated island sanctuary offers a peaceful and secure respite. Lush gardens, views of Biscayne Bay, original artwork and guests sipping martinis by the pool as yachts dock at the marina below, create the ambience of a private luxury residence. Accommodations feature Italian marble bathrooms, iron four-poster beds, and balconies with views of the bay and shoreline of Miami. BALEENmiami, the fine dining restaurant, serves Euro-Asian fare that can also be enjoyed "Dining on the Rocks" in a tropical ocean-front setting. Alternately, choose the Palapa Bar for lighter poolside bites, island-style cuisine on the open-air loggia or an evening meal in the comfort of your very own room. The 6000 sq. ft. SpaTerre offers exotic Balinese spa treatments and Thai body rituals with a private couple's Zen steam room, outdoor yoga deck, Watsu pool and full-service salon.

CASA TUA

1700 JAMES AVENUE, MIAMI BEACH, FLORIDA 33139
Tel: +1 305 673 0973 **Fax:** +1 305 673 0974
Web: www.johansens.com/casatua **E-mail:** hotel@casatualifestyle.com

This stylish boutique hotel, set in the heart of the art-deco district of Miami's South Beach, will make you feel like you're staying in a private luxury home. Mediterranean Revival in style, Casa Tua hides behind wrought-iron gates and neatly trimmed hedges, just 1 block from the beach. 5 sophisticated guest rooms are individually decorated with soft cashmere throws, crisp white Italian linens, original artwork and impressive antiques. Attentive personalized service is their forte. Casa Tua's own casual-chic restaurant serves classic Italian and Mediterranean food. Enjoy Chef Sergio Sigala's specialty risotto while dining by candlelight in the library, garden or at the popular Chef's table.

Our inspector loved: *Dining at the "friends table" next to the open kitchen at Casa Tua Restaurant.*

Price Guide: (including breakfast)
rooms $750-$1,050

Attractions: Lincoln Road, 2-min walk; Art Deco Historic District, 2-min walk; Bass Museum of Art, 2-min walk; South Beach, 5-min walk
Towns/Cities: Miami, 11 miles; Key Biscayne, 15 miles; North Miami Beach, 17 miles; Hollywood, 21 miles
Airports: Miami International Airport, 12 miles

Hotel Victor

1144 OCEAN DRIVE, MIAMI BEACH, FLORIDA 33139
Tel: +1 305 428 1234 **Fax:** +1 305 421 6281
Web: www.johansens.com/hotelvictor **E-mail:** salesvicto@hotelvictorsouthbeach.com

Our inspector loved: *The very relaxing "reVitalizing" body treatment at Spa V.*

Price Guide:
rooms $325-$709
suites $875-$10,000

88 500 SPA

Attractions: Versace Mansion, 1-min walk; South Beach, 1-min walk; Upscale Shopping, Restaurants and Nightclubs, 2-min walk; Bass Museum of Art, 1 mile
Towns/Cities: Miami, 8 miles; Sunny Isle, 10 miles; Coconut Grove, 12 miles; Coral Gables, 12 miles
Airports: Miami International Airport, 11 miles; Fort Lauderdale/Hollywood International Airport, 28 miles; Palm Beach International Airport, 72 miles

Hotel Victor is the epitome of glamour and style. And as such, has received various awards including North America's Leading Boutique Hotel and Florida's Leading Boutique Hotel at the World Travel Awards and recognition as One of the Best New Hotels in the World by Condé Nast Traveler. The vibe is hip yet elegant, and all vibrant guest rooms have custom furniture, designer fabrics and views of the ocean or South Beach. Open bathrooms feature oversized soaking tubs, rain showers, 350-count Fili d'Oro Egyptian cotton linens, L.C.D. T.V.s and Big Bars. The opulent Penthouse occupies the entire eighth floor and has a private entrance, gourmet kitchen, infinity-edge tub and outdoor entertainment areas with hot tubs and 360° views. Dining at VIX is an exciting experience: displaying a jellyfish tank and original artwork, it offers an exciting spiced and culturally inspired cuisine. Visit Spa V's Cool Down Room and signature Turkish-style hammam for the ultimate pampering!

U.S.A. - FLORIDA (MIAMI BEACH)

THE SETAI

2001 COLLINS AVENUE, MIAMI BEACH, FLORIDA 33139
Tel: +1 305 520 6000 **Fax:** +1 305 520 6600
Web: www.johansens.com/setai **E-mail:** setai@ghmamericas.com

Our inspector loved: *The tranquil serenity.*

Price Guide:
suites $1,150-$9,700
penthouse $30,000-$35,000

130 40 SPA

Awards/Ratings: Condé Nast Traveler Gold List '07-'08; Wine Spectator Award of Excellence '06-'07

Attractions: Ocean Drive, 1-min walk; Art Deco Historic District, 3-min walk; The Bass Museum of Art, 3-min walk; Lincoln Road, 10-min walk
Towns/Cities: Downtown Miami, 10 miles; Hollywood, 22 miles; Fort Lauderdale, 30 miles; West Palm Beach, 73 miles
Airports: Miami International Airport, 12 miles; Fort Lauderdale International Airport, 29 miles

Affiliations: The Leading Hotels of the World

The Setai is a magnificently renovated art deco landmark that has quickly become one of the crown jewels of South Beach. Invoking Asian traditions of simplicity and elegance, the hotel's ambience is one of serenity and style. The ideal setting for a small wedding, this stunning ocean-front resort hotel, adjoined by a 40-story residential tower, offers strikingly elegant rooms set above an oasis of tropical gardens, shimmering pools and sundecks leading to the gorgeous white sand beach. Dining is unparalleled at The Grill, which serves the finest meats and aritsan products from around the world, and at The Restaurant, where exceptional, authentic Asian cuisine is available. The Pool & Beach Bar provides excellent Mediterranean-style fare. The Bar and Courtyard is the perfect place to start your evening or end your night in the buzzing South Beach. Visit The Spa at The Setai to restore your mind, body and soul.

LaPlaya Beach & Golf Resort

9891 GULF SHORE DRIVE, NAPLES, FLORIDA 34108
Tel: +1 239 597 3123 **Fax:** +1 239 597 8283 **U.S./Canada Toll Free:** 1 800 237 6883
Web: www.johansens.com/laplaya **E-mail:** sales@laplayaresort.com

Our inspector loved: *The huge private balconies overlooking the beach and bay.*

Price Guide:
rooms $199-$799
suites $805-$2,600

189 250 SPA

Awards/Ratings: Condé Nast Johansens Most Excellent Resort, U.S.A. & Canada 2008

Attractions: Waterside Shops, 5 miles; Historic Fifth Avenue Shopping, 9 miles; Miromar Outlets, 20 miles
Towns/Cities: Naples, on-site; Fort Myers, 25 miles
Airports: Southwest Florida International Airport, 27 miles; Miami International Airport, 125 miles

This is the place for sun worshippers and all who like the attractions of year-round sub-tropical weather, warm turquoise waters and sugar-white sandy beaches. The resort is situated on Vanderbilt Beach and revolves around a magnificent meandering pool complex. The interior is equally stunning. French doors attractively span the width of the first floor, and the elegant main lobby is adorned with crystal chandeliers and plush cane and wicker furnishings. Bedrooms are oversized and luxuriously appointed and decorated in fresh greens and warm yellows with bamboo-patterned bedcovers, four-poster beds, balconies and superb ocean views. An evening in Baleen, the resort's signature restaurant, begins indoors and ends on the long shoreline terrace. Adjacent to the fitness center is a fully-equipped spa decorated in 1920s décor.

U.S.A. - FLORIDA (PALM BEACH)

THE BRAZILIAN COURT

301 AUSTRALIAN AVENUE, PALM BEACH, FLORIDA 33480
Tel: +1 561 655 7740 **Fax:** +1 561 655 0801 **U.S./Canada Toll Free:** 1 800 552 0335
Web: www.johansens.com/braziliancourt **E-mail:** info@thebraziliancourt.com

Our inspector loved: *The intimacy and hidden sitting areas within this lovely property.*

Price Guide:
luxury studios $299-$750
1/2-bedroom suites $399-$3,000

80 200 SPA

Awards/Ratings: Condé Nast Traveler Gold List 2008; Wine Spectator Award of Excellence 2007

Attractions: Worth Avenue Shopping and Beach, 2-min walk; Henry Flagler Museum, 0.7 miles; Kravis Center and Beach Place, 1.1 miles
Towns/Cities: Jupiter, 16 miles; Boca Raton, 24 miles; Fort Lauderdale, 40 miles; Miami, 68 miles
Airports: Palm Beach Intl., 4 miles; Fort Lauderdale/Hollywood Intl., 55 miles

Affiliations: The Leading Small Hotels of the World; Preferred Hotels & Resorts

This intimate European-designed hotel, privately set on a quiet tree-lined street in glamorous Palm Beach, is a haven for guests seeking elegant accommodations, exquisite dining and personalized service. Beautifully appointed guest rooms are sophisticated and comfortable, each unique in design and décor. Café Boulud Palm Beach, overlooking the highly recognized central fountain and courtyard, will tempt your palate with French-American cuisine by world-renowned Chef Daniel Boulud. Meander through the hotel to the art gallery where Brazilian Court's very own curator will take you through the local and international artwork on display. For the ultimate in pampered luxury, spend a day at the Frederic Fekkai Palm Beach Salon and Spa located within the hotel.

WaterColor Inn & Resort

34 GOLDENROD CIRCLE, SANTA ROSA BEACH, FLORIDA 32459
Tel: +1 850 534 5000 **Fax:** +1 850 534 5001 **U.S./Canada Toll Free:** 1 866 426 2656
Web: www.johansens.com/watercolor **E-mail:** info@watercolorreservations.com

Our inspector loved: *The powder-white sand beach and clear gulf water.*

Price Guide:
rooms $245-$595
suites $745-$845
vacation homes $230-$2,500

Attractions: Shopping, 8 miles
Towns/Cities: Destin, 8 miles; Panama City, 36 miles; Pensacola, 75 miles
Airports: Okaloosa Regional Airport, 24 miles; Panama City-Bay County International Airport, 36 miles; Pensacola Regional Airport, 75 miles

Affiliations: Preferred Hotels & Resorts

WaterColor nestles between the shores of Florida's Emerald Coast and the banks of a 220-acre dune lake. Embraced by wind-sculptured oak groves, palmettos and sea grasses, the inn is surrounded by a maze of pathways and parks that meander from the Gulf of Mexico to the lake. With the intimacy and hospitality of a traditional Southern grand hotel the inn has magnificent David Rockwell-designed architecture and spacious guest rooms with king-size beds and sofa sleepers, walk-in showers and beach views from private balconies. There are also 150 beautifully appointed, fully-equipped vacation homes, with 1-6 bedrooms. The casual Fish Out of Water restaurant takes an imaginative approach to traditional cuisine, while the BaitHouse and the BeachClub, with its pool deck and grill, are great alternatives.

U.S.A. - FLORIDA (ST. PETE BEACH)

Don CeSar Beach Resort, A Loews Hotel

3400 GULF BOULEVARD, ST. PETE BEACH, FLORIDA 33706

Tel: +1 727 360 1881 **Fax:** +1 727 367 6952 **U.S./Canada Toll Free:** 1 800 282 1116

Web: www.johansens.com/doncesar **E-mail:** doncesarinfo@loewshotels.com

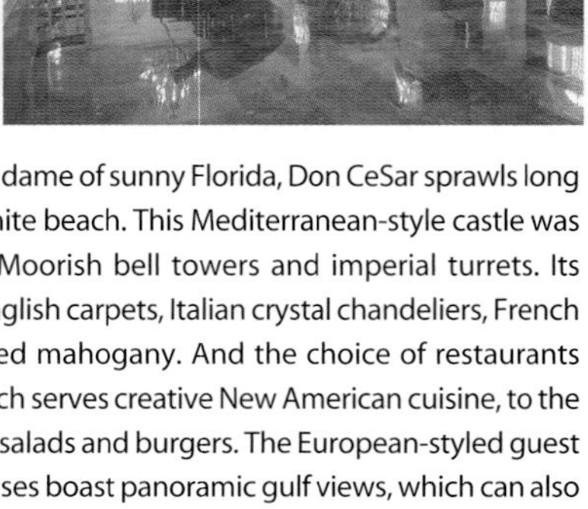

Our inspector loved: *The old fashioned ice-cream parlor, and the beautiful beach.*

Price Guide:
rooms $204-$569
suites $324-$3,000

277 400 SPA NR HP

Attractions: St. Petersburg Pier, 11 miles; Florida Aquarium, 32 miles; Busch Gardens, 38 miles; Cypress Gardens, 81 miles
Towns/Cities: St. Petersburg, 10 miles; Tampa, 30 miles
Airports: St. Petersburg/Clearwater International Airport, 19 miles; Tampa International Airport, 28 miles

Affiliations: Loews Hotels

Affectionately referred to as a grand dame of sunny Florida, Don CeSar sprawls long and high on the edge of a sugar-white beach. This Mediterranean-style castle was built in 1928 and is accented by Moorish bell towers and imperial turrets. Its luxurious interior is adorned with English carpets, Italian crystal chandeliers, French candelabras, fountains and polished mahogany. And the choice of restaurants ranges from the Maritana Grille, which serves creative New American cuisine, to the poolside Beachcomber Grill with its salads and burgers. The European-styled guest rooms, spacious suites and penthouses boast panoramic gulf views, which can also be admired from the spa's whirlpool and rooftop garden. Loews Spa Oceana uses the therapeutic elements of a collection of worldwide, organic sea salts, and comprises 16 treatment rooms including a private reception area for soothing meditation, deluxe couples' treatment rooms and suite areas for private parties.

TENNESSEE
NORTH CAROLINA
SOUTH CAROLINA
ALABAMA
FLORIDA
ATLANTIC OCEAN
Hendersonville
Charlotte
Cleveland
Chattanooga
Greenville
Camden
Dalton
Toccoa
COLUMBIA
Calhoun
Summerville
Abbeville
Gainesville
Payne
Canton
Rome
Elberton
Athens
Aiken
Cedartown
ATLANTA
Monroe
Augusta
Thomson
Barnwell
Douglasville
Covington
Hartsfield-Jackson Atlanta Int. Airport
Eatonton
Walterboro
Carrollton
Fayetteville
Waynesboro
ladega
Griffin
Milledgeville
La Grange
Thomaston
Macon
Swainsboro
Statesboro
Dublin
Savannah Int. Airport
Opelika
Fort Valley
Lyons
Savannah
Colombus
Eastman
Hinesville
ONTGOMERY
Americus
Cordele
Fitzgerald
Jesup
Dawson
Douglas
Brunswick
Albany
Tifton
Waycross
Nashville
Camilla
Adel
Blakely
Fernandina Beach
Andalusia
Dothan
Cairo
Valdosta
Thomasville
Bainbridge
Jacksonville
Marianna
TALLAHASSEE
Panama City
Gainseville
146
148
147
150
151
149

Barnsley Gardens Resort

597 BARNSLEY GARDENS ROAD, ADAIRSVILLE, GEORGIA 30103
Tel: +1 770 773 7480 **Fax:** +1 770 877 9155 **U.S./Canada Toll Free:** 1 877 773 2447
Web: www.johansens.com/barnsleygardens **E-mail:** bgr_reservations@barnsleyresort.com

37 charming cottages built to resemble a 19th-century English-style village are nestled in 1,300 acres of lush gardens and historic land at the foothills of the beautiful Blue Ridge Mountains. All the gabled, fretted and shingled cottages edge tree-lined walkways and are decorated with warmth and comfort in mind. Each suite and room is individually styled. Many suites feature antiques and fine furnishings, fireplaces, king or queen-size sleigh or poster beds and bathrooms with cast-iron ball and claw-foot tubs. Dominated by the ruins of the Italian-style manor's historic mansion, the original ornamental gardens have been stunningly restored and feature more than 150 types of roses. There is a choice of 3 excellent dining areas: Continental cuisine with a memorable twist at the Rice House, the Woodlands Grill steakhouse or German beer and sausages in the Beer Garden.

Our inspector loved: *The quaint village, unique cottages, and all the activities on-site.*

Price Guide:
rooms $299
suites $375-$1,675

87 150 SPA NR HP

Attractions: Spa at Barnsley Gardens, on-site; Jim Fazio-designed 18-hole Golf Course and Historic Ruins and Gardens, 5-min walk; Orvis Wing-Shooting and Fly-Fishing Schools, 100 yards; Spring Bank Plantation Quail Hunting Preserve, 5-min drive
Towns/Cities: Atlanta, 61 miles; Chattanooga, TN, 68 miles; Birmingham, AL, 137 miles; Nashville, TN, 199 miles
Airports: Chattanooga Airport, TN, 65 miles; Atlanta Hartsfield Jackson Airport, 75 miles

Affiliations: Preferred Boutique

TWELVE Atlantic Station

361 17TH STREET, ATLANTA, GEORGIA 30363
Tel: + 1 404 961 1212 **Fax:** +1 404 961 1221
Web: www.johansens.com/twelvehotelsas **E-mail:** reservations@twelvehotels.com

Our inspector loved: *The latest technology at your fingertips and the fantastic dining and entertainment outside your door.*

Price Guide:
1-bedroom suites $189-$229
2-bedroom suites $279-$359

101 · 400

Attractions: High Museum of Art; 20-min walk; Georgia Aquarium, 3 miles; Georgia World Congress Center, 3 miles; World of Coca Cola, 3 miles
Towns/Cities: Madison, 64 miles; Charlotte, NC, 245 miles; Nashville, TN, 246 miles; Savannah, 252 miles
Airports: Dekalb-Peachtree Airport, 9 miles; Hartsfield-Jackson Atlanta International Airport, 20-min drive; Birmingham International Airport, 140 miles

Affiliations: Preferred Boutique

A luxurious all-suite hotel in midtown Atlanta, TWELVE Atlantic Station is in the heart of wonderful shopping, dining and entertainment options. Each 1 or 2-bedroom suite comes with a full kitchen, separate living area and a chic and unique design. The rooms are also equipped with special Internet access which allows guests to take advantage of all hotel services from the convenience of a computer. Dine at the LOBBY at TWELVE, which serves seasonally driven dishes with a comfort food edge. Also visit the Cellar at LOBBY, available for interactive wine tasting, cocktail parties or meetings. Relax by the swimming pool or in the guest lounge with flat-screen televisions and comfortable couches. If it is excitement you crave, rent one of the hotel's BMWs or Mini Coopers and explore the city by car.

U.S.A. - GEORGIA (ATLANTA)

TWELVE Centennial Park

400 WEST PEACHTREE STREET, N.W. ATLANTA, GEORGIA 30308
Tel: +1 404 418 1212 **Fax:** +1 404 418 1221
Web: www.johansens.com/twelvehotelscp **E-mail:** reservations@twelvehotels.com

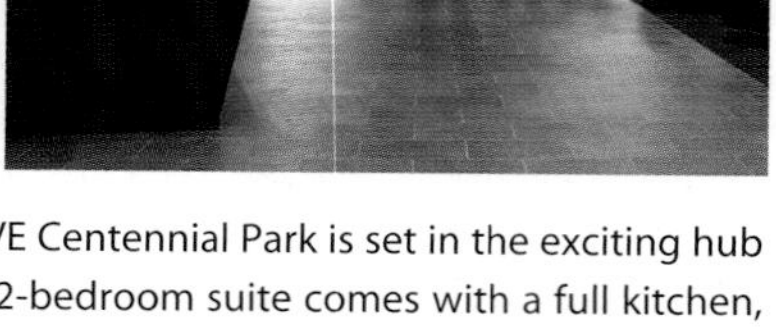

A luxurious all-suite hotel, TWELVE Centennial Park is set in the exciting hub of downtown Atlanta. Each 1 or 2-bedroom suite comes with a full kitchen, separate living area and a chic and unique design. The rooms are also equipped with special Internet access which allows guests to take advantage of all hotel services from the comfort of a computer. Dine at ROOM, a new take on the classic American grill, serving exceptional steaks as well as sushi and handcrafted cocktails. Relax by the swimming pool with an elevated deck or visit one of Atlanta's many attractions. If it is excitement you crave, rent one of the hotel's BMWs or Mini Coopers and explore the city by car.

Our inspector loved: *The luxury of the extra large rooms complete with a full kitchen and computer.*

Price Guide:
1 bedroom suites $189-$229
2 bedroom suites $279-$359

102 250 DVD WiFi

Attractions: Georgia Aquarium, 10-min walk; World of Coca-Cola, 10-min walk; CNN Center, 15-min walk; Georgia Dome, 20-min walk
Towns/Cities: Madison, 64 miles; Charlotte, NC 245 miles; Augusta, 150 miles; Nashville, TN, 246 miles
Airports: Dekalb - Peachtree Airport, 11 miles; Hartsfield - Jackson Atlanta International Airport, 15-min drive; Birmingham International Airport, 146 miles

Affiliations: Preferred Boutique

GREYFIELD INN

CUMBERLAND ISLAND, GEORGIA
Tel: +1 904 261 6408 **Fax:** +1 904 321 0666 **U.S./Canada Toll Free:** 1 866 410 8052
Web: www.johansens.com/greyfieldinn **E-mail:** seashore@greyfieldinn.com

Our inspector loved: *The unbelieveable trip back in time. This is the most intriguing, restful vacation spot in America.*

Price Guide: (including round-trip ferry service, 3 meals per day, guided wilderness outing and use of bicycles, kayaks and fishing equipment)
rooms $395-$525
suites $525-$595

16 M 25 5 NR HP

Attractions: 17-mile Long Protected National Seashore, close by; Wildlife and Bird-watching, close by; Fernandina Beach, Amelia Island, 10 miles
Towns/Cities: Fernandina Beach, Amelia Island, 10 miles; Savannah, 120 miles; Hilton Head, 150 miles
Airports: Jacksonville Airport, 30-min drive; Savannah Airport, 120 miles

Affiliations: Classic Inns of the South; Preferred Hotels & Resorts

Cumberland Island is the largest and most southern of Georgia's 120-mile long coastal archipelago. Steel baron Thomas Carnegie and his wife built Greyfield as a wedding gift for their daughter Margaret Ricketson in 1901. In 1962 the home was converted into an inn by her daughter Lucy Ferguson, whose descendants now oversee the daily operations. Filled with original furnishings that date from the turn-of-the-century, added luxuries and contemporary amenities are found throughout. Relax in the Baronial living room, in the cozy bar, well-stocked library, on the shady veranda or in the exquisite bedrooms with fabulous views. This is the only overnight accommodation on an island the size of Manhattan and is reached by ferry or small private plane. Surrounded by 17 miles of protected national seashore of pristine beaches and ancient oaks, there is an abundance of wildlife here including deer, wild horses, bobcats, boar, alligators and 230 species of birds.

THE JAMES MADISON INN

260 WEST WASHINGTON STREET, MADISON, GEORGIA 30650
Tel: +1 706 342 7040 **Fax:** +1 706 342 8100
Web: www.johansens.com/jamesmadison **E-mail:** reservations@jamesmadisoninn.com

Our inspector loved: *This inn that is like no other. Take a carriage ride to see the antebellum home that your luxurious room is named after!*

Price Guide: (including upscale Continental breakfast)
king rooms $250-$275
suites $325-$350

19 M 35

Attractions: Shopping, Dining, Galleries and City Park in Historic Downtown Madison, 5-min walk
Towns/Cities: Lake Oconee, 25 miles; Atlanta, 65 miles; Augusta, 80 miles
Airports: Hartsfield Jackson International Airport, Atlanta, 65 miles; Greenville - Spartanburg Airport, 120 miles

This landmark in the historic town of Madison, Georgia, is a "gem of the Antebellum Trail." Combining the splendor and charm of the pre-war South with modern comfort, James Madison has been designed to complement the architecture of the town and comprises 17 luxury guest rooms and 2 suites. Each room has been named after one of Madison's historic houses and features a painting of its namesake above the mantle of the fireplace. The in-room library, filled with works by local authors and artists, furthers the sense of local pride apparent in this elegant hotel. Rooms are individually appointed with custom-designed furniture, 600 thread-count linens on sumptuous king-sized beds, soft-lighting and neutral hues. They also include a furnished porch, flat-screen television, wireless Internet and an oversized walk-in black and white tile shower in every bathroom.

The Presidents' Quarters Inn

225 EAST PRESIDENT STREET, SAVANNAH, GEORGIA 31401-3806
Tel: +1 912 233 1600 **Fax:** +1 912 238 0849 **U.S./Canada Toll Free:** 1 800 233 1776
Web: www.johansens.com/presidentsquarters **E-mail:** info@presidentsquarters.com

Our inspector loved: *The staff that provide the ultimate in charming Southern hospitality.*

Price Guide: (including breakfast, on-site parking available)
rooms $229-$325

Attractions: Owens-Thomas House, across the street; City Market and Riverfront, 10-min walk; Juliette Gordon Low Birthplace, 10-min walk; Forsyth Park, 15-minute walk
Towns/Cities: Beaufort, 1-hour drive; St. Simons Island, 60 miles; Charleston, 120 miles
Airports: Savannah Airport, 10 miles; Hilton Head Airport, 60 miles; Charleston International Airport, 70 miles

Built in 1855, The Presidents' Quarters Inn represents the epitome of Southern hospitality and gracious living. Newly restored to its former grandeur, the extremely spacious rooms are named after U.S. Presidents such as George Washington and John F. Kennedy who visited Savannah during their presidency. Each bedroom is fitted with luxurious bedding and features working fireplaces. Guests enjoy evening wine and hors d'oeuvres as well as bedtime cordials in the lovely parlor. With its own intriguing stories to tell, such as the time when Robert E. Lee visited General Lawton of the Court of Vienna while staying here, the history of this place is reflected in lovely touches found throughout the bedrooms, making you almost feel transported back in time. Enjoy a light and tasty breakfast in the front parlor or courtyard gazebo before exploring the historic downtown and its museums, monuments and Savannah College of Art and Design.

Idaho

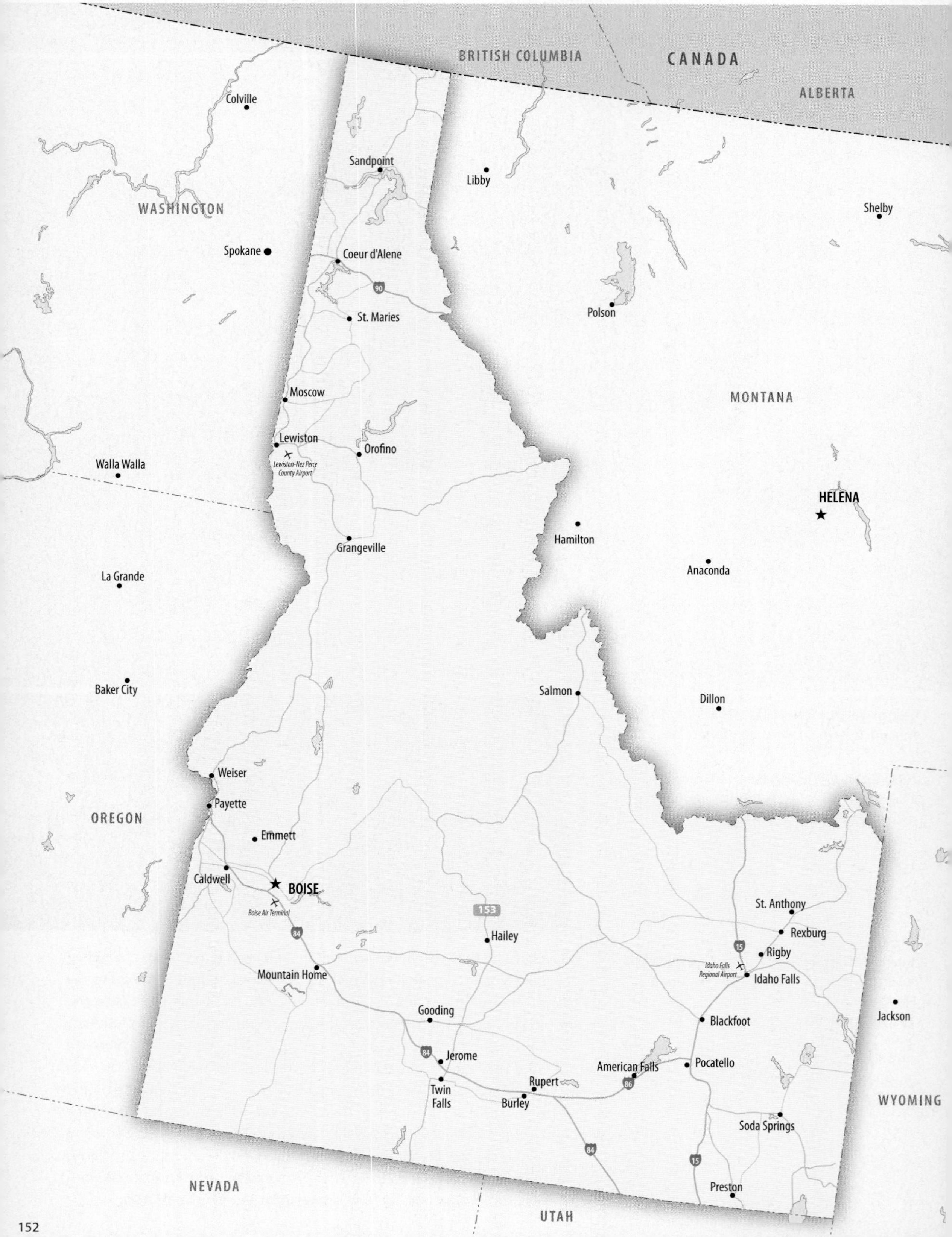

BRITISH COLUMBIA
CANADA
ALBERTA
Colville
Sandpoint
Libby
WASHINGTON
Shelby
Spokane
Coeur d'Alene
90
St. Maries
Polson
Moscow
MONTANA
Lewiston
Orofino
Walla Walla
Lewiston-Nez Perce County Airport
HELENA
Hamilton
Grangeville
Anaconda
La Grande
Baker City
Salmon
Dillon
Weiser
Payette
OREGON
Emmett
Caldwell
BOISE
Boise Air Terminal
153
St. Anthony
Rexburg
84
Hailey
15
Rigby
Idaho Falls Regional Airport
Idaho Falls
Mountain Home
Gooding
Blackfoot
Jackson
84
Jerome
Pocatello
American Falls
Rupert
86
Twin Falls
Burley
WYOMING
Soda Springs
84
15
NEVADA
Preston
UTAH

KNOB HILL INN

960 NORTH MAIN STREET, P.O. BOX 800, KETCHUM, IDAHO 83340
Tel: +1 208 726 8010 **Fax:** +1 208 726 2712 **U.S./Canada Toll Free:** 1 800 526 8010
Web: www.johansens.com/knobhillinn **E-mail:** khi@knobhillinn.com

Our inspector loved: *The breathtaking mountain views.*

Price Guide: (including breakfast, excluding 10% tax and gratuities)
rooms $275-$350
suites $425-$525

26 M 25

Awards/Ratings: Wine Spectator Outstanding Wine List 2008

Attractions: Sun Valley Resort, 1 mile; Big Wood River, 1 mile; Bald Mountain, 1 mile; Sun Valley Championship 18-hole Golf Course, 1.5 miles
Towns/Cities: Ketchum, on-site; Boise, 150 miles
Airports: Hailey Airport, 12 miles

Knob Hill Inn is an Austrian-style inn set in the heart of Hemingway country, Ketchum. Centrally located and ideal for those who enjoy both winter skiing and summer-type activities, the inn is in America's first destination ski resort overlooking the world-famous Bald Mountain, the majestic Sawtooths and the Boulder Mountain ranges. Most of the charming rooms have dressing rooms, marble bathrooms with an oversized tub and separate shower. Each room has glass doors that open out to breathtaking views of the mountain peaks. Each morning, you are treated to a buffet of fresh pastries, breads and muffins with daily entrées made to order. Fine dining in the restaurant is a modern American feast with dishes expertly prepared by Chef Michael Zentner who takes time to find the freshest of local and imported ingredients. To complement the cuisine, the fine wine list comprises regional samples and the best of Old World vintages.

Illinois

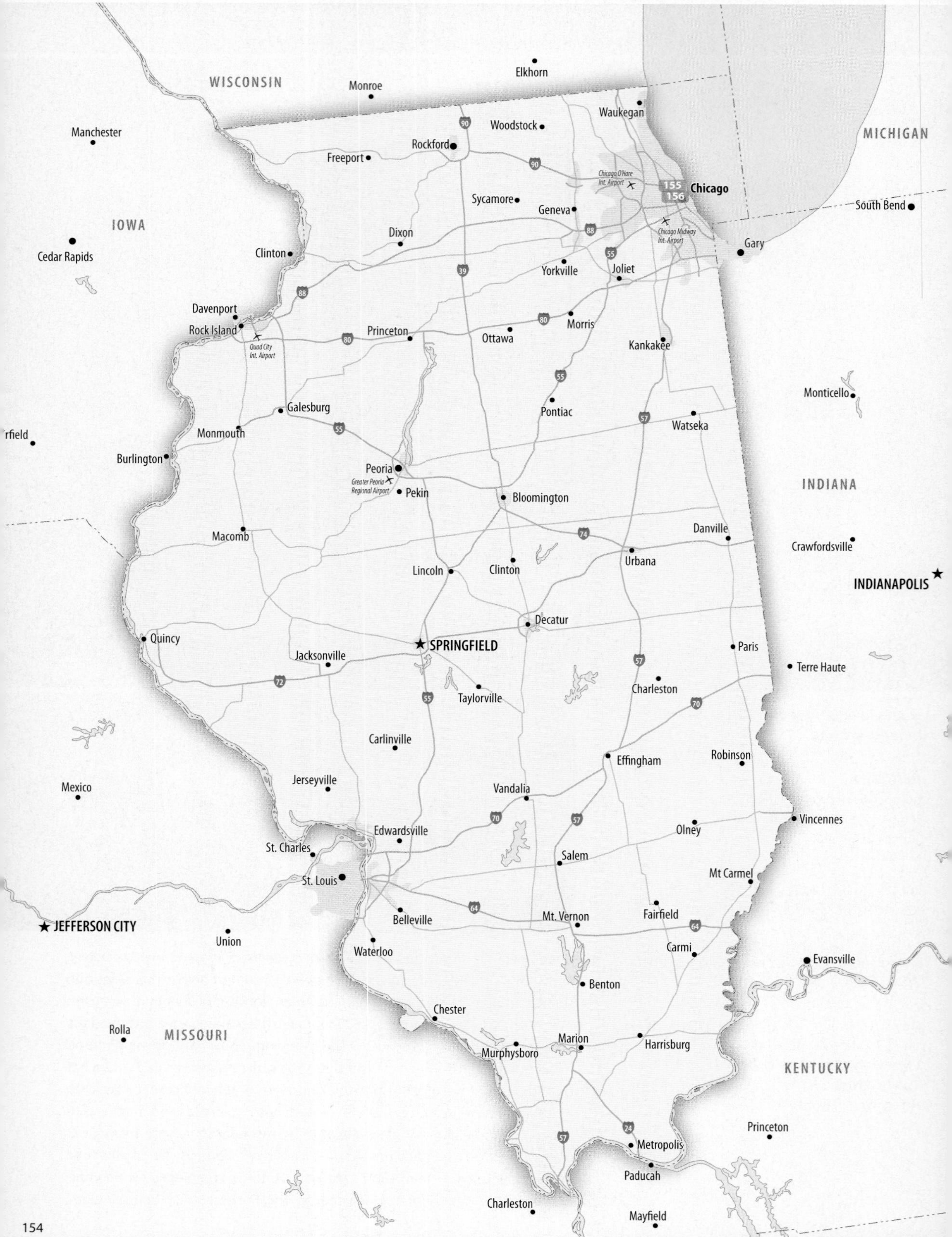
WISCONSIN
IOWA
MICHIGAN
INDIANA
MISSOURI
KENTUCKY
Elkhorn
Monroe
Waukegan
Woodstock
Manchester
Rockford
Freeport
Chicago O'Hare Int. Airport
155
156
Chicago
Sycamore
Geneva
South Bend
Chicago Midway Int. Airport
Dixon
Cedar Rapids
Clinton
Gary
Yorkville
Joliet
Davenport
Rock Island
Quad City Int. Airport
Princeton
Ottawa
Morris
Kankakee
Monticello
Pontiac
Galesburg
Watseka
Monmouth
Burlington
Peoria
Greater Peoria Regional Airport
Pekin
Bloomington
Macomb
Danville
Crawfordsville
Urbana
Lincoln
Clinton
INDIANAPOLIS
Decatur
Quincy
SPRINGFIELD
Paris
Jacksonville
Terre Haute
Charleston
Taylorville
Carlinville
Effingham
Robinson
Jerseyville
Mexico
Vandalia
Vincennes
Olney
Edwardsville
St. Charles
Salem
St. Louis
Mt Carmel
Fairfield
JEFFERSON CITY
Mt. Vernon
Belleville
Union
Carmi
Waterloo
Evansville
Benton
Chester
Rolla
Marion
Harrisburg
Murphysboro
Princeton
Metropolis
Paducah
Charleston
Mayfield
90
88
39
80
55
57
74
72
70
64
24

Hotel Sax Chicago

333 NORTH DEARBORN STREET, CHICAGO, ILLINOIS 60654
Tel: +1 312 245 0333 **Fax:** +1 312 923 2444 **U.S./Canada Toll Free:** 1 877 569 3742
Web: www.johansens.com/hotelsax **E-mail:** reservations@hotelsaxchicago.com

Our inspector loved: *The edgy, urban attitude and the multiple dining and entertainment options available within, and adjacent to the hotel.*

Price Guide:
rooms $149-$569
suites $239-$1000

353 400

Attractions: Soldier Field, 3 miles; Theater District, 5-min walk; Magnificent Mile Shopping, 10-min walk; Field Museum/Shedd Aquarium, 20-min walk
Airports: Chicago Midway, 11 miles; Chicago O'Hare, 20 miles

On Condé Nast Traveler's Hot List 2008, Hotel Sax Chicago is an architectural oasis discovered in the heart of downtown Chicago, amidst the bustling city streets. After entering the crisp red and white lobby and being welcomed by the staff, head to your room to enjoy wonderful views of the city. Each guest room has a 42" H.D. T.V. and Special Entertainment Technology rooms, built in partnership with Microsoft, are equipped with up-to-date gadgets such as gaming devices, stereos with headphones and laptop computers. The hotel's Crimson Lounge is the hottest new nightspot in Chicago with its beautiful crimson touches and an intriguing cocktail menu. Step outside the door to experience everything Chicago has to offer: jazz, blues and rock 'n' roll music, high-end shopping, Broadway-caliber theater and fascinating architectural history.

U.S.A. - ILLINOIS (CHICAGO)

THE TALBOTT HOTEL

20 E. DELAWARE PLACE, CHICAGO, ILLINOIS 60611
Tel: +1 312 944 4970 **Fax:** +1 312 944 7241 **U.S./Canada Toll Free:** 1 800 TALBOTT
Web: www.johansens.com/talbotthotel **E-mail:** info@thetalbott.com

This luxury boutique hotel is located steps from the famed Michigan Avenue, and is ideal for the most discerning business and leisure travelers. Boasting some of the largest rooms and luxury suites in the city, the hotel exudes classic and elegant European décor and the latest in high-tech and modern conveniences. Expansive hospitality suites are available for both business and entertaining. The acclaimed Italian BICE Bistro serves hearty regional northern and southern Italian cuisine where in season, you can enjoy outdoor dining. As a guest of the hotel, you can also take advantage of the complimentary access to Equinox, a world-class health complex, located just steps from the hotel. The award-winning concierges and attentive staff will ensure personalized service to make sure your stay is a relaxing one.

Our inspector loved: *The Old World style, comfort and service combined with New World technology.*

Price Guide:
rooms $249-$649
suites $349-$899

149 100

Attractions: Michigan Avenue Shopping, 5-min walk; Museum of Contemporary Art, 15-min walk; Navy Pier, 1.5 miles; Field Museum, 3 miles
Airports: Chicago O'Hare Airport, 17 miles; Chicago Midway Airport, 12 miles

Affiliations: Small Luxury Hotels of the World

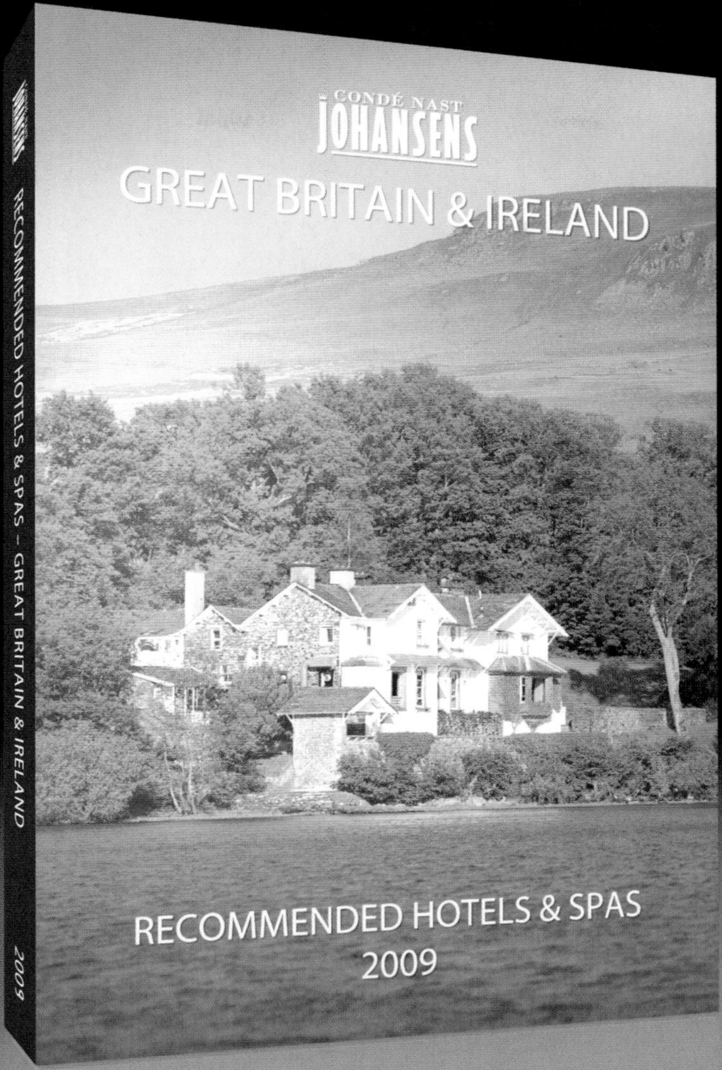

Small Hotels, Inns & Restaurants, Great Britain & Ireland 2009 • Hotels & Spas, Europe & The Mediterranean 2009
Hotels, Inns, Resorts & Spas, The Americas, Atlantic, Caribbean & Pacific 2009 • Luxury Spas Worldwide 2009
International Venues for Meetings & Special Events 2009

New Guides • New Destinations • New Experiences

Available at all good bookshops or by calling TOLL FREE 1 800 564 7518

Order online at www.johansens.com

Kansas

NEBRASKA
IOWA
MISSOURI
OKLAHOMA
TEXAS
Sioux City
Broken Bow
Lexington
York
LINCOLN
Clarinda
Maryville
McCook
Falls City
Burlington
St. Francis
Norton
Smith Center
Marysville
Hiawatha
Troy
Concordia
Atchison
Colby
Hill City
Osborne
Leavenworth
Kansas City Int. Airport
Manhattan
Kansas City
Kansas City
Oakley
Junction City
TOPEKA
Lawrence
Olathe
Harrisonvil
Sharon Springs
Hays
Salina
Abilene
Council Grove
Ottawa
Leoti
Ness City
Great Bend
McPherson
Emporia
Syracuse
Garden City
Kinsley
Hutchinson
Newton
Fort Scott
Iola
Neva
Dodge City
Wichita
El Dorado
Wichita Mid-Continent Airport
Ulysses
Pratt
Howard
Wellington
Columbus
Meade
Coldwater
Winfield
Independence
Elkhart
Liberal
Neosho
Guymon
Bartlesville
Perryton
Woodward
Enid
Tulsa
OKLAHOMA CITY
Amarillo
Wichita Falls
Durant
70
135
335
35
159

THE ELDRIDGE HOTEL

701 MASSACHUSETTS, LAWRENCE, KANSAS 66044
Tel: +1 785 749 5011 **Fax:** +1 785 749 4512 **U.S./Canada Toll Free:** 1 800 527 0909
Web: www.johansens.com/eldridge **E-mail:** info@eldridgehotel.com

Our inspector loved: *The history that has been preserved with integrity and care.*

Price Guide:
suites $149-$295

48 150 NR HP

Awards/Ratings: Wine Spectator Award of Excellence 2007 and 2008

Attractions: Booth Family Hall of Athletics, 2 miles; University of Kansas, 2 miles; Lied Center for Performing Arts, 3 miles; Clinton Lake, 10 miles
Towns/Cities: Kansas City, 40 miles
Airports: Kansas City International Airport, 45 miles

The Eldridge was originally built as temporary quarters for families of the New England Emigrant Aid Society who came to Kansas from Massachusetts and other areas in the mid 1800s. Over the years it became the Free State Hotel, then the Hotel Eldridge. Restored to its original grandeur, it is now a 48-room luxury boutique hotel that combines history with hospitality. The original furnishings have been updated with black leather chairs and hardwood furnishings alongside black and white photographs for a contemporary feel. Suites are spacious with beautiful furnishings, cozy living areas and modern amenities, while the Honeymoon Suite is perfect for a weekend getaway or romantic escape. TEN serves casual and hearty fare as well as a sumptuous Sunday brunch. The Jayhawker Bar, popular for its jazz nights, has an extensive wine list.

Louisiana

LITTLE ROCK
Batesville
ARKANSAS
Camden
Texarkana
El Dorado
Greenville
Louisville
Bastrop
Lake Providence
Minden
Ruston
Shreveport
20
Monroe
Tallulah
Vicksburg
JACKSON
MISSISSIPPI
49
Winnsboro
Waynesboro
Carthage
Mansfield
Winnfield
Natchitoches
Jena
Natchez
Hattiesburg
Alexandria
Marksville
Leesville
Greensburg
Bunkie
Jasper
49
New Roads
Baton Rouge Metropolitan Airport
55
Covington
Biloxi
De Ridder
Ville Platte
12
Bay St. Louis
TEXAS
Opelousas
BATON ROUGE
Plaquemine
Louis Armstrong New Orleans Int. Airport
10
Crowley
Lafayette
Lake Charles
10
Donaldsonville
10
161
Jennings
St. Martinville
New Orleans
Beaumont
Orange
10
Abbeville
New Iberia
Thibodaux
Franklin
Pointe a la Hache
Houma
Galveston
GULF OF MEXICO

SONIAT HOUSE

1133 CHARTRES STREET, NEW ORLEANS, LOUISIANA 70116
Tel: +1 504 522 0570 **Fax:** +1 504 522 7208 **U.S./Canada Toll Free:** 1 800 544 8808
Web: www.johansens.com/soniathouse **E-mail:** stay@soniathouse.com

Our inspector loved: *The gracious staff and exquisitely unique rooms.*

Price Guide: (including breakfast)
rooms $240-$295
suites $425-$695

Attractions: Jackson Square, 2-min walk; Convention Center, 10-min walk; New Orleans Museum of Art, 2 miles
Airports: New Orleans International Airport, 13 miles

Affiliations: Small Luxury Hotels of the World

In the heart of the French Quarter, this small luxury hotel is in fact 3 historic town houses. Its beautifully appointed rooms overlook lush tropical patios or open out onto wide verandas. It is an owner-managed property and both French and Spanish are spoken by the staff. Filled with period French antiques and furnished with Frette linen and Anick Goutal amenities, this is a great choice when visiting New Orleans. Breakfast consisting of home-made biscuits, fresh orange juice and café au lait can be served in your room or on the courtyard. Why not start your evenings with cocktails by candlelight before venturing out to the one of the many nearby Quarter restaurants? This is a totally non-smoking hotel.

Maine

Edmundston
Madawaska
Grand Falls
(Grand Sault)
Van Buren
Perth-Andover
Caribou
CANADA
Presque Isle
FREDERICTON
Montmagny
Woodstock
Houlton
NEW BRUNSWICK
QUÉBEC
Millinocket
Saint-
Stephen
St-Georges
Calais
163
95
Lincoln
Lac-Mégantic
Machias
Dover-Foxcroft
Bangor
Int. Airport
Bangor
Ellsworth
Pittsfield
Skowhegan
Bar Harbor
Belfast
Waterville
Farmington
Rumford
AUGUSTA
Rockland
Lewiston
Norway
Bath
St. Johnsbury
495
Brunswick
NEW
HAMPSHIRE
Portland
165
Portland Int.
Jetport
ATLANTIC
OCEAN
Saco
Sandford
95
164
Kennebunk
Laconia
York Village
CONCORD
Dover

THE LODGE AT MOOSEHEAD LAKE

368 LILY BAY ROAD, P.O. BOX 1167, GREENVILLE, MAINE 04441
Tel: +1 207 695 4400 **Fax:** +1 207 695 2281 **U.S./Canada Toll Free:** 1 800 825 6977
Web: www.johansens.com/lodgeatmooseheadlake **E-mail:** innkeeper@lodgeatmooseheadlake.com

Our inspector loved: *The Maine décor in the Lodge and throughout the individually decorated guest rooms.*

Price Guide: (including breakfast)
rooms $267.50-$422.65
suites $410.25-$727.60

9 35 12

Attractions: Moose Sightings, 1 mile; Moosehead Lake, 1 mile; Lily Bay State Park, 12 miles; Mount Kineo, 20 miles
Towns/Cities: Bar Harbor, 126 miles; Québec City, QC, 159 miles; Kennebunkport, 184 miles; Manchester, NH, 248 miles
Airports: Bangor Airport, 89 miles; Portland Airport, 158 miles; Boston Logan International Airport, MA, 259 miles

Perched gracefully atop a rise on 7.5 acres with beautifully landscaped gardens overlooking the broad waters of Moosehead Lake, this award-winning inn offers spectacular lake views, a peaceful atmosphere and warm hospitality. Built in 1917, this stately Colonial property is an ultra-private hideaway that combines elegance and comfort with an interior filled with unique imports, rich custom-designer fabrics and bespoke furnishings. You will especially enjoy the ever-changing vista across Moosehead Lake that is both stunning by day and magical by moonlight. Savor your favorite cocktail at Chloe's Pub before heading to the recently renovated Lakeview Dining Room, an enchanting setting where the service is impeccable.

THE WHITE BARN INN

37 BEACH AVENUE, KENNEBUNKPORT, MAINE 04043
Tel: +1 207 967 2321 **Fax:** +1 207 967 1100
Web: www.johansens.com/whitebarninn **E-mail:** innkeeper@whitebarninn.com

Since welcoming its first travelers in the 1800s, The White Barn Inn has earned an envious reputation for its wonderfully relaxing atmosphere, charm, luxury, attentive service and superb cuisine. The interior is beautifully decorated and furnished, and guest rooms are the epitome of luxury and comfort. Each has every amenity from flatscreen plasma T.V.s to voicemail and fresh flowers. Some have a fireplace, steam shower, whirlpool bath and private deck looking out to the manicured grounds. There are also fully-equipped waterfront cottages close by with a private marina clubhouse alongside the inn's 44-ft. Hinkley Talaria jet cruiser, which can be chartered for coastal tours. Enjoy the outdoor heated pool, canoeing, cycling and full-service spa with treatment suites, skin services, Kohler soak tub and Swiss shower.

Our inspector loved: *The warm New England charm.*

Price Guide:
rooms $395-$460
suites $699-$750
waterfront cottages $799-$860

28 20 12
SPA

Awards/Ratings: AAA 5 Diamond Award; Mobil 5 Star

Attractions: Beaches, 0.25 miles; Former President Bush's Summer Home, 2 miles; Ogunquit Play House, 14 miles; Portland Headlight, 32 miles
Towns/Cities: Portland, 30 miles; Portsmouth, NH, 32 miles; Boston, MA, 87 miles; New York City, NY, 295 miles
Airports: Portland Intl. Jetport, 27 miles; Manchester, NH, 79 miles; Boston, MA, 85 miles

Affiliations: Relais & Châteaux

PORTLAND HARBOR HOTEL

468 FORE STREET, PORTLAND, MAINE 04101
Tel: +1 207 775 9090 **Fax:** +1 207 775 9990 **U.S./Canada Toll Free:** 1 888 798 9090
Web: www.johansens.com/portlandharbor **E-mail:** resmgr@harthotels.com

Our inspector loved: *The downtown location, close to the harbor, quaint shops and cobbled streets.*

Price Guide:
rooms $189-$350
suites $289-$700

101 65

Attractions: Portland Observatory, 1 mile; Portland Head Light, 4 miles; Two Lights State Park, 7 miles; Freeport/L.L. Bean, 15 miles
Towns/Cities: Augusta, 35 miles; North Conway, NH, 45 miles; Portsmouth, NH, 50 miles; Boston, MA, 110 miles
Airports: Portland Airport, 4 miles; Manchester Airport, NH, 80 miles; Boston Logan International Airport, MA, 110 miles

Experience Old World charm and exceptional service in the heart of the Old Port, just 1 block from the Portland waterfront. Enjoy views of the city skyline or the hotel's lush garden from the well-appointed guest rooms. Each room is distinctive with custom-made his and her armoires and luxury bathrooms include granite surround and an enclosed shower or soaking tub. Pampering touches include high-thread count bed linens, feather pillows and comforters, and plush towels and robes. Within easy walking distance from the hotel, the lovingly restored shops and restaurants reflect the charm of the Victorian Old Port district, and Portland's vibrant waterfront is a must-see, with cobblestone streets, historic landmarks and full-service marinas on both sides of the harbor. Reflect on the day's experiences over a candle-lit dinner at the award-winning Eve's restaurant overlooking the garden.

Maryland

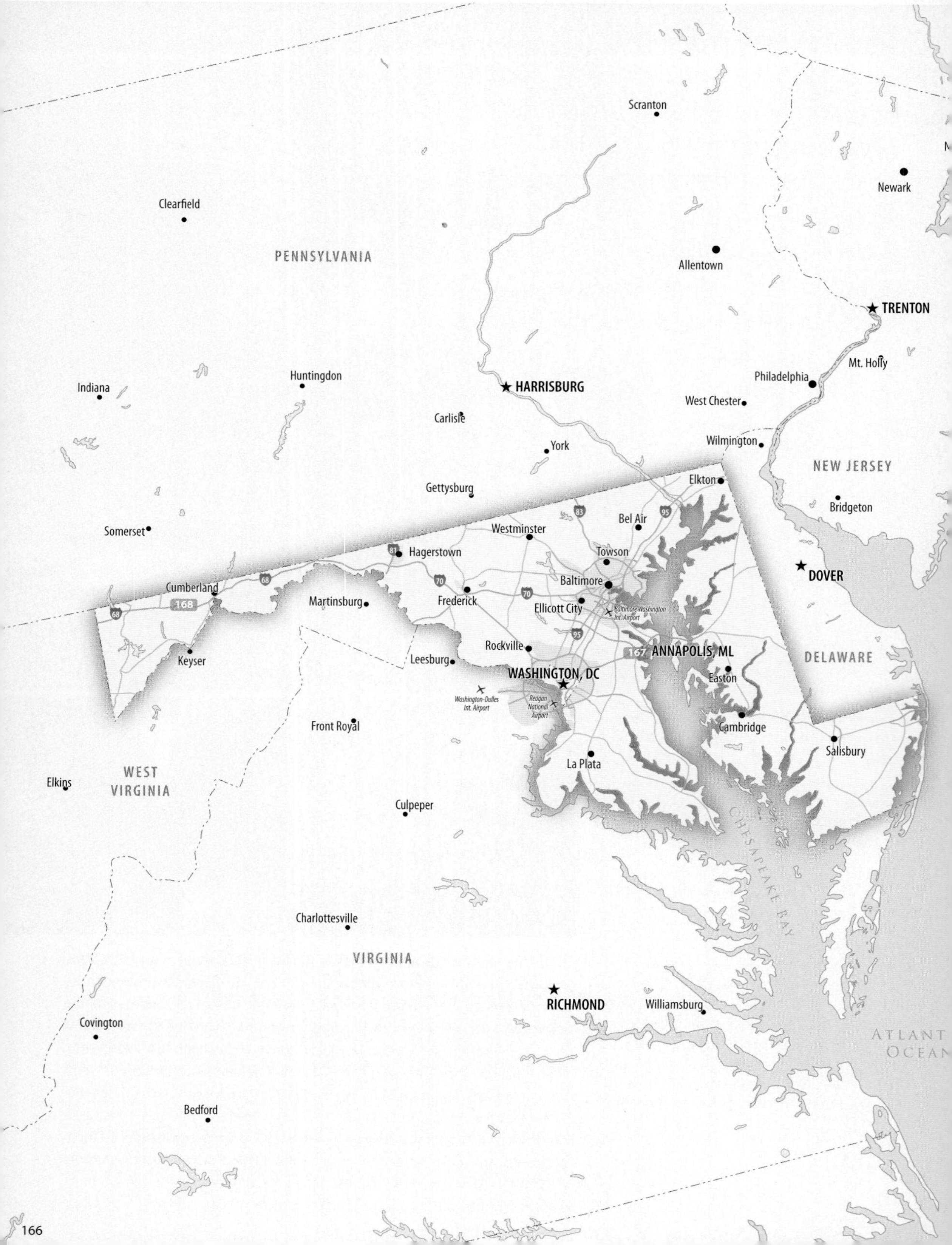
Scranton
Newark
Clearfield
PENNSYLVANIA
Allentown
TRENTON
Mt. Holly
Huntingdon
Indiana
HARRISBURG
Philadelphia
West Chester
Carlisle
York
Wilmington
NEW JERSEY
Gettysburg
Elkton
Bridgeton
Bel Air
Somerset
Westminster
Hagerstown
Towson
DOVER
Cumberland
Baltimore
Martinsburg
Frederick
Ellicott City
Baltimore-Washington Int. Airport
Rockville
ANNAPOLIS, ML
DELAWARE
Keyser
Leesburg
WASHINGTON, DC
Easton
Washington-Dulles Int. Airport
Reagan National Airport
Cambridge
Front Royal
Salisbury
La Plata
Elkins
WEST VIRGINIA
Culpeper
CHESAPEAKE BAY
Charlottesville
VIRGINIA
RICHMOND
Williamsburg
Covington
Bedford
168
167
68
81
70
83
95

The Annapolis Inn

144 PRINCE GEORGE STREET, ANNAPOLIS, MARYLAND 21401-1723
Tel: +1 410 295 5200 **Fax:** +1 410 295 5201
Web: www.johansens.com/annapolisinn **E-mail:** info@annapolisinn.com

Our inspector loved: *The sumptuous breakfast, gracious hosts and fascinating history.*

Price Guide: (including breakfast)
rooms $259-$439
suites $379-$479

3 M 8 17 DVD WiFi NR HP

Attractions: Downtown Annapolis, 1-min walk; Naval Academy, 1-min walk; Annapolis Harbor, 1-min walk; State Capitol, 2-min walk
Towns/Cities: Baltimore, 30 miles; Washington D.C., 35 miles
Airports: Baltimore Washington International Airport, 25 miles; Reagan National Airport, 37 miles; Dulles International Airport, 65 miles

Nestled between the U.S. Naval Academy, city harbor and the stunning State Capitol, The Annapolis Inn is in one of the few historic cities whose entire downtown is on the National Register of Historic Places. A gorgeous example of Georgian and Greek revival, it was built circa 1770 and holds just 3 guest bedrooms within whose expansive opulence take you back to a bygone era. The accompanying attentive levels of service, including an elegant and delicious breakfast, will sweep your cares away. Each room of the inn features classical moldings, beautiful antiques and elaborate wood carvings. Bathrooms feature heated marble floors, towel warmers and Jacuzzi baths. Downtown Annapolis beckons, with history, shopping, dining and a variety of nautical pursuits at your doorstep.

U.S.A. - MARYLAND (FROSTBURG)

SAVAGE RIVER LODGE

1600 MT. AETNA ROAD, FROSTBURG, MARYLAND 21532
Tel: +1 301 689 3200 **Fax:** +1 301 689 2746
Web: www.johansens.com/savageriver **E-mail:** info@savageriverlodge.com

Our inspector loved: *The privacy of the luxurious cabins, the excellent cuisine and the extensive list of outdoor activities to choose from.*

Price Guide: (including Continental breakfast)
cabins $185-$275

Awards/Ratings: Wine Spectator Award of Excellence 2008

Attractions: Hiking, Cross-Country Skiing, Snowshoeing, Geocaching, Fly-Fishing and Biking the Great Allegheny Passage, 5 miles; C&O Canal, 20-min walk; Frank Lloyd Wright's "Falling Water," 45-min walk

Towns/Cities: Frostburg, 5 miles; Cumberland, 20 miles

Airports: Pittsburgh Airport, 125 miles; Baltimore/Washington Airport, 150 miles; Dulles International Airport, 150 miles

A rustic lodge, log cabins, porches with rocking chairs, gourmet dining, excellent service, mountain-side location encircled by 700 acres of forest teeming with wildlife and nature - if that is what you want from a vacation then this is it! Nestling in 42 acres, 18 cabins are scattered along a tree-lined road and provide every solace from overstuffed furniture to down comforters on queen-size beds and oversized soaking tubs. There are telephones but no televisions. The lodge itself is for relaxing with friends or a place in which to curl up by the fire or window with a book. Dining is a casual experience where the Wine Enthusiast award-winning wine list offers a great array of choice and an open view into the kitchen enhances the informality. Continental breakfast is delivered to cabins in a picnic basket.

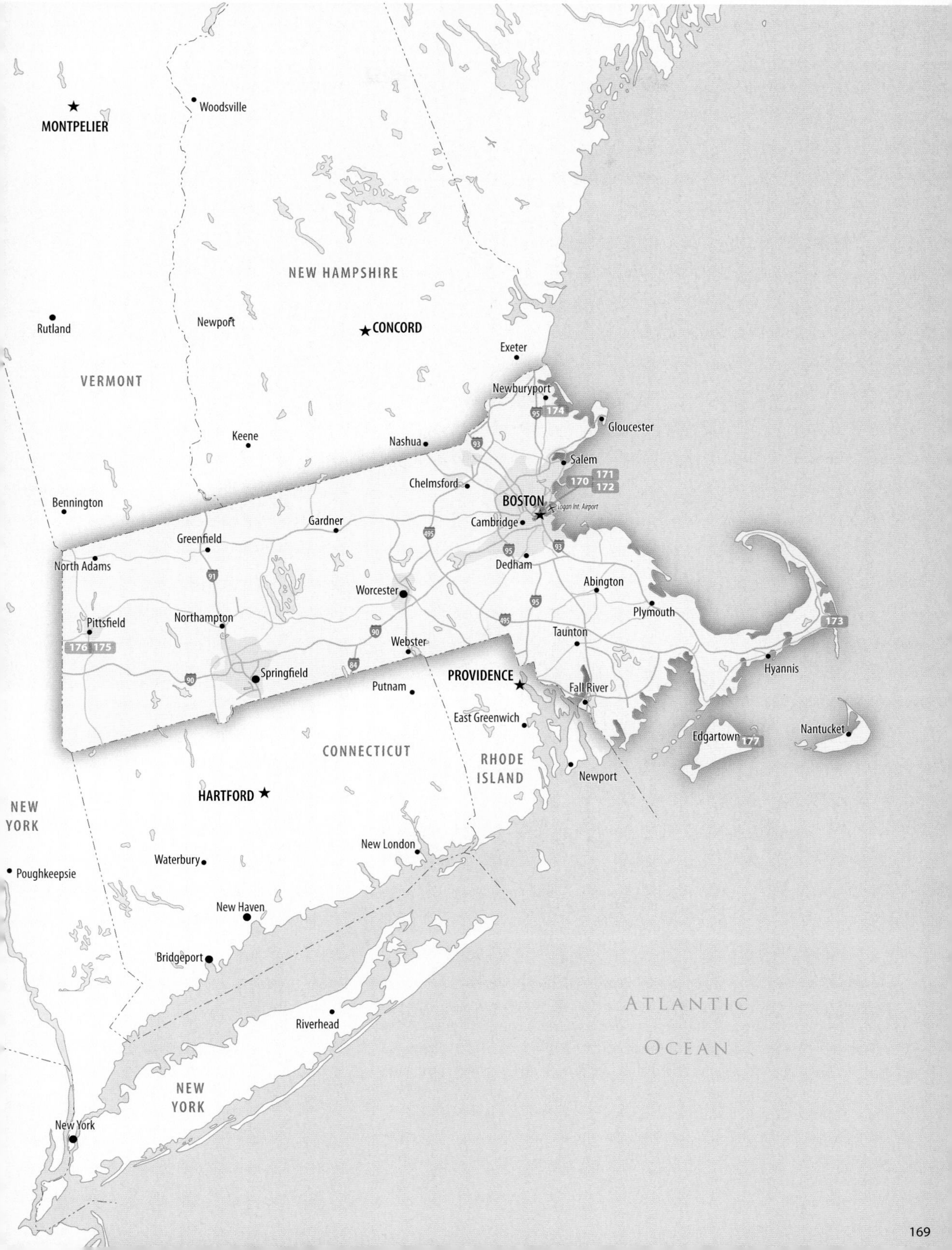
Woodsville
MONTPELIER
NEW HAMPSHIRE
Rutland
Newport
CONCORD
Exeter
VERMONT
Newburyport
174
Gloucester
Keene
Nashua
Salem
171
170
172
Chelmsford
Bennington
BOSTON
Logan Int. Airport
Gardner
Cambridge
Greenfield
North Adams
Dedham
Abington
Worcester
Plymouth
Pittsfield
Northampton
Taunton
173
176
175
Webster
Hyannis
PROVIDENCE
Springfield
Putnam
Fall River
East Greenwich
Nantucket
Edgartown
177
CONNECTICUT
RHODE ISLAND
Newport
HARTFORD
NEW YORK
New London
Waterbury
Poughkeepsie
New Haven
Bridgeport
ATLANTIC OCEAN
Riverhead
NEW YORK
New York

U.S.A. - MASSACHUSETTS (BOSTON)

Boston Harbor Hotel

70 ROWES WHARF, BOSTON, MASSACHUSETTS 02110
Tel: +1 617 439 7000 **Fax:** +1 617 345 6799 **U.S./Canada Toll Free:** +1 800 752 7077
Web: www.johansens.com/bhh **E-mail:** reservations@bhh.com

One of Boston's landmarks, this elegant hotel is ideally located on historic Rowes Wharf overlooking celebrated Boston Harbor. Inside this distinctive luxury hotel you are welcomed with sincere and attentive service. A warm lobby detailed with beautifully hand-carved wood and exquisite Italian marble enhance the experience. Each of the accommodations reflects a residential feel of elegance with graceful and distinctive Boston styles and breathtaking city skyline or scenic harbor views. Meritage, a Mobil 4 Star restaurant takes the unique approach of matching wine and food by offering small and large plates paired with specific wine characteristics. For the ultimate in relaxation, renew and rejuvenate at the Spa at Rowes Wharf, one of the most luxurious health and modern fitness centers in New England.

Our inspector loved: *The beautiful views.*

Price Guide: (room only, excluding 12.45 tax)
superiors from $320
deluxes from $440
suites $695-$4,500

230 500 SPA

Awards/Ratings: Condé Nast Traveler Gold List 2006-2008; Mobil 5 Star 2008; Wine Spectator Award of Excellence, 2004-2007

Attractions: Quincy Market, Faneuil Hall, Freedom Trail and New England Aquarium, 5-min walk; Children's Museum, Institute of Contemporary Art, Little Italy and Chinatown, 10-min walk
Towns/Cities: Cambridge, 2 miles
Airports: Boston Logan International Airport, 3.6 miles; Airport Water Shuttle, 7-min boat ride

Affiliations: Preferred Hotels & Resorts

FIFTEEN BEACON

15 BEACON STREET, BOSTON, MASSACHUSETTS 2108
Tel: +1 617 670 1500 **Fax:** +1 617 670 2525 **U.S./Canada Toll Free:** 1 877 XVBEACON
Web: www.johansens.com/xvbeacon **E-mail:** hotel@xvbeacon.com

Our inspector loved: *The complimentary in-town chauffeur-driven Lexus Sedan service available to all guests.*

Price Guide:
rooms $295-$700
suites $995-$1,400
2-bedroom suite (1,375 sq. ft.) $1,900-$2,500

60 75 NR HP

Awards/Ratings: Condé Nast Traveler Gold List 2008; Wine Spectator Award of Excellence 2007; DiRoNA 2007

Attractions: Boston Common, 2-min walk; State House, 2-min walk; Beacon Hill, 2-min walk; Quincy Market/Faneuil Hall, 5-min walk
Towns/Cities: Cambridge, 3 miles; Providence, RI, 51 miles; Cape Cod, 65 miles; Portland, ME, 108 miles
Airports: Boston Logan Intl. Airport, 5 miles

Affiliations: Preferred Boutique

Stylish and modern, Fifteen Beacon is a popular luxury boutique hotel in the heart of Boston with all the comforts and intimacy of a private residence. Situated in a 1903 Beaux Arts Building, this stylish landmark property is modernist in design with only 7 guest rooms per floor and no two are alike. Each luxury guest room and suite is richly decorated and has cozy working gas fireplaces, poster beds with custom-designed 300 count Italian linens and marble baths with rainforest showers. Several suites have lovely views of historic Beacon Street. Ideal for both business and pleasure, take advantage of the hotel's complimentary, in-town chauffeur-driven Lexus Sedan service to explore all that Boston has to offer. Fifteen Beacon's new modern steakhouse with exceptional wine cellar is not to be missed!

U.S.A. - MASSACHUSETTS (BOSTON)

THE LIBERTY HOTEL

215 CHARLES STREET, BOSTON, MASSACHUSETTS 02114
Tel: +1 617 224 4000 **Fax:** +1 617 399 4259 **U.S./Canada Toll Free:** 1 866 507 5245
Web: www.johansens.com/liberty **E-mail:** reservations@libertyhotel.com

Once the storied Charles Street Jail, this hotel offers you the unique experience of staying in a newly renovated historic landmark in the heart of Boston's famed Beacon Hill. The striking granite edifice welcomes you into the building's grand interior, which is linked by catwalks below a breathtaking 90-ft. central rotunda and cupola built in 1851. Original jail cells have been preserved within the hotel lobby bar, Clink, and feature striking oversized windows. Rooms are sophisticated in décor with rich mahogany woods, touches of stainless steel and high-tech conveniences. You will find some of Boston's best Charles River views from the hotel suites. Sip champagne at the new Veuve Clicquot La Grande Dame Bar before dining at the award-winning Lydia Shire's Scampo restaurant.

Our inspector loved: *The new Veuve Clicquot La Grande Dame Bar located under the soaring 90-ft. rotunda.*

Price Guide:
rooms $299-$595
escape suites from $899
presidential suite $5,500-$6,000

298 350 NR HP

Attractions: Beacon Hill, 2-min walk; Charles River and Esplanade, 3-min walk; Freedom Trail, 5-min walk; State House, 5-min drive
Towns/Cities: Cambridge, 3 miles; Brookline, 5 miles; Gloucester, 37 miles; Cape Cod, 67 miles
Airports: Boston Logan International Airport, 3.5 miles

Affiliations: The Leading Hotels of the World

Wequassett Resort and Golf Club

ON PLEASANT BAY, CHATHAM, MASSACHUSETTS 02633
Tel: +1 508 432 5400 **Fax:** +1 508 430 3131 **U.S./Canada Toll Free:** 1 800 225 7125
Web: www.johansens.com/wequassett **E-mail:** info@wequassett.com

Our inspector loved: *The new lavish Signature Collection rooms with incredible views.*

Price Guide: (excluding tax)
rooms $185-$925
suites $600-$3,500

Awards/Ratings: Condé Nast Traveler Gold List 2007 and 2008

Attractions: Cape Cod National Golf Club, 5 miles; Chatham Railroad Museum, 5 miles; Nauset Beach, 9 miles
Towns/Cities: Orleans, 9 miles; Brewster, 10 miles; Hyannis, 18 miles; Provincetown, 35 miles
Airports: Chatham Municipal Airport, 4 miles; Boston Logan International Airport, 90 miles

Affiliations: Preferred Hotels & Resorts

Combining old fashioned elegance with modern-day comforts, this historic Cape Cod resort sits high atop a rise with magnificent views of Pleasant Bay and the Atlantic Ocean. The secluded grounds overlook the salt marshes and woodlands and invite you to explore through meandering pathways filled with beautiful, seasonal flowers. Cozy weathered cottages and suites are comfortable and charming; all have private decks, patios or balconies. There are 4 distinct dining options: LiBAYtion, a beach-front bar offering cocktails and light fare looking out to the best water views from a fashionable pergola; the Outer Bar and Grille for sophisticated yet casual dining; and the relaxed lounge-style Thoreau's. Exceptional cuisine is served in Twenty-Eight Atlantic, decorated in an eclectic fashion with Shaker décor, nautical etchings and exquisite chandeliers.

THE INN AT CASTLE HILL

280 ARGILLA ROAD, IPSWICH, MASSACHUSETTS 01938
Tel: +1 978 412 2555 **Fax:** +1 978 412 2556
Web: www.johansens.com/castlehill **E-mail:** theinn@ttor.org

This elegantly restored sanctuary is quietly nestled at the foot of Castle Hill in the heart of the Crane Estate. The warm and serene atmosphere perfectly complements the glorious countryside of Boston's North Shore. The rooms at the inn are individually appointed and many feature impressive views over the salt marshes, sand dunes and Atlantic Ocean. There is no need for televisions or radios here. Start your day with a hearty breakfast then a leisurely picnic lunch. Later in the day sit on a rocking chair to savor afternoon tea or a glass of wine on the wraparound veranda. Crane Estate is a designated conservation area containing historical buildings, a wildlife refuge and rare maritime forest. The Inn is a property of The Trustees of Reservations and all proceeds from the inn contribute to the conservation efforts of the area.

Our inspector loved: *Drinking tea on the veranda while enjoying the spectacular coastline views.*

Price Guide: (including full breakfast and afternoon tea)
rooms $140-$385

10 22 12 NR HP

Attractions: Crane Beach, 0.25 miles; Castle Hill at the Crane Estate, 0.25 miles; Agassiz Rock, 8 miles; Peabody Essex Museum, 17 miles
Towns/Cities: Cape Ann, 8 miles; Newburyport, 14 miles; Salem, 15 miles; Rockport, 15 miles
Airports: Boston Logan International Airport, 31 miles

BLANTYRE

16 BLANTYRE ROAD, P.O. BOX 995, LENOX, MASSACHUSETTS 01240
Tel: +1 413 637 3556 **Fax:** +1 413 637 4282
Web: www.johansens.com/blantyre **E-mail:** welcome@blantyre.com

Our inspector loved: *The delightful dinner.*

Price Guide: (incl. full breakfast, excl. 20% service charge and 9.7% tax) rooms $550-$850
suites $725-$1,800

24 22 13 DVD WiFi SPA

Awards/Ratings: Condé Nast Johansens Most Excellent Country House Hotel 2008; Condé Nast Traveler Gold List 2007; Mobil 5 Star; Wine Spectator Best of Award of Excellence 2008

Attractions: Tanglewood, 10-min drive; Norman Rockwell Museum, 15-min drive; Hancock Shaker Village, 30-min drive; Museum of Art, 45-min drive
Towns/Cities: Lee, 3 miles; Stockbridge, 6 miles; North Adams, 29 miles
Airports: Albany Intl., 58 miles; Hartford, CT/Bradley Intl., 66 miles; Boston Logan, 131 miles

Affiliations: Relais & Châteaux

Blantyre is an exquisite 1902 family-owned manor house hotel located in the picturesque Berkshires. The beautiful décor is highlighted with striking leaded glass windows and richly burnished woods. The impeccably designed guest rooms and suites feature romantic four-poster beds, exceptional furnishings with luxurious fabrics and spacious marble bathrooms with relaxing soaking tubs. Period pieces and treasured heirlooms are a focal point of the main floor's Baronial Main Hall, while inviting plush chairs and fresh flowers are welcoming in the sunlit Music Room. Fine French cuisine is served in the elegant dining room; the inn boasts an impressive wine collection of more than 1,600 vintages. Magnificent picnic baskets are perfect for a summer's day lunch on the grounds or an afternoon of music at nearby Tanglewood. Ice skating, snow shoeing and cross-country skiing are available in the winter season with refreshments served in the Warming Hut.

CRANWELL RESORT, SPA & GOLF CLUB

55 LEE ROAD, ROUTE 20, LENOX, MASSACHUSETTS 01240
Tel: +1 413 637 1364 **Fax:** +1 413 637 4364 **U.S./Canada Toll Free:** 1 800 272 6935
Web: www.johansens.com/cranwell **E-mail:** info@cranwell.com

This Historic Hotels of America, AAA 4 Diamond property stands in the heart of the Berkshires, surrounded by 380 scenic acres. The year-round resort features a Gilded-Age mansion carefully restored to preserve its original 19th-century grandeur. Cranwell provides exceptional accommodation, fine dining, modern amenities and unforgettable service. The property has beautifully decorated bedrooms and 3 restaurants serving a variety of cuisine. Views of the picturesque golf course can be enjoyed from Sloane's Tavern and the romantic will enjoy an intimate candle-lit meal in the Wyndhurst or Music Room Restaurants. With a mountain backdrop, the panoramic 18-hole championship golf course is a real challenge to be explored on your very own G.P.S. equipped golf cart; a driving range is also available. And for those in need of pampering, visit the 35,000 sq. ft. spa with 16 treatment rooms offering over 50 services. This is a memorable setting for conferences and weddings.

Our inspector loved: *Golfing on the beautiful 18-hole championship course with my very own G.P.S. cart.*

Price Guide:
rooms $255-$395
suites $305-$1,150

114 200 DVD WiFi SPA NR HP

Awards/Ratings: Wine Spectator Award of Excellence 2001-2007

Attractions: Shakespeare & Company, 2 miles; Tanglewood, 4 miles; Norman Rockwell Museum, 9 miles; Jiminy Peak Mountain Resort, 21 miles
Towns/Cities: Stockbridge, 6 miles; Great Barrington, 15 miles; Williamstown, 30 miles
Airports: Albany International Airport, 58 miles; Hartford, CT, and Bradley International Airport, 66 miles; Boston Logan International Airport, 131 miles

THE CHARLOTTE INN

27 SOUTH SUMMER STREET, EDGARTOWN, MASSACHUSETTS 02539
Tel: +1 508 627 4151 **Fax:** +1 508 627 4652
Web: www.johansens.com/charlotte **E-mail:** charlotteinn@aol.com

Our inspector loved: *The magnificent Carriage House with its antiques and super outlook over the courtyard.*

Price Guide:
rooms $295-$695
suites $550-$895

25 14

Attractions: Edgartown, 2-min walk; Vineyard Golf Club, 2 miles
Towns/Cities: Edgartown, 2-min walk
Airports: Hyannis Cape Cod Airport, 30 miles; Boston Logan International Airport, 120 miles

Affiliations: Relais & Châteaux

Ideally situated, just a short walk from the vibrant and historic Edgartown, this delightful inn is nestled amongst chestnut and linden trees. Originally built for a wealthy merchant in 1864, this grand house has recently been restored to recreate the ambience of a bygone era. 19th-century oil paintings line the walls and antiques including grandfather clocks remain. Each of the individually designed Victorian-style bedrooms has traditional mahogany furniture, leather-bound books, silver dressing table sets, goose-down bedding and European draperies. The inn's restaurant serves some of the finest New England cuisine in the area at its romantic candle-lit dining room or on a summer night, on the ivy-clad terrace. The attentive yet unobtrusive service will encourage you to return year after year.

Michigan

Marathon
CANADA
Thunder Bay
ONTARIO
LAKE SUPERIOR
Sud
Houghton
Sault Ste. Marie
Sault Ste. Marie
Marquette
75
Cheboygan
Iron Mountain
Escanaba
Petoskey
LAKE HURAN
Rhinelander
Alpena
Menominee
Marinette
75
Merrill
Traverse City
Cadillac
Stevens Point
Green Bay
Appleton
Manistee
75
Manitowoc
Ludington
Midland
Bay City
Big Rapids
Mt. Pleasant
WISCONSIN
Saginaw
Lapeer
Port Huron
69
Flint
Muskegon
St. Johns
Bishop Int. Airport
94
Ionia
75
Grand Haven
96
Capital Region Int. Airport
69
Gerald R. Ford Int. Airport
Pontiac
179
Mount Clemens
Grand Rapids
96
LANSING
Howell
96
Charh
Milwaukee
Mason
Detroit
MADISON
Hastings
Charlotte
Ann Arbor
Windsor
LAKE MICHIGAN
69
Wayne County Airport
Elkhorn
94
Kalamazoo
Marshall
Jackson
Monroe
Waukegan
94
Adrian
Rockford
St. Joseph
Coldwater
Hillsdale
Toledo
Norwalk
Chicago
Angola
ILLINOIS
INDIANA
OHIO
Clinton
Gary
Warsaw
As
Findlay
Joliet

Royal Park Hotel

600 E. UNIVERSITY DRIVE, ROCHESTER, MICHIGAN 48307
Tel: +1 248 652 2600 **Fax:** +1 248 453 8600 **U.S./Canada Toll Free:** 1 800 339 2761
Web: www.johansens.com/royalparkmi **E-mail:** reservations@royalparkhotel.net

Our inspector loved: *The impeccable attention to detail in everything from the architecture to the amenities.*

Price Guide:
rooms $249-$349
suites $499-$1,499

143 1200

Attractions: Historic Downtown Rochester, 5-min walk; Meadow Brook Festival Theater, 4 miles; Walter P. Chrysler Museum, 5 miles; The Palace of Auburn Hills, 7 miles
Towns/Cities: Troy, 5 miles; Auburn Hills, 6 miles; Birmingham, 14 miles; Royal Oak, 15 miles
Airports: Oakland International Airport, 20 miles; Detroit International Airport, 43miles; Bishop International Airport, 43 miles

This luxury boutique hotel in the Detroit area combines privacy, thoughtful design and relaxed elegance in the style of a classic English manor estate. Rich woodwork, marble, Murano glass chandeliers and blue slate are blended to create a sanctuary for discerning guests. The well-appointed rooms and suites have large airy windows offering beautiful views. In addition, some have cozy fireplaces, bathrooms with Japanese soaking tubs and spacious, fully appointed kitchens. Enjoy a made-to-order breakfast each morning and experience exceptional fine dining at the Brookshire Restaurant where daily classic European fare is served. For lighter dishes or drinks and entertainment visit The Commons Lounge. Relax in the Library, with its inviting burled walnut paneling and fireplace, or on the tranquil outdoor Terrace, overlooking the Paint Creek, featuring seasonal alfresco dining.

Mississippi

Fairview Inn & Restaurant

734 FAIRVIEW STREET, JACKSON, MISSISSIPPI 39202
Tel: +1 601 948 3429 **Fax:** +1 601 948 1203 **U.S./Canada Toll Free:** 1 888 948 1908
Web: www.johansens.com/fairviewinn **E-mail:** reservations@fairviewinn.com

Our inspector loved: *The charming residential ambience.*

Price Guide: (including breakfast)
rooms $139-$199
suites $179-$304

18 100 SPA NR HP

Attractions: Mississippi Museum of Art, 0.1 miles; Eudora Welty Home, 0.3 miles; Old Capitol Museum, 0.3 miles; Natural Science Museum, 2.2 miles
Towns/Cities: Madison, 13 miles; Vicksburg, 49 miles; Natchez, 117 miles
Airports: Jackson Airport, 6.5 miles

Proprietors Peter and Tamar Sharp invite you to experience their unique inn. This 1908 Colonial revival mansion is one of the few architecturally designed homes of its period left standing and exudes the rich history of Jackson. In the Belhaven historic neighborhood, adjacent to Millsaps and Belhaven Colleges, the inn offers the charm, ambience and hospitality of a small bed and breakfast with the full-service amenities of a luxury hotel. Perfect for leisure and business travelers alike, the tranquil setting is complete with over an acre of pristine gardens. The guest rooms and suites are individually decorated and provide modern conveniences, and Sophia's Restaurant serves lunch Monday to Friday and dinner from Tuesday to Saturday and Sunday brunches. There is also nomiSpa to enjoy where massages, Dr. Hauschka facials, body scrubs/wraps, detoxification, reflexology and manicures and pedicures are all available. Only the purest of products are used in the spa.

MONMOUTH PLANTATION

36 MELROSE AVENUE, NATCHEZ, MISSISSIPPI 39120
Tel: +1 601 442 5852 **Fax:** +1 601 446 7762 **U.S./Canada Toll Free:** 1 800 828 4531
Web: www.johansens.com/monmouthplantation **E-mail:** luxury@monmouthplantation.com

This is truly one of the grand old ladies of the South. Lovingly restored to her original 1818 glory by owners Ron and Lani Riches, Monmouth Plantation offers complete luxury alongside great Southern hospitality. Many distinguished guests have visited this magnificent estate of 26 immaculate acres with rose gardens, ponds and walking trails, and each of the well-appointed rooms and suites has its own personality and charm. Every modern comfort has been considered without compromising the building's architecture, resulting in a perfect blend of comfort and Southern splendor. A 5-course dinner is served by candlelight each evening, and the chef plans daily menus to incorporate traditional favorites and regional ingredients.

Our inspector loved: *The experience of staying in such a magnificently restored plantation.*

Price Guide: (including breakfast)
rooms $195-$240
suites $265-$390

30 M 100 14 NR HP

Awards/Ratings: Condé Nast Traveler Gold List 2008

Attractions: Golf Course, 1.5 miles; Antique Shopping District, 1.5 miles; Antebellum Home Tours, 5 miles; Seasonal Festivals, 5-min drive
Towns/Cities: Natchez, 5-min walk; Vicksburg, 66 miles; Jackson, 122 miles; New Orleans, LA, 175 miles
Airports: Baton Rouge, LA, 85 miles; Jackson, 122 miles; New Orleans, LA, 175 miles

Affiliations: Small Luxury Hotels of the World

Bonne Terre Country Inn

4715 CHURCH ROAD WEST, NESBIT, MISSISSIPPI 38651
Tel: +1 662 781 5100 **Fax:** +1 662 781 5466
Web: www.johansens.com/bonneterre **E-mail:** info@bonneterre.com

Our inspector loved: *The relaxing ambience and friendly service.*

Price Guide: (including breakfast)
rooms from $165
suites $250

14 250

Attractions: Graceland, 10 miles; Beale Street, 20 miles; Memphis Zoo, 22 miles; Brooks Museum of Art, 22 miles
Towns/Cities: Memphis, TN, 22 miles; Tunica, 28 miles; Oxford, 66 miles; Tupelo, 101 miles
Airports: Memphis International Airport, 15 miles

In a quiet, romantic location surrounded by 24 wooded acres of Mississippi highlands, this elegant inn is the perfect retreat from the stresses of daily life. The décor is simply impeccable, and the tastefully, individually decorated guest rooms have sumptuous beds and are filled with fine art and French and English antiques. Fresh flowers and whirlpool tubs complete the feeling of utter luxury and relaxation. The 4 downstairs guest rooms have access to a quaint Southern porch, while the balconies of the rooms upstairs have stunning views of the magnificent grounds. Start your day with a full country breakfast served on the indoor veranda of the Café, and in the evenings, enjoy innovative gourmet cuisine complemented by fine wines in the sophisticated, intimate restaurant.

Missouri

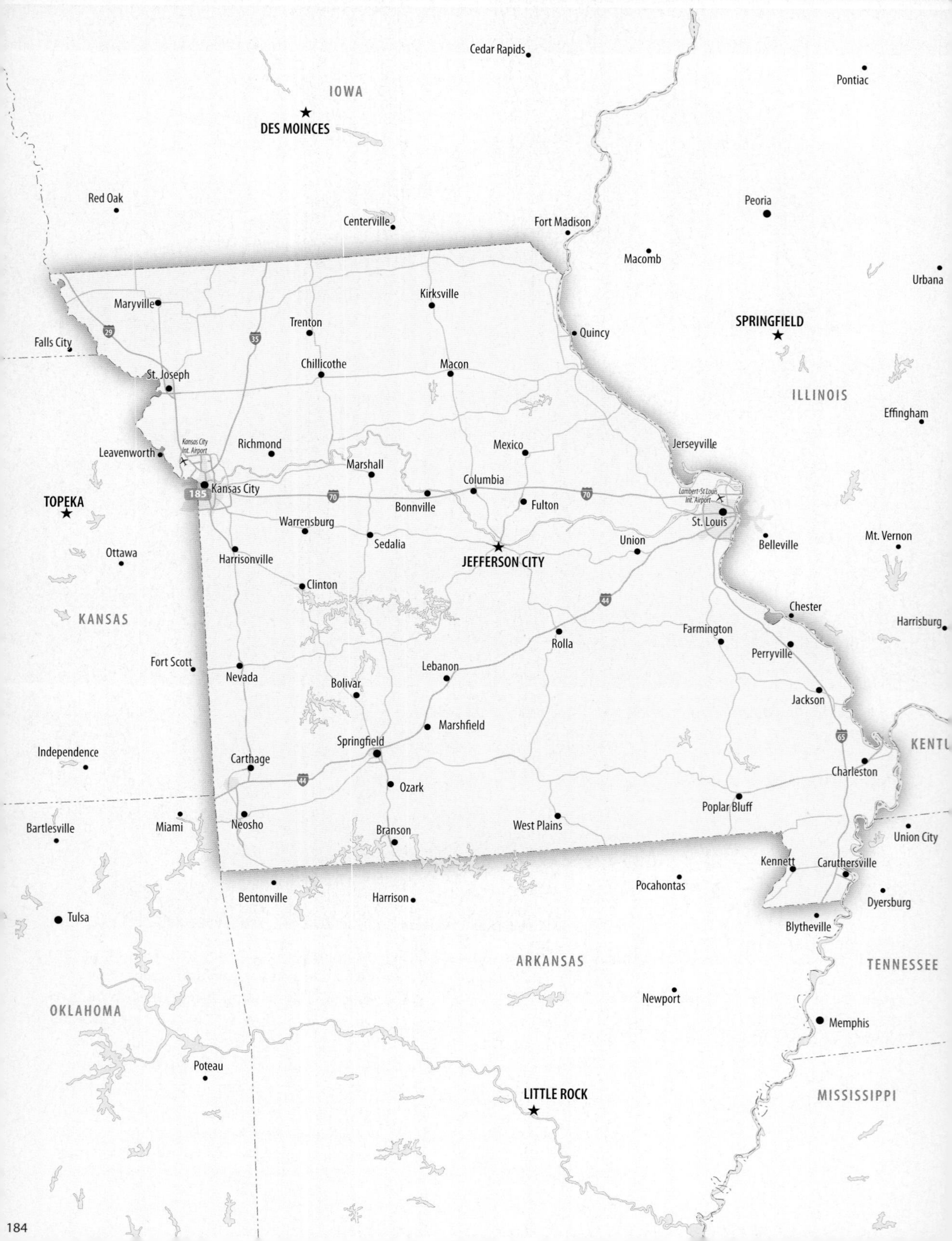
IOWA
Cedar Rapids
DES MOINCES
Pontiac
Red Oak
Centerville
Fort Madison
Peoria
Macomb
Urbana
Maryville
Kirksville
Trenton
Quincy
SPRINGFIELD
Falls City
Chillicothe
Macon
St. Joseph
ILLINOIS
Effingham
Kansas City Int. Airport
Leavenworth
Richmond
Mexico
Jerseyville
Marshall
Columbia
Lambert-St Louis Int. Airport
Kansas City
TOPEKA
Bonnville
Fulton
St. Louis
Warrensburg
Union
Belleville
Mt. Vernon
Sedalia
Ottawa
Harrisonville
JEFFERSON CITY
Clinton
KANSAS
Chester
Harrisburg
Farmington
Rolla
Perryville
Fort Scott
Nevada
Lebanon
Bolivar
Jackson
Marshfield
KENTU
Independence
Springfield
Carthage
Charleston
Ozark
Poplar Bluff
Bartlesville
Miami
Neosho
Branson
West Plains
Union City
Kennett
Caruthersville
Bentonville
Harrison
Pocahontas
Dyersburg
Tulsa
Blytheville
ARKANSAS
TENNESSEE
Newport
OKLAHOMA
Memphis
Poteau
LITTLE ROCK
MISSISSIPPI
29
35
70
185
44
65

THE RAPHAEL HOTEL

325 WARD PARKWAY, KANSAS CITY, MISSOURI 64112
Tel: +1 816 756 3800 **Fax:** +1 816 802 2131 **U.S./Canada Toll Free:** 1 800 821 5343
Web: www.johansens.com/raphael **E-mail:** information@raphaelkc.com

Our inspector loved: *The relaxing, elegant accommodations in the heart of the Country Club Plaza.*

Price Guide: (room only)
rooms $154-$209
suites $185-$255

Attractions: Country Club Plaza Shopping District, 0.1 miles; Nelson Atkins Museum of Art, 1 mile; 18th & Vine Historical District, 5 miles; Kansas City Convention Center, 5 miles
Towns/Cities: Lawrence, 43 miles; Topeka, 65 miles; Manhattan, 123 miles
Airports: Kansas City International Airport, 25 miles

The Raphael offers a unique Kansas City experience in the heart of the city's popular Country Club Plaza. This historic, one-of-a-kind boutique hotel embodies the spirit of Europe's finest small hotels. It combines the distinct character of a locally significant landmark with a relaxing atmosphere, intimacy and highly individualized service. A total makeover designed to preserve the hotel's history while providing for every modern amenity is scheduled for completion in 2009. The all-new guest rooms are stylish and sophisticated. The Raphael's famously romantic restaurant features neo-classic Continental/American cuisine and a well-edited wine list including international, California and surprisingly pleasant regional wines. The inviting lounge has a fantastic piano bar and live entertainment most evenings.

Montana

EDMONTON
Red Deer
Prince Albert
Saskatoon
CANADA
BRITISH COLUMBIA
ALBERTA
SASKATCHEWAN
Calgary
Brooks
Elkford
Nelson
Cranbrook
Lethbridge
Medicine Hat
Swift Current
Moose Jaw
REGINA
Assiniboia
Weyburn
Sandpoint
Libby
Glacier Park Int. Airport
Cut Bank
Shelby
Kalispell
Conrad
Havre
Polson
St. Maries
Glasgow
Wolf Point
Great Falls Int. Airport
Great Falls
Sidney
Missoula Int. Airport
Missoula
Lewistown
Hamilton
Deer Lodge
HELENA
Glendive
Grangeville
187
Anaconda
Butte
Miles City
Bozeman
Billings Logan Int. Airport
Salmon
Livingston
Billings
Hardin
Dillon
15
90
94
IDAHO
BOISE
Cody
Buffalo
Gillette
Belle Fourche
St. Anthony
Hailey
Idaho Falls
Thermopolis
Newcastle
Rapid City
Gooding
Jackson
SOUTH DAKOTA
Lander
WYOMING
Douglas
Preston
NEVADA
Kemmerer
Torrington
Brigham City
UTAH
Green River
Rawlins
NEBRASKA
SALT LAKE CITY
CHEYENNE
Kimball
Tooele

Triple Creek Ranch

5551 WEST FORK ROAD, DARBY, MONTANA 59829
Tel: +1 406 821 4600 **Fax:** +1 406 821 4666 **U.S./Canada Toll Free:** 1 800 654 2943
Web: www.johansens.com/triplecreek **E-mail:** info@triplecreekranch.com

Our inspector loved: *Waking up to elk in the front of my cottage!*

Price Guide: (including all meals, cocktails and house wines, double occupancy)
rooms $650-$2,495

Awards/Ratings: Condé Nast Johansens Most Excellent Ranch 2006; Wine Spectator Award of Excellence 2006 and 2008

Attractions: Fly-Fishing, 2-min walk; Cross-Country Skiing, 3-min walk; Hiking, 3-min walk
Towns/Cities: Darby, 12 miles; Hamilton, 40 miles; Missoula, 75 miles; Salmon, ID, 75 miles
Airports: Missoula Airport, 75 miles; Bozeman Airport, 215 miles; Kalispell Airport, 220 miles

Affiliations: Relais & Châteaux

Named for the 3 creeks that border the property, Triple Creek is a spectacular ranch-style hideaway deep in the Montana Mountains. Surrounded by some of the most beautiful wilderness, the snow-covered peaks are awe-inspiring in winter, while the babbling creeks turn magnificent in springtime. Alpine and cross-country skiing are popular activities during the colder months, and in springtime fly-fishing on the Bitterroot River is a delight. Accommodation is available in a series of traditional log cabins throughout the grounds, each carefully designed and decorated to take advantage of the environment. Dining in the candle-lit dining room is a particular treat; the rooftop lounge offers a more informal menu with views over the West Fork of the Bitterroot River.

New Hampshire

Mountain View Grand Resort & Spa

101 MOUNTAIN VIEW ROAD, WHITEFIELD, NEW HAMPSHIRE 03598
Tel: +1 603 837 2100 **Fax:** +1 603 837 8720 **U.S./Canada Toll Free:** 1 866 484 3843
Web: www.johansens.com/mountainview **E-mail:** info@mountainviewgrand.com

Our inspector loved: *The panoramic view from the hot tub located in the spa's tower.*

Price Guide:
rooms $129-$299
suites $239-$679

145 350 SPA NR HP

Attractions: Santa's Village, 8 miles; Cannon Mountain Tram & Ski Area, 20 miles; Storyland, 30 miles; N. Conway Outlet Shopping, 40 miles
Towns/Cities: Manchester, 100 miles; Portland, ME, 100 miles; Boston, MA, 150 miles; Montréal, QC, 170 miles
Airports: Mount Washington Regional Airport, 4 miles; Manchester-Boston Regional Airport, 100 miles; Boston Logan International Airport, 150 miles

This magnificent resort's legendary charm is matched only by its stunning location within 1,700 acres, in the heart of the White Mountains. Its tradition of hospitality dates back to 1865 and provides intimate guest areas such as the lobby with baby grand piano, Dodge Parlor and Eisenhower Library, named in honor of the frequent presidential visitor. Spacious rooms and suites display custom-made mahogany furnishings and the Main Dining Room offers a sophisticated atmosphere. There is also the wine cellar dining area, the casual Tavern, and alfresco, poolside selections from The Club House. Perched high within the Colonial revival observation tower is the comprehensive Mountain View Grand Spa. Other activities include golf on the resort's 100-year-old course, snowshoeing, sleigh rides and the chance to visit the on-site animal farm.

New Mexico

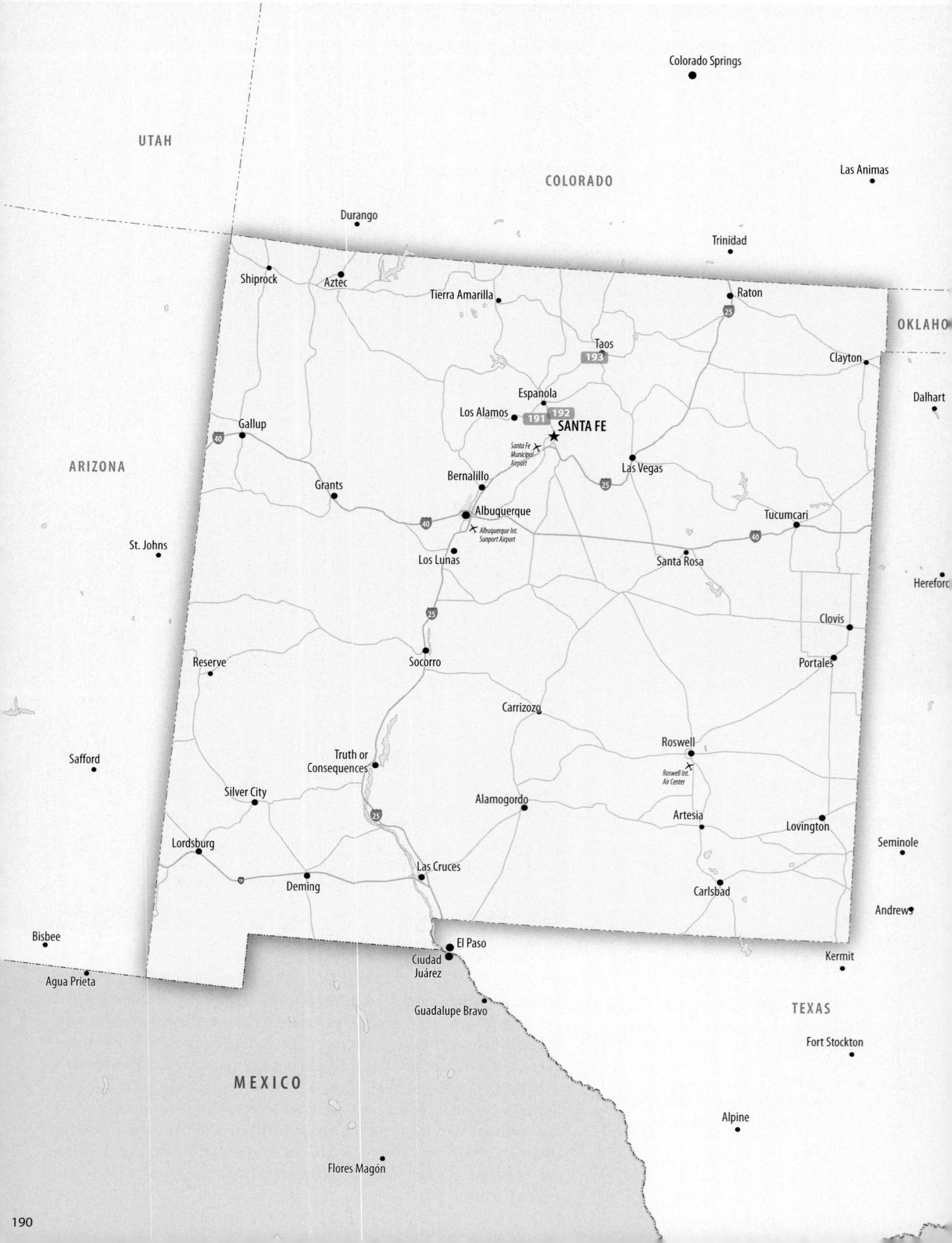

Colorado Springs
UTAH
COLORADO
Las Animas
Durango
Trinidad
Shiprock
Aztec
Tierra Amarilla
Raton
OKLAHO
Taos
193
Clayton
Espanola
Los Alamos
191
192
SANTA FE
Dalhart
Gallup
40
Santa Fe Municipal Airport
ARIZONA
Las Vegas
Grants
Bernalillo
25
Albuquerque
Tucumcari
Albuquerque Int. Sunport Airport
St. Johns
Los Lunas
Santa Rosa
Hereford
Clovis
Reserve
Socorro
Portales
Carrizozo
Roswell
Safford
Truth or Consequences
Roswell Int. Air Center
Silver City
Alamogordo
Artesia
Lovington
Lordsburg
Seminole
Las Cruces
Deming
Carlsbad
Andrews
Bisbee
El Paso
Ciudad Juárez
Kermit
Agua Prieta
Guadalupe Bravo
TEXAS
Fort Stockton
MEXICO
Alpine
Flores Magón

RANCHO DE SAN JUAN

P.O. BOX 4140, HIGHWAY 285, ESPAÑOLA, NEW MEXICO 87533
Tel: +1 505 753 6818 **Fax:** +1 505 753 4641
Web: www.johansens.com/ranchosanjuan **E-mail:** ranchosj@windstream.net

Our inspector loved: *The stunning high desert beauty and the exquisite gourmet dining.*

Price Guide: (excluding tax and service)
rooms $285-$385
suites $485-$685

13 30 12

Awards/Ratings: Condé Nast Johansens Most Excellent Romantic Hideaway, U.S.A. & Canada 2007; Wine Spectator Award of Excellence 2007; Condé Nast Traveler Gold List 2006

Attractions: Hot Springs, 12 miles; Georgia O'Keefe Museum/Home, 18 miles; Art Galleries and Museums, 38 miles
Towns/Cities: Santa Fe, 38 miles, Taos, 48 miles
Airports: Santa Fe Airport, 38 miles; Albuquerque Airport, 100 miles

Affiliations: Relais & Châteaux

Amidst 225 acres of astonishing natural beauty, Rancho de San Juan is a Spanish hacienda with wildflower-filled courtyards. Public rooms are adorned with the owners' private art and antique collections, and bedrooms feature kiva fireplaces and private terraces with glorious views. Each room is decorated with eclectic furnishings, Egyptian cotton sheets, frette bath towels and Aveda toileteries. Dining is a gourmet delight served on custom-designed porcelain alongside family sterling silver. The weekly changing à la carte menu uses traditional Norteño ingredients to create classic meals combined with worldwide flavors. A diverse range of seasonal activities can be organized nearby, including white-water rafting and hiking trails. Alternately, enjoy a massage in the privacy of your own room or terrace.

ENCANTADO, AN AUBERGE RESORT

198 STATE ROAD 592, SANTA FE, NEW MEXICO 87506
Tel: +1 505 988 9955 **Fax:** +1 505 820 1223 **U.S./Canada Toll Free:** 1 877 262 4666
Web: www.johansens.com/encantado **E-mail:** info@encantadoresort.com

Set against the foothills of the Sangre de Cristo Mountains, Encantado is a relaxing and private sanctuary with elegantly designed accommodations, a world-class spa and exceptional dining. Suites and casitas offer stunning views of the Jemez Mountains and Rio Grande Valley, and are carefully designed in the native New Mexico style with fine amenities distinctive of an Auberge Resort. The full-service Spa at Encantado, the region's first ever luxury spa, provides an extensive array of signature treatments. The spa also provides steam rooms, soaking pools, relaxation areas, a labyrinth, a state-of-the-art fitness facility and movement studio. For an exceptional culinary experience, the signature restaurant offers the freshest seasonal cuisine in an intimate setting with beautiful mountain views or alfresco on the courtyard patio.

Our inspector loved: *The captivating location near the famed Santa Fe Opera, with the enticement of Santa Fe galleries and shopping just minutes away.*

Price Guide:
casitas $380-$711
suites $767-$1,098

65 150 SPA

Attractions: Hiking, on-site; Santa Fe Opera, 2 miles; Santa Fe Shopping, Historic Plaza, Musuems, Restaurants, Canyon Road Famed Artist Row, 8 miles; Hot-Air Ballooning, 45 miles
Towns/Cities: Santa Fe, 8 miles; Albuquerque, 60 miles
Airports: Santa Fe Municipal Airport, 15 miles; Santa Fe International Airport, 60 miles; Albuquerque International Airport, 60 miles

EL MONTE SAGRADO LIVING RESORT & SPA

317 KIT CARSON ROAD, TAOS, NEW MEXICO 87571
Tel: +1 575 758 3502 **Fax:** +1 575 737 2985 **U.S./Canada Toll Free:** 1 800 828 TAOS
Web: www.johansens.com/elmontesagrado **E-mail:** info@elmontesagrado.com

Our inspector loved: *The magical ambience, and the art, culture, fine dining and excitement of Taos just minutes away.*

Price Guide:
rooms U.S.$199-U.S.$349
suites U.S.$299-U.S.$719

84 250 SPA

Awards/Ratings: Condé Nast Traveler Gold List 2008; Wine Spectator Award of Excellence 2007

Attractions: Art Galleries, 5-min walk; Shopping, 5-min walk; Hiking, 20-min drive; Skiing, 25-min drive
Towns/Cities: Santa Fe, 58 miles
Airports: Santa Fe Airport, 68 miles; Albuquerque Airport, 130 miles

Affiliations: Kessler Collection; Preferred Hotels & Resorts

Tucked away in the shadow of the Sangre de Cristo Mountains, Taos has long been considered a place of artistic and spiritual inspiration. The Sacred Circle is an area set aside for quiet events or contemplation and forms the heart of this unusual compound. It sets the theme of celebrating, embracing and respecting nature and local traditions. The Biolarium is a holistically designed structure, and the Spa offers specialized treatments and therapies. Choose to stay in one of the uniquely designed and furnished Treasure of Taos casitas, constructed by local craftsman and artists, or in a Native American Suite featuring kiva-style fireplaces, stone tiles and stained-wood furnishings. Alternately, the lavishly appointed Global Suites offer total immersion in international art and culture. The eclectic and diverse dining options include the Anaconda Bar that often provides live entertainment and displays a 1,100 gallon salt-water aquarium and a giant anaconda sculpture.

New York

CANADA
QUÉBEC
ONTARIO
MONTRÉAL
OTTAWA
TORONTO
Orillia
Belleville
Kingston
Oshawa
Hamilton
Erie
Meadville
Warren
Pittsburgh
PENNSYLVANIA
Williamsport
Lewisburg
HARRISBURG
Gettysburg
Scranton
Allentown
Philadelphia
Honesdale
MARYLAND
ANNAPOLIS
DELAWARE
DOVER
NEW JERSEY
TRENTON
Newton
Somerville
Newark
Newark Liberty Int. Airport
New York
La Guardia Airport
John F Kennedy Int. Airport
Long Island
Riverhead
Stamford
Bridgeport
New Haven
New London
HARTFORD
Bristol
CONNECTICUT
R.I.
PROVID
Springfield
Worcester
MASSACHUSETTS
BOSTON
Pittsfield
Bennington
VERMONT
Rutland
MONTPELIER
St. Albans
St. Johnsbury
Newport
NEW HAMPSHIRE
Laconia
CONCORD
Dover
Nashua
Norway
MAINE
QUÉBEC
ATLANTIC OCEAN
Plattsburgh
Malone
Canton
Saranac Lake
Elizabethtown
Watertown
Lake Pleasant
Hudson Falls
Oswego
Utica
Herkimer
Johnstown
Albany Int. Airport
ALBANY
Syracuse Hancock Int. Airport
Syracuse
Rochester
Rochester Int. Airport
Albion
Lockport
Batavia
Niagara Falls
Buffalo
Buffalo Niagara Int. Airport
Geneseo
Canandaigua
Auburn
Waterloo
Penn Yan
Cortland
Norwich
Ithaca
Binghamton
Bath
Elmira
Wellsville
Salamanca
Jamestown
Hudson
Kingston
Poughkeepsie
Monticello
Goshen
New City
201
197
195
196
198
199
200
203
204
205
90
81
87
88
84
390

THE MANSION ON DELAWARE AVENUE

414 DELAWARE AVENUE, BUFFALO, NEW YORK 14202
Tel: +1 716 886 3300 **Fax:** +1 716 883 3923
Web: www.johansens.com/mansionondelaware **E-mail:** info@mansionondelaware.com

Our inspector loved: *This architectural treasure in the heart of downtown; a culturally rich neighborhood.*

Price Guide:
rooms $179-$319
suites $425

28 165

Attractions: Allentown Art and Theater District, on-site; Niagara Falls, 25-min drive
Towns/Cities: Buffalo, on-site; Niagara-on-the-Lake, 32 miles; Toronto, 96 miles
Airports: Buffalo Airport, 9 miles; Toronto Airport, ON, 96 miles

The Mansion on Delaware Avenue is, without a doubt, a Buffalo landmark with international status. Built as a private residence in 1869, it has since experienced a colorful history, yet stood vacant for 25 years until 2001. A 3-year, multi-million dollar restoration elevated the hotel to sought-after status with high-style design, butler service and grand luxury, and offers highly-acclaimed culinary quality, design and personal service. Upon entering through the Second Empire mahogany doors, you will be greeted by a butler who will show you to a fully prepared whirlpool bath with complimentary bath salts. Butlers will mix the perfect beverage, press your attire and organize free downtown transportation or helipad access. The exquisitely decorated guest rooms, including 3 parlor suites, are impeccably appointed with every modern amenity and first-class level of comfort.

OHEKA CASTLE HOTEL & ESTATE

135 WEST GATE DRIVE, HUNTINGTON, NEW YORK 11743
Tel: +1 631 659 1400 **Fax:** +1 631 592 5991
Web: www.johansens.com/oheka **E-mail:** reservations@oheka.com

OHEKA CASTLE is a magnificent French-style château set amidst 23 acres of formal gardens with pebble-paths, statues and fountains. This historic estate was named after Otto Hermann Kahn, the wealthy philanthropist who built it as a summer home in 1919 during the golden age of American history. The castle and estate, converted to a hotel following $30 million of restoration, is lavishly decorated and boasts 32 guest rooms and a grand library sumptuously furnished with Oriental rugs, authentic portraits, a regal fireplace and grand piano. The guest rooms are equally impressive, individually appointed in rich, luxurious tones with exquisite details such as French-print wallpaper, chandeliers and claw-footed bathtubs. For a special treat, order a spa treatment from the hotel's extensive in-room menu.

Our inspector loved: *The location of this historic house in the country yet so close to New York City.*

Price Guide: (including Continental breakfast, excluding taxes)
rooms $495-$595
suites $695-$1,195

32 400 NR HP

Attractions: Old Bethpage Restoration, 12-min drive; Historic Gold Coast Mansions, 15-25-min drive; Belmont Race Track, 30-min drive; Long Island Vineyards, 45-min drive
Towns/Cities: Huntington, 11 miles; New York City, 32 miles; The Hamptons, 44 miles
Airports: J.F.K. Airport, 40-min drive

Affiliations: Small Luxury Hotels of the World

Barton Hill Hotel & Spa

100 CENTER STREET, LEWISTON, NEW YORK 14092
Tel: +1 716 754 9070 **Fax:** +1 716 754 9075 **U.S./Canada Toll Free:** 1 800 718 1812
Web: www.johansens.com/bartonhillhotel **E-mail:** reservations@bartonhillhotel.com

Our inspector loved: *The yesteryear feeling in this brand new hotel overlooking the beautiful Niagara River.*

Price Guide: (including breakfast, double occupancy)
portage retreats $169-$252
sunset suites $259-$369

78 250 SPA

Attractions: Whirlpool Jet Boat Tour, 2-min walk; Artpark, 5-min walk; Underground Railroad Tours; Niagara Falls State Park, 10-min drive
Towns/Cities: Buffalo, 20-min drive; Niagara Falls, 10-min drive; Niagara-on-the-Lake, ON, 40-min drive
Airports: Buffalo Airport, 30-min drive

Set in the landmark town of Lewiston that dates back to the 1600s, Barton Hill Hotel & Spa mixes heritage with modern elegance and accommodation to create a "historically hip" atmosphere. The stunning rooms, designed with an Old World charm, and the attentive staff, make every visit incredibly relaxing. Take time to enjoy an aromatherapy massage or revitalizing body scrub at the hotel's tranquil spa. Also, sample the impressive wine list at the Lookout Bar. Venture outside and discover the exciting town of Lewiston, where the first U.S. invasion of a foreign country began, the cocktail was invented, and where slaves made their last stop on the way to freedom. All year the town hosts festivals and art events, and from May through to October, exciting whirlpool jet boats - rated one of the top 5 adventure rides in the U.S. - leave from the docks opposite the hotel. Alternatively, head slightly further afield to experience Niagara Falls.

U.S.A. - NEW YORK (NEW YORK CITY)

Hôtel Plaza Athénée

37 EAST 64TH STREET, NEW YORK CITY, NEW YORK 10065
Tel: +1 212 734 9100 **Fax:** +1 212 772 0958 **U.S./Canada Toll Free:** 1 800 447 8800
Web: www.johansens.com/athenee **E-mail:** res@plaza-athenee.com

Conveniently and fashionably situated on the East Side of Manhattan, Hôtel Plaza Athénée is nestled amidst a line of town houses on a quiet tree-lined street. Rooms feature Asian silks and soothing earth tones, and offer complimentary services such as 24-hour concierge, business center facilities, tea and coffee at 5.30-7am, use of the fitness center and WiFi Internet access. Some suites have a sweeping view over the rooftops of Manhattan from a private balcony and atrium terrace. Modern American cuisine is served in Arabelle, a romantic gold-domed room with lovely murano glass. Enjoy an after-dinner drink in the exotic Bar Seine, where a fusion of Moroccan, African, European and Asian art are complemented by animal print fabrics and leather flooring.

Our inspector loved: *The impeccable attention to detail and service.*

Price Guide: (room only, excluding tax)
rooms $695
suites $1,470

149 100

Awards/Ratings: Condé Nast Johansens Most Excellent Business Partner, The Americas, Caribbean, Atlantic & Pacific Islands 2008; DiRoNA 2007; Condé Nast Traveler Gold List 2007

Attractions: Central Park, 0.5 miles; Museum of Modern Art, 0.5 miles; Children's Zoo, 0.5 miles; Madison Avenue Shopping, 0.5 miles
Airports: J.F.K. Airport, 13 miles; Newark Airport, 13 miles

Affiliations: The Leading Hotels of the World

The Inn at Irving Place

56 IRVING PLACE, NEW YORK, NEW YORK CITY 10003
Tel: +1 212 533 4600 **Fax:** +1 212 533 4611 **U.S./Canada Toll Free:** 1 800 685 1447
Web: www.johansens.com/irving **E-mail:** innatirving@aol.com

Our inspector loved: *High tea in Lady Mendl's Tea Salon.*

Price Guide:
rooms $445-$645

Attractions: Union Square and Gramercy Park, 2-min walk; New York Univeristy, 10-min walk; Empire State Building, 15-min walk; Times Square and Broadway, 20-min walk
Airports: La Guardia International Airport, 30-min drive; J.F.K. International Airport, 50-min drive

Affiliations: Small Luxury Hotels of the World

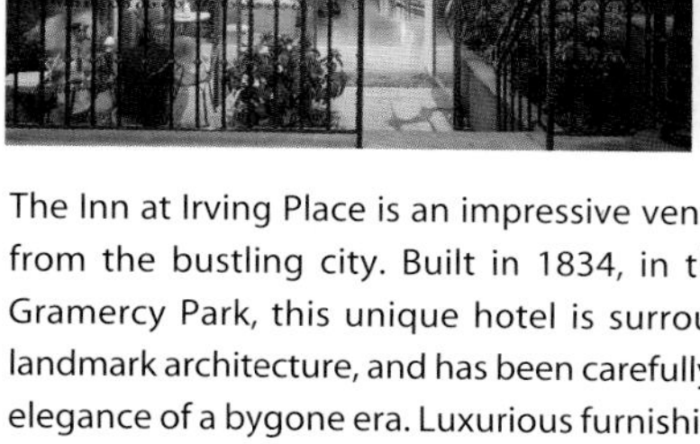

The Inn at Irving Place is an impressive venue to visit and a peaceful respite from the bustling city. Built in 1834, in the heart of New York's historic Gramercy Park, this unique hotel is surrounded by tree-lined streets and landmark architecture, and has been carefully renovated to reflect the timeless elegance of a bygone era. Luxurious furnishings and beautiful antiques adorn the 12 immaculate bedrooms and residences, which are reminiscent of Edith Wharton's New York. A delicious breakfast can be served to your bed or in the famous Lady Mendl's Tea Salon, renowned for its idyllic setting and fine teas. Your hosts will be happy to recommend one of the many excellent restaurants nearby, and for health enthusiasts, there is a fitness club a few minutes away.

U.S.A. - NEW YORK (TARRYTOWN)

Castle On The Hudson

400 BENEDICT AVENUE, TARRYTOWN, NEW YORK 10591
Tel: +1 914 631 1980 **Fax:** +1 914 631 4612 **U.S./Canada Toll Free:** 1 800 616 4487
Web: www.johansens.com/hudson **E-mail:** info@castleonthehudson.com

This elegant medieval-style castle was built during the turn of the 20th century by New York writer, businessman and socialite, Howard Carroll, in order to flaunt his wealth. Following his death, the castle was converted into an opulent hotel offering traditional, warm hospitality and impeccable service. Each of the individually appointed bedrooms and bathrooms has been lavished with rich fabrics, ornate artworks, antiques and beautiful wooden furniture. The magnificent Tower Suites are the ultimate in style with four-poster beds, wood-burning fireplaces, marble bathrooms, turret alcoves and panoramic vistas over the hillside, Hudson River and Manhattan. Dining at the hotel is sublime: there are 3 different rooms, each with their own unique ambience in which to enjoy the creative gourmet dishes. The spectacular outdoor terrace is perfect for romantic alfresco meals and cocktails.

Our inspector loved: *Dining at the hotel, an exceptional experience that should not be missed!*

Price Guide:
rooms $340-$450
suites $510-$820

31 M 125 NR HP

Attractions: Antiquing, 5-min drive; Lyndhurst Castle, 7-min drive; Kykuit (Rockefeller Family Mansion), 10-min drive; The Westchester (Shopping), 10-min drive
Towns/Cities: New York City, 31 miles
Airports: LaGuardia Airport, 28 miles; J.F.K. Airport, 36 miles; Newark Airport, 42 miles

Affiliations: Small Luxury Hotels of the World

THE LODGE AT TURNING STONE

5218 PATRICK ROAD, VERONA, NEW YORK 13478
Tel: +1 315 361 8525 **Fax:** +1 315 361 8686 **U.S./Canada Toll Free:** 1 877 784 8375
Web: www.johansens.com/turningstone **E-mail:** info@turningstone.com

Our inspector loved: *The American-Indian influence apparent throughout Skana, the Spa at Turning Stone.*

Price Guide:
rooms $295-$595
suites $3,000-$3,500

95 SPA

Awards/Ratings: Condé Nast Johansens Most Excellent Resort, U.S.A. & Canada 2007

Attractions: International Boxing Hall of Fame, 10 miles; Fort Stanwix National Monument, 12 miles; National Baseball Hall of Fame, 61 miles; Finger Lakes Wine Country, 90 miles
Towns/Cities: Syracuse, 35 miles; New York City, 260 miles; Philadelphia, PA, 293 miles; Washington, D.C., 409 miles
Airports: U.C.A. Oneida County Airport, 16 miles; Syracuse Hancock International Airport, 35 miles; Albany International Airport, 111 miles

This luxury boutique hotel surrounds its guests with sophistication and comfort while providing personal, intuitive service. Feel like a V.I.P. during your stay and request the advanced service of a personal butler who will anticipate your every need. At The Lodge's heart is the magnificent Great Room with its open fire, luxury seating, superb décor and interesting artwork. This is an ideal spot in which to relax and enjoy stunning views before enjoying a memorable gourmet dinner in the elegant Wildflowers restaurant, where traditional Continental dishes are prepared to exact preferences. Suites are lavishly furnished and appointed with every modern amenity and comfort with wonderful balcony views over 2 of the country's finest and most challenging 18-hole championship golf courses. Expansive and intimately indulgent, the Presidential Suite is an opulent retreat with 3 bedrooms, mini-spa, kitchen, and deluxe media center.

The Perfect Gift...

Condé Nast Johansens Gift Certificates

Condé Nast Johansens Gift Certificates make a unique and much valued gift for birthdays, weddings, anniversaries, special occasions or as a corporate incentive.

Certificates are available in denominations of $150, $75, £100, £50, €140, €70 and may be used as payment or part payment for your stay or a meal at any Condé Nast Johansens 2009 Recommended property.

To order, call +44 207 152 3558

or purchase direct at www.johansens.com

THE BAKER HOUSE 1650

181 MAIN STREET, EAST HAMPTON, NEW YORK 11937
Tel: +1 631 324 4081 **Fax:** +1 631 329 5931
Web: www.johansens.com/bakerhouse **E-mail:** info@bakerhouse1650.com

Our inspector loved: *The delicious gourmet breakfast, and the fantastic pool.*

Price Guide: (including breakfast, excluding tax)
rooms $250-$895

5 SPA

Attractions: Shops and Restaurants, 5-min walk; Ocean Beach, 15-min walk
Towns/Cities: Southampton, 10 miles; New York City, 100 miles
Airports: J.F.K. Airport, 94 miles; LaGuardia Airport, 97 miles

The charming Baker House 1650 exudes elegance and will delight those of you in search of an exclusive hideaway with a romantic ambience. Featuring wood craftwork derived from medieval English architecture and a Colonial revival staircase, the wood-burning fireplaces and William Morris wallpaper contrast with the flat-screen T.V.s and state-of-the-art cable and D.V.D. players. Surrounded by flowering perennials and shrubs, delicately scented herbs and English gardens, the outdoor terraces are perfect for alfresco dining, and the outdoor infinity-edge pool, with teak chaises for sunbathing, is utterly relaxing. The Baker Spa, with lap pool, steam shower and sauna, is the ideal retreat. In the summer, you will receive coveted East Hampton Village beach parking passes, as well as beach towels, umbrellas and chairs.

U.S.A. - NEW YORK/LONG ISLAND (EAST HAMPTON)

THE MILL HOUSE INN

31 NORTH MAIN STREET, EAST HAMPTON, NEW YORK 11937
Tel: +1 631 324 9766 **Fax:** +1 631 324 9793
Web: www.johansens.com/millhouse **E-mail:** innkeeper@millhouseinn.com

The Mill House Inn is in the heart of the village surrounded by spectacular beaches, pristine bays and picturesque country roads. Warm, inviting interiors create a relaxed ambience that is friendly and welcoming while the attention to detail, combined with old-fashioned hospitality, makes each visit truly memorable. Rooms are individually decorated with fine quality linens, lofty featherbeds, gas fireplaces and private baths. The spacious, dog-friendly suites have 6-foot serenity air baths, double marble showers and private decks where you can enjoy beautiful sunsets and starry skies. Views of the historic Old Hook Windmill are seen from the front porch. Wake up to imaginative breakfasts with dishes such as crawfish and Andouille omelette or 4-cheese frittata each morning, and set off to explore the eastern end of Long Island, which is a fisherman's playground, a vintner's paradise and an artist's inspiration.

***Our inspector loved:** The Mill House breakfast that is simply remarkable!*

Price Guide: (including breakfast)
rooms $295-$750
suites $450-$1,195

10 18 DVD WiFi NR HP

Attractions: Ocean Beach, 1 mile; World-Class Shops and Restaurants, 5-min walk; Galleries and Theaters, 10-min walk; Wineries, 15-min drive
Towns/Cities: Southampton, 12 miles; Newport, RI, 80 miles; New York City, 105 miles; Boston, MA, 130 miles
Airports: MacArthur I.S.P. Airport, 52 miles; J.F.K. Airport, 94 miles; LaGuardia Airport, 96 miles

1708 House

126 MAIN STREET, SOUTHAMPTON, NEW YORK 11968
Tel: +1 631 287 1708 **Fax:** +1 631 287 3593
Web: www.johansens.com/1708house **E-mail:** 1708house@hamptons.com

Our inspector loved: *The charming wine cellar where you can have a drink, relax or play games.*

Price Guide: (including breakfast)
rooms $150-$395
suites $175-$450
cottages $295-$675

15

NR
HP

Attractions: Shops and Restaurants, on the doorstep; Beaches, 1-3 miles; Wineries, 1-6 miles
Towns/Cities: Sag Harbor, 11 miles; East Hampton, 18 miles; Montauk, 35 miles; New York City, 100 miles
Airports: McArthur Islip Airport, 40 miles; LaGuardia Airport, 95 miles; J.F.K. Airport, 95 miles

This stylish, historic and charming boutique hotel exudes a quiet, romantic atmosphere that is complemented by personalized and unobtrusive service. At every turn you are reminded of the historical significance of this hotel. The cellar dates back to 1648 and has oak beams and stone walls with an original brick fireplace. Guest rooms have wooden panels and exposed beams and are beautifully decorated with luxurious antique beds, antique furnishings and sumptuous fabrics. There are also 3 cottages on the property; 2 are fitted with a kitchen and living room. The reading room is perfect for quiet reflection or the more formal parlor is ideal for meeting up with friends and family. Breakfast is served in the dining room overlooking the patio and garden, which boasts the finest Limoges china.

North Carolina

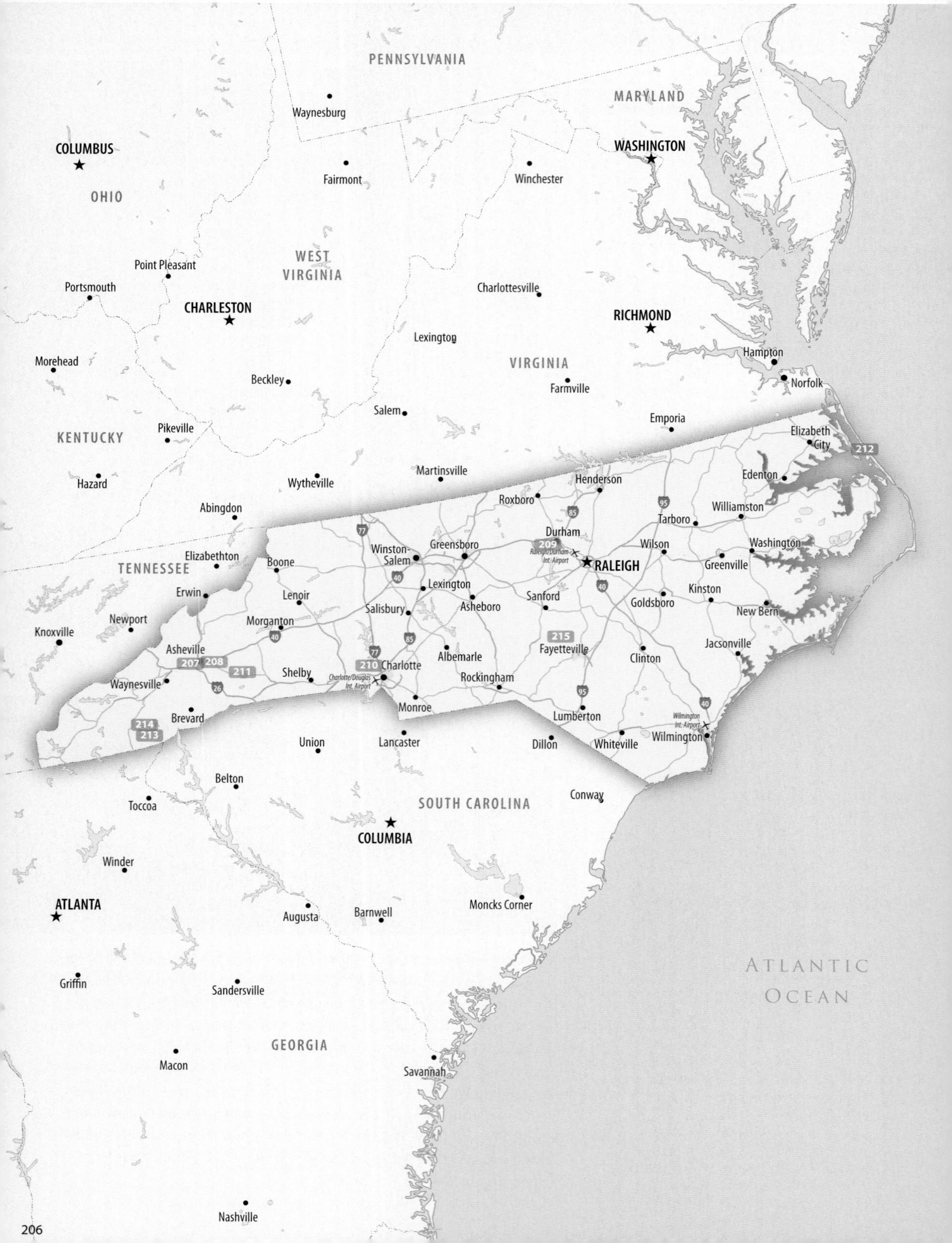

Haywood Park Hotel

ONE BATTERY PARK AVENUE, ASHEVILLE, NORTH CAROLINA 28801
Tel: +1 828 252 2522 **Fax:** +1 828 253 0481 **U.S./Canada Toll Free:** 1 800 228 2522
Web: www.johansens.com/haywoodpark **E-mail:** hotelsales@haywoodpark.com

Our inspector loved: *The spacious rooms, breakfast on a silver tray and access to all of the activity in downtown Asheville right outside the front door!*

Price Guide: (room only)
rooms from $220
suites from $475

33 60

Attractions: Biltmore House, 5 miles
Towns/Cities: Hendersonville, 30 miles
Airports: Asheville Airport, 15-min drive

For a truly all-encompassing getaway, visit this great hotel in the heart of Asheville, known as the Paris of the South for its art deco architecture and abundance of museums, shopping options, and restaurants. The hotel's expansive atrium offers enough shopping, dining, and galleries to keep you busy for days! When you're ready to explore your surroundings a bit further, Asheville's historic atmosphere and variety of attractions and tours provide endless entertainment, and the surrounding Blue Ridge Mountains facilitate a variety of outdoor activities. At the end of an action-packed day, you may return to the hotel to enjoy the flavors of The Flying Frog Café, which offers diverse menu options including French, German, and Indian cuisines.

INN ON BILTMORE

ONE ANTLER HILL ROAD, ASHEVILLE, NORTH CAROLINA 28803
Tel: +1 828 225 1600 **Fax:** +1 828 225 1629 **U.S./Canada Toll Free:** 1 800 858 4130
Web: www.johansens.com/biltmore **E-mail:** innsales@biltmore.com

Set within 8,000 acres enveloped by rolling hills, vineyards and views of the Blue Ridge Mountains, this is an elegant retreat amidst quiet, beautiful surroundings. In the vast lobby, with its marble floor and elegant seating, peaceful jazz plays as guests sip complimentary coffee in front of the stone fireplace, admiring the views from the huge windows. The Dining Room offers creative regional interpretations of Continental cuisine, and afternoon tea in the library is a distinguished affair with a delightful array of finger sandwiches, chocolate pastries, fruit tarts, jams and clotted cream. Biltmore House has countless treasures and there are acres of landscaped gardens to explore. Biltmore Estate Winery offers award-winning wines and production tours, alternately, indulge yourself with a visit to the intimate spa.

Our inspector loved: *The magnificent view, great food and wine, and the elegance of the inn.*

Price Guide:
rooms $299-$499
suites $700-$2,000

213 180 SPA

Awards/Ratings: Condé Nast Traveler Gold List 2005, 2006 and 2007

Attractions: Biltmore Estate, 10-min complimentary shuttle ride; Downtown Asheville, 15-min drive
Towns/Cities: Charlotte, 2-hour drive; Atlanta, GA, 3.5-hour drive; Raleigh, 4-hour drive
Airports: Asheville Regional Airport, 16 miles

The Franklin Hotel

311 WEST FRANKLIN STREET, CHAPEL HILL, NORTH CAROLINA 27516
Tel: +1 919 442 9000 **Fax:** +1 919 442 4040 **U.S./Canada Toll Free:** 1 866 831 5999
Web: www.johansens.com/franklinhotelnc **E-mail:** reservations@franklinhotelnc.com

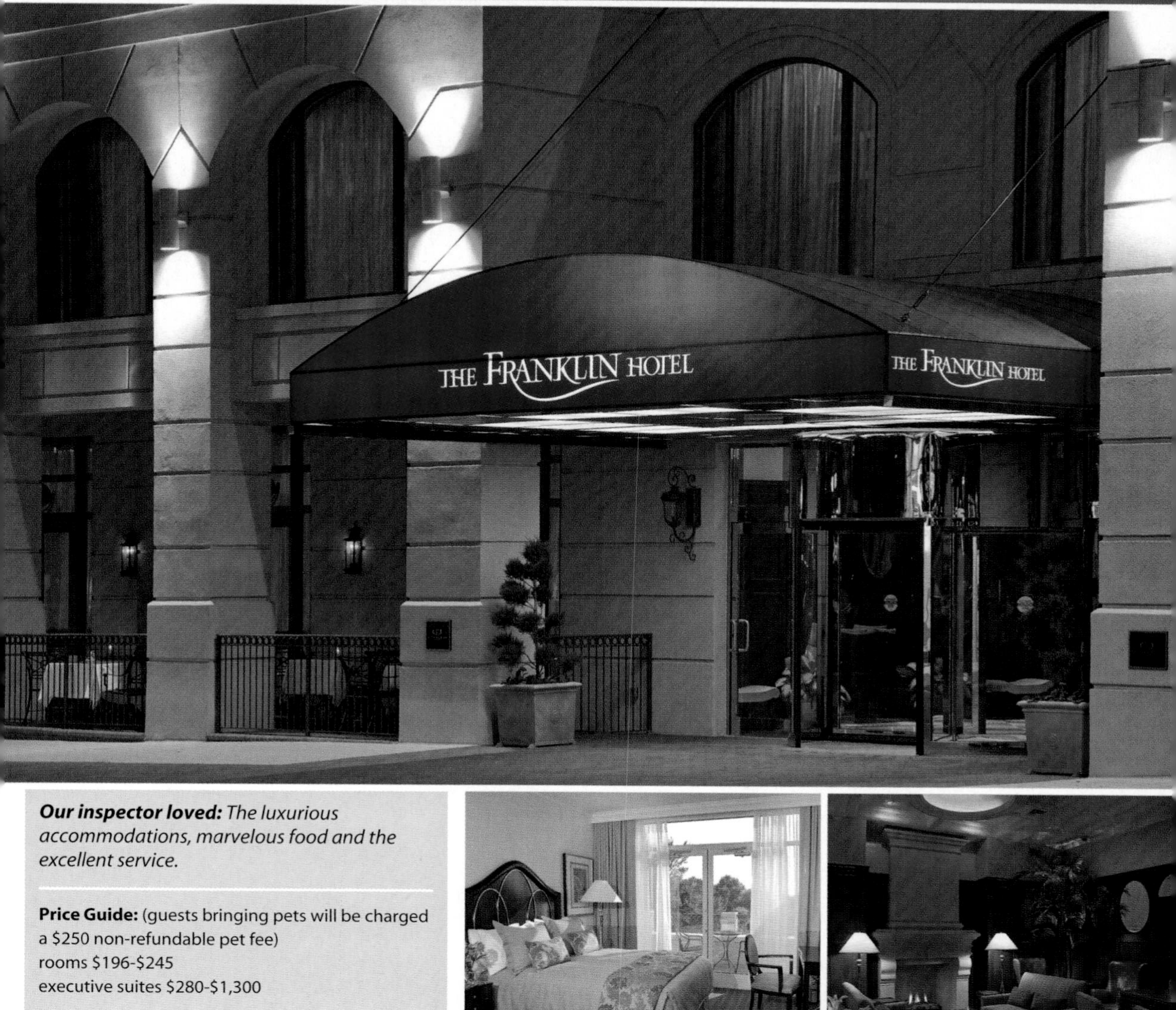

Our inspector loved: *The luxurious accommodations, marvelous food and the excellent service.*

Price Guide: (guests bringing pets will be charged a $250 non-refundable pet fee)
rooms $196-$245
executive suites $280-$1,300

67 M 288 WiFi

Attractions: Award-Winning Restaurants, 2-min walk; A Southern Season, 5-min drive; Carolina Performing Arts at Memorial Hall, 10-min walk; World-Class Golf, 5-60-min drive
Towns/Cities: Durham, 20-min drive; Raleigh, 30-min drive; Charlotte, 2.5-hour drive; Wilmington 2.5-hour drive
Airports: Raleigh Durham International Airport (RDU), 20-min drive; Greensboro Airport (GSO), 66 miles; Charlotte/Douglas International Airport (CLT), 145 miles

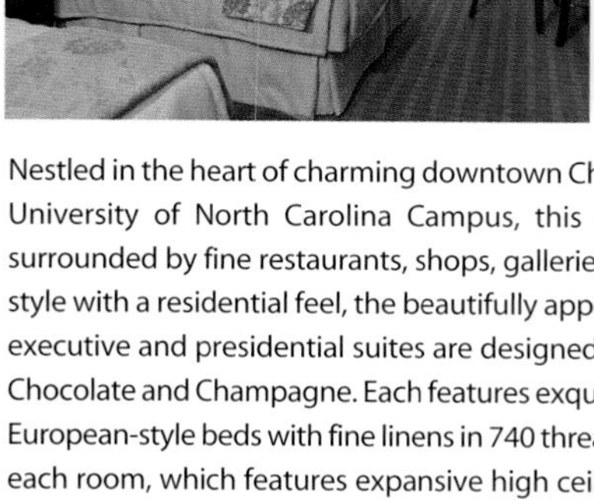

Nestled in the heart of charming downtown Chapel Hill, just a short stroll from The University of North Carolina Campus, this elegant luxury boutique hotel is surrounded by fine restaurants, shops, galleries, theaters and museums. Classic in style with a residential feel, the beautifully appointed guest rooms and penthouse executive and presidential suites are designed in a soothing palette of Sea Spray, Chocolate and Champagne. Each features exquisite fabrics, custom furnishings and European-style beds with fine linens in 740 thread count. Abundant natural light fills each room, which features expansive high ceilings and either double glass doors that open to your own private furnished patio balcony, or beautiful arched windows that bring in fresh air. Every room boasts impressive tree-top or panoramic views of Chapel Hill. Pamper yourself with an in-room spa service before enjoying a special evening of live music, cocktails and the bistro menu in Roberts At The Franklin.

BALLANTYNE RESORT

10000 BALLANTYNE COMMONS PARKWAY, CHARLOTTE, NORTH CAROLINA 28277
Tel: +1 704 248 4000 **Fax:** +1 704 248 4005 **U.S./Canada Toll Free:** 1 866 248 4824
Web: www.johansens.com/ballantyneresort **E-mail:** info@ballantyneresort.com

Our inspector loved: *The great food, golf, spa, and the most elegant rooms in Charlotte!*

Price Guide:
rooms $209-$429
suites $700-$5,000

214 500 SPA

Awards/Ratings: Condé Nast Johansens Most Excellent Golf Resort, U.S.A. & Canada 2008

Attractions: Dana Rader Golf School, 1-min walk; Carowinds, 13-min drive; U.S. National Whitewater Center, 20-min drive; Downtown Charlotte, 18 miles
Towns/Cities: Asheville, 120 miles; Chapel Hill, 120 miles; Charleston, 3-hour drive; Atlanta, 4-hour drive
Airports: Charlotte Douglas Airport, 20-min drive

Ballantyne Resort, a member of The Luxury Collection by Starwood Hotels and Resorts, offers the affluent traveler luxurious rooms, golf, a spa, Dana Rader Golf School, meeting and event facilities, dining and shopping all in the beautiful 2,000-acre Ballantyne community. The Spa at Ballantyne Resort practises an array of soothing and revitalizing treatments, and the health facility provides fitness classes as well as an indoor and outdoor pool. Golf lovers will enjoy the par 71 course designed to challenge players of all levels while professional tennis and golf instruction are available for individuals and groups. Gallery Restaurant, with its distinguished art collection, defines Charlotte's upscale dining with its contemporary take on American fare. Leisure activities include afternoon tea, weekly wine tastings and entertainment. A helipad on the property allows for a convenient transportation option.

The Esmeralda

910 MAIN STREET, CHIMNEY ROCK, NORTH CAROLINA 28720
Tel: +1 828 625 2999 **Fax:** +1 828 625 2959 **U.S./Canada Toll Free:** 1 888 897 2999
Web: www.johansens.com/esmeralda **E-mail:** info@theesmeralda.com

***Our inspector loved:** The warm and luxurious guest rooms with excellent views of the Rocky Broad River and the surrounding Hickory Nut Gorge.*

Price Guide: (including breakfast)
rooms $225-$395

14 12

Attractions: Chimney Rock, 10-min walk; Lake Lure, 5-min drive; Pisgah National Forest, 30-min drive; Biltmore Estate, 1-hour drive
Towns/Cities: Tryon, 20 miles; Rutherfordton, 21 miles; Hendersonville, 18 miles; Asheville, 25 miles
Airports: Asheville Airport, 1-hour drive; Greenville Spartanburg Airport, 1-hour drive; Charlotte Airport, 90-min drive

Set within the scenic Hickory Nut Gorge of the splendid Blue Ridge Mountains in the quaint village of Chimney Rock, this peaceful hotel offers you a rustic and elegant setting with a contemporary flair. Each of the guest rooms is beautifully designed with exquisite Anichini luxury linens, Bose Wave music systems and incredible views of Chimney Rock, the Rocky Broad River and the surrounding areas. Spend the afternoon quietly on a rocking chair taking in the amazing views or go hiking at the nearby Chimney Rock Park. The new Prime restaurant is a wonderful choice for dinner with its French, Spanish, pan-Asian and Latin influenced menu. An ideal hotel all year round, couples will enjoy the Romance Package, which includes champagne and chocolate covered strawberries.

U.S.A. - NORTH CAROLINA (DUCK)

THE SANDERLING RESORT & SPA

1461 DUCK ROAD, DUCK, NORTH CAROLINA 27949

Tel: +1 252 261 4111 **Fax:** +1 252 261 1638 **U.S./Canada Toll Free:** 1 800 701 4111

Web: www.johansens.com/sanderling **E-mail:** reservations@thesanderling.com

Our inspector loved: *The spacious rooms with spectacular views, and the excellent food at The Left Bank Restaurant.*

Price Guide:
rooms $150-$475
suites $210-$550
villas $600-$1,050

93 100 SPA

The Outer Banks' only true resort, The Sanderling touches the shores of both the Atlantic Ocean and Currituck Sound. Miles of unspoiled beaches provide serenity, which, like the ocean waves, ensure your inevitable return. Relax at The Sanderling Spa with its beautiful backdrop of the tranquil waters of Currituck Sound making the experience complete. The luxurious lodging reflects classic Outer Banks architecture: each of the 3 distinctive 2-story inns is decorated with a rare collection of fine wildlife art and sculptures, and each building offers private porches, most with ocean or sound views. 4 ocean-side cottages and 1 ocean-front cottage are also available. Dine casually among nautical artefacts in a restored 1899 U.S. Lifesaving Station or play the epciure in the AAA 4 Diamond award-winning The Left Bank Restaurant, where spectacular views of Currituck Sound complement the fine cuisine.

Attractions: Currituck Lighthouse, 8 miles; Wright Brothers Memorial and Visitors Center, 15 miles; North Carolina Aquarium, 30 miles

Towns/Cities: Kitty Hawk, 20 miles; Nags Head, 30 miles

Airports: Norfolk Virginia Airport, 75 miles

INN AT HALF MILE FARM

P.O. BOX 2769, 214 HALF MILE DRIVE, HIGHLANDS, NORTH CAROLINA 28741
Tel: +1 828 526 8170 **Fax:** +1 828 526 2625 **U.S./Canada Toll Free:** 1 800 946 6822
Web: www.johansens.com/halfmilefarm **E-mail:** mail@halfmilefarm.com

Our inspector loved: *The serenity of the mountains, walking around the beautiful grounds of the inn and sitting by the pond.*

Price Guide: (including gourmet country breakfast and wine and apéritifs each evening)
rooms $220-$950

23 30 12

Attractions: Fly Fishing, 1 mile; White-Water Rafting, 4 miles
Towns/Cities: Cashiers, 10 miles; Asheville, 60 miles
Airports: Asheville International Airport, 70 miles; Atlanta International Airport, 90 miles

Tucked away on the outskirts of town, this lovely rambling inn is a paradise for nature lovers and those who hanker for the great outdoor life. There's hiking, fly-fishing, lake canoeing, white-water rafting and just about every mountain activity. Originally a mid-19th-century farmhouse, the inn is surrounded by beautiful grounds, which feature a lake, pool and an abundance of wild flowers and greenery. Sit and watch the sun rise and set over the mountain peaks while enjoying an early morning coffee or a glass of complimentary wine and hors d'oeuvres in the evening. Tennessee fieldstone fireplaces, pine floors and local wood decorations are particularly attractive features of the 4 guest rooms in the main house and those that surround a colorful courtyard and fountain.

Old Edwards Inn and Spa

445 MAIN STREET, HIGHLANDS, NORTH CAROLINA 28741
Tel: +1 828 526 8008 **Fax:** +1 828 526 8301 **U.S./Canada Toll Free:** 1 866 526 8008
Web: www.johansens.com/oldedwards **E-mail:** info@oldedwardsinn.com

This is the ultimate getaway in the heart of the Blue Ridge Mountains. In Highlands, a delightful main-street town filled with eclectic shops and an abundance of cultural activities, you will find Old Edwards Inn and Spa. Wide screen plasma T.V.s and elegant frette linens set the scene for the bedrooms, while the bathrooms have heated tile floors, Bulgari bath amenities, rainfall showers and more. Madison's Restaurant and Wine Garden, an AAA 3 Diamond winner, is the place to find New South cuisine at its finest. The Spa at Old Edwards features some of the most exotic and contemporary treatments, limestone heated terrace flooring and European influenced antiques throughout. The Farm, located nearby, is a magnificent backdrop for that fairy-tale wedding, elegant corporate retreat or family gathering. The property of Old Edwards Inn also boasts an Executive Conference Center, state-of-the-art fitness center and heated mineral pool.

Our inspector loved: *The first-class spa, magnificent dining and picturesque setting.*

Price Guide: (including breakfast)
rooms $250-$350
suites $275-$1,100
cottages $1,400-$2,000

57 130 SPA NR HP

Awards/Ratings: Condé Nast Johansens Most Excellent Inn, U.S.A. & Canada 2008; Wine Spectator Award of Excellence 2005-2008

Attractions: Spa, on-site; Shopping, on-site and close by; Golf, close by; Hiking, 1 mile
Towns/Cities: Cashiers, 10 miles; Franklin, 20 miles; Clayton, GA, 20 miles; Asheville, 70 miles
Airports: Asheville International Airport, 70 miles; Atlanta Hartsfield Airport, 120 miles

Affiliations: Preferred Boutique

The Jefferson Inn

150 WEST NEW HAMPSHIRE AVENUE, SOUTHERN PINES, NORTH CAROLINA 28387
Tel: +1 910 692 9911 **Fax:** +1 910 692 9986
Web: www.johansens.com/jeffersoninn **E-mail:** info@JeffersonInnSouthernPines.com

Our inspector loved: *The true Southern experience, the large, luxury guest rooms, restaurant and tavern, all located on-site.*

Price Guide: (including Continental breakfast)
rooms $185-$210
suites $250-$285

15 M 60 WiFi

Attractions: Historic Shopping District, on-site; 42 Golf Courses, close by
Towns/Cities: Pinehurst, 10-min drive; Raleigh, 75-min drive; Chapel Hill, 75-min drive; Charlotte, 2-hour drive
Airports: Raleigh Airport, 90-min drive

The Jefferson Inn is a century-old landmark located in Southern Pines' downtown historic district. The inn recently completed a multi-million dollar restoration to recreate the history and lifestyle of the area while providing all the amenities of a luxury boutique hotel. Charming rooms and suites are welcoming with cottage-style furniture, plantation shutters, 600 thread count Egyptian cotton sheets, and elegant baths with rain showers and claw foot tubs. For a comfortable stay, rooms are equipped with modern conveniences. One Fifty West, the inn's upscale restaurant, serves delicious American cuisine in a casual setting. Relax in the tavern or enjoy seasonal live music in the courtyard where local and regional musicians play. Avid golfers will enjoy the inn's Southern Pines and Pinehurst golf packages.

Oklahoma

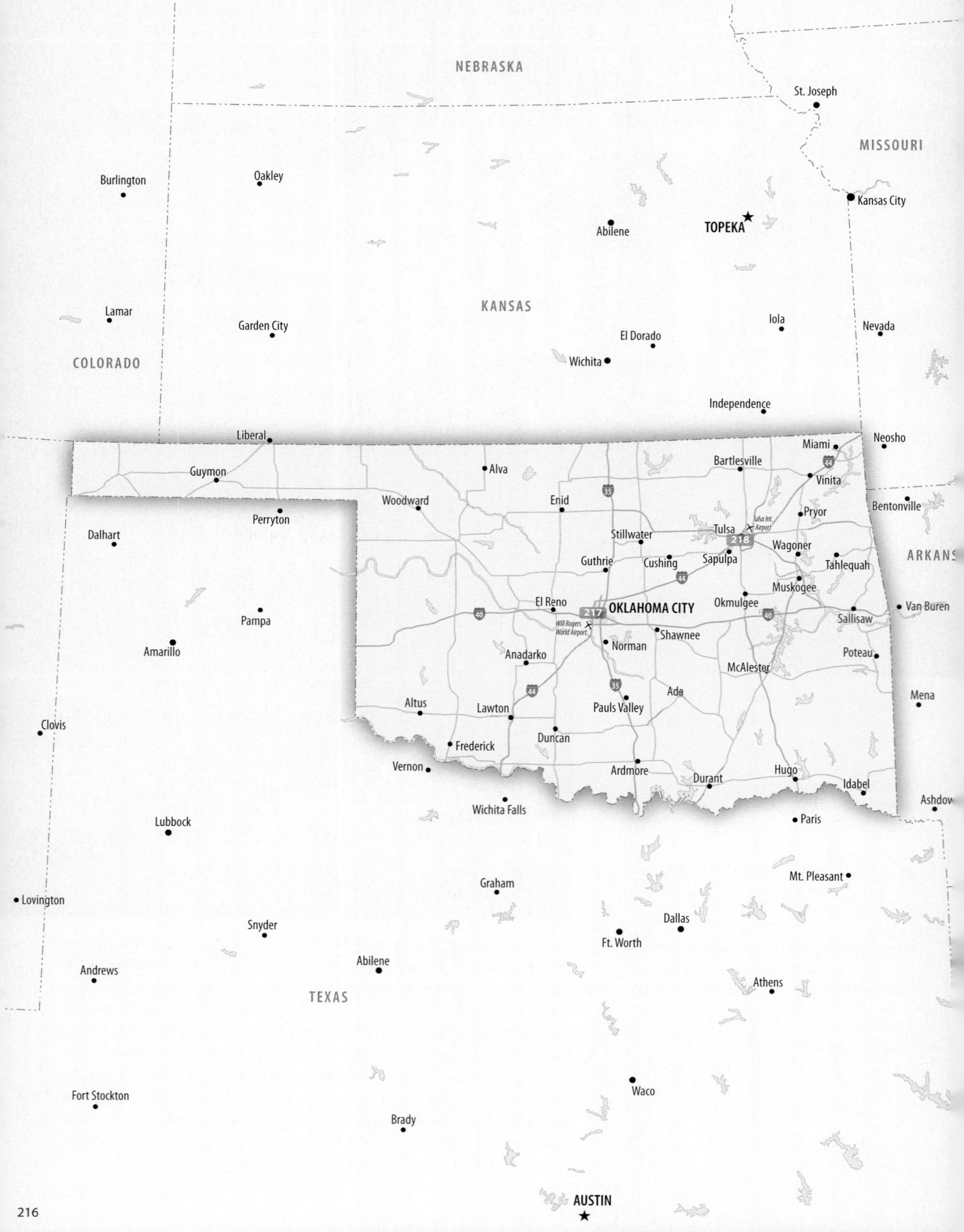
NEBRASKA
St. Joseph
MISSOURI
Burlington
Oakley
Kansas City
Abilene
TOPEKA
KANSAS
Lamar
Garden City
Iola
Nevada
El Dorado
COLORADO
Wichita
Independence
Liberal
Neosho
Miami
Guymon
Alva
Bartlesville
Vinita
Woodward
Enid
Bentonville
Perryton
Pryor
Dalhart
Stillwater
Tulsa
Tulsa Int. Airport
Wagoner
ARKANS
Guthrie
Cushing
Sapulpa
Tahlequah
Muskogee
El Reno
OKLAHOMA CITY
Okmulgee
Van Buren
Pampa
Will Rogers World Airport
Sallisaw
Shawnee
Amarillo
Norman
Anadarko
Poteau
McAlester
Ada
Mena
Altus
Lawton
Pauls Valley
Clovis
Frederick
Duncan
Vernon
Ardmore
Hugo
Durant
Idabel
Wichita Falls
Ashdow
Paris
Lubbock
Mt. Pleasant
Graham
Lovington
Dallas
Snyder
Ft. Worth
Abilene
Andrews
Athens
TEXAS
Fort Stockton
Waco
Brady
AUSTIN

Colcord Hotel

15 NORTH ROBINSON, OKLAHOMA CITY, OKLAHOMA 73102
Tel: +1 405 601 4300 **Fax:** +1 405 208 4399 **U.S./Canada Toll Free:** 1 866 781 3800
Web: www.johansens.com/colcord **E-mail:** reservations@colcordhotel.com

Our inspector loved: *The fabulous architecture in the heart of downtown.*

Price Guide:
rooms $179-$299
suites $299-$1,299

Attractions: Cox Convention Center, close by; Myriad Botanical Gardens, close by; Oklahoma City National Memorial, 5-min walk; Bricktown Entertainment District, 5-min walk
Towns/Cities: Edmond, 20-min drive; Norman, 30-min drive; Tulsa, 108 miles; Dallas, TX, 200 miles
Airports: Will Rogers World Airport, 15-min drive; Wiley Post Airport, 20-min drive

Oklahoma City's first skyscraper when built in 1910, the 12-story Colcord has been meticulously restored into a sophisticated boutique hotel with a celebrated past. Listed on the National Register of Historic Places since 1976, this elegant hotel combines historic décor with classic modern style. Built by Charles Francis Colcord, the original polished elevators and moldings of decorative terracotta still adorn the first and second floors. The original magnificent staircase also remains. The trendy XO Lounge, located in the basement, is a wonderful place to have a specialty mixed drink or a glass of wine. The extremely popular restaurant, Soleil, headed by celebrated Chefs Michel and Alain Buthion, will tempt your palate with exquisite French cuisine.

Hotel Ambassador

1324 SOUTH MAIN STREET, TULSA, OKLAHOMA 74119
Tel: +1 918 587 8200 **Fax:** +1 918 587 8208 **U.S./Canada Toll Free:** 1 888 408 8282
Web: www.johansens.com/ambassador **E-mail:** sales@hotelambassador-tulsa.com

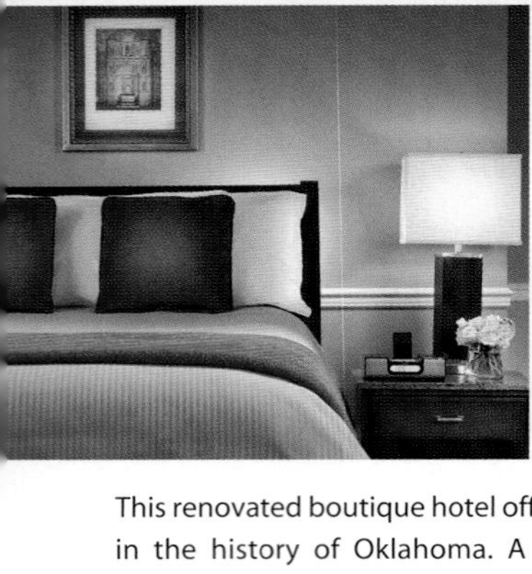

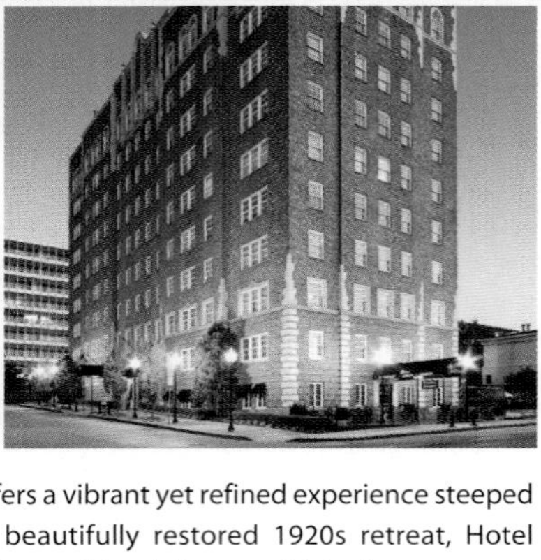

Our inspector loved: *The hospitality and attention of the staff, which create a warm atmosphere.*

Price Guide:
rooms $219-$239
suites $279-$359

55 70 NR HP

This renovated boutique hotel offers a vibrant yet refined experience steeped in the history of Oklahoma. A beautifully restored 1920s retreat, Hotel Ambassador showcases the craftsmanship of the era with Italian terracotta relief panels and limestone cornices. The recessed desk area and other architectural details add charming touches to each guest room, while the soothing neutral decor, pillow top mattresses and triple sheeted beds enhance the calm, spa-like ambience. The Hurley library, named after the founder of Hotel Ambassador, offers an intimate space to recline with a book, enjoy a peaceful game of chess, or simply relax in the tranquility of the room. The lively Chalkboard restaurant serves Northern Californian-style breakfasts, lunches and dinners in the main dining room, wine cellar or alfresco on the patio.

Attractions: Tulsa Performing Arts Center, 1 mile; BOK Center (Opening Fall 2008), 1 mile; Utica Square, 1 mile; The Philbrook Museum and Gardens, 2 miles
Towns/Cities: Oklahoma City, OK, 100 miles
Airports: Tulsa International Airport, 10 miles

PACIFIC OCEAN
CANADA
WASHINGTON
IDAHO
CALIFORNIA
NEVADA
VICTORIA
Bellingham
Osoyoos
Nelson
Trail
Creston
Mount Vernon
Port Angeles
Colville
Seattle
Sandpoint
Shelton
Tacoma
OLYMPIA
Wenatchee
Spokane
Ephrata
Chehalis
St. Maries
Astoria
Seaside
Kelso
Yakima
St. Helens
Moscow
Tillamook
Vancouver
Pasco
Hillsboro
Portland Int. Airport
221
Portland
Orofino
McMinnville
Hood River
Walla Walla
Oregon City
The Dalles
Pendleton
Grangeville
SALEM
Dallas
Newport
Heppner
Albany
84
La Grande
5
Fossil
Madras
Florence
Mahlon Sweet Field Airport
Eugene
Prineville
Canyon City
Baker City
Bend
Coss Bay
Roseburg
Vale
Burns
5
Caldwell
Gold Beach
Grants Pass
BOISE
Rogue Valley / Medford Int. Airport
Medford
Brookings
220
Ashland
Klamath Falls
Mountain Home
Lakeview
Eureka
Redding
Red Bluff
Susanville
Winnemucca
Battle Mountain
Elko
Willows
Ukiah
Oroville
Colusa
Reno
Fallon

The Winchester Inn & Restaurant

35 SOUTH SECOND STREET, ASHLAND, OREGON 97520
Tel: +1 541 488 1113 **Fax:** +1 541 488 4604 **U.S./Canada Toll Free:** 1 800 972 4991
Web: www.johansens.com/winchester **E-mail:** Innkeeper@theWinchesterInn.com

With large windows and attractive roof peaks, this intimate lodging encourages you to relax, take a stroll to the nearby shops and enjoy the surrounding attractions. Owned, restored, refurbished and managed since 1983 by Laurie and Michael Gibbs, the inn has expanded from the original 1886 Victorian family home and today's 4 buildings and restaurant are surrounded by an English cottage-style garden. The main house has 7 Victorian guest rooms and 1 suite. The adjacent Heritage House features 3 suites and 4 bedrooms. The Carriage House offers 2 suites and the Larkspur Cottage, a short brick-lined walk away, has 2 private suites. Its crowning glory is the food: exquisite meals are served in the elegant main house restaurant where the kitchen uses organically grown local products whenever possible.

Our inspector loved: *The wonderful restaurant featuring the wines and fresh cuisine of the Pacific Northwest.*

Price Guide: (including breakfast)
rooms $140-$225
suites $190-$325

19

Awards/Ratings: Wine Spectator Award of Excellence 2006, 2007 and 2008; Condé Nast Traveler Gold List 2006

Attractions: Shopping, 2-min walk; Ashland Restaurants, 2-min walk; Ashland Theaters, 5-min walk
Towns/Cities: Medford, 15 miles
Airports: Medford Airport, 15 miles

The Heathman Hotel

1001 S.W. BROADWAY, PORTLAND, OREGON 97205
Tel: +1 503 241 4100 **Fax:** +1 503 790 7110 **U.S./Canada Toll Free:** 1 800 551 0011
Web: www.johansens.com/heathman **E-mail:** reservations@heathmanhotel.com

Our inspector loved: *The customized "books by your bedside."*

Price Guide:
rooms $229-$329
suites $329-$3,000

150 125 NR HP

Awards/Ratings: Wine Spectator Award of Excellence 2008

Attractions: Pearl District, 0.5 miles; Portland Art Museum, 2-min walk; Pioneer Court House Square Shopping, 5-min walk; Portland Zoo, 5 miles
Towns/Cities: Beaverton, 7 miles; Newport, 25 miles; Hood River, 60 miles; Cannon Beach, 80 miles
Airports: Portland International Airport, 20-min drive

Successfully evoking Old World atmosphere with a modern twist, The Heathman is full of intimate charm even with its 150 rooms. This is partly due to the warm décor of the Lobby and Tea Court Lounge, and the absence of a check-in desk. Energy Star Certified, the hotel is a superior energy efficient property that also boasts the first ever "Art of Sleep Bed Menu." Each guest has the opportunity to choose from 3 mattress types: Tempur Pedic, European Pillow Top or European Feather Bed. And the special treatment continues as each guest is assigned a "personal concierge" who provides a seamless, personal service achieving a sense of intimacy you might expect at a smaller hotel. The beautiful Mezzanine holds curated art exhibits and looks down over the art deco Lobby and Lounge where jazz artists play most nights.

Orillia
Belleville
Watertown
Lake Pleasant
Hudson Fal
CANADA
Oshawa
Oswego
Johnstown
TORONTO
Syracuse
ALBAN
Albion
Rochester
Norwich
Hamilton
Niagara Falls
ONTARIO
Buffalo
NEW YORK
Kingston
Binghamton
Pough
Monticello
Wellsville
Salamanca
Honesdale
Erie
Erie Int./ Tom Ridge Field Airport
Bradford
Scranton
Warren
Wilkes Barre
Newton
Williamsport
Stroudsburg
Meadville
Lock Haven
Bloomsburg
NEW JERSEY
Lewisburg
Lehigh Valley Int. Airport
Easton
Franklin
Clarion
Sunbury
Pottsville
Clearfield
Bellefonte
Allentown
Warren
Doylestown
New Castle
Reading
Lewistown
Lebanon
Kittanning
Norristown
Philadelphia
Huntingdon
HARRISBURG
Indiana
Harrisburg Int. Airport
Philadelphia Int. Airport
Beaver
Carlisle
Lancaster
OHIO
Hollidaysburg
York
Pittsburgh Int. Airport
Wilmington
Pittsburgh
Greensburg
Chambersburg
Gettysburg
Elkton
Bridgeton
Washington
Somerset
Westminster
Uniontown
Baltimore
DOVER
St. Clairsville
Waynesburg
Cumberland
MARYLAND
Martinsburg
Rockville
ANNAPOLIS
Morgantown
DELAWARE
Winchester
WASHINGTON
WEST VIRGINIA
VIRGINIA
Charlottesville
CHARLESTON
RICHMOND
Lexington
Hampton

THE INN AT BOWMAN'S HILL

518 LURGAN ROAD, NEW HOPE, PENNSYLVANIA 18938
Tel: +1 215 862 8090 **Fax:** +1 215 862 9362
Web: www.johansens.com/bowmanshill **E-mail:** info@theinnatbowmanshill.com

Our inspector loved: *The exceptional ambience through all seasons!*

Price Guide: (including full breakfast)
rooms $325-$455
suites $455-$595

Attractions: Bowman's Hill Wildflower Preserve, 5-min walk; Delaware Canal State Park, 1 mile; Wine Tasting and Touring, 3 miles; Washington Crossing State Park, 4 miles
Towns/Cities: Princeton, NJ, 35-min drive; Philadelphia, 45-min drive; New York City, NY, 2-hour drive; Washington D.C., 3-hour drive
Airports: Trenton Mercer Airport, NJ, Private and Commercial Jet Service, 15-min drive; Philadelphia International Airport, 1-hour drive; Newark Liberty International Airport, NJ, 1-hour drive

The charming and eclectic riverside town of New Hope is a vibrant tourist destination with a rich and diverse history. Independent and non-conformist, the rich cultural heritage of New Hope is today alive and well in theater, cabaret, piano bars, art and antiques. Close to New York and Philadelphia, yet a world apart, you can also enjoy unique dining experiences and local wine tastings. The Inn at Bowman's Hill is an intimate retreat nestled within a 5-acre manicured and gated estate just 2 miles from the town center. Private, luxurious, romantic and memorable! Indulge your senses in a 2-person heated whirlpool; relax on a king-size featherbed; enjoy an in-suite massage or simply warm your body and soul by your very own fireplace. Multi-course gourmet breakfast with daily à la carte choices is served in the fireside dining room or in bed. Celebrate, relax, connect and remember!

U.S.A. - PENNSYLVANIA (PHILADELPHIA)

RITTENHOUSE 1715, A BOUTIQUE HOTEL

1715 RITTENHOUSE SQUARE, PHILADELPHIA, PENNSYLVANIA 19103
Tel: +1 215 546 6500 **Fax:** +1 215 546 8787 **U.S./Canada Toll Free:** 1 877 791 6500
Web: www.johansens.com/rittenhouse **E-mail:** reservations@rittenhouse1715.com

Rittenhouse 1715 is a traditional 19th-century carriage house in the fashionable Rittenhouse Square district of downtown Philadelphia that has been restored and combined with the neighboring 18th-century Georgian town houses to make it one of Philadelphia's most exclusive and luxurious boutique hotels. An intimate, comfortable retreat that exudes style, sophistication and charm, the hotel is adorned with fine furnishings, exquisite artwork and upholds a careful attention to detail. All guest rooms feature marble bathrooms, plush robes, triple sheeting with fine European linens, 37" plasma T.V.s and nightly turndown service. A lovely complimentary Continental breakfast is served in the Parisian-style café, and an evening wine reception is held in the drawing room each day.

Our inspector loved: *The evening wine receptions held in the drawing room.*

Price Guide: (room only)
rooms from $250
suites from $459

Attractions: Philadelphia Museum of Art, 1 mile; The Kimmel Center, 5-min walk
Towns/Cities: Westchester, 45-min drive; Lancaster, 1.5-hour drive
Airports: Philadelphia Airport, 30-min drive

Skytop Lodge

ONE SKYTOP, SKYTOP, PENNSYLVANIA 18357
Tel: +1 570 595 7401 **Fax:** +1 570 595 7285 **U.S./Canada Toll Free:** 1 800 345 7759
Web: www.johansens.com/skytop **E-mail:** reservations@skytop.com

Our inspector loved: *The porch with rocking chairs overlooking the mountains!*

Price Guide: (double occupancy, including breakfast, lunch and dinner, excluding taxes and gratuities)
rooms $299-$605
suites $540-$745

125 250 SPA

Attractions: The Pocono Mountains Tourist Region
Towns/Cities: Canadensis, 3 miles
Airports: Allentown-Bethlehem-Easton Airport, 40 miles; Wilkes-Barre-Scranton Airport, 45 miles

Inspired by nature and enveloped in 5,500 acres of pristine forest, this is an awe-inspiring holiday retreat with year-round activities as well as plenty of quiet places to relax and take in the views. Accommodations are variable and range from spacious standard rooms to stream-side cottages ideal for families. Savor the delicious tastes of American cuisine in the historical main lodge, or outstanding Continental dishes and fine wines at the lake view restaurant. A variety of activities can be arranged: during winter, sledding and skiing is superb and there is also a huge weather protected skating rink nearby. In the summer months the lake offers boating, canoeing and other water sports. The forests have many nature trails to explore, and there is a spa and health club.

Rhode Island

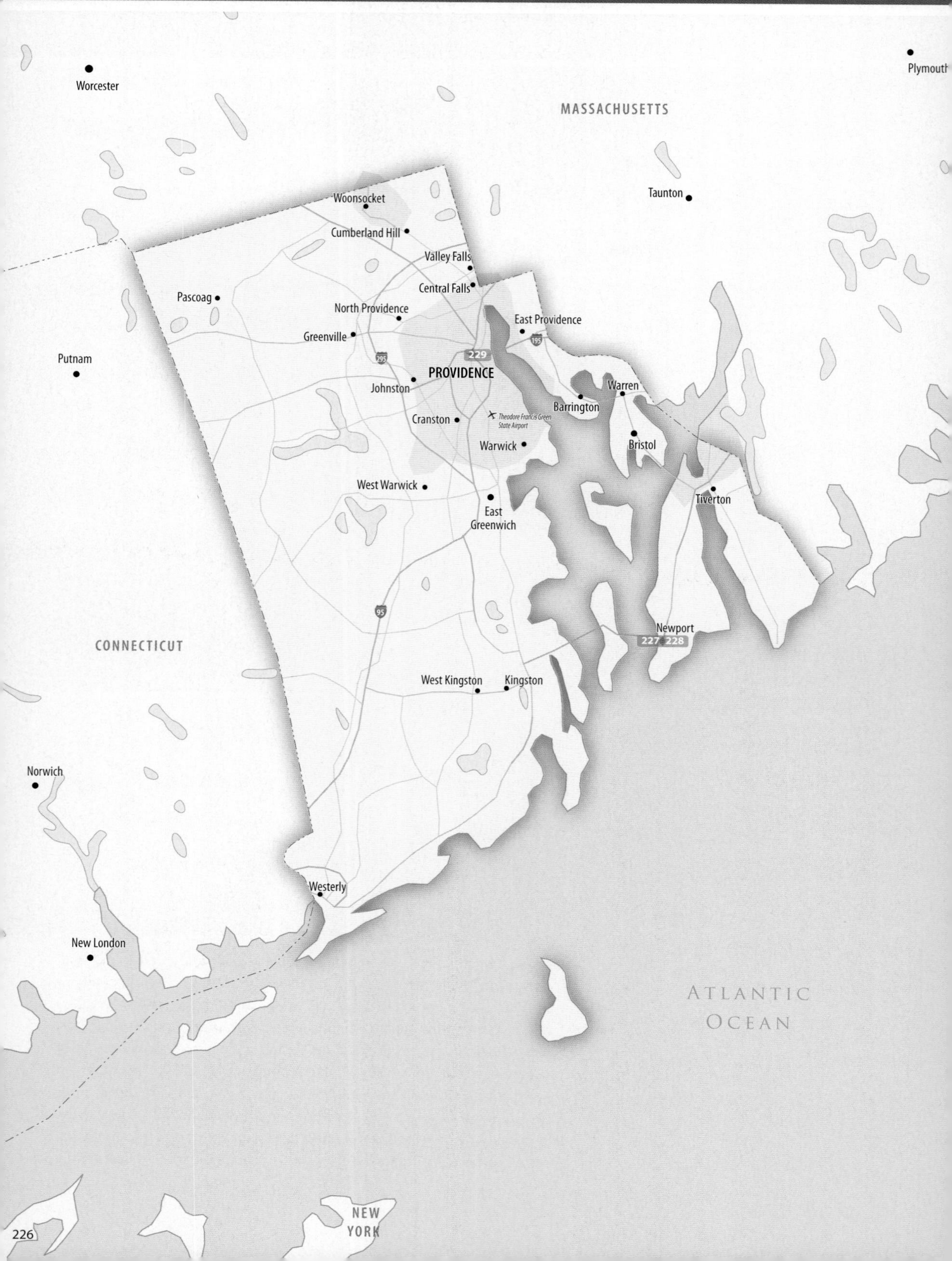

Chanler at Cliff Walk

117 MEMORIAL BOULEVARD, NEWPORT, RHODE ISLAND 02840
Tel: +1 401 847 1300 **Fax:** +1 401 847 3620 **U.S./Canada Toll Free:** 1 866 793 5664
Web: www.johansens.com/chanler **E-mail:** reservations@thechanler.com

Our inspector loved: *The exclusive Beach Butler service for a pampered experience at the beach.*

Price Guide: (excluding tax)
rooms from $295

Attractions: Cliff Walk, 0.5 miles; Beach, 0.5 miles; Newport Mansions, 1 mile; Downtown, 1 mile
Towns/Cities: Providence, 38 miles; Middletown, 38 miles; Boston, MA, 75 miles;
Airports: Quonset (F.B.O.) Airport, 17 miles; T.F. Green Airport, 28 miles; Boston Logan International Airport, MA, 75 miles

Located at the start of Newport's famous Cliff Walk, through majestic iron gates and along beautifully landscaped gardens with fountains, the Chanler is the epitome of romance. The sense of history is awe-inspiring: the authentic furniture, stunning antiques and a rich opulence is reminiscent of a bygone era. Rooms are separated into Manor Rooms, Estate Rooms and Signature Rooms, each designed to reflect a different period or theme. From your private patio, watch the waves roll in before heading outdoors to Terazza to enjoy romantic Tuscan dishes and fine wines on the terrace with breathtaking views. The acclaimed Spiced Pear restaurant serves gourmet New England seafood where you can participate in the popular Chef's Table.

U.S.A. - RHODE ISLAND (NEWPORT)

LA FARGE PERRY HOUSE

24 KAY STREET, NEWPORT, RHODE ISLAND 02840
Tel: +1 401 847 2223 **Fax:** +1 401 847 1967 **U.S./Canada Toll Free:** 1 877 736 1100
Web: www.johansens.com/lafargeperry **E-mail:** innkeeper@lafargeperry.com

Our inspector loved: *The delicious gourmet breakfasts prepared by the welcoming innkeeper.*

Price Guide: (including breakfast)
rooms $175-$395
suites $295-$565

5 M 70 DVD WiFi

Attractions: International Tennis Hall of Fame, 1 mile; Newport Mansions, 2 miles; Cliff Walk, 2 miles; Newport Harbor, 2 miles
Towns/Cities: Fall River, 20 miles; Providence, 40 miles; Boston, MA, 70 miles
Airports: T. F. Green State Airport, 26 miles; Boston Logan International Airport, MA, 78 miles; Hartford Airport, 89 miles

This quaint Victorian-style inn, named after the renowned painter and stained-glass artist, John La Farge, and his wife Margaret Perry La Farge, is set in a quiet residential neighborhood of Newport. The beautiful rooms are designed to immerse you in history yet feature touches of modern luxury such as H.D. flat-screen T.V.s. Each room evokes the personality of one of Newport's most famous figures and displays wonderful fresh flowers cut from the inn's vibrant gardens, and personalized stationery that add to the warm nature of this great little inn. The innkeeper, a former restaurant chef, will tempt your palate with sumptuous breakfasts in the grand dining room each morning followed by her signature chocolate chip macaroons and tea in the afternoon, so popular with guests that she will send you home with the secret recipe!

HOTEL PROVIDENCE

311 WESTMINSTER STREET, PROVIDENCE, RHODE ISLAND 02903
Tel: +1 401 861 8000 **Fax:** +1 401 861 8002 **U.S./Canada Toll Free:** 1 800 861 8990
Web: www.johansens.com/providence **E-mail:** info@thehotelprovidence.com

Our inspector loved: *The hotel's new restaurant, Aspire, that serves contemporary American and regional Rhode Island cuisine.*

Price Guide:
rooms $199-$349
suites $429-$829

80 150

Attractions: Providence Performing Arts Center, 0.2 miles; Johnson and Wales University, 1 mile; Rhode Island School of Design, 1 mile; Brown University, 1 mile
Towns/Cities: Newport, 30 miles; Boston, MA, 45 miles; New York City, NY, 3-hour drive
Airports: T.F. Green Airport, 10 miles; Boston Logan International Airport, MA, 55 miles

This landmark property is ideally located in the heart of Providence's downtown arts and entertainment district. From vibrant theaters and shopping to world-class educational institutions and the bustling convention center, Hotel Providence is within a short walking distance of all the excitement the city has to offer. With some of the most luxurious accommodations in town, its spacious suites and guest rooms will satisfy a variety of tastes ranging from hip and chic designs to a more traditional and elegant style. All rooms are richly appointed with a mix of lavish elements with high-end finishes such as rich fabrics and tiger maple accents. The superb personalized service adds to the luxurious atmosphere. Aspire and the A-bar are the hotel's newest additions to the city's bustling restaurant scene with inviting menus, a global wine list and gracious staff, that all contribute to the sophisticated and relaxing surrounding.

South Carolina

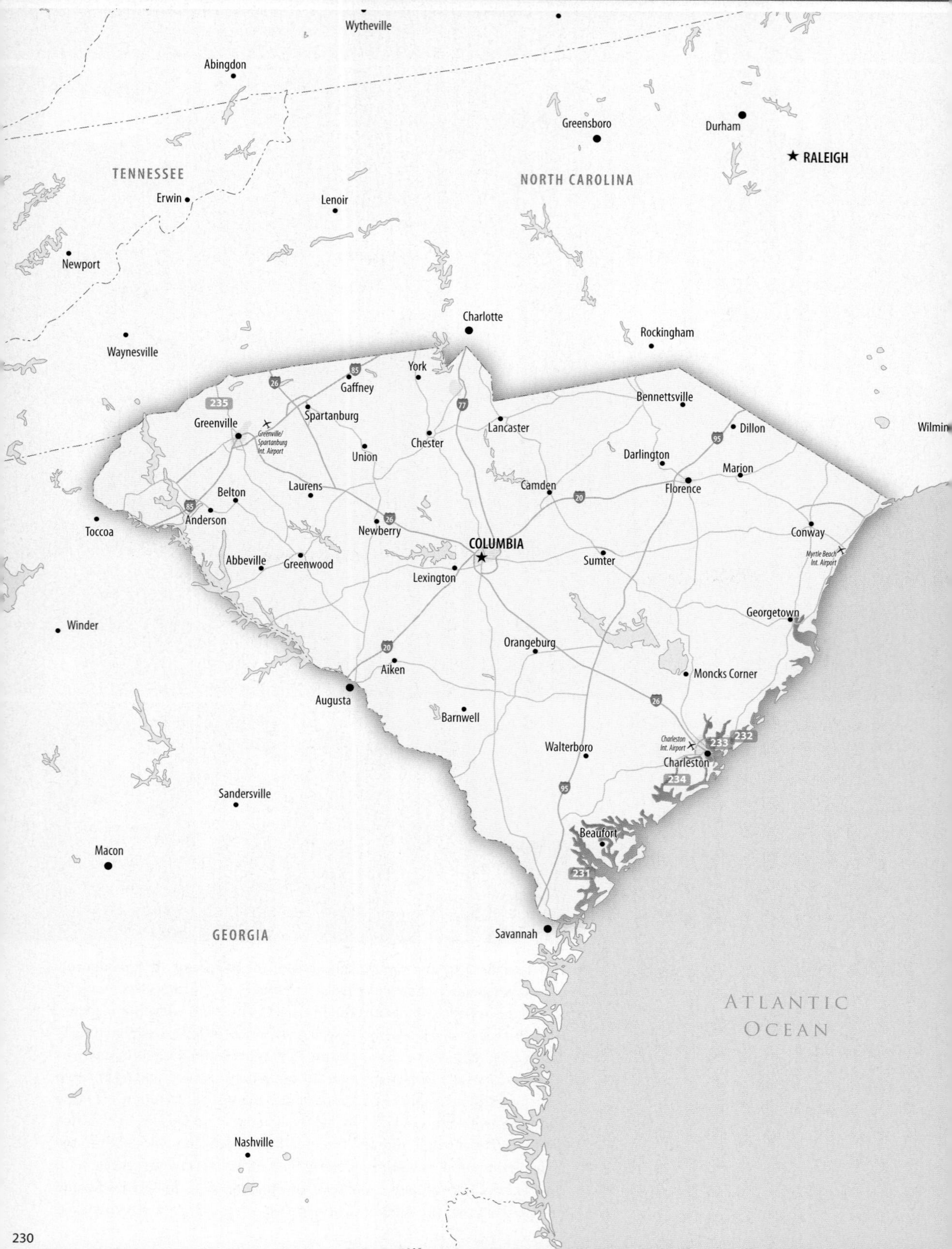

THE INN AT PALMETTO BLUFF

476 MOUNT PELIA ROAD, BLUFFTON, SOUTH CAROLINA 29910
Tel: +1 843 706 6500 **Fax:** +1 843 706 6550 **U.S./Canada Toll Free:** 1 866 706 6565
Web: www.johansens.com/palmettobluff **E-mail:** reservations@palmettobluffresort.com

Our inspector loved: *The spacious cottages, variety of activities and unique spa treatments!*

Price Guide:
rooms $475-$950

50 100 SPA

Awards/Ratings: Condé Nast Johansens Most Excellent Golf Resort, U.S.A. & Canada 2007

Attractions: May River Golf Course, 5-min walk; Daufuskie Island History Tours, 30-min drive; Historic Savannah, 45 miles
Towns/Cities: Hilton Head, 20 miles; Savannah, 45 miles; Charleston, 100 miles
Airports: Hilton Head Airport, 30-min drive; Savannah Airport, 45-min drive; Charleston Airport, 100 miles

Affiliations: The Leading Small Hotels of the World

Capturing the essence of Southern hospitality in South Carolina's Lowcountry, The Inn at Palmetto Bluff is one of the region's premier golf and spa resorts. This graceful and romantic 50-room cottage inn offers a private and spacious hideaway feel perfect for a relaxing escape or golf break. Each well-appointed room has beautiful water views, vaulted ceilings, pine floors and luxury linens. You can choose from the exceptional fine dining at the River House Dining Room, with its signature South Carolina Lowcountry dishes, the more casual May River Grille, the new Canoe Club Restaurant or Buffalo's. After a day of golf at the 18-hole Jack Nicklaus Signature May River Golf Club, why not relax in the full-service Spa at Palmetto Bluff, set beside serene waterways, lush gardens and moss-laden oak trees. The Inn is an idyllic location for weddings, corporate retreats and family getaways.

U.S.A. - SOUTH CAROLINA (CHARLESTON)

The Boardwalk Inn at Wild Dunes Resort

5757 PALM BOULEVARD, ISLE OF PALMS, SOUTH CAROLINA 29451
Tel: +1 843 886 6000 **Fax:** +1 843 886 2916 **U.S./Canada Toll Free:** 1 877 221 0901
Web: www.johansens.com/boardwalk **E-mail:** reservations@wilddunes.com

The Boardwalk Inn is an impeccable AAA 4 Diamond hotel, named one of the Readers' Choice Top 10 U.S. Resort Hotels in Condé Nast Traveler, 2007. In the heart of the premier ocean-front Wild Dunes Resort overlooking the Grand Pavilion, the newly refurbished combination of elegant Charleston architecture with informal island style, exudes Old World charm. Each guest room and suite is spacious and comfortable, and the relaxed coastal décor complements the light, airy atmosphere. There are several dining options: The Sea Island Grill offering fresh seafood dishes; and the 2 newest additions, the laid-back Lettered Olive, serving modern à la carte and buffet-style meals and the gourmet Hudson's Market. Outdoor facilities available to adults and children alike are superb: there are 2 award-winning golf courses, 17 Har-Tru tennis courts, a marina, beautifully landscaped tropical pool complex and fitness center.

Our inspector loved: *The spectacular view of the ocean, and the comfort of the rooms.*

Price Guide:
rooms $120-$450
suites $170-$875

93 350 SPA

Attractions: Boone Hall Plantation, 9 miles; Patriot's Point, 9 miles; Fort Sumter, 10 miles; South Carolina Aquarium, 10 miles
Towns/Cities: Charleston, 15 miles; Pawleys Island, 90 miles; Savannah, 120 miles
Airports: Charleston International Airport, 25 miles; Myrtle Beach Airport, 100 miles

Charleston Harbor Resort & Marina

20 PATRIOTS POINT ROAD, CHARLESTON, SOUTH CAROLINA 29464
Tel: +1 843 856 0028 **Fax:** +1 843 856 8333 **U.S./Canada Toll Free:** 1 888 856 0028
Web: www.johansens.com/charlestonharbor **E-mail:** reservations@charlestonharborresort.com

Our inspector loved: *The beautifully decorated rooms and wonderful views of the harbor and Charleston from the balconies.*

Price Guide:
rooms $129-$300
suites $225-$995

130 250

Attractions: Patriots Point Golf Course and U.S.S. Yorktown, 0.5 miles; Fort Sumter, 1 mile; Beaches, 8 miles; South Carolina Aquarium, 10 miles
Towns/Cities: Pawleys Island, 90 miles; Savannah, 100 miles
Airports: Charleston International Airport, 12 miles; Myrtle Beach Airport, 100 miles

Offering an uncommon blend of unique Low Country culture, exciting downtown revelry and resort-style pampering, Charleston Harbor includes a full-service marina and stunning championship golf course that meanders along the Atlantic coast. With 459 slips, the marina ranks as South Carolina's largest pleasure boat refuge with concierge service extended to all marina guests. In return, the marina launches sailboat charters, romantic dinner cruises and fishing trips for land-based guests. Most rooms and suites have private balconies or Juliette terraces with views of the water, city skyline or historic Fort Sumter. The Grille restaurant has an international focus, and drinks are served at the beachfront Tiki Bar or the Reel Bar, decorated with antique fishing reels from the 1920s. The harbor-side pool and private beach are ideal settings for oyster roasts and island-style theme parties.

The Sanctuary at Kiawah Island Golf Resort

ONE SANCTUARY BEACH DRIVE, KIAWAH ISLAND, SOUTH CAROLINA 29455
Tel: +1 843 768 6000 **Fax:** +1 843 768 5150 **U.S./Canada Toll Free:** 1 877 683 1234
Web: www.johansens.com/sanctuary **E-mail:** reservations@thesanctuary.com

The shores of Kiawah Island are home to this luxurious ocean-front hideaway where the custom-made furniture and quality fabrics add to the unflinching attention to detail in this grand yet inviting resort. The Ocean Room restaurant seats 110 and the private wine room and spacious ocean view terrace add a sense of grandeur. Casual dining can be enjoyed in the Jasmine Porch, and drinks taken at the martini bar and grand lobby bar. Enjoy a round of golf at the 5 championship courses including Pete Dye's Ocean Course, host of the 2007 Senior PGA and 2012 PGA Championships, or play tennis on the 23 clay or 5 hard courts before relaxing in the Mobil 5 Star spa, one of only 3 spas in North America earning Mobil's highest accolade.

***Our inspector loved:** The spectacular views of the ocean from every luxurious room.*

Price Guide:
rooms $299-$4,500

255 500 SPA

Awards/Ratings: AAA 5 Diamond; Mobil 5 Star; Condé Nast Johansens Most Excellent Golf Resort 2006; Condé Nast Traveler Gold List 2007; Wine Spectator Best of Award of Excellence 2007

Attractions: Charleston Museum, 25 miles; Charles Towne Landing, 25 miles; Fort Sumter, 25 miles; Cypress Gardens, 50 miles
Towns/Cities: Charleston, 45-min drive; Hilton Head, 70 miles; Savannah, 80 miles
Airports: Private Executive Airport, 15-min drive; Charleston International Airport, 45-min drive

Affiliations: Preferred Hotels & Resorts

La Bastide

10 ROAD OF VINES, TRAVELERS REST, SOUTH CAROLINA 29690
Tel: +1 864 836 8463 **Fax:** +1 864 836 4820 **U.S./Canada Toll Free:** 1 877 836 8463
Web: www.johansens.com/labastide **E-mail:** frontdesk@cliffscommunities.com

Our inspector loved: *The magnificent view of the vineyards from the most luxurious room! You will never want to leave!*

Price Guide: (including breakfast)
rooms $260-$310

13 16 7

Attractions: Table Rock State Park, 15 miles; The Greenville Museum of Art and Tryon Fine Arts Center, 20 miles; Lake Keowee, 25 miles; Blue Ridge Parkway, 45 miles
Towns/Cities: Greenville, 20 miles; Hendersonville, NC, 20 miles; Asheville, NC, 45 miles
Airports: Greenville/Spartanburg International Airport, 25 miles; Charlotte Douglas Airport, 110 miles

Framed by lush vineyards at the foothills of the Blue Ridge Mountains, La Bastide is an intimate country inn and restaurant. Relax in a hand-made bed within your individually decorated room, or cozy up by the fire and sip a glass of wine in the living room lounge. Alternately, take a leisurely stroll through the vineyards. For those wishing to explore the area, the inn's central location affords easy access to Greenville and the Lakes Region of South Carolina as well as the historic towns of Hendersonville and Asheville, North Carolina. The restaurant emphasizes upscale farm fresh cuisine from the inn's very own organic farm and the highest quality natural meats and seafood.

Tennessee

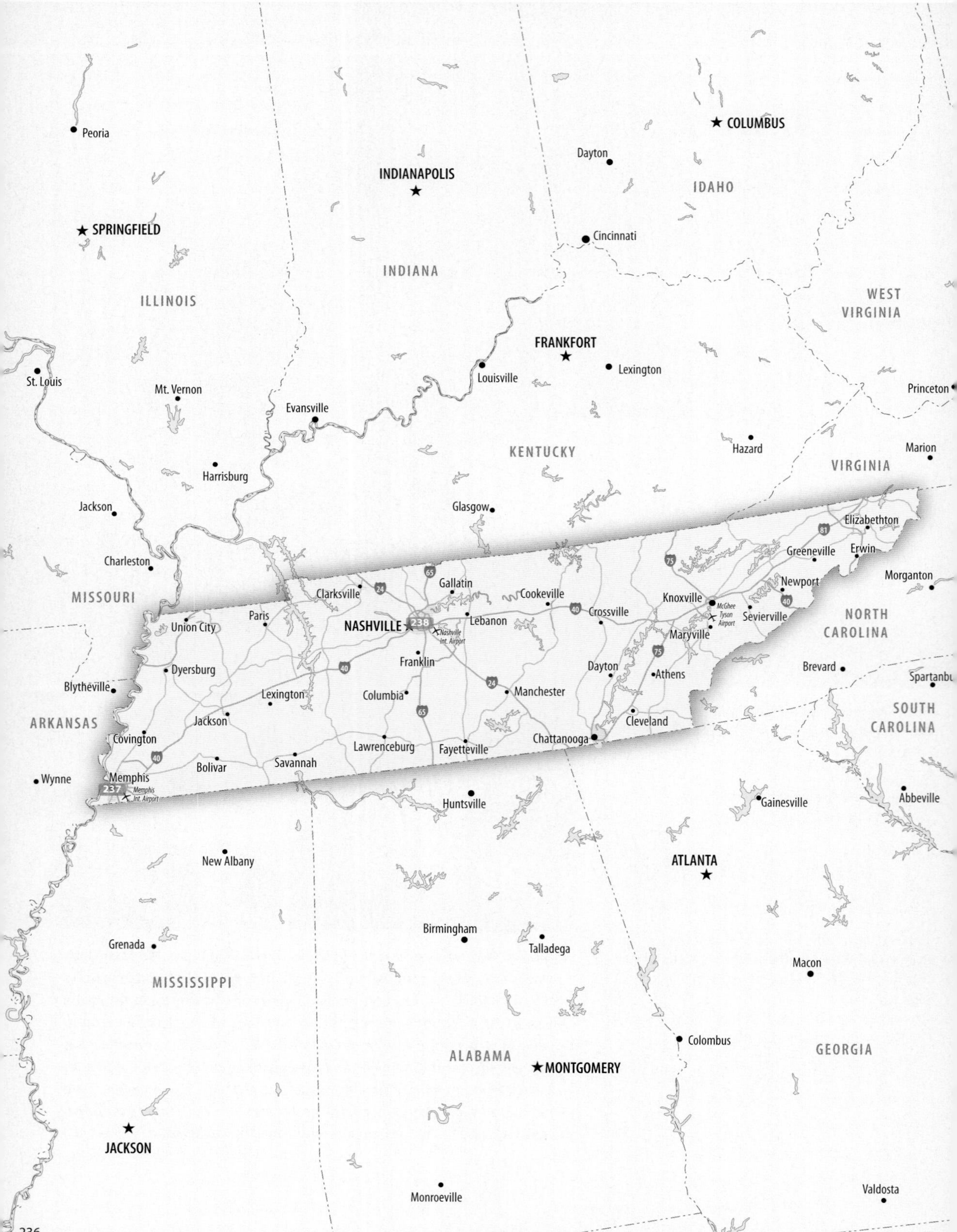
Peoria
SPRINGFIELD
ILLINOIS
INDIANAPOLIS
INDIANA
COLUMBUS
Dayton
IDAHO
Cincinnati
WEST VIRGINIA
FRANKFORT
Louisville
Lexington
St. Louis
Mt. Vernon
Evansville
Princeton
KENTUCKY
Hazard
Marion
VIRGINIA
Harrisburg
Jackson
Glasgow
Elizabethton
Charleston
Greeneville
Erwin
MISSOURI
Gallatin
Clarksville
Cookeville
Knoxville
Newport
Morganton
Union City
Paris
NASHVILLE
238
Lebanon
Crossville
McGhee Tyson Airport
Sevierville
NORTH CAROLINA
Nashville Int. Airport
Maryville
Dyersburg
Franklin
Dayton
Athens
Brevard
Spartanbu
Blytheville
Lexington
Columbia
Manchester
ARKANSAS
Jackson
Cleveland
SOUTH CAROLINA
Covington
Lawrenceburg
Fayetteville
Chattanooga
Bolivar
Savannah
Wynne
Memphis
237
Memphis Int. Airport
Huntsville
Gainesville
Abbeville
New Albany
ATLANTA
Birmingham
Talladega
Grenada
Macon
MISSISSIPPI
Colombus
GEORGIA
ALABAMA
MONTGOMERY
JACKSON
Monroeville
Valdosta

U.S.A. - TENNESSEE (MEMPHIS)

THE RIVER INN OF HARBOR TOWN

50 HARBOR TOWN SQUARE, MEMPHIS, TENNESSEE 38103
Tel: +1 901 260 3333 **Fax:** +1 901 260 3290 **U.S./Canada Toll Free:** 1 877 222 1531
Web: www.johansens.com/riverinnmemphis **E-mail:** reservation@riverinnmemphis.com

Our inspector loved: *The excellent service in this elegant inn that overlooks the Mississippi River.*

Price Guide: (including breakfast)
rooms $245-$340
suites $375-$595

Awards/Ratings: Wine Spectator Award of Excellence 2008

Attractions: Beale Street and Orpheum Theatre, 5-min drive; Memphis Zoo, 10-min drive; Graceland, 15-min drive
Towns/Cities: Nashville, 120 miles; Little Rock Arkansas, 130 miles; St. Louis Missouri, 280 miles; New Orleans, 400 miles
Airports: Memphis Airport, 20-min drive; Nashville Airport, 2-hour drive

Affiliations: Preferred Boutique

The charm of the Old South and European style mix together to form The River Inn of Harbor Town, located on the banks of the majestic Mississippi River. The lobby is reminiscent of the antique South, with chandeliers, a New Orleans mantel and wood flooring from a Virginia textile mill. Guest rooms include four-poster beds, fine linens, white duvets and luxurious pillows, as well as windows with flowering window boxes and lovely views. Currents Restaurant offers a fine dining experience, or there is Tug's Bar and Grill with more casual fare. Relax with a glass of port or wine in the Little Bar. While in Memphis make sure to take a riverboat cruise on the Mississippi or experience a tour of Beale Street and the legendary jazz, blues and rock 'n' roll.

THE HERMITAGE HOTEL

231 SIXTH AVENUE NORTH, NASHVILLE, TENNESSEE 37219
Tel: +1 615 244 3121 **Fax:** +1 615 254 6909 **U.S./Canada Toll Free:** 1 888 888 9414
Web: www.johansens.com/hermitagetn **E-mail:** info@thehermitagehotel.com

Situated in the heart of Nashville, The Hermitage is a picture of elegant grandeur. This historic hotel opened in 1910 and was recently renovated to feature paneled walls, ornate vaulted ceilings and polished floors in its public spaces. Luxurious refinement pervades its guest rooms, many of which offer views of the Nashville skyline, and special touches such as afternoon tea and evening cocktails are served in the grand lobby. Complimentary newspapers are delivered to your room in the morning, and a Pampering Pet Program and special Family Offerings lend this opulent hotel a feeling of personal warmth. Fine dining is offered in the Capitol Grille, which uses only the freshest local ingredients and serves 3 meals a day. The distinguished, rich wood-paneled Oak Bar serves drinks.

Our inspector loved: *The exquisite décor and furnishings as well as the convenient location for so many attractions.*

Price Guide:
rooms $249-$439
suites $800-$2,200

122 200

NR
HP

Awards/Ratings: AAA 5 Diamond; Mobil 5 Star

Attractions: Broadway, 5-min walk; Schermerhorn Symphony Center, 5-min walk; Tennessee Performing Arts Center, 5-min walk; Country Music Hall of Fame, 5-min walk
Towns/Cities: Knoxville, 180 miles; Memphis, 197 miles
Airports: Nashville International Airport, 10 miles; Knoxville Airport, 180 miles

Affiliations: Preferred Hotels & Resorts

DENVER
COLORADO
Colorado Springs
KANSAS
Kansas City
JEFFERSON CITY
JEFFERSON CITY
Wichita
MISSOURI
Branson
Raton
SANTA FE
Albuquerque
NEW MEXICO
Roswell
as Cruces
Woodward
Dalhart
Perryton
Pampa
Amarillo
Amarillo Int. Airport
OKLAHOMA
Tulsa
OKLAHOMA CITY
Batesville
LITTLE ROCK
Mena
Duncan
Childress
Plainview
Littlefield
Lubbock Preston Smith Int. Airport
Lubbock
Brownfield
ARKANSAS
Wichita Falls
Sherman
New Boston
Magnolia
Greenville
Dallas/Fort Worth Int. Airport
Ft. Worth
Dallas
Shreveport
Longview
Tyler
Snyder
Abilene
Stephenville
Corsicana
Big Spring
El Paso Int. Airport
El Paso
Odessa
Midland
Palestine
Lufkin
Alexandria
Pecos
San Angelo
Waco
Jasper
LOUISIANA
Brady
Belton
Fort Stockton
Huntsville
Alpine
Jennings
AUSTIN
George Bush Intercontinental Airport
Beaumont
Kerrville
Austin-Bergstrom Int. Airport
Houston
San Anonio Int. Airport
Del Rio
Uvalde
San Antonio
Cuero
Wharton
Galveston
CHIHUAHUA
Eagle Pass
Victoria
Port Lavaca
Beeville
Alice
Corpus Christi
Nuevo Laredo
Laredo
Monclova
MEXICO
Zapata
Raymondville
GULF OF MEXICO
Brownsville
Reynosa
Matamoros
Gómoz Palacio
Torreón
SALTILLO
MONTERREY
DURANGO
CIUDAD VICTORIA
ZACATECAS
240
241
242
243
244

Mansion at Judges' Hill

1900 RIO GRANDE, AUSTIN, TEXAS 78705
Tel: +1 512 495 1800 **Fax:** +1 512 495 1869 **U.S./Canada Toll Free:** 1 800 311 1619
Web: www.johansens.com/judgeshill **E-mail:** reservations@judgeshill.com

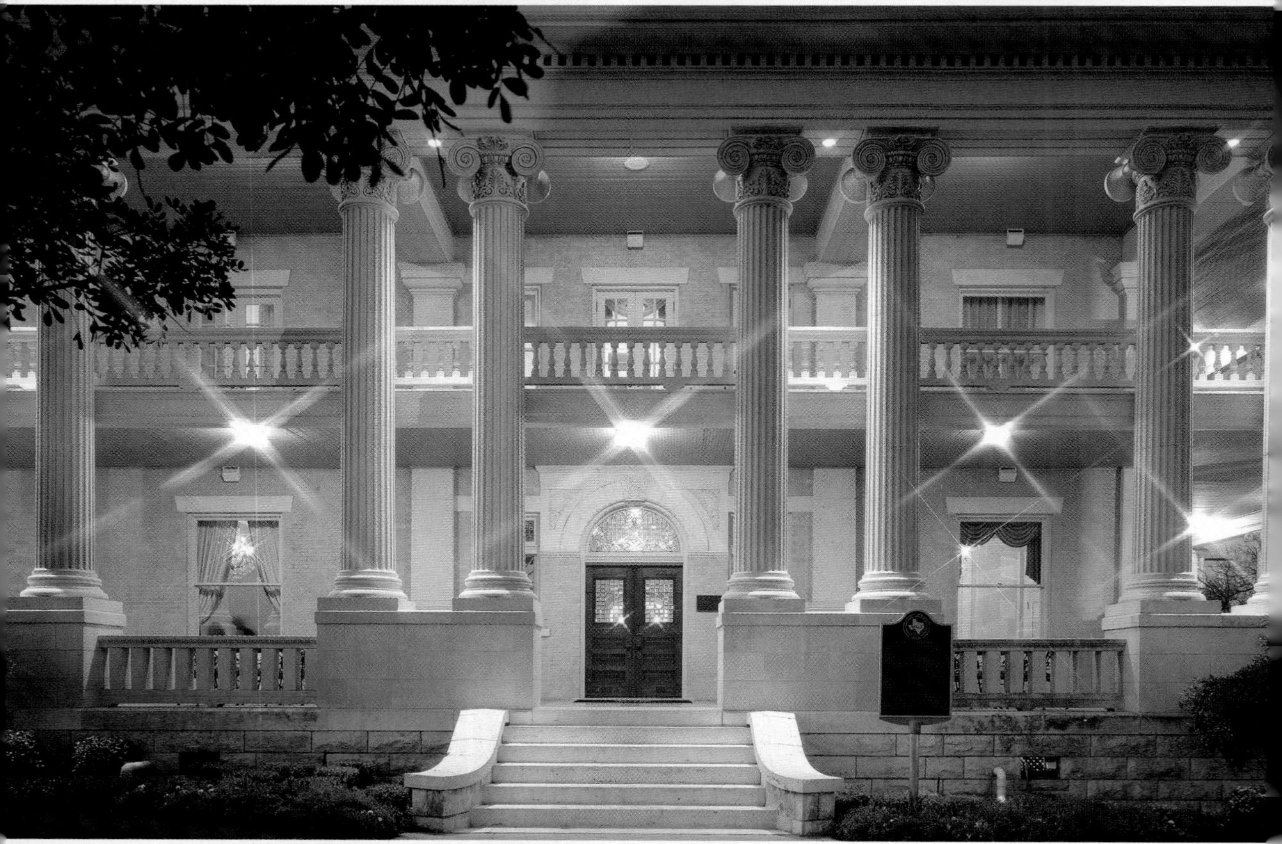

Our inspector loved: *The food at Judges' Hill restaurant that should not be missed!*

Price Guide: (room only)
rooms $169-$399
suites $299-$399

48 300 NR HP

Attractions: 6th Street, 1 mile; Convention Center, 2 miles; University of Texas, 5-min walk; State Capitol, 10-min walk
Towns/Cities: Georgetown, 35 miles; San Antonio, 60 miles
Airports: Austin Bergstrom International Airport, 12 miles

Built in 1900, the Goodall Wooten House is now home to Austin's premier luxury boutique hotel and fine dining restaurant. This restored 19th-century mansion offers a serene, refined atmosphere reminiscent of a bygone era. While located deep within the heart of Austin, the Mansion is set in a secluded area away from the business district traffic and day-to-day noise of downtown Austin. The 48 guest rooms feature rich colors, textures and tapestries along with bathrooms decorated in mosaic tiles and marble flooring. From the seasonal menu to the ever-expanding wine list, Judges' Hill Restaurant & 1900 Bar offer a memorable dining experience whether sitting in the exquisite dining room or outside on the breezy veranda. The Mansion is also a wonderfully unexpected setting for meetings, weddings and special events; the highly-trained, professional staff can transform any space to create the perfect ambience for any occasion.

U.S.A. - TEXAS (DALLAS)

THE JOULE

1530 MAIN STREET, DALLAS, TEXAS 75201

Tel: +1 214 748 1300 **Fax:** +1 214 261 4499 **U.S./Canada Toll Free:** 1 888 625 4988

Web: www.johansens.com/thejoule **E-mail:** thejoule@luxurycollection.com

Our inspector loved: *The innovative design features of the hotel, especially the rooftop pool cantilevered over Main Street.*

Price Guide:
rooms $270-$1,345

129 100 NR HP

Attractions: Dallas Cultural District, 1 mile; Dallas Convention Center, 1 mile; American Airlines Area, 1 mile
Towns/Cities: Airports: Dallas/Fort Worth Airport, 20 miles; Dallas Love Field Airport, 6 miles; Fort Worth, 32 miles
Airports: Dallas Love Field Airport, 6 miles; Dallas/Fort Worth Airport, 20 miles; Fort Worth, 32 miles

The Joule, a member of The Luxury Collection by Starwood Hotels and Resorts, is a beautifully restored property with a 1920s, neo-Gothic façade and elegant, striking interiors. Spacious guest rooms are sleek in design and include duplex suites and a penthouse with private access and a rooftop terrace. Each room has high-end finishes and the latest in modern conveniences and amenities. Inspired décor and original furniture, with rich color palates and black and white historic photographs, create an eye-catching contemporary feel. The heated rooftop pool is yours to enjoy seasonally. The acclaimed chef and restaurateur, Charlie Palmer, has created a distinctive American menu including a stylish underground bar where you can enjoy late night cocktails. The hotel is ideally located at one of Dallas's most prestigious addresses.

THE INN ON LAKE GRANBURY

205 WEST DOYLE STREET, GRANBURY, TEXAS 76048
Tel: +1 817 573 0046 **Fax:** +1 817 573 0047 **U.S./Canada Toll Free:** 1 877 573 0046
Web: www.johansens.com/lakegranbury **E-mail:** info@innonlakegranbury.com

Our inspector loved: *The tranquil lake views and memorable gourmet breakfasts!*

Price Guide: (including appetizers, beverages and a full breakfast)
rooms $225-$325
suites $325-$375

Attractions: Granbury Opera House, 5-min walk; Granbury Live Entertainment, 5-min walk; Barking Rocks Winery, 5 miles; Fossil Rim Wildlife Park, 20 miles
Towns/Cities: Forth Worth, 35 miles; Dallas, 80 miles
Airports: Dallas Fort Worth Airport, 75 miles

This private oasis, on approximately 2 acres of landscaped gardens and scenic lake-front views, provides a tranquil environment to renew your vitality. Cozy up to fire pits, relax by the flagstone pool or bask at the soothing waterfall with tanning ledge. Each guest room at the inn is luxurious and unique; some have sitting areas and outside porches, all have feathered beds and fine linens. Recreational options abound on the scenic Lake Granbury, and downtown offers fine dining options and Broadway plays and musicals. With its spacious conference room and grounds, this is an idyllic setting for a corporate retreat, business meeting, family reunion or wedding.

HOTEL GRANDUCA

1080 UPTOWN PARK BOULEVARD, HOUSTON, TEXAS 77056
Tel: +1 713 418 1000 **Fax:** +1 713 418 1001 **U.S./Canada Toll Free:** 1 888 GRANDUCA
Web: www.johansens.com/granduca **E-mail:** info@granducahouston.com

Our inspector loved: *The wonderful books about all things Italian, architecture, food, wine and history that are in every room of the hotel.*

Price Guide: (including breakfast)
rooms $305-$325
suites $375-$2,400

Attractions: Houston Galleria, 1 mile; Houston Ballet, 5 miles; Houston Rockets Basketball, 10 miles; Houston Astros - Minute Maid Park, 10 miles
Towns/Cities: Galveston, 50 miles; Austin, 150 miles; San Antonio, 200 miles; Dallas, 230 miles
Airports: Houston Hobby Airport, 25 miles; George Bush Intercontinental Airport, 25 miles

Affiliations: The Leading Hotels of the World

Hotel Granduca is a new luxury hotel in the Uptown/Galleria area. The spacious guest rooms range in size from standard rooms at 425 sq. ft. to a 3-bedroom suite at 2,100 sq. ft. These lavish accommodations include plasma H.D.T.V.s, concierge, valet and luxury courtesy transportation anywhere within a 3-mile radius and to the Medical Center. The complimentary Business Center will meet your business needs as well as 2 state-of-the-art Conference rooms. For your social needs enjoy Salone Rialto. Dine in the warm and intimate Ristorante Cavour, which serves Northern Italian gourmet cuisine with a French accent, or relax in the beautiful courtyard, refined lounge or billiard room. Unwind by the pool just steps away from the fitness facility, or step across the street to the renowned Uptown Park Shopping Center.

Inn at Dos Brisas

10,000 CHAMPIONS DRIVE, WASHINGTON, TEXAS 77880
Tel: +1 979 277 7750 **Fax:** +1 979 277 7751
Web: www.johansens.com/dosbrisas **E-mail:** reservations@dosbrisas.com

The Inn at Dos Brisas is an impressive retreat on 300 beautiful acres offering the best in fine dining and casita-style luxury accommodations. Welcomed with keys to the ranch, you will find your own Spanish-styled casita has views of the meadows, horse paddocks and a pond with a golf cart for exploring the grounds. Relax by the infinity pool, enjoy an en-suite spa service or partake in an array of outdoor activities. Executive Chef Jason Robinson will provide you with a sophisticated culinary experience with his award-winning organic cuisine in the most romantic of settings. Savor the 8-course "grand collection" menu, breakfast on the patio of your own casita or a gourmet picnic lunch. On special request, the inn will schedule a private tasting for you in their 5,000 bottle wine cellar.

Our inspector loved: *The quiet luxury of the inn's country setting, and the amazing epicurean offerings.*

Price Guide: (including breakfast and Chef's Choice lunch, excluding 12.75% state tax)
Casitas $650

Awards/Ratings: Mobil 5 Star 2008; Wine Spectator's Best of Award of Excellence 2008

Attractions: Monastery of Saint Clare, 4 miles; Festivals at Chappell Hill, 6 miles; Blue Bell Ice Cream Factory, 12 miles; Washington on Brazos, 11 miles
Towns/Cities: Brenham, 13 miles; College Station, 42 miles; Houston, 70 miles; Austin, 105 miles
Airports: Brenham Municipal, 8 miles; Houston Bush Intl, 75 miles; Austin Bergstrom, 100 miles

Affiliations: Relais & Châteaux

American Falls
IDAHO
Lander
WYOMING
Preston
84
15
Logan
Kemmerer
Brigham City
NEVADA
Green River
Ogden
Evanston
84
80
Farmington
80
Salt Lake City Int. Airport
80
Manila
SALT LAKE CITY
247
Tooele
Heber City
Provo
Vernal
Duchesne
15
Nephi
Ely
Price
Delta
Manti
Castle Dale
Fillmore
Grand Junction
70
Richfield
70
Moab
246
Beaver
Loa
Delta
Panguitch
Cedar City
Monticello
COLORADO
15
Blanding
St George Municipal Airport
St. George
Kanab
Cortez
Colorado City
Kayenta
Aztec
ARIZONA
NEW MEXICO
Tusayan

U.S.A. - UTAH (MOAB)

Sorrel River Ranch Resort & Spa

MILE 17 SCENIC BYWAY 128, H.C. 64 BOX 4002, MOAB, UTAH 84532
Tel: +1 435 259 4642 **Fax:** +1 435 259 3016 **U.S./Canada Toll Free:** 1 877 359 2715
Web: www.johansens.com/sorrelriver **E-mail:** stay@sorrelriver.com

On a bend in the Colorado River, amid dramatic Red Rock cathedrals, Sorrel River Ranch Resort & Spa basks in peaceful seclusion beneath a flawless desert sky. Luxury accommodations, abundant outdoor activities, gourmet dining and full-service spa complete this impressive CloudNine Resort's resumé. Well-appointed guest rooms have kitchenettes, private decks and charming Western appeal. Some offer fireplaces and stunning river or mountain views. Those who yearn for adventure will enjoy mountain biking, hiking, 4x4 off-road driving and river-rafting on the Colorado, followed by a riverside gourmet dining experience at the acclaimed Sorrel River Grill. For the perfect complement to your active vacation, the Health Spa's skilled therapists provide pampering and rejuvenation preparing you for more excitement tomorrow!

Our inspector loved: *Watching the Colorado River flow by the porch.*

Price Guide: (incl daily in-room mini-bar, excl. tax)
mountain/river views $359-$429
family suites $649

52 M 200 SPA

Awards/Ratings: Condé Nast Johansens Most Excellent Ranch, U.S.A. & Canada 2007

Attractions: Colorado River, on-site; Fisher Towers, 5 miles; Arches National Park, 19 miles; Canyonlands National Parks, 46 miles
Towns/Cities: Moab, 20 miles; Grand Junction, Colorado, 80 miles; Salt Lake City, 250 miles; Las Vegas, NV, 480 miles
Airports: Moab, 30 miles; Grand Junction Colorado, 80 miles; Salt Lake City, 250 miles

Affiliations: Small Luxury Hotels of the World

The Sky Lodge

201 HEBER AVENUE AT MAIN STREET, P.O. BOX 683300, PARK CITY, UTAH 84068
Tel: +1 435 658 2500 **Fax:** +1 435 615 6751 **U.S./Canada Toll Free:** 1 888 876 2525
Web: www.johansens.com/skylodge **E-mail:** reservations@TheSkyLodge.com

Our inspector loved: *The amazing views of Old Town Park City and ski areas from the warm fireplace of the SkyClub.*

Price Guide:
1-bedroom suites $375-$925
2-bedroom suites $525-$1,525
penthouses $650-$3,000

33 SPA

Attractions: Sundance Film Festival, 1-min walk; Art Galleries, 1-min walk; Ski In/Ski Out via Town Lift to Deer Valley, 5-min walk; Outdoor Concerts, 10-min drive
Towns/Cities: Salt Lake City, 25 miles; Sundance, 41 miles; Moab, 250 miles
Airports: Heber Airport with Private Jet Service, 20-min drive; Salt Lake City International Airport, 25-min drive

Affiliations: Small Luxury Hotels of the World

The Sky Lodge is a stylish and modern 5-star luxury CloudNine Resort, unique for its Rocky Mountain loft design. Its ultra-chic suites are bold and modish and feature private radiant-heated decks, outdoor hot tubs, luxury bedding and custom Kohler bathrooms. Huge picture windows allow you to take in the scenic views of Park City Mountain Resort, Bald Mountain and historic Old Town. No detail has been overlooked and the resort boasts no antlers in sight. Après-ski, unwind at the Amatsu Spa, which was inspired by an 800-year-old Japanese tradition of Ofuro Baths. Savor the cuisine at the new seafood restaurant, Fin, or opt for the romantic brasserie featuring international cuisine. Cocktails at Bar Boheme will make you feel you are in Paris in the middle of Park City.

Vermont

St-Hyacinthe
Granby
Montréal
CANADA
QUÉBEC
Newport
MAIN
Swanton
89
91
Guildhall
North Hero
St. Albans
Hyde Park
St. Johnsbury
Plattsburgh
Winooski
Burlington Int. Airport
Burlington
S. Burlington
MONTPELIER
Barre
NEW HAMPSHIRE
Vergennes
251
Chelsea
Randolph
Middlebury
NEW YORK
Bethel
White River Jct.
Laconia
Woodstock
Rutland
Ludlow
249
Newport
CONCORD
Wallingford
Springfield
Bellows Falls
Hudson Falls
250
Manchester Center
Newfane
Keene
Brattleboro
Bennington
MASSACHUSETTS
Johnstown
Greenfield
Worcester
Schenectady
Troy

Castle Hill Resort & Spa

JCT. ROUTES 103 AND 131, CAVENDISH, VERMONT 05142
Tel: +1 802 226 7361 **Fax:** +1 802 226 7301 **U.S./Canada Toll Free:** 1 888 764 6836
Web: www.johansens.com/castlehillvt **E-mail:** sales@thecastle-vt.com

Our inspector loved: *The spa, located in the circa 1860 carriage house, with heated walkways that melt snow.*

Price Guide:
deluxe rooms $275-$375
suites $325-$425
resort homes $275-$975

20 60 SPA NR HP

Attractions: Okemo Mountain Resort, 3 miles; President Coolidge Historic State Site, 12 miles; Marsh-Billings-Rockefeller National Historical Park, 21 miles; Manchester Village, 35 miles
Towns/Cities: Weston, 15 miles; Woodstock, 20 miles; Burlington, 122 miles; Montréal, QC, 220 miles
Airports: Hartford Bradley Intl., 126 miles; Boston Logan, 158 miles; New York City Airports, 248 miles

Affiliations: Small Luxury Hotels of the World

Set in Vermont's scenic Green Mountains, Castle Hill Resort & Spa offers intimate and elegant accommodations and serves as the perfect destination for a wedding, honeymoon or just for a relaxing getaway. Choose to stay in the mansion where rooms exude a sense of historic elegance updated with modern comforts, or in one of Castle Hill's Resort Homes, which provide plenty of privacy and room for friends and family. The Green Mountains offer an abundance of daytime activities, including snowboarding and snow shoeing in the winter. Hiking, biking and fly-fishing are popular during the summer months. Castle Hill's classic dining room, with its wood-paneled walls and subtle antique flair, provides a cozy and historic atmosphere for you to enjoy French-inspired American cuisine made from fresh local produce and meats.

EQUINOX GOLF RESORT & SPA

3567 MAIN STREET, MANCHESTER, VERMONT 05254
Tel: +1 802 362 4700 **Fax:** +1 802 362 4861 **U.S./Canada Toll Free:** 1 800 270 2132
Web: www.johansens.com/equinoxresort **E-mail:** reservations@equinoxresort.com

The Equinox Golf Resort & Spa is a luxurious base from which to explore everything Vermont has to offer. Choose from diverse options for accommodation, from rooms and suites with custom-made beds and plush pillows in the main inn to luxury town homes and historic, refurbished country inns. Any choice will offer stunning views of Vermont's rolling hills and striking landscape. Indulge in an oversized steak at the Chop House, dine in history at the Marsh Tavern or experience a traditional clambake outdoors at the Dormy Grill. Enjoy 18 holes at the Equinox Golf Club, relax at the Spa, go fly-fishing, shooting or take a day to explore the lovely shops and restaurants in nearby Manchester Village. Lastly, learn how to handle a hawk at the British School of Falconry, located close by.

Our inspector loved: *Sitting in a rocking chair on the great porch and enjoying the view of the village green.*

Price Guide:
deluxe $299-$499
superior $369-$549
suites $499-$1,400

195 200 SPA

Attractions: Hildene-Lincoln Family Home, 1 mile; Manchester Designer Outlets, 2 miles; Stratton and Bromley Ski Resorts, 15 miles; VT Country Store, 40 miles;
Towns/Cities: Albany, NY, 70 miles; Burlington, 120 miles; Boston, MA, 189 miles; New York City, NY, 204 miles
Airports: Albany International Airport, 70 miles; Bradley International/Hartford Airport, CT, 146 miles

THE PITCHER INN

275 MAIN STREET, P.O. BOX 347, WARREN, VERMONT 05674
Tel: +1 802 496 6350 **Fax:** +1 802 496 6354
Web: www.johansens.com/pitcherinn **E-mail:** info@pitcherinn.com

Our inspector loved: *The wonderfully appointed Mallard Room with the built-in nature sounds.*

Price Guide: (Sunday - Thursday rates include a 3-course dinner)
rooms $425-$800

11 M 14 WiFi SPA

Attractions: Warren Country Store, 2-min walk; Sugarbush Golf Course, 5 miles; Skiing/ Snowboarding, 5 miles; Mad River Valley Soaring, 10 miles
Towns/Cities: Burlington, 45 miles; Montréal, QC, 140 miles; Boston, MA, 190 miles; New York City, NY, 325 miles
Airports: Burlington Intl. Airport, 45 miles; Albany Intl. Airport, 135 miles; Boston (Logan) Intl. Airport, MA, 190 miles

Affiliations: Relais & Châteaux

The Pitcher Inn is a delightful 11-room and suite inn located in the heart of Vermont's Green Mountains, at the foot of Sugarbush Resort. Welcoming guests since the early 1850s, each charming Vermont-themed room is located in the main house or in the adjacent barn brimming with original art, memorabilia and antiques. The Main Dining Room offers à la carte menus or for more casual fare there is Tracks. Chef Sue Schickler's seasonal menus highlight some of Vermont's freshest ingredients including lamb, quail, rabbit, organic vegetables, artisanal cheeses and seafood. The smell of freshly baked goods will wake you up each morning, and in the afternoon, enjoy tea and afternoon cocktails in the Library. Go ahead and treat yourself to some time at the Alta Day Spa where an array of spa and beauty treatments is available.

Virginia

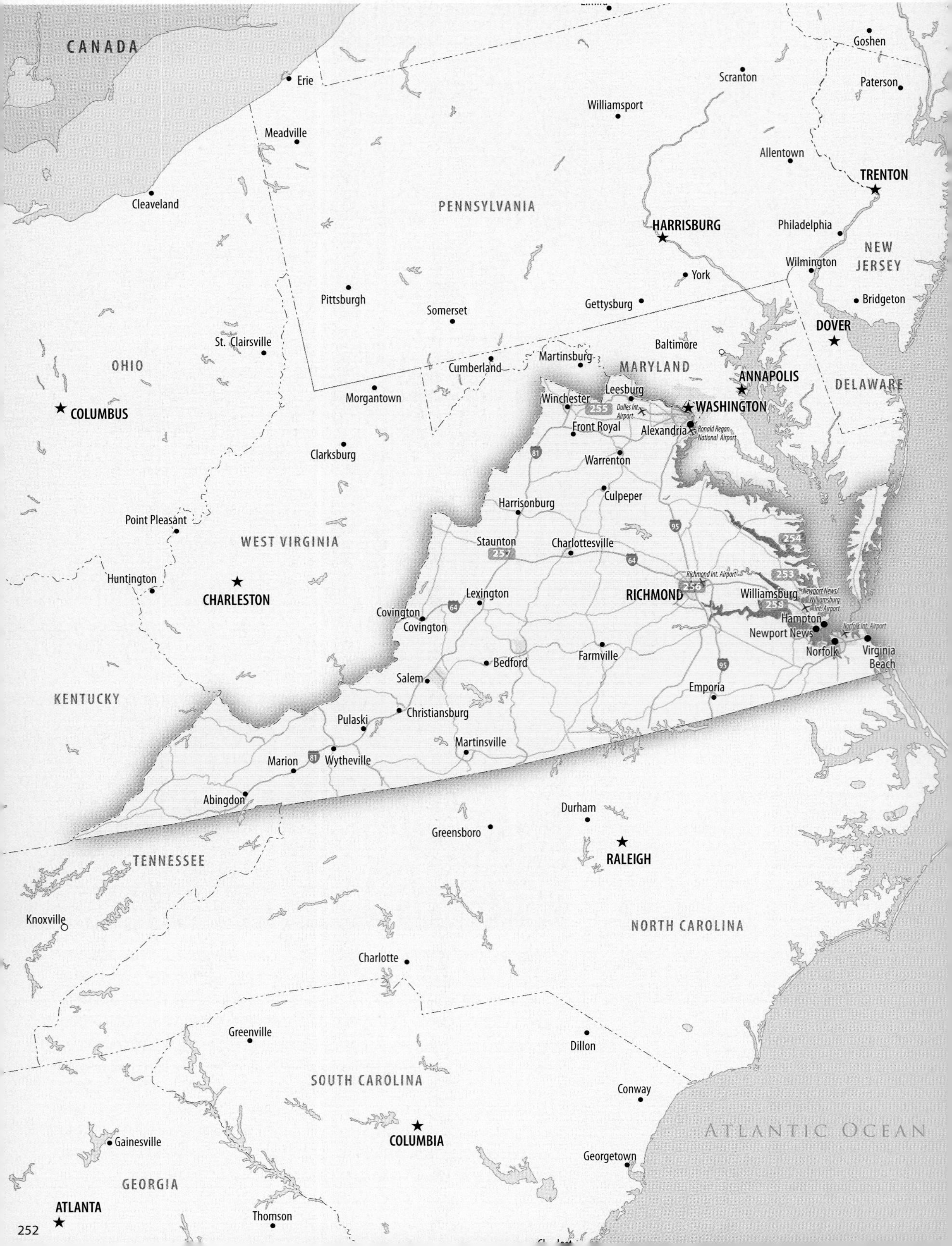
CANADA
Erie
Meadville
Cleaveland
PENNSYLVANIA
Scranton
Goshen
Paterson
Williamsport
Allentown
TRENTON
HARRISBURG
Philadelphia
NEW JERSEY
Wilmington
York
Bridgeton
Gettysburg
Pittsburgh
Somerset
DOVER
Baltimore
St. Clairsville
OHIO
Cumberland
Martinsburg
MARYLAND
ANNAPOLIS
DELAWARE
Morgantown
Winchester
Leesburg
255
Dulles Int. Airport
WASHINGTON
COLUMBUS
Front Royal
Alexandria
Ronald Regan National Airport
Clarksburg
81
Warrenton
Culpeper
Harrisonburg
Point Pleasant
95
WEST VIRGINIA
Staunton
257
Charlottesville
254
64
Richmond Int. Airport
253
Huntington
CHARLESTON
Lexington
RICHMOND
256
Williamsburg
Newport News/ Williamsburg Int. Airport
258
Covington
Hampton
Norfolk Int. Airport
Newport News
Norfolk
Virginia Beach
Farmville
Bedford
Salem
Emporia
KENTUCKY
Christiansburg
Pulaski
Martinsville
Marion
Wytheville
Abingdon
Durham
Greensboro
RALEIGH
TENNESSEE
Knoxville
NORTH CAROLINA
Charlotte
Greenville
Dillon
SOUTH CAROLINA
Conway
COLUMBIA
ATLANTIC OCEAN
Gainesville
Georgetown
GEORGIA
ATLANTA
Thomson

The Inn at Warner Hall

4750 WARNER HALL ROAD, GLOUCESTER, VIRGINIA 23061
Tel: +1 804 695 9565 **Fax:** +1 804 695 9566 **U.S./Canada Toll Free:** 1 800 331 2720
Web: www.johansens.com/warnerhall **E-mail:** info@warnerhall.com

Our inspector loved: *The large, elegant and immaculate rooms that reflect a fascinating history.*

Price Guide:
rooms $175-$245

Attractions: Yorktown 11 miles; Colonial Williamsburg, 25 miles; Jamestown Settlement, 32 miles
Towns/Cities: Norfolk, 40 miles; Richmond, 45 miles; Virginia Beach, 50 miles
Airports: Williamsburg Airport, 28 miles

Established as a plantation by George Washington's great-great grandfather in 1642, this Colonial-Revival waterfront manor house has been restored to its original grandeur and transformed into a modern country inn. Many famous historic figures have ties to the inn, including Meriwether Lewis, General Robert E. Lee and Queen Elizabeth II. Each of the rooms has period antiques and Schumacher fabrics as well as comfortable seating areas, private baths and Gilchrist Soames products. The 38 acres of grounds include the tranquil Severn River where complimentary kayaks, canoes, fishing equipment and bicycles are available, and native wildlife and natural wonders of tidewater Virginia can be enjoyed. Formal dining is available on weekends, while during the week, sumptuous supper baskets can be enjoyed at the location of your choice.

HOPE AND GLORY INN

65 TAVERN ROAD, IRVINGTON, VIRGINIA 22480
Tel: +1 804 438 6053 **Fax:** +1 804 438 5362 **U.S./Canada Toll Free:** 1 800 497 8228
Web: www.johansens.com/hopeandglory **E-mail:** inquiries@hopeandglory.com

Our inspector loved: *The fun and hopelessly romantic outdoor shower.*

Price Guide:
rooms $185-$295
cottages $250-$350
tents $310-$695

Attractions: Downtown Irvington, 0.1 miles; White Fences Vineyard & Winery, 0.3 miles; Waterfront, 0.4 miles; Colonial WIlliamsburg, 53 miles
Towns/Cities: Williamsburg, 53 miles; Richmond, 70 miles; Norfolk, 77 miles; Washington D.C., 145 miles
Airports: Richmond International Airport, 64 miles; Reagan National Airport, 143 miles

Set on the picturesque Chesapeake Bay Shore, Hope and Glory is a whimsical and elegantly restored schoolhouse with several guest cottages, each with their own private gardens. Children are welcome in the cottages only. The inn caters more to adult travelers looking for serenity. The surrounding English gardens are a gardener's delight, filled with old fashioned single hollyhocks, David Austin roses, artemesias and flowers rare to Virginia. A favorite area of the inn is the winding pathway that leads to a private outdoor shower, complete with a claw-foot tub and sink. In the evenings relax in the dreamy moon garden, and on a Friday night take part in the crab feast on the inn's 42-foot boat, The Faded Glory, and the prix-fixe wine paired "Dinner at our Chef's Table" on a Saturday. 7 additional cottages called "tents" are located within White Fences Vineyard & Winery.

THE GOODSTONE INN & ESTATE

36205 SNAKE HILL ROAD, MIDDLEBURG, VIRGINIA 20117
Tel: +1 540 687 4645 **Fax:** +1 540 687 6115 **U.S./Canada Toll Free:** 1 877 219 4663
Web: www.johansens.com/goodstoneinn **E-mail:** information@goodstone.com

Our inspector loved: *The gorgeous grounds and beauty surrounding this historic estate.*

Price Guide: (including full country breakfast, afternoon tea and golf at Stoneleigh Golf Club)
rooms $250-$515
junior suites $285-$530
suites $300-$610

17 40 10 Wi Fi

Attractions: Steeplechase Races, 2 miles; Downtown Middleburg, 3 miles; Shenandoah National Park, 50 miles; Washington D.C., 50 miles
Towns/Cities: Middleburg, 2 miles
Airports: Dulles International Airport, 25 miles

Affiliations: Small Luxury Hotels of the World

This superb inn is located in the heart of Virginia's famous hunt country and wine region. Situated on 265 acres of estate grounds with the Blue Ridge Mountains visible in the distance, each of the individually decorated guest rooms and suites is located in residences renovated in elegant English and French country styles. The heart of the inn is the Carriage House where afternoon tea is served daily and Hilltoppers is located. Complimentary recreational activities include mountain biking, canoeing, woodland nature trails and gardens. On-site massage and horse-trail rides in the foothills of the mountains can be arranged.

THE JEFFERSON

101 W. FRANKLIN STREET, RICHMOND, VIRGINIA 23220
Tel: +1 804 788 8000 **Fax:** +1 804 225 0334 **U.S./Canada Toll Free:** 1 800 424 8014
Web: www.johansens.com/jeffersonva **E-mail:** reservationsdept@jeffersonhotel.com

A historic hotel nestled in downtown Richmond, The Jefferson has welcomed an extensive number of celebrities and notable guests including 11 U.S. Presidents. Known for its grand setting and exceptionally gracious hospitality, the beautiful Beaux Arts and Renaissance Revival architectural styles and impressive public spaces make for a stately setting, while luxurious guest rooms offer a warm and welcoming residential feel. Throughout the hotel are high ceilings and windows, elegant custom furnishings such as beautiful mahogany armoires, sophisticated artwork and decorative carpets. And there are 2 restaurants: Lemaire Restaurant, providing upscale Southern cuisine and the more casual T.J.'s Restaurant and Lounge. Other dining options include excellent afternoon tea and Sunday brunch. The Salon at The Jefferson offers a unique variety of pampering services but if you wish to explore Richmond, the hotel's courtesy car is at your service.

***Our inspector loved:** The spectacular lobby.*

Price Guide:
superior and deluxe rooms $270-$395
suites $415-$2,100

262 450 NR HP

Awards/Ratings: AAA 5 Diamond 2008; Mobil 5 Star 2008; DiRoNA 2007; Wine Spectator Award of Excellence 2007

Attractions: State Capitol, 5-min walk; Children's Museum of Richmond, 1.5 miles; Museum of Fine Arts, 2 miles; Carytown Shopping District, 2 miles
Towns/Cities: Williamsburg, 50 miles; Charlottesville, 69 miles; Virginia Beach, 106 miles; Washington, D.C., 110 miles
Airports: Richmond Intl, 10 miles; Reagan National, Washington D.C., 107 miles

Affiliations: Preferred Hotels & Resorts

FREDERICK HOUSE

28 NORTH NEW STREET, STAUNTON, VIRGINIA 24401
Tel: +1 540 885 4220 **Fax:** +1 540 885 5180 **U.S./Canada Toll Free:** 1 800 334 5575
Web: www.johansens.com/frederickhouse **E-mail:** stay@frederickhouse.com

Our inspector loved: *The personalized concierge service.*

Price Guide: (including breakfast)
oversized guest rooms $139-$189
1-bedroom suites $169-$199
2-bedroom suites $209-$269

23 25

Attractions: American Shakespeare Center, 0.1 miles; Woodrow Wilson Presidential Library, 0.1 miles; Frontier Cultural Museum, 2 miles; Skyline Drive/Blue Ridge Parkway, 15 miles
Towns/Cities: Charlottesville, 30 miles; Roanoke, 90 miles; Richmond, 120 miles; Washington D.C., 180 miles
Airports: Shenandoah Valley Regional Airport, 15 miles; Charlottesville Airport, 30 miles; Richmond Airport, 120 miles

3 adjoining 19th-century town houses and 2 mid-1800 residences lie in the quiet downtown of historic Staunton; a great starting point for a tour of Virginia's sites. Frederick House's intimate ambience reflects the conviviality of this small town, and its impeccable hospitality now includes a personalized concierge service that allows you to order custom room touches like birthday cakes, flowers and more. The earliest of the Frederick houses dates back to 1809 and is the epitome of period elegance with its Federal staircase. Each of the rooms has been painstakingly designed to incorporate period features and charm with modern facilities. Each is also uniquely decorated with original antiques, books and pictures. Making careful use of the building's hillside setting, the balconies, terraces and front porches are the perfect location to enjoy a glass of wine before attending the theater or enjoying the many restaurants nearby.

Wedmore Place

5810 WESSEX HUNDRED, WILLIAMSBURG, VIRGINIA 23185
Tel: +1 757 941 0310 **Fax:** +1 757 941 0318 **U.S./Canada Toll Free:** 1 866 933 6673
Web: www.johansens.com/wedmoreplace **E-mail:** info@wedmoreplace.com

A European-themed country hotel on the outskirts of Colonial Williamsburg, Wedmore Place is situated on 300 acres of vineyards, forest and meadowlands and is rich in culture and history. Each of the elegant, luxuriously appointed rooms is styled in the theme of a different European province and period of history. The Corinthian Room, inspired by ancient Greece, features a large marble statue, white ceramic tiling, and Corinthian columns. The sumptuous Venetian Suite has an impressive 20-foot, frescoed ceiling. Each room has wood-burning fireplaces, antique furnishings, king-size beds and reading material about the history the room is depicting. The hotel has an English club-inspired library, a pool set within woodland, and a main dining room, Café Provençal, which serves Mediterranean cuisine. The Williamsburg Winery and Gabriel Archer Tavern are located adjacent to the property and offers special food and wine pairing dinners every Thursday night.

***Our inspector loved:** The European style and state-of-the-art amenities that enhance the wonderful guest experience.*

Price Guide: (including European Continental breakfast and a tour and wine tasting at The Williamsburg Winery)
rooms $190-$395
suites $300-$750

28 48 12 WiFi

Attractions: Colonial Williamsburg, 3 miles; Jamestowne/Yorktown Settlements, 5 miles; Busch Gardens, 5 miles; Outlet Shopping, 10 miles
Towns/Cities: Williamsburg, on-site; Richmond, 50 miles; Virginia Beach, 65 miles
Airports: Newport News/Williamsburg International Airport, 26 miles; Richmond International Airport, 50 miles; Norfolk/Virginia Beach International Airport, 55 miles

Affiliations: Small Luxury Hotels of the World

CANADA
Kamloops
BRITISH COLUMBIA
Kelowna
Vancouver
Hope
Princeton
Nelson
Grand Forks
Creston
VICTORIA
261
Bellingham
5
Mount Vernon
Port Angeles
Port Townsend
Everett
266
Okanogan
Republic
Colville
PACIFIC OCEAN
262
267
264
260
263
Seattle
Seattle/Tacoma Int. Airport
Shelton
Tacoma
90
OLYMPIA
Wenatchee
Newport
Sandpoint
Spokane
265
Spokane Int. Airport
Ephrata
Grant County Int. Airport
Ellensburg
Ritzville
South Bend
Chehalis
82
St. Maries
Yakima
Seaside
Kelso
Colfax
St. Helens
Moscow
Grandview
Pasco
Vancouver
Clarkston
Goldendale
Portland
Hood River
Walla Walla
IDAHO
Pendleton
Grangeville
SALEM
Newport
OREGON
Eugene
Prineville
Baker City
Weiser
BOISE

THE BELLEVUE CLUB HOTEL

11200 S.E. 6TH STREET, BELLEVUE, WASHINGTON 98004
Tel: +1 425 455 1616 **Fax:** +1 425 688 3197 **U.S./Canada Toll Free:** 1 800 579 1110
Web: www.johansens.com/bellevue **E-mail:** hotel@bellevueclub.com

Our inspector loved: *The wonderful 180,000 sq. ft. athletic facility adjacent to the hotel.*

Price Guide:
rooms $265-$335
suites $625-$1,500

67 M300 WiFi SPA

Attractions: Bellevue Square, 15-min walk; Newcastle Golf and Country Club, 7 miles; Downtown Seattle, 12 miles
Towns/Cities: Redmond, 8 miles; Seattle, 12 miles; Woodinville, 12 miles
Airports: Seattle/Tacoma International Airport, 17 miles

Affiliations: Small Luxury Hotels of the World

Surrounded by lush green gardens, yet in close proximity to downtown Seattle, The Bellevue Club Hotel is an ideal oasis with a distinct air of seclusion and luxury. The hotel offers a truly all-inclusive experience where guests can enjoy the Club's extensive athletic and social resources, or simply unwind in the comfortable living room setting of The Terrace Room with coffee each morning and tea and cookies in the afternoon. There are no less than 3 restaurants ranging from Polaris's sophisticated and chic atmosphere to the Luna Express Café's menu of espresso drinks, sandwiches and salads. Set just 15 minutes from Seattle's waterfront, and in the heart of downtown Bellevue, this is the perfect location to enjoy the innumerable dining, gallery and outdoor activities in the area.

THE CHRYSALIS INN AND SPA

804 10TH STREET, BELLINGHAM, WASHINGTON 98225
Tel: +1 360 756 1005 **Fax:** +1 360 647 0342 **U.S./Canada Toll Free:** 1 888 808 0005
Web: www.johansens.com/chrysalis **E-mail:** info@thechrysalisinn.com

Our inspector loved: *The large window seats in every room with the panoramic view of Bellingham Bay.*

Price Guide: (including breakfast)
rooms $209-$249
suites $299-$349

42 50 SPA

Attractions: Walking Trails; Kayaking, 5-min walk; Vineyards, 14 miles; Mount Baker, 50 miles
Towns/Cities: Bellingham, 20-min walk; Vancouver, BC, 45 miles; Seattle, 90 miles
Airports: Bellingham Airport, 7 miles

Set on the waterfront in the historic Fairhaven district, this peaceful inn captures the essence of the Northwest. The architectural style is modern and distinct and is ideal for a romantic weekend or undisturbed business meeting. The bedrooms are cleverly designed with corner fireplaces and deep window seats perfect for relaxing with a glass of wine. Modern cherrywood bathrooms feature 2-person tubs with marvelous views of the Northwest seascape. The Inn's restaurant, Fino Wine Bar, serves classic European food and wine and features a popular "exhibition" kitchen where the chef produces regional and international specialties. The Chrysalis Spa is a sensory delight with stone floors, glass art and soothing music.

U.S.A. - WASHINGTON (KIRKLAND)

The Heathman Hotel

220 KIRKLAND AVENUE, KIRKLAND, WASHINGTON 98033
Tel: +1 425 284 5800 **Fax:** +1 425 284 5888 **U.S./Canada Toll Free:** 1 800 551 0011
Web: www.johansens.com/heathmanwa **E-mail:** infokirkland@heathmanhotel.com

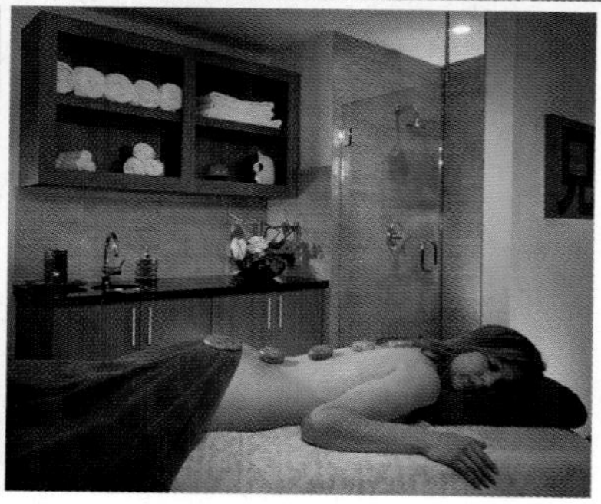

Our inspector loved: *The bed and pillow menu, and the fantastic spa and gym.*

Price Guide:
rooms $239-$279
suites $309-$3,000

91 M 200 SPA

Attractions: Downtown Kirkland, 1-min walk; Marina Park, 1-min walk; Bellevue Museum, 3 miles; Wineries, 10 miles
Towns/Cities: Bellevue, 3 miles; Redmond, 4 miles; Seattle, 8 miles
Airports: SEA-TAC International Airport, 18 miles

Understated elegance awaits you at The Heathman Hotel, located in downtown Kirkland. Each guest room is designed with a sense of nature, reflecting the waterfront community in which it is located. But before enjoying your stay, select the type of pillow and mattress for your bed! There are 3 options to choose from, each designed for different preferences and sleeping styles. Make sure to dine at Trellis, where the farm-to-table cuisine includes produce from the chef's very own 3-acre farm and fare from local foragers and ranchers. Trellis also offers a wine list of over 200 local and international wines. Venture outside and take a stroll along Kirkland's tree-lined boulevards, jog by the shore of Lake Washington, or visit Wednesday's local Farmer's Market. And then treat yourself after a long day of exploring by relaxing at Penterra Spa with one of their many signature treatments.

U.S.A. - WASHINGTON (SEATTLE)

HOTEL ÄNDRA

2000 FOURTH AVENUE, SEATTLE, WASHINGTON 98121
Tel: +1 206 448 8600 **Fax:** +1 206 441 7140 **U.S./Canada Toll Free:** 1 877 448 8600
Web: www.johansens.com/hotelandra **E-mail:** hotelandra@hotelandra.com

Our inspector loved: *The lovely wooden ceiling to floor length mirrors in every room.*

Price Guide:
ändra studios-ändra rooms $309-$329
ändra suites-ändra lux suites $339-$400

119 30

Attractions: Pike Place Market, 5-min walk; Downtown Shopping, 5-min walk; Space Needle, 15-min walk; Waterfront, 15-min walk
Towns/Cities: Seattle, on-site; Bellevue, 11 miles
Airports: Seattle Airport, 15 miles

Affiliations: Small Luxury Hotels of the World

Close to the fashionable and thriving retail neighborhood of Belltown, which is renowned for its innovative art, music and dining scene, Hotel Ändra is a stylish retreat with a welcoming atmosphere. The interior features strong Northwestern décor with Scandinavian design influences, rich wooden furnishings and ambient lighting. The impressive Lobby Living Room is filled with rich woods and wool hand-knotted rugs, and each bedroom and suite displays original artwork and has a plush bed fitted with goose-down comforters, an oversized walnut desk and modern features. Highly-acclaimed chef/author Tom Douglas oversees the Northwest ingredients served in the Greek-inspired Lola restaurant. Alternately, Assaggio Ristorante serves authentic Italian cuisine.

INN AT THE MARKET

86 PINE STREET, SEATTLE, WASHINGTON 98101
Tel: +1 206 443 3600 **Fax:** +1 206 448 0631 **U.S./Canada Toll Free:** 1 800 446 4484
Web: www.johansens.com/innatthemarket **E-mail:** info@innatthemarket.com

Nestled in the heart of Seattle's famous Pike Place Market is this stylish boutique hotel offering stunning views of both the bustling market and beautiful Elliot Bay, as well as a great location minutes from downtown tourist attractions, shopping and dining. The elegant lobby and friendly staff welcome you the minute you step through the door. Contemporary Pacific Northwest-styled guest rooms, for either leisure or business travelers, have every amenity including complimentary WiFi access and tempur-pedic beds. After a day of shopping and sightseeing, relax in the courtyard and dine at Campagne, where Southern France cuisine is served. Other dining choices include Café Campagne, a French bistro, and Bacco, an inventive juice bar. This is a great choice for exploring everything downtown Seattle has to offer.

Our inspector loved: *The rooftop garden chairs for a great view of the sunset and island ferries on the sparkling waterways.*

Price Guide:
rooms $235-$625

70 25

Awards/Ratings: Condé Nast Traveler Gold List 1994-2008

Attractions: Pike Place Market, on-site; Downtown Shopping, 5-min walk; Seattle Art Museum, 5-min walk; Ferries, 15-min walk
Towns/Cities: Seattle, on-site; Bellevue, 11 miles
Airports: Seattle, 12 miles

THE DAVENPORT HOTEL AND TOWER

10 SOUTH POST STREET, SPOKANE, WASHINGTON 99201
Tel: +1 509 455 8888 **Fax:** +1 509 624 4455 **U.S./Canada Toll Free:** 1 800 899 1482
Web: www.johansens.com/davenport **E-mail:** reservations@thedavenporthotel.com

Our inspector loved: *The custom-made Davenport beds wrapped in the finest linens, and the historical walking tour of the property.*

Price Guide:
rooms $299-$369
suites $419-$2,500

611 500 SPA NR HP

Awards/Ratings: Condé Nast Traveler Gold List 2008

Attractions: Bing Crosby Theater, 1-min walk; River Park Square Shopping, 2-min walk; Fox Theater, 2-min walk; Riverfront Park, 5-min walk
Towns/Cities: Spokane, on the doorstep; Coeur D' Alene, 26 miles; Idaho, 26 miles
Airports: Spokane Airport, 8 miles

This stately hotel was established in 1914 and retains its classical architecture and large formal rooms that create the perfect atmosphere for meetings, parties and weddings. Each guest room and suite is spacious and well-planned. The Penthouse floor houses the most spectacular collection of suites. The Venetian-inspired Hall of the Doges and the Grand Pennington Ballroom combine to accommodate 500 guests for banquets, and some smaller meeting rooms seat 150. The Palm Court Grill restaurant serves a selection of Northwest-inspired cuisine accompanied by a fine wine selection, and the Lobby fireside is great for breakfast, tea or cocktails. The Tower's Safari Room Fresh Grill and Bar Restaurant offers seasonally-inspired dishes. The 328-room Tower, located across the street, adds a contemporary flavor of world travel.

Sun Mountain Lodge

P.O. BOX 1,000, WINTHROP, WASHINGTON 98862
Tel: +1 509 996 2211 **Fax:** +1 509 996 3133 **U.S./Canada Toll Free:** 1 800 572 0493
Web: www.johansens.com/sunmountain **E-mail:** sunres@methow.com

***Our inspector loved:** The wonderful views of the North Cascade Mountains and the 124 miles of trails on the property.*

Price Guide:
rooms $175-$400
suites $275-$450

96 300 SPA

Awards/Ratings: Wine Spectator Award of Excellence 2008

Attractions: Miles of Hiking and Biking Trails, on-site; Wineries, 10 miles; North Cascade National Park, 25 miles; Lake Chelan, 60 miles
Towns/Cities: Winthrop, 10 miles
Airports: Winthrop Airport, 12 miles; Seattle Airport, 212 miles

Set against the magnificent North Cascade Mountain Range and surrounded by pristine countryside, the AAA 4 Diamond awarded Sun Mountain Lodge is an ideal getaway for nature-lovers, as well as those simply seeking a first-class resort experience in a beautiful setting. The Lodge, situated amidst the second largest cross-country ski trail system in the U.S., offers a myriad of outdoor activities, features large, spacious interiors framed with huge Douglas Fir beams and floors laden with Idaho Quartz. The rooms are filled with hand-made wood furniture and original artwork; many have fireplaces, and all offer breathtaking views. Enjoy innovative dishes using fresh, locally-grown Northwest ingredients in the award-winning Dining Room, and the extensive, 450-label wine list.

THE HERBFARM

14590 NORTH EAST 145TH STREET, WOODINVILLE, WASHINGTON 98072
Tel: +1 425 485 5300 **Fax:** +1 425 424 2925
Web: www.johansens.com/herbfarm **E-mail:** reservations@theherbfarm.com

Our inspector loved: *The 9-course dinner showcasing the foods and wines of the Pacific Northwest.*

Price Guide: (including breakfast)
rooms $300-$395

150 SPA

Awards/Ratings: Wine Spectator Best of Award of Excellence 2008; AAA 5 Diamond

Attractions: Sammamish River Trail, 1-min walk; Wineries, 5-min walk/drive; Redmond Town Center, 9 miles
Towns/Cities: Downtown Woodinville, 4-min drive; Redmond, 9 miles; Seattle, 20 miles
Airports: Seattle Airport, 28 miles

Bask in the warm and personalized hospitality of owners, husband and wife Ron Zimmerman and Carrie Van Dyck, and enjoy the exceptional cuisine, which is the centerpiece of this magnificent place. Themed dinner evenings run throughout the year with menus created just hours before service to utilize the best produce at the peak of its perfection. The majestic 9-course dinners are accompanied by a selection of 5 or 6 fine wines chosen by The Herbfarm's sommeliers. The Herbfarm offers 2 luxurious suites on the property in romantic Willows Lodge. The Orchard House Suite is decorated in rich hues of red and gold embellished with paintings and sculptures, while the Herb Garden Suite features serene shades of green and mauve complemented by delicate lighting.

Wisconsin

MINNESOTA
Houghton
Duluth
Superior
Ashland
Marquette
MICHIGAN
Escanaba
Iron Mountain
Rhinelander
Menominee
Marinette
Merrill
Antigo
Wausau
Sturgeon Bay
Shawano
Minneapolis
ST PAUL
Hudson
Chippewa Falls
Menomonie
Eau Claire
Green Bay
Austin Straubel Int. Airport
Stevens Point
Appleton
Outagamie County Regional Airport
Wisconsin Rapids
Waupaca
Red Wing
Manitowoc
Oshkosh
Sheboygan
Rochester
Winona
Owatonna
Sparta
Fond du Lac
West Bend
Portage
Port Washington
Baraboo
Austin
Richland Center
Milwaukee
Decorah
Jefferson
Waukesha
General Mitchell Int. Airport
MADISON
Dane County Regional Airport
Charles City
Prairie du Chien
Racine
Elkhorn
Janesville
Kenosha
IOWA
Monroe
Waukegan
Dubuque
Waterloo
Manchester
Rockford
ILLINOIS
Freeport
Chicago
Geneva
Maquoketa
Dixon
Cedar Rapids
94
39
90
43
269

THE CLARKE HOTEL

314 WEST MAIN STREET, WAUKESHA, WISCONSIN 53186
Tel: +1 262 549 3800
Web: www.johansens.com/clarkehotel **E-mail:** info@theclarkehotelwi.com

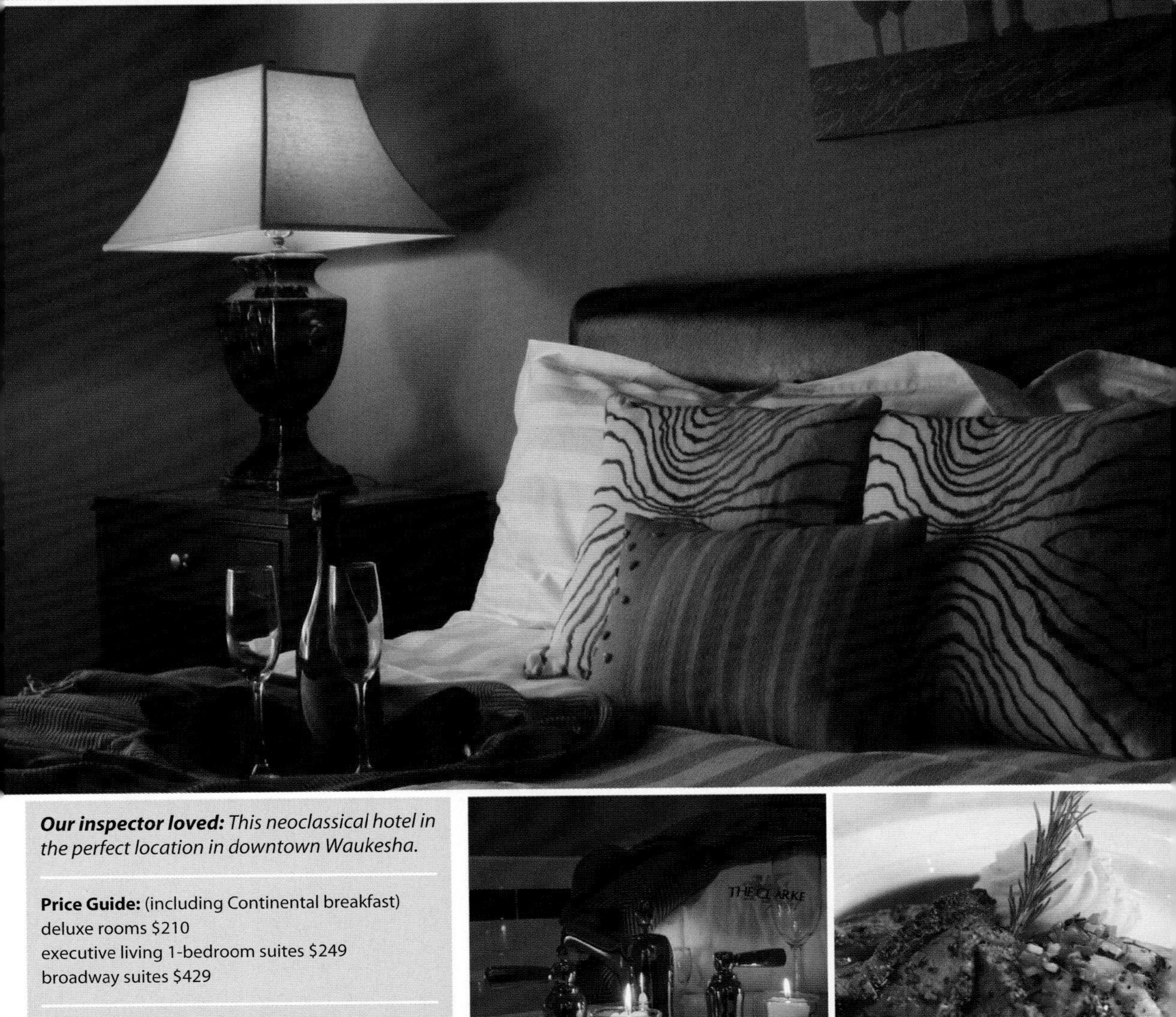

Our inspector loved: *This neoclassical hotel in the perfect location in downtown Waukesha.*

Price Guide: (including Continental breakfast)
deluxe rooms $210
executive living 1-bedroom suites $249
broadway suites $429

Attractions: Shops, Theater, Cafés, Restaurants, Art Galleries, Outdoor Music (Seasonal), 1-min walk; Riverwalk, 2-min walk; Retzer Nature Center and Planetarium, 10-min drive; Ten Chimneys National Historic Landmark, 15-min drive
Towns/Cities: Milwaukee, 10 miles; Madison, 60 miles; Chicago, 100 miles; Green Bay, 130 miles
Airports: Waukesha Crites Field, 5 miles; Milwaukee General Mitchell International Airport, 20 miles; Madison Dane Co. Regional Airport, 63 miles

Located in the historic downtown area of Waukesha, The Clarke Hotel is designed in a neoclassical style and blends beautifully with the surrounding area. Each guest room has a spa-style bathroom with massage tub and/or a body-spray shower system, as well as elegantly appointed furniture and linens. The meeting and banquet rooms are intimate and detailed, ideal for small corporate gatherings with top quality service. The Black Trumpet restaurant on the first floor serves neoclassic cuisine, combining tradition with creativity, giving preference to local sources. And guests can even choose to have a private Wine Locker stocked with their favorite wines. After dinner, relax in the Clarke Bar, offering martinis, vintage wines and top liquors, all set in a unique and exciting way.

Belize

MEXICO
Chetumal
Corozal
Sarteneja
Xcalak
Libertad
Buena Vista
San Roman
Icaiché
Orange Walk
Ambergris Cay
271
August Pine Ridge
Neustadt
272
San Pedro
San Felipe
Corozalito
Crooked Tree
Sond Hill
Burrell Boom
Gallon Jug
Rancho Dolores
Belize
274
Turneffe Islands
Freetown Sibun
Tu-tu Camp
Tikal
BELMOPAN
San Ignacio
273
Gales Point
Melchor de Mencos
San Antonio
BenqueViego del Carmen
CARIBBEA SEA
El Cruce
Dangriga
Hopkins
Cohune Ridge
GUATEMALA
Alabama
Riversdale
Dolores
Placentia Village
Monkey River Town
San Antonio
San Luis
Punta Gorda
Crique Sarco
Barranco
GULF OF HONDURAS
Modesto Méndez
Chahal
Puerto Cortés
HONDURAS

MATACHICA BEACH RESORT

5 MILES NORTH OF SAN PEDRO, AMBERGRIS CAYE
Tel: +501 220 5010/11 **Fax:** +501 220 5012
Web: www.johansens.com/matachica **E-mail:** info@matachica.com

Our inspector loved: *Its unique and very chic, artistic décor.*

Price Guide: (incl. Continental breakfast, and transfers to and from San Pedro Airstrip, excluding 9% hotel tax and 10% service charge)
beach-front casitas U.S.$295-U.S.$415
sea-view suites U.S.$265-U.S.$360
sea-breeze bunglaows U.S.$215-U.S.$280

14 WiFi SPA

Attractions: Hol Chan Marine Reserve, Stingray and Shark Alley, 30-min boat ride; Blue Hole and Atolls for Diving, 2-hour boat ride; Mayan River Jungle Tours, 2-hour boat ride
Towns/Cities: San Pedro, 5 miles; Belize City, 15-min flight; Corozal, 20-min flight; Caye Caulker, 15 miles, 30-min boat ride and 10-min flight
Airports: San Pedro Airstrip, 12-min boat ride; Caye Caulker Airstrip, 10-min flight; Belize International Airport, 20-min flight from San Pedro Airstrip

This rustically elegant boutique hotel, with diverse accommodation options ideal for romantic breaks or family vacations, is partially surrounded by tropical nature and steps away from Belize's Great Barrier Reef. With spacious thatched-roof casitas, bungalows, villas and the beach mansion to choose from, the hotel is Bohemian in style with authentic Central American artefacts and fabrics. The beach-front bar lounge is the perfect place to enjoy music while savoring cognac and Cuban cigars. Enjoy snorkeling, sailing or quietly relaxing in a hammock overlooking the Caribbean Sea. The Jade Spa will pamper you with treatments using only local organic products. At night, dine at the contemporary Mambo restaurant offering fresh seafood and pastas, one of the finest restaurants in Belize. Then enjoy a classic film in the stylish Cinema-Martini Lounge.

BELIZE - AMBERGRIS CAYE (SAN PEDRO)

Victoria House

P.O. BOX 22, SAN PEDRO, AMBERGRIS CAYE
Tel: +501 226 2067 **Fax:** +501 226 2429 **U.S./Canada Toll Free:** 1 800 247 5159
Web: www.johansens.com/victoriahouse **E-mail:** info@victoria-house.com

Situated along a pristine stretch of white sand beach, palm trees and clear turquoise water, this island resort offers the utmost in comfort and tranquility. The absence of radios and telephones ensures that nothing will disturb your relaxation and quiet enjoyment of the abundant natural beauty surrounding this plantation-style property. The varied accommodations include charming thatched-roof casitas with locally handcrafted mahogany beds, the Rainforest Suite, a spacious casita featuring frescoed walls and bamboo furniture, and elegant, fully-equipped infinity poolside private villas. Each accommodation is set in lush gardens with a private balcony or veranda offering sea views. The poolside Restaurant Palmilla serves fresh fish and a variety of Mayan-inspired Caribbean dishes, and Admiral Nelson's Bar features live music under a palapa thatched roof.

***Our inspector loved:** Staying at the beautiful "Infinity Suite" and enjoying its privacy.*

Price Guide:
casitas/plantation-style rooms U.S.$225-U.S.$345
suites/villas U.S.$500-U.S.$1,900

42

Attractions: Hol Chan Marine Reserve, 20-min boat ride; Caye Chapel (18-Golf Course), 45-min boat ride; Great Blue Hole, 90-min boat ride; Caye Caulker, 25-min flight
Towns/Cities: San Pedro Town, 2 miles; Belize City, 17-min flight; Corozal Town, 20-min flight; Dangriga, 40-min flight
Airports: San Pedro Airstrip, 10-min drive; Belize International Airport, 17-min flight; Caye Caulker Airstrip, 25-min flight

THE LODGE AT CHAA CREEK

P.O. BOX 53, SAN IGNACIO, CAYO
Tel: +501 824 2037 **Fax:** +501 824 2501 **U.S./Canada Toll Free:** 1 877 709 8708
Web: www.johansens.com/chaacreek **E-mail:** reservations@chaacreek.com

Our inspector loved: *Taking a very cooling and refreshing swim in the Macal River during the midday heat.*

Price Guide: (including breakfast)
cottages U.S.$135-U.S.$150 per person
suites/macal cottages U.S.$400-U.S.$450
spa villa U.S.$550-U.S.$575

23 75 SPA

Attractions: Guided Nature and Birdwatching Tours, Mountain Biking and Canoeing, on-site; Nearby: Daily Scheduled Maya Archeological Temple, Ceremonial Cave Tours, Tubing and River Floats in the Mountain Pine Ridge, Ziplining and Helicopter Tours
Towns/Cities: San Ignacio, 7 miles; Benque Viejo, 11 miles; Belmopan, 30 miles; Belize City, 77 miles
Airports: Belize Municipal Airport, 70 miles; Belize International Airport, 74 miles; Flores Airport, 84 miles

Perched on the edge of a grassy knoll overlooking the sleepy Macal River in the foothills of the Maya Mountains, The Lodge at Chaa Creek's individually designed thatched cottages reflect an atmosphere of elegance. Charmingly decorated villas and suites blend fine fabrics, elegant furnishings, and antiques to create a romantic ambience in a stunning rainforest setting. Recognized by Travel & Leisure Magazine's Top 25 Best Hotels in Mexico, Central and South America, the recipient of notable environmental accreditations and Condé Nast Traveler Readers' Choice Award in 2007, this 365-acre private reserve offers you a truly unforgettable rainforest experience. Miles of forested trails lead to a Natural History Center, Butterfly Farm, Rainforest Medicine Trail, an Organic Maya Farm and a full-service Spa. Country-wide tours offering easy access to Belize's richest Maya archeological sites, national parks, and Reef and Rainforest Adventures are always available.

Chan Chich Lodge

GALLON JUG, ORANGE WALK DISTRICT
Tel: +501 223 4419 **Fax:** +501 223 4419 **U.S./Canada Toll Free:** 1 800 343 8009
Web: www.johansens.com/chanchich **E-mail:** reservations@chanchich.com

Our inspector loved: *Spotting the spectacle owl and a baby ocelot/leopard during the incredible jungle night walk.*

Price Guide:
regular/standard cabañas U.S.$175-U.S.$250
deluxe cabañas U.S.$200-U.S.$300
villa U.S.$795-U.S.$895

13

This unique jungle lodge is set in the heart of La Selva Maya, beautifully surrounded by the forest within a 130,000-acre private nature reserve. Awarded the Wilderness Lodge of the Year 2007 by Andrew Harper, the Lodge consists of 12 individual thatched-roof cabanas and a beautifully appointed 2-bedroom villa, perfect for family stays. The comfortable thatched-roof cabanas are made with local exotic hardwoods and have fully-screened wraparound verandas. After a day of wandering the extensive trails retracing Mayan footsteps, relax in a hammock, swim in the pool while watching the monkeys swing in the trees or enjoy a tropical drink at sunset. The Lodge serves exquisite Belizean cuisine using the freshest of local ingredients. Wildlife enthusiasts and beginners will enjoy this authentic jungle experience where you might even spot a rare jaguar in its natural habitat!

Attractions: Hiking Trails, Nature Walks and Bird Spotting Excursions, on-site; Canoeing on Laguna Verde, 4 miles; Gallon Jug Estate Farm, Coffee and Cacao Plantations, 20-min drive; Laguna Seca (Bird Habitat), 45-min drive
Towns/Cities: Gallon Jug, 20-min drive; Sylvester Village, 30-min drive; Orange Walk, 95-min drive; Belize City, 30-min flight and 3-hour drive
Airports: Gallon Jug Airstrip, 20-min drive; San Pedro Airstrip, 30-min flight; Belize International Airport, 30-min flight and 3-hour drive

Masaya
Granada
notepe
NICARAGUA
Rivas
Cárdenas
San Carlos
La Cruz
El Castillo
San Juan
del Norte
Upala
Santa Rosa
CARIBBEAN
SEA
Barra del Colorado
Liberia
San Rafael
277
Puerto
Viejo
Cañas
Quesada
Parismina
Santa Cruz
279
Puerto
Moreno
276
Guápiles
Río Jiménez
Naranjo
San Juanillo
Puntarenas
Heredia
Alajuela
SAN JOSÉ
Puerto Limón
San Mateo
Sámara
278
Paquera
Santiago
Cartago
Moravia
Cóbano
Cahuita
Santa María
Esterillos Oeste
281
Quepos
282
San Isidro
Changuinola
Bocas del Toro
Juntas
Almirante
Dominical
Buenos Aires
Palmar
Norte
San Vito
PANAMA
Rincón
Ciudad Neily
Jiménez
280
David
PACIFIC
OCEAN
Puerto Armurelles

EL SILENCIO LODGE & SPA

BAJOS DEL TORO, ALAJUELA
Tel: +506 2291 3044 **Fax:** +506 2232 2183
Web: www.johansens.com/elsilencio **E-mail:** info@elsilenciolodge.com

Situated within a 500-acre private tropical cloud forest reserve next to a gently flowing river, the appropriately named El Silencio Lodge & Spa is an ideal retreat for those seeking peace and quiet in a serene natural setting. Built with environmentally friendly materials, the lodge features 16 luxury suites offering views of either the river or the forest. Each includes a whirlpool tub, gas fireplace and complimentary mini-bar. Rejuvenation and relaxation is taken seriously at El Silencio, with a full-service spa providing a variety of treatments enhanced by the surrounding nature and a yoga platform set within the forest. The daily rate includes 3 meals composed of Costa Rican specialties with an innovative, international flare using fresh, organic ingredients.

Our inspector loved: *The beautiful lush location, and having a personal Eco-Concierge Guide.*

Price Guide: (including 3 daily meals, 2-night minimum stay, price per person, double occupancy)
suites U.S.$210-U.S.$280

16 50 8 SPA

Attractions: Nature Hiking, Lake Kayaking, Horseback Riding and Canopy Zip-lining, 1-hour drive; Sarapiqui River Rafting, 1-hour drive; Arenal and Poas Volcanos, 1-hour drive
Towns/Cities: Sarchi Arts and Crafts Town, 30-min drive; San José, 90-min drive; La Fortuna, 90-min drive
Airports: San José International Juan Santamaria Airport, 90-min drive; San José Tobias Bolanos Domestic Airport, 90-min drive

Tabacón Grand Spa Thermal Resort

LA FORTUNA DE SAN CARLOS, ARENAL
Tel: +506 2519 1999 **Fax:** +506 2519 1940 **U.S./Canada Toll Free:** 1 877 2277 8291
Web: www.johansens.com/tabacon **E-mail:** sales@tabacon.com

Our inspector loved: *Enjoying a meal prepared by my very own personal chef in the beautiful private bungalow.*

Price Guide:
rooms U.S.$260-U.S.$375
suites U.S.$350-U.S.$575

114 60 SPA

Attractions: Arenal Volcano National Park, 10-min drive; Hanging Bridges, 10-min drive; Canopy Tours, Sky Tram & Trek, 20-min drive; White-Water Rafting, 90-min drive
Towns/Cities: La Fortuna, 9 miles; Liberia, 75 miles; San José, 78 miles
Airports: La Fortuna Domestic Airport, 9 miles; San José International Airport - Juan Santamaria, 72 miles; Liberia International Airport - Daniel Oduber International, 81 miles

Affiliations: The Leading Hotels of the World

Set in the heart of the Costa Rican rainforest, this luxury resort serves as the perfect place to rejuvenate and explore stunning natural surroundings. Each of the 114 rooms features deep-soaking tubs and floor-to-ceiling windows allowing you to relax and enjoy the resort's environs from the comfort and privacy of your own room. In Tabacón's Grand Spa you can enjoy the unique experience of soaking in outdoor thermal mineral springs at the base of the Arenal Volcano, and daytime activities, including nature cruises and zip lines, are endless. A hike up the Arenal Volcano, Costa Rica's most active (and closely monitored) volcano, is an unforgettable experience not to be missed. There are both casual and elegant dining options including a private dinner set in a romantic rainforest bungalow prepared for you by your own personal chef.

Hotel Punta Islita

GUANACASTE
Tel: +506 2231 6122 **Fax:** +506 2231 0715
Web: www.johansens.com/hotelpuntaislita **E-mail:** reservas@hotelpuntaislita.com

Hotel Punta Islita offers an authentic Costa Rican experience courtesy of its close ties with surrounding villages and internationally lauded responsible tourism model focusing on community, art and the environment. Spanning 35 acres, its tiered layout discreetly tucks away rooms, suites and family-friendly villas offering privacy and ocean views. Many have private outdoor whirlpools or plunge pools. The 1492 Restaurant, with its open layout and native-inspired 50-foot thatched palm ceiling, serves Costa Rican fusion cuisine, and the Borrancho Beach Club Restaurant provides casual poolside dining. You can participate in unique activities led by local guides such as zip-lining over the forest canopy, monkey safaris or surfing. The on-site Casa Spa offers a menu of stress-reducing treatments including the Punta Islita Ritual, a relaxing blend of Costa Rican healing traditions.

Our inspector loved: *Enjoying the jungle and ocean views from the infinity pool.*

Price Guide:
deluxe rooms U.S.$250-U.S.$350
suites U.S.$360-U.S.$495
villas U.S.$570-U.S.$760

35 30 SPA

Awards/Ratings: CN Johansens Most Excellent Hotel 2008; CN Johansens Most Excellent Eco Resort 2007; Condé Nast Traveler Gold List 2007

Attractions: Contemporary Art Museum, 1 mile; Camaronal Wildlife Refuge, 3 miles; Playa Samara, 9 miles; Cabo Blanco Nature Reserve, 30 miles
Towns/Cities: Samara, 9 miles; Nosara, 15 miles; Tamarindo, 50 miles
Airports: Punta Islita Airport, 2 miles; Liberia Intl. Airport, 70 miles; San José Intl. Airport, 120 miles

Affiliations: Small Luxury Hotels of the World

Paradisus Playa Conchal

BAHÍA BRASILITO, PLAYA CONCHAL, SANTA CRUZ, GUANACASTE
Tel: +506 2654 4123 **Fax:** +506 2654 4181 **U.S./Canada Toll Free:** 1 888 956 3542
Web: www.johansens.com/paradisusplayaconchal **E-mail:** info@paradisusplayaconchal.com

Our inspector loved: *The lovely beach location and the wide selection of water sports.*

Price Guide: (all inclusive)
royal suites U.S.$375-U.S.$1,800

Attractions: Sailing and Snorkeling Tours, 15-min drive; Canopy Tours, 30-min drive; Rafting and River Tours, 45-min drive; Rincon De La Vieja Volcano, 44 miles
Towns/Cities: Brasilito, 10-min walk; Tamarindo, 20-min drive; Arenal, 78 miles
Airports: Tamarindo Domestic Airport, 6 miles; Liberia International Airport, 37 miles; San José International Airport, 124 miles

Affiliations: The Leading Hotels of the World

Enchantment awaits you at the 406-room Paradisus Playa Conchal, a luxurious seaside retreat amidst green forests in the North-Pacific Riviera. Surrounded by meandering walkways, fountains, shimmering lakes and lush tropical gardens, this is a top-of-the-line, all-inclusive beach and golf resort in Costa Rica. The luxurious guest suites, which Condé Nast Johansens recommends, are spacious with private terraces, and a personalized concierge and butler service for a truly indulgent experience. There are 7 restaurants to choose from where fine Italian, Mexican and Asian-fusion cuisine will surely delight the senses. Entertainment options include nightly musical reviews, 4 bars, a casino, kids' center, spa and water sports along the resort's 1½-mile white sand beach. A championship eco-golf course, Reserva Conchal Golf Club, incorporates majestic ocean vistas, while the adventurous can enjoy white-water rafting, deep-sea fishing and scuba diving nearby.

COSTA RICA - OSA PENISULA (PUERTO JIMENEZ)

LAPA RIOS ECO LODGE

PUERTO JIMENEZ, OSA PENISULA
Tel: +506 2735 5130 **Fax:** +506 2735 5179
Web: www.johansens.com/laparios **E-mail:** info@laparios.com

Set in a private nature reserve encompassing over 1,000 acres of untouched natural beauty, Lapa Rios Eco Lodge is the embodiment of paradise. John and Karen Lewis, the hotel's founders, envisioned this special place as a refuge for wildlife and guests alike, where travelers could come to relax and enjoy their pristine rainforest surroundings. Overlooking the Gulfo Dulce and the Pacific Ocean, the hotel's 16 private bungalows offer comfortable and luxurious accommodations that evoke the tranquility and natural beauty of their setting, each with its own private wooden deck. A variety of tours and activities are available to help you explore your unique environment, including bird watching, rainforest walks and surf lessons. Meals are prepared by local chefs who create gourmet dishes that draw upon Costa Rican flavors and culture.

Our inspector loved: *Relaxing on my bungalow's porch and watching 2 scarlet macaws playing in the tree above, and of course the morning wake up calls from the howler monkeys!*

Price Guide: (per person, all inclusive, including transfer to and from Puerto Jimenez Airport) bungalows U.S.$330-U.S.$490

16 5

Attractions: Beach, Surfing and Kayaking, 15-min walk; Dolphin Tours, 45-min drive; Corcovado National Park, 37 miles
Towns/Cities: Puerto Jimenez, 45-min drive; Drake Bay, 28 miles; Quepos, 124 miles; San José, 230 miles
Airports: Puerto Jimenez Airport, 45-min drive

Arenas del Mar

KM 3.7 CARRETERA QUEPOS, MANUEL ANTONIO, PUNTARENAS
Tel: +506 2777 2777 **Fax:** +506 2777 2777
Web: www.johansens.com/areanasdelmar **E-mail:** reservations@arenasdelmar.com

Our inspector loved: *The lovely location set between 2 secluded beaches.*

Price Guide: (including breakfast)
ocean or rainforest view rooms U.S.$220-U.S.$260
ocean view suites U.S.$340-U.S.$480
ocean view apartments U.S.$560-U.S.$795

38

SPA

Attractions: Manuel Antonio National Park, 2 miles; Canopy Tour, 6 miles; Damas Island Mangrove by Kayak, 8 miles; White-Water Rafting, 12 miles
Towns/Cities: Manuel Antonio, 2 miles; Quepos, 3 miles; Dominical, 35 miles; San José, 112 miles
Airports: Quepos Airport, 4 miles; San José - Juan Santamaria International Airport, 112 miles

This unique beach resort, set on the Pacific coast of Costa Rica, combines the beauty of the beach with a rainforest setting in an eco-friendly environment. Guest rooms and apartments, located on a secluded beach, are well-appointed and have spectacular views of the Manuel Antonio National Park, the Pacific Ocean and the tropical rainforest. With its small spa and abundance of outdoor activities, the resort is ideal for an active honeymoon. You can enjoy white-water rafting, mangrove kayak and boat tours, guided rainforest hikes, ocean kayaking, sport fishing, canopy tours and horseback riding. Or simply relax on one of the resort's 2 unparalleled beaches, Playa Espadillas and Playitas Beach. Take in the beautiful sunsets while dining at El Mirador featuring Costa Rican cuisine with an international flavor.

COSTA RICA - PUNTARENAS (MANUEL ANTONIO)

Gaia Hotel & Reserve

KM 2.7 CARRETERA QUEPOS, MANUEL ANTONIO, PUNTARENAS
Tel: +506 2777 9797 **Fax:** +506 2777 9126 **U.S./Canada Toll Free:** 1 800 226 2515
Web: www.johansens.com/gaiahr **E-mail:** reservations@gaiahr.com

Nestled high on a hill above Costa Rica's Pacific coastline, Gaia offers the ultimate in luxury and personal service amidst pristine wilderness. The sleek Bauhaus design is fresh and modern, and each room has amazing views of the surrounding jungle and ocean. Your personal concierge will cater to your every need. Spend your afternoons at the spectacular 3-tiered, infinity-edge pool with its unique in-water table dining. La Luna restaurant offers exceptional cuisine featuring international and local dishes and special dietary requirements can be accommodated. Take time to tour Gaia's 12.1 acres of nature reserve with a certified nature guide. The reserve contains a wide range of rare flora, fauna and mammals such as the White Face and Squirrel monkeys, 3-toed sloths and red-eyed tree frogs.

Our inspector loved: *The spectacular setting and view from the infinity-edge pool.*

Price Guide: (including full breakfast)
studios U.S.$220-U.S.$360
suites U.S.$330-U.S.$880
villas U.S.$760-U.S.$970

20 15 16 SPA

Awards/Ratings: Condé Nast Johansens Most Excellent Hotel, Mexico & Central America 2007

Attractions: Nature Reserve, on-site; Manuel Antonio National Park, 2 miles; Quepos Marina Sport Fishing, 2 miles; Damas Island, 5 miles
Towns/Cities: Manuel Antonio, 2 miles; Quepos, 2 miles; Jaco, 40 miles; San José, 110 miles
Airports: Quepos Airport, 2 miles; San José-Juan Santamaria International Airport, 110 miles

Affiliations: Small Luxury Hotels of the World

MEXICO
Emiliano Zapata
Tenosique
Cristóbal
e las Casas
Comitán de Domínguez
pachula
Carmelita
Flores
Mundo Maya Int. Airport
Sayaxché
San Luis
Orange Walk
Belize
BELMOPAN
San Ignacio
Dangriga
BELIZE
San Antonio
Punta Corda
CARIBBEAN SEA
Modesto Méndez
Sebol
San Mateo Ixtatán
Puerto Cortés
Puerto Barrios
Puerto Barrios Airport
Cobán
San Pedro Sula
Morales
Mariscos
Uspantán
Huehuetenango
Salama
Santa Cruz del Quiché
San Marcos
Totonicapán
Zacapa
El Progreso
HONDURAS
Coatepeque
Quezaltenango
Chiquimula
Chimaltenango
Santa Rosa de Copán
284
285
286
GUATEMALA
Antigua
La Aurora Int. Airport
Jalapa
Retalhuleu
Mazatenango
Champerico
Pueblo Nuevo Tiquisate
Sta Lucia Cotzulmalguapa
Escuintla
Cuilapa
Jutiapia
Santa Ana
San José Airport
Tecojate
San José
EL SALVADOR
Las Lilas
PACIFIC OCEAN
SAN SALVADOR

GUATEMALA - SACATEPÉQUEZ (LA ANTIGUA GUATEMALA)

El Convento Boutique Hotel Antigua Guatemala

2A AVENUE NORTE 11, LA ANTIGUA GUATEMALA, ANTIGUA
Tel: +502 7720 7272 **Fax:** +502 7720 7272
Web: www.johansens.com/elconventoantigua **E-mail:** reservaciones@elconventoantigua.com

This brand new all-suite, boutique hotel combines Colonial style with Guatemalan tradition to inspire tranquility and rest. Its delicate, elegant and comfortable atmosphere is modern yet classic in style and each of the luxurious suites is carefully designed to offer you a relaxing stay. There are 2 grand suites, 6 suites and 6 junior suites to choose from; all are spacious and have private gardens, cedar-beamed ceilings and bedrooms fitted with the finest linens. Restaurant Sitz', Mayan for delight, offers exceptional international cuisine. Be sure not to miss the passionate, young chef's deserts! Try the Antigua coffee delicacies such as miniature-sized coffee crème brûlée, tiramisu and coffee and nutella ice cream created from exceptional Guatemalan coffee. The hotel is ideally located in a quiet residential area, in front of the traditional Convent of Capuchinas, just a few blocks away from the historical sites, plazas, parks and markets.

Our inspector loved: *The beautiful "new construction" in Colonial style, in contrast with the very modern details and décor.*

Price Guide: (excluding 22% tax)
junior suites U.S.$190
suites U.S.$240
grand suites U.S.$300

14

Attractions: Convent of Capuchinas, 1-min walk; Central Park, 5-min walk; Cathedral, 5-min walk; Ruins of San Gerónimo, 12-min walk
Towns/Cities: Escuintla, 19 miles; Guatemala City, 28 miles; Sololá, 47 miles; Retalhuleu, 15 miles
Airports: Guatemala City Airport, 28 miles; Petén Airport, 342 miles

Hotel Vista Real La Antigua

3A CALLE ORIENTE 16, LA ANTIGUA GUATEMALA
Tel: +502 7832 9715/6 **Fax:** +502 7832 9716
Web: www.johansens.com/vistareal **E-mail:** info@vistareal.com

Our inspector loved: *The "privacy" of the Special Grand Class Suite and its very romantic atmosphere.*

Price Guide: (excluding 22% tax)
master suite U.S.$175
grand class suites U.S.$225
special grand class suites U.S.$275

Awards/Ratings: Condé Nast Traveler Gold List 2008

Attractions: Cathedral, 5-min walk; Antigua's Central Park, 5-min walk; Capuchinas Convent, 5-min walk; Church and Monastery La Merced, 8-min walk
Towns/Cities: Jocotenango, 2 miles; Ciudad Vieja, 4 miles; Guatemala City, 28 miles; Panajachel on Lake Atitlan, 62 miles
Airports: Guatemala City Airport, 28 miles; Petén Airport, 341 miles

The historic Hotel Vista Real La Antigua is the ideal boutique hotel for those searching for privacy and inviting hospitality. Located just 300 meters from the main street of La Antigua Guatemala, it is conveniently situated for all the city has to offer. Behind its beautiful 18th-century façade, Colonial wood carvings, sculptures, ceramics and paintings have all been preserved, and cozy rooms with fireplaces and patios are peaceful resting places. Choose to stay in one of the Special Grand Class Suites, Grand Class Suites or the Master Suite. Each is fitted with high-tech amenities and features magnificent beds draped in fine Egyptian linen. The highly regarded Romarin Restaurant serves the finest international cuisine with Grand Class Service perfect for an enjoyable lunch or business dinner.

Filadelfia Coffee Resort & Spa

150 METERS NORTH OF THE SAN FELIPE CHAPEL, LA ANTIGUA GUATEMALA
Tel: +502 7728 0800 **U.S. Tel:** +1 646 257 4957
Web: www.johansens.com/filadelfia **E-mail:** hotel@filadelfiaresort.com

Sitting on a working coffee plantation for more than 130 years, Filadelfia Coffee Resort & Spa comprises 750-acres of coffee and ecological reserve, including a mountain of 7,000 to 8,000 feet high. Capturing Old World charm the resort also provides modern-day comfort with spacious rooms decorated in warm hues and creams evoking Guatemalan elegant simplicity and feature very comfortable beds prepared with Egyptian cotton sheets. Most offer a panoramic view of the Agua Volcano and the poolside garden. Contemporary lifestyle luxuries include iPods with sound bases, large televisions and WiFi connection. Pergaminos Restaurant serves international, beautifully presented gourmet dishes, and Cafetenango Restaurant presents delicious local dishes. The resort's specialty coffee-based drinks are prepared with beans harvested from their award-winning coffee plantation.

Our inspector loved: *Having a delicious romantic dinner in front of the hotel's main chimney.*

Price Guide: (including breakfast)
standard rooms U.S.$260
superior double rooms U.S.$307
master suites U.S.$550

20 50

Attractions: Iximché Archeological Park, 37 miles; Monterrico Beach, 72 miles; Panajachel in Lake Atitlan, 75 miles; Chichicastenango, 75 miles
Towns/Cities: Jocotenango, 1 mile; Ciudad Vieja, 3 miles; Guatemala City, 26 miles; Puerto San José, 56 miles
Airports: Guatemala City Airport, 26 miles; Petén Airport, 342 miles

Affiliations: Small Luxury Hotels of the World

Honduras

EXICO
Belize
BELOMOPAN
BELIZE
San Antonio
Punta Corda
CARIBBEAN SEA
Roatan
290
289
Islas de la Bahia
Puerto Castilla
Trujillo
Puerto Cortés
Tela
La Ceiba
Puerto Barrios
ATEMALA
San Pedro Sula
288
El Progrese
Pueblo Viejo
San Esteban
Puerto Lempira
Dulce Nombre de Culmí
Nuevo Arcadia
Santa Rita
Yoro
Santa Barbara
Auasbila
Salamá
Catacamas
Siguatepeque
Juticalpa
Nuevo otepeque
Gracias
Comayagua
La Esperanza
La Paz
Danlí
TEGUCIGALPA
LVADOR
Yuscaran
Ocotal
EL SALVADOR
Nacaome
San Miguel
Choluteca
Matagalpa
NICARAGUA
Chinandega
Juigalpa
MANAGUA
PACIFIC OCEAN
San Carlos
La Cruz
Los Chiles
COSTA RICA

HONDURAS - ATLÁNTIDA (LA CEIBA)

THE LODGE AT PICO BONITO

A. P. 710, LA CEIBA, ATLÁNTIDA, C. P. 31101
Tel: +504 440 0388 **Fax:** +504 440 0468 **U.S./Canada Toll Free:** 1 888 428 0221
Web: www.johansens.com/picobonito **E-mail:** picobonito@caribe.hn

Cradled between the Caribbean Sea and the 8,000-foot mountains of Pico Bonito National Park, this incredible lodge lies in the heart of the rainforest, surrounded by nearly 400 private acres bursting with exotic flora and fauna. Luxury accommodations are provided in enchantingly secluded pine and hardwood cabins. Each cabin has its own private veranda, which is a refreshing place to start or finish the day's activities. English speaking guides provide interpretive tours through a lush tropical jungle inhabited by jaguars, tapirs, monkeys, parrots, toucans and a list of over 400 bird species. Boat trips into the nearby manatee preserve are an absolute must, and for the more intrepid The Lodge offers guided night hikes into the forest. The Lodge's chefs pride themselves on their authentic Meso-American cuisine, served either in the beautifully appointed restaurant, or on one of the many relaxing outdoor decks.

Our inspector loved: *The "marañon" juice!*

Price Guide: (including breakfast, airport transfer, taxes, welcome drink, loop trail hike and visits to Butterfly Farm and Serpentarium)
standard cabins U.S.$245.70-U.S.$321.30
standard plus cabins U.S.$289.80-U.S.$371.70
superior plus cabins U.S.$333.90-U.S.$422.10

22 M 60

Awards/Ratings: Condé Nast Traveler Gold List 2008; Condé Nast Johansens Eco Resort 2006

Attractions: World-Class Bird-Watching, on-site; Butterfly Farm, Serpentarium and Iguana Breeding Facility, 5-min walk; Rio Zacate Waterfalls, 2 miles; Cuero y Salado Wildlife Refuge, 5 miles
Towns/Cities: La Ceiba, 15 miles; Tela, 49 miles; San Pedro Sula, 124 miles; Tegucigalpa, 264 miles
Airports: La Ceiba, 9 miles; San Pedro Sula, 124 miles; Tegucigalpa, 264 miles

Affiliations: Small Luxury Hotels of the World

BAREFOOT CAY

ROATAN, BAY ISLANDS
Tel: +504 455 6235 **Fax:** +1 270 918 3621 **U.S./Canada Toll Free:** 1 866 246 3706
Web: www.johansens.com/barefootcay **E-mail:** info@barefootcay.com

Our inspector loved: *The privacy of the cay, which makes you feel at home on your very own private island!*

Price Guide: (excluding 16% tax)
1-bedroom bungalows U.S.$185
2-bedroom villas U.S.$325
please inquire about exclusive hire of the property

6 12 10

Attractions: Snorkeling by the Reef Wall, 5-min swim; Pirates of the Caribbean Canopy, 5-min drive; Scuba Diving in Mary's Place and John's Spot, 5-min boat ride
Towns/Cities: Dixon's Cove, 5-min drive; French Harbour, 8-min drive; West End, 25-min drive; West Bay, 35-min drive
Airports: Roatan Airport, 10-min drive; La Ceiba Airport, 15-min flight and 15-min drive; San Pedro Airport, 1-hour flight and 20-min drive

Barefoot Cay is a private 4-acre cay centrally located on Roatan in the Bay Islands of Honduras, an ideal oasis for a quiet escape. This intimate luxury resort offers 4 private and spacious beach-front retreats. The two 1-bedroom bungalows and two 2-bedroom villas are well-appointed with Heavenly beds, complete kitchens and large Balinese open-air showers. Each tropical bungalow or villa has views and a covered deck overlooking the Caribbean Sea, capturing the cool breezes passing by. Curl up with your book on a window seat, relax in a palm-shaded hammock or try "valet diving." A dive center is on-site and the reef is within swimming distance; perfect for diving and snorkeling. Add meal service to your stay and feast on sumptuous local specialties such as shrimp, lobster and fish. Dine in the pool cabana or in the privacy of your very own bungalow or villa. You'll enjoy falling asleep to the sound of waves in the distance.

MAYOKA LODGE

SANDY BAY, ROATAN, BAY ISLANDS
Tel: +504 445 3043
Web: www.johansens.com/mayokalodge **E-mail:** enquiries@mayokalodge.com

Located on Roatan's unspoiled northern coast of the Western Caribbean, Mayoka Lodge is a stunning 6,500 square foot beach-front home offering all the amenities of a luxury resort. Beautifully decorated bedrooms feature natural stone and tile throughout, 5 of which are called "pods" because of their unique shape. The sixth suite, the master bedroom, is the most private at the top of the Lodge. The beautiful views of the turquoise sea are unparalleled and well-manicured, landscaped tropical gardens of flowers, fruit and nut trees are just steps from the sea. The residence is complete with its own private infinity pool and 300 feet of white sandy beach. Your private chef will create sumptuous international cuisine and wine enthusiasts will enjoy the well-stocked cellar.

Our inspector loved: *The most spectacular 180° views from the Master Suite of the hotel's infinity pool to the Caribbean ocean beyond.*

Price Guide: (per week, all inclusive, max group 12, excluding 16% tax and gratuities)
house group rental U.S.$15,550-U.S.$24,300

6

Attractions: Dolphin Experience, 2-min drive; Carambola Botanical Gardens, 2-min drive; Deep Water Submarine and Sailing, 5-min drive; South Shore Canopy Tour, 10-min drive
Towns/Cities: Half Moon Bay, 5-min drive; West End, 5-min drive; Coxen Hole, 10-min drive; West Bay, 12-min drive
Airports: Roatan International Airport, 10-min drive; La Ceiba Airport, 15-min flight; San Pedro Sula Airport, 45-min flight

BOLIVIA
Villazón
Mariscal Estigarribia
Calama
Orán
PARAGUAY
Pedro Juan Caballero
Dourados
Marília
Maringá
San Salvador de Jujuy
San Pedro
Salta
Cascavel
ASUNCIÓN
Paranaguá
Presidencia Roque Sáenz Peña
Formosa
Chapecó
El Salvador
San Miguel de Tucumán
Resistencia
Encarnación
Posadas
Corrientes
Florianópolis
BRAZIL
Santiago del Estero
San Fernando del Valle de Catamarca
Goya
Santa Maria
Uruguaiana
Porto Alegre
La Rioja
Rivera
Coquimbo
Concordia
Santa Fé
Paraná
Córdoba
Tacuarembó
Rio Grande
Melo
San Juan
Gualeguaychu
Rosario
URUGUAY
Río Cuarto
Mendoza
San Luis
San Nicolas de los Arroyos
PACIFIC OCEAN
SANTIAGO
Mercedes
BUENOS AIRES
MONTEVIDEO
292 293 294
295 296 297
San Rafael
Curicó
CHILE
Santa Rosa
Olavarría
Mar del Plata
Bahía Blanca
Concepción
Necochea
Neuquén
Viedma
299
300
301
San Carlos de Bariloche
Puerto Montt
298
ATLANTIC OCEAN
Rawson
Comodoro Rivadavia
Coihaique
Patagonia represented by shaded area
El Calafate
Stanley
Río Gallegos
Punta Arenas
Ushuaia

HOME BUENOS AIRES

HONDURAS 5860, 1414 CIUDAD DE BUENOS AIRES, BUENOS AIRES
Tel: +54 11 4778 1008 **Fax:** +54 11 4779 1006
Web: www.johansens.com/homebuenosaires **E-mail:** info@homebuenosaires.com

Our inspector loved: *Enjoying a drink at the charming RestoBar after a walk in the cool Palermo Viejo.*

Price Guide: (including breakfast)
rooms U.S.$145-U.S.$405

SPA

Attractions: Palermo Soho Boutiques, 5-min walk; Historical Center, 20-min drive
Airports: Buenos Aires Domestic Airport, 15-min drive; Ezeiza International Airport, 45-min drive

Located in a trendy district of the city, Home Buenos Aires is hip and stylish, while maintaining a cozy, intimate atmosphere. Owned and realized by spouses Patricia O'Shea and London music producer Tom Rixton, the hotel combines O'Shea's Argentine heritage and Rixton's music savvy with superb results. The modern, glass-walled RestoBar serves up innovative and exciting cocktails as well as traditional Argentinian tapas by the pool and landscaped garden, and features a D.J. and dancing on Friday nights. The colorful rooms, decorated with French vintage wallpaper and modern, comfortable furniture, feature stereo-systems on which to play C.D.s from the hotel's extensive music library. A spa, outdoor heated pool, and weekly Argentinian barbecues round off this intimate boutique hotel's impressive résumé.

KRISTA HOTEL BOUTIQUE

BONPLAND 1665, CP1414 CIUDAD DE BUENOS AIRES, BUENOS AIRES
Tel: +54 11 4771 4697 **Fax:** +54 11 4776 4650
Web: www.johansens.com/kristahotel **E-mail:** reservas@kristahotel.com.ar

Our inspector loved: *The charming "patios" and the well restored woodwork of this early 20th-century house.*

Price Guide: (including breakfast)
rooms U.S.$136-U.S.$217

Attractions: Palermo Soho Boutiques, 5-min walk; Historical Center, 20-min drive
Airports: Aeroparque Domestic Airport, 15-min drive; Ezeiza International Aiport, 45-min drive

The hotel is located in the heart of Palermo Hollywood, one of the most exclusive and trendiest neighborhoods in Buenos Aires. This amazing location is surrounded by restaurants, bars and fashion boutiques. Krista Hotel Boutique, with 10 exclusive rooms, offers a home-away-from-home and a relaxing atmosphere. Originally a house from the early 20th century, it has been fully remodeled, taking care to restore the internal patios to give the rooms an abundance of light. The chandeliers and tastefully chosen furniture contribute to the chic and welcoming ambience, accompanied by a high quality service. Each room has king-size beds, free Internet access, cable T.V. and every modern amenity to make your stay comfortable. Visit the "Palermo Woods," a lovely park in the neighborhood.

Legado Mitico

GURRUCHAGA 1848, C1414DIL CIUDAD DE BUENOS AIRES, BUENOS AIRES
Tel: +54 11 4833 1300 **Fax:** +54 11 4833 1300
Web: www.johansens.com/legadomitico **E-mail:** reservasbsas@legadomitico.com

Our inspector loved: *The unique concept and sophistication of the bedrooms.*

Price Guide: (including breakfast, excluding tax)
classic rooms U.S.$220
superior rooms U.S.$250
deluxe rooms U.S.$280

11 12 DVD WiFi

Attractions: Palermo Soho Boutiques, 5-min walk; Art Gallery, 5-10-min walk; Restaurants and Parks, 5-10-min walk; Historical Center, 20-min drive
Airports: Jorge Newbery Domestic Airport, 15-min drive; Exeiza International Airport, 45-min drive

In the Bohemian neighborhood of Palermo Viejo, Legado Mitico sits amongst tree-lined roads and cosmopolitan galleries and restaurants. Reflecting the famous and infamous of Argentina's history and myths, each room subtly reflects the person who inhabits it, from Eva Peron to Che Guevara. The decorations are all very refined and sophisticated, and a complete learning experience for the guest. The library complements the rooms, and offers guests a chance to research and explore the characters, or simply relax next to the fireplace with a glass of wine. Enjoy the solarium and patio on a sunny afternoon, or take a leisurely meal in the breakfast room. The staff is multilingual and prepared to help you with any need or interest in the exciting area of Palermo.

Mine Hotel Boutique

GORRITI 4770, PALERMO SOHO, C1414BJL CIUDAD DE BUENOS AIRES, BUENOS AIRES
Tel: +54 11 4832 1100 **Fax:** +54 11 4832 7400
Web: www.johansens.com/minehotel **E-mail:** info@minehotel.com

Our inspector loved: *The inviting décor and welcoming staff.*

Price Guide: (including breakfast and Internet access)
rooms U.S.$180-U.S.$280

20

Attractions: Palermo Soho Boutiques, 5-min walk; La Rural Convention Center: 10-min walk; Latin American Art Museum of Buenos Aires: 10-min drive; Historical Center, 20-min drive
Airports: Aeroparque Domestic Airport, 15-min drive; Ezeiza International Airport, 45-min drive

Located in the Palermo Soho neighborhood of Buenos Aires is the chic Mine Hotel Boutique. The hotel is designed to make each guest feel right at home with a décor that creates an atmosphere of harmony and cordiality, hence the concept of "mine," and friendly staff who immediately make you feel welcome. They truly seem to love what they do. Each guest room includes every modern amenity, features accents of rattan, wood and white, and has either a lovely garden or city view. There is also a small pool and charming garden for relaxing, yet the nearby attractions of Buenos Aires await discovery: subway lines, the zoo, botanical gardens, polo, shopping, art galleries, cafés, bars and restaurants. And if those don't interest you, tango lessons or a personal shopper can be arranged!

Moreno Hotel Buenos Aires

MORENO 376, C1091AAH CIUDAD DE BUENOS AIRES, SAN TELMO, BUENOS AIRES
Tel: +54 11 6091 2000 **Fax:** +54 11 6091 2001
Web: www.johansens.com/moreno **E-mail:** info@morenobuenosaires.com

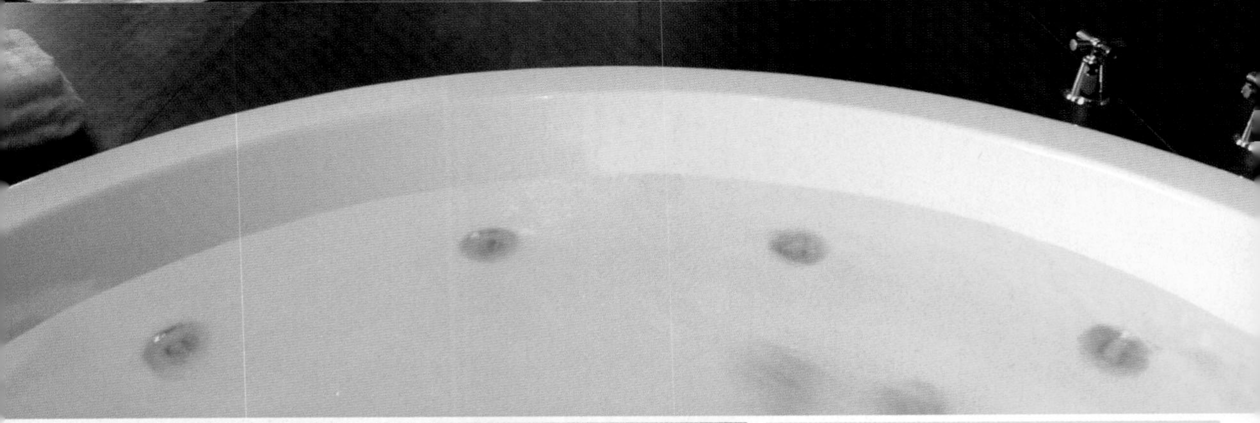

Moreno Hotel offers everything a discerning modern traveler's heart could desire from a boutique hotel - with style. Its 39 rooms are spacious and strikingly designed so as to epitomize modern elegance. The hotel, which occupies a 1920s art-deco building in the heart of Buenos Aires, features, among other luxuries, a gym open 24 hours, an on-site 130-seat theater that regularly hosts a variety of live shows, and a rooftop terrace complete with Jacuzzi and river-views. Food-lovers will enjoy the Latin-American-inspired cuisine at the hotel's upscale restaurant, and wine-aficionados will delight in the bar's 300 labels of Argentinean wine. A traditional Argentinean barbecue is served on the rooftop terrace for an authentic taste of Buenos Aires.

Our inspector loved: *The extra-large and trendy bedrooms.*

Price Guide: (including Continental breakfast, Internet and gym access)
rooms U.S.$100-U.S.$200
lofts U.S.$250-U.S.$400

39 M 200 WiFi

Attractions: Puerto Madero, 0.3 miles; San Telmo's Flea Market, 0.4 miles; La Boca, 1.9 miles; Recoleta, 2 miles
Airports: Jorge Newbery-Aeroparque Domestic Airport, 4 miles; Ministro Pistarini-Ezeiza International Airport, 19 miles

Vain Boutique Hotel

THAMES 2226/8, C1425FIF CIUDAD DE BUENOS AIRES, BUENOS AIRES
Tel: +54 11 4776 8246 **Fax:** +54 11 4776 8246
Web: www.johansens.com/vainuniverse **E-mail:** info@vainuniverse.com

Our inspector loved: *Reading on the charming rooftop terrace before going shopping at nearby boutiques.*

Price Guide: (including breakfast and welcome drink, excluding taxes)
rooms U.S.$125-U.S.$220

15

Attractions: Palermo Soho Boutiques, 5-min walk; Historical Center, 20-min drive
Airports: Aeroparque Domestic Airport, 15-min drive; Ezeiza International Airport, 45-min drive

In the heart of Palermo Soho, Vain Boutique Hotel is only 15 minutes away from a multitude of tourist attractions. It preserves the feeling of the Portenos downtown, while creating an atmosphere of relaxation and serenity. The rooms are comfortable and modern, with all contemporary amenities to make your stay more than comfortable, and with only 15 rooms, the staff are more than prepared to assist. The hotel offers a welcome massage, Jacuzzis, bilingual staff and a wine-bar ready with your welcome drink. Relax on the terrace and solarium after a busy day of designer shopping and dining in the bohemian inspired neighborhood of Palermo Viejo. If that still leaves you wanting more, arrange for a tango or Spanish lesson, a personalized city tour guide, a tango tour or arrange to view a polo match.

TERRITORIO

BOULEVARD ALTE. G. BROWN 3251, U9120ACG PUERTO MADRYN, PATAGONIA - CHUBUT
Tel: +54 11 4114 6029 **Fax:** +54 2965 47 1524
Web: www.johansens.com/hotelterritorio **E-mail:** informes@hotelterritorio.com.ar

Our inspector loved: *Eating a delicious regional dish at the restaurant while watching whales in the bay.*

Price Guide: (including breakfast)
rooms U.S.$123-U.S.$726

36 M 45 SPA

Península Valdés, a World Heritage Site, is the outstanding natural location of Territorio. Each guest room offers unparalleled views of the bay, the sea and the steppe and is designed in a gentle curve to reflect the geography of Patagonia. Experience the spa and fitness center, a special environment in which guests can relax and enjoy the sauna, massages and the unique Scottish shower. Dine at the Territorio restaurant, which serves the best of local Patagonian cuisine, and is complemented by a wine cellar full of Argentinean wines. This hotel offers an ideal base from which to explore Atlantic Patagonia, with is exceptional flora and fauna, as well as the intriguing history, which can be explored in the historic Punta Cuevas.

Attractions: Whale-Watching Expedition, 40-min drive; Península Valdés, 45-min drive
Towns/Cities: Trelew, 50-min drive; Gaiman, 1-hour drive; Rawson, 1-hour drive
Airports: Trelew Airport, 50-min drive

CORRENTOSO LAKE & RIVER HOTEL

AV. SIETE LAGOS 4505, VILLA LA ANGOSTURA, PATAGONIA
Tel: +54 11 4803 0030 **Fax:** +54 11 4803 0030
Web: www.johansens.com/correntoso **E-mail:** info@correntoso.com

Our inspector loved: *Enjoying a superb dinner overlooking Nahuel Huapi Lake.*

Price Guide: (including breakfast)
rooms U.S.$290-U.S.$400

29 SPA

Awards/Ratings: Condé Nast Johansens Most Excellent Romantic Hideaway, South America 2008

Attractions: Parque Los Arrayanes, 10-min drive; Cerro Bayo, 15-min drive; Villa Traful, 90-min drive
Towns/Cities: Bariloche, 90-min drive
Airports: Bariloche International Airport, 1-hour drive

Affiliations: Small Luxury Hotels of the World

A traditional hotel, Correntoso is situated at the mouth of the Correntoso River where it enters Nahuel Huapi Lake at the foot of the Andes. Accommodations are beautifully decorated with fine woodwork and elegant furnishings, and the fine dining restaurant and wine bar specializes in Mediterranean cuisine fused with traditional Patagonian dishes and regionally produced wines. Correntoso serves more casual fare on a deck overlooking the lake, while at teatime, a variety of home-made pastries, chocolates and special tea blends are available. The hotel's Spirit & Adventures department can arrange custom-designed excursions, with gourmet picnics or asado (Argentine barbecue) lunches on most tours. For a relaxing day, enjoy a massage, the herbal hammam, heated pool or a good book in the Patagonian-themed library.

Hotel Las Balsas

BAHÍA LAS BALSAS S/N, 8407 VILLA LA ANGOSTURA, NEUQUÉN
Tel: +54 2944 494308 **Fax:** +54 2944 494308
Web: www.johansens.com/lasbalsas **E-mail:** info@lasbalsas.com.ar

Our inspector loved: *Enjoying the gourmet food and first-class service after relaxing in the great Spa by the Lake.*

Price Guide: (including breakfast and access to spa)
single/double standards U.S.$480
single/double suites U.S.$770

15 M 40 WiFi SPA

Attractions: Wine Tastings, on-site; Cooking Classes, on-site
Towns/Cities: Villa La Angostura, 2 miles; Cardenal Samore, 28 miles; Villa Traful, 39 miles; Bariloche, 50 miles
Airports: San Carlos de Bariloche International Airport, 50 miles

Affiliations: Relais & Châteaux

In this most serene and romantic of locations stands the fantastic Hotel Las Balsas. Magnificently set within the Nahuel Huapi National Park of Argentine Patagonia, with a backdrop of snow-capped mountains and green forests, Las Balsas looks out to the tranquil Nahuel Huapi Lake. Exclusivity and comfort are hallmarks of this idyllic retreat where additional services such as babysitting, concierge advice and private use of the dock and beach are available. Each guest room and suite is individually styled and has a lake view, which is also enjoyed from the gourmet restaurant. A visit to the wine-tasting lounge and wine cellar, where over 150 samples are kept, is well worth your while, as is a day of indulgence at the relaxing spa. Outdoor activities abound in the spectacular surroundings, making Hotel Las Balsas an ideal destination for those looking both to unwind and explore.

Isla Victoria Lodge

ISLA VICTORIA, PARQUE NACIONAL NAHUEL HUAPI, C.C. 26 (R8401AKU)
Tel: +54 43 94 96 05 **Fax:** +54 11 43 94 95 99
Web: www.johansens.com/islavictoria **E-mail:** maresur@maresur.com

Our inspector loved: *The overwhelming natural beauty of the island, and the atmosphere of the Lodge.*

Price Guide: (all inclusive and all transfers included)
2-night stay per person U.S.$740
3-night stay per person U.S.$1,088

22 M 35 12 SPA

Awards/Ratings: Condé Nast Johansens Most Excellent Lodge, South America 2007

Attractions: Circuito Chico, 30-min drive; Cerro Cathedral, Bariloche, 45-min drive
Towns/Cities: Bariloche, 30-min boat ride; Villa La Angostura, 2-hour drive
Airports: Bariloche International Airport, 45-min drive

Situated on a cliff overlooking the lake and forests of cohiues and cypresses, Isla Victoria Lodge is part of the Nahuel Huapi National Park, one of the most unique areas of the Argentinean Patagonia. Bilingual guides are available to lead outdoor activities including deer sighting, photographic safari, kayaking and trekking. Every activity is carefully designed to make sure that you enjoy and learn all about the area, get closer to nature and find out the infinite world that Victoria Island offers. The Lodge itself has 3 living rooms, a cozy bar with fireplace, a spa-solarium and a wine cellar with some of the best wines the area has to offer, as well as an inviting library offering a relaxing environment. The restaurant looks out to a breathtaking view while serving delightful local cuisine.

Brazil

GEORGETOWN
VENEZUELA
PARAMARIBO
GUYANA
Cayenne
Puerto Ayacucho
SANTA FE
DE BOGOTÁ
SURINAM
FRENCH
GUIANA
Boa Vista
ATLANTIC
OCEAN
OLOMBIA
Roraima
Amapa
Macapá
Belém
Santarém
Manaus
São Luís
Fortaleza
Fernando
de Noronha
313
Teresina
Ceara
Maranhao
Maraba
Rio Grande
Do Norte
Natal
322
Amazonas
Para
João
Pessoa
Paraiba
Araguaína
Humaitá
Piaui
Pernambuco
Recife
314
uzeiro do Sul
Cachimbo
303
Alagoas
Acre
Pôrto Velho
Palmas
Tocantins
Maceió
Sergipe
Rio Branco
Rondonia
Aracaju
Pimena Bueno
Cobija
Barreiras
Bahia
Mato
Grosso
309
Puerto
Maldonado
Salvador
308
307
PERU
Goias
Trinidad
Cuiabá
BRASÍLIA
Cáceres
LA PAZ
Goiânia
304
Arequipa
310
BOLIVIA
Minas
Gerais
306
305
Tacna
Mato Grosso
do Sul
Espirito
Santo
SUCRE
Belo Horizonte
Vitória
Fuerte Olimpo
Campo Grande
Sao
Paulo
311
312
Rio De
Janeiro
318
319
320
Tarija
Campinas
329
PARAGUAY
321
315
São Paulo
331
332
Rio de Janeiro
316
Calama
Concepción
333
330
317
Salta
ASUNCIÓN
Parana
Curitiba
Encarnación
Chañaral
Resistencia
Santa
Catarina
326
327
328
Florianópolis
ARGENTINA
Rio Grande
Do Sul
323
324
325
Porto Alegre
La Rioja
Coquimbo
Santa Fé
Salto
Chimbas
URUGUAY
San Luis
SANTIAGO
BUENOS AIRES
MONTEVIDEO

BRAZIL - ALAGOAS (SÃO MIGUEL DOS MILAGRES)

Pousada do Toque

RUA FELISBERTO DE ATAIDE, POVOADO DO TOQUE, SÃO MIGUEL DOS MILAGRES, 57940-000 ALAGOAS
Tel: +55 82 3295 1127 **Fax:** +55 82 3295 1127
Web: www.johansens.com/pousadadotoque **E-mail:** pousadadotoque@uol.com.br

Our inspector loved: *The coziness and comfort of all the guest rooms, in addition to the owner's attentive service.*

Price Guide: (including dinner)
rooms U.S.$160-U.S.$210
suites U.S.$290-U.S.$430

13

Awards/Ratings: Condé Nast Johansens Most Excellent Beach Hotel, South America 2008

Attractions: Ocean Pools of Maragogi, 45-min drive
Towns/Cities: Porto de Galinhas, 90-min drive; Maceió, 90-min drive
Airports: Maceió International Airport, 90-min drive

Located on the private and pristine beach of Praia do Toque, this pleasant pousada has quickly become a favorite beach retreat. Combining intimacy, rusticity and charm, owners Nilo Burgarelli and his wife Gilda Peixoto have created an inspiring retreat where its simplicity and comfort provides the ultimate escape. Blending in beautifully with the surrounding coconut grove plantation, there are 13 guest rooms called chalets, which include private pools, sundecks, Jacuzzis and verandas with hammocks. Nilo is a former restaurateur and uses his talents to create international cuisine featuring fresh local seafood and local dishes from fresh vegetables supplied by the pousada's garden. Spend the day at the beach-front pool, chill out at the rustic gazebos situated near the lawn, or have a relaxing massage in the small massage parlor.

Maitei Hotel

ESTRADA DO MUCUGÊ 475, ARRAIAL D'ÁJUDA, PORTO SEGURO, BAHIA 45816-000
Tel: +55 73 3575 3877 **Fax:** +55 73 3575 3799
Web: www.johansens.com/maitei **E-mail:** hotelmaitei@hotmail.com

Our inspector loved: *The amazing view while sipping a drink by the pool, and taking an evening stroll to the lively village.*

Price Guide: (including breakfast)
rooms U.S.$235-U.S.$315

17 15 DVD WiFi

Attractions: Arraial Beach; Arraial's Boutiques, 2-min walk; Pitinga Beach, 20 meters
Towns/Cities: Trancoso, 15 miles
Airports: Porto Seguro International Airport, 6 miles

Flanked by clear aquamarine waves on one side and forest dense with palm trees on the other, Maitei Hotel combines Brazilian flare with sophisticated design to create the perfect beach getaway for the discerning traveler. The interior design and architecture of this tile-roofed hotel is simple yet stylish, with interesting touches such as modern art, elegant pottery, lamps with paper shades and sponge-painted Stucco walls alongside luxury amenities such as Jacuzzis in all rooms. Outside, cushioned white lounge chairs are plentiful on the many decks and around the 2 pools, and each room offers a balcony with hammock overlooking the sea, encouraging you to lounge outside and enjoy the breathtaking view afforded by the hotel's location. Meals are served in the restaurant, which also offers a view, and the pool bar serve drinks and snacks.

FAZENDA SÃO FRANCISCO

PONTA DO CORUMBAU S/N, PRADO, BAHIA
Tel: +55 11 3078 4411 **Fax:** +55 73 3294 2250
Web: www.johansens.com/fazenda **E-mail:** reservas@corumbau.com.br

Our inspector loved: *The great feeling of staying at a farmhouse with its comfortable rooms located directly in front of the exclusive beach.*

Price Guide: (including breakfast, lunch, dinner and coconut water, excluding tax)
suites from U.S.$500
bungalows from U.S.$750

10

Attractions: A Variety of Schooner Trips; Canoe Trips; Visit to the Indian Reserve at Monte Pascoal National Park; Corumbau River, 15-min walk
Towns/Cities: Corumbau Village, 5-min walk; Caraiva, 1-hour drive
Airports: Porto Seguro International Airport, 124 miles

Set on a coconut palm farm surrounded by virgin mangrove swamps and a mile-long pristine golden beach, Fazenda São Francisco combines modern architecture with rustic simplicity to create a retreat offering unparalleled serenity. Interiors are characterized by bright colors and bold patterns tranquilized by dark Brazilian woods and clean whites, fusing innovative design and a natural elegance in perfect harmony with the resort's unspoiled location. The spacious and sophisticated suites and bungalows, situated on the beach and shaded by palm fronds, afford guests ultimate privacy and stunning views, which can be enjoyed over a glass of wine or gourmet meal served on large, private terraces. Those seeking adventure will appreciate the fantastic diving to be found on the farm's front doorstep.

Vila Naiá - Paralelo 17º

PONTA DO CORUMBAU, BAHIA
Tel: +55 11 3061 1872 **Fax:** +55 11 3061 1872
Web: www.johansens.com/vilanaia **E-mail:** info@vilanaia.com.br

Our inspector loved: *The tropical influence and relaxed atmosphere.*

Price Guide: (all meals included)
rooms U.S.$460-U.S.$600
bungalow U.S.$615-U.S.$800

Attractions: Visit to an Indian Community, 40-min drive; The Reefs and Natural Pools, 2-hour boat ride; Monte Pascoal, 2-hour drive; Tour of Jubarte Whale, 5-hour boat ride
Towns/Cities: Corumbau Village, 10-min walk; Caraíva, 1-hour drive
Airports: Porto Seguro International Airport, 124 miles

Set on the 9-mile stretch of white sandy Corumbau Beach and surrounded by spit wood and palm trees, Vila Naiá combines the simplistic charm of a Brazilian fisherman's village with modern sophistication. Its bungalows and suites, connected by a web of tree-lined platforms, are of rustic design made with re-used timber and feature interiors laden with traditional, hand-made tiles with colorful accents such as sheer flowing curtains and modern furniture that complement the rich wood floor and walls. Dining is a special treat with sophisticated dishes including seafood caught by local fishermen and ingredients from Vila Naiá's own organic farm. Cool drinks are served by the beach and at the Quadrado, an open-air, hammock-adorned lounge area.

TXAI RESORT

ROD. ILHÉUS-ITACARÉ KM 48, ITACARÉ, BAHIA 45530-000
Tel: +55 73 2101 5000 **Fax:** +55 73 2101 5251
Web: www.johansens.com/txairesort **E-mail:** reserva@txairesort.com.br

Our inspector loved: *The excellent service provided by the staff, and the natural beauty of the area.*

Price Guide: (including breakfast)
rooms U.S.$553-U.S.$1,737

40 SPA

Awards/Ratings: Condé Nast Johansens Most Excellent Resort, South America 2007

Attractions: Surfing Lessons, on-site; Cycling routes, close by; Mansions and Historical Sites of Itacaré, 15-min drive
Towns/Cities: Itacaré Village, 15-min drive
Airports: Ilhéus International Airport, 37 miles

Located on a 100-hectare coconut plantation set along Itacarezinho beach and surrounded by unspoiled Atlantic rainforest, this sophisticated beach resort comprises 40 comfortable bungalows tucked amidst the coconut palms. Bungalows are built on stilts with wooden decks, palm-thatch detailing and look out to beautiful natural vistas. Each has been decorated in earth tones with king beds, open-air showers, whirlpool baths and massage and relaxation beds. The ocean-view restaurant, with its traditional Bahia architecture, serves both regional and international cuisine accompanied by a great choice of wines. After dinner rest in the Colonial-style lounge, filled with Brazilian art and furniture, surrounded by a reflecting pool, and enjoy the views. Txai's blue-tiled pool is just a few yards from the beach, and the Txai Health Spa offers a tempting variety of massages, treatments and classes.

Kiaroa Eco-Luxury Resort

LOTEAMENTO DA COSTA, ÁREA SD6, DISTRITO DE BARRA GRANDE, MUNICIPIO DE MARAÚ, BAHIA, CEP 45 520-000
Tel: +55 71 3272 1320 **Fax:** +55 71 3272 1320
Web: www.johansens.com/kiaroa **E-mail:** reservas@kiaroa.com.br

Situated in the Maraú Peninsula eco-sanctuary, Kiaroa Eco-Luxury Resort provides luxurious accommodations that blend seamlessly into their natural surroundings. Experience the unique setting by taking a boat trip, snorkeling or great day's surf in the warm clear waters before resting in one of just 28 intimate rooms and bungalows where seclusion, comfort and sophistication are paramount. Take a trip to the newly opened Armonia SPA where an abundance of massages, spa treatments and rituals are practised. And dine on fresh, local seafood and ingredients that create mouth-watering dishes in this naturally inspired, yet sophisticated atmosphere. With the recent addition of the Directory Room, the resort is now able to host meetings and events in a stress-free, conducive environment. Overall, Kiaroa is a welcoming tropical oasis for those seeking to submerge in nature while still enjoying the comforts of a luxury hotel.

Our inspector loved: *The sense of isolation at this beach-front place where top service and a wonderful mix of regional and international food is guaranteed.*

Price Guide: (including breakfast and dinner, excluding taxes)
Tropical luxury rooms U.S.$525
Moorea luxury bunglows U.S.$760
Bali luxury bungalows U.S.$1,076

28 M 50 12 WiFi
SPA H

Attractions: Península de Maraú, on-site; Natural Swimming Pools and Reefs, on-site; Camamu Bay, 15-min drive; Land Excursions, 20/30-min drive
Towns/Cities: Barra Grande Village, 15-min drive; Ilheus, 106 miles; Salvador, 230 miles
Airports: Private Air Strip, on-site; Ilheus National Airport, 106 miles; Salvador International Airport, 230 miles

Tivoli Ecoresort Praia do Forte

AVENIDA DO FAROL, PRAIA DO FORTE - MATA DE SÃO JOÃO, BAHIA
Tel: +55 71 36 76 40 00 **Fax:** +55 71 36 76 11 12
Web: www.johansens.com/praiadoforte **E-mail:** reservas.htpf@tivolihotels.com

Our inspector loved: *The beauty, and wide range of services and treatments offered at both the thalasso spa and resort.*

Price Guide: (including breakfast and dinner)
rooms U.S.$390-U.S.$495

293 200 SPA

Awards/Ratings: Condé Nast Johansens Most Excellent Spa Hotel 2006

Attractions: Turtles Preservation Project, 10-min walk
Towns/Cities: Praia do Forte Village, 10-min walk
Airports: Salvador International Airport, 34 miles

This is one of the most beautiful coastal regions in Brazil where ecological reserves adjoin semi-deserted white sand beaches surrounded by natural Atlantic forests, coral reefs, lagoons and lush tropical gardens, enormous coconut groves and quiet beaches. With intricate piaçava straw roofs thatched by local craftsmen, the resort's buildings are made from locally sourced natural materials that blend effortlessly into the environment. Thoughtful attention to detail is evident in the spacious and peaceful bedrooms, and friendly staff create a welcoming atmosphere. A feast of 115 different items on the breakfast buffet include exotic fruits, fresh breads and local specialties such as tapioca couscous and beiju. For dinner, there is a large selection of home-made, mouth-watering dishes. The prawn kiosk is popular and serves unique fish and fresh lobster as well as tropical drinks during the day.

Etnia Pousada and Boutique

TRANCOSO, BAHIA 45818-000
Tel: +55 73 3668 1137 **Fax:** + 55 73 3668 1780
Web: www.johansens.com/etnia **E-mail:** etniabrasil@etniabrasil.com.br

Our inspector loved: *The comfortable bedrooms and the relaxed atmosphere at this perfectly located pousada.*

Price Guide: (including breakfast, excluding taxes)
suites U.S.$243-U.S.$399

8 14 SPA

Attractions: Trancoso Square (Quadrado), 5-min walk; Trancoso Beach, 15-min walk
Towns/Cities: Arraial D'Ájuda, 45-min drive
Airports: Porto Seguro International Airport, 1-hour drive

Located amidst natural rainforest vegetation in the small Bohemian-chic coastal town of Trancoso, Etnia is exotic and ethnic while maintaining a simple, barefoot elegance. The hotel, which consists of 8 bungalows scattered throughout the woodland, is an ideal spot for those of you seeking rest and relaxation, with massage, yoga, meditation and artistic therapy on-hand to enhance your well-being. The hotel features a pool, a wooded garden with hammocks and open-air bar-restaurant, which serves a sumptuous breakfast each morning and light fare later in the day. Each bungalow, designed to evoke a particular culture with theme-appropriate names such as Tribal, Kyoto, and Morocco, is stylishly appointed with ethnic touches including African-inspired art in the Tribal bungalow and Japanese prints in Kyoto.

Pousada dos Inconfidentes

RUA JOÃO RODRIGUES SOBRINHO 91, 36325-000, TIRADENTES, MINAS GERAIS
Tel: +55 32 3355 2135 **Fax:** +55 32 3355 2135
Web: www.johansens.com/inconfidentes **E-mail:** reservas@pousadadosinconfidentes.com.br

Our inspector loved: *Reading a book in the garden as the sun sets behind the beautiful mountains.*

Price Guide:
rooms U.S.$308-U.S.$370

Attractions: Historical Center, 5-min drive
Towns/Cities: São João Del Rei, 15-min drive
Airports: Rio de Janeiro International Airport, 213 miles

Located in a quiet street, Pousada dos Inconfidentes is an elegant, new Colonial-style inn with 13 nicely outfitted suites decorated by a famous Brazilian interior designer. The inn itself is named after the "Inconfidentes," 18th-century Colonial rebels who stood against the Portuguese crown, and each suite bears the name of a different local rebellion hero. There is a lovely library where you can enjoy a good read with a cup of tea or coffee and cookies, and beautiful gardens that are equally pleasant on sunny days. In the evenings, savor a drink at the cozy piano bar or take advantage of the inn's home theater. There is also a semi-Olympic outdoor swimming pool and poolside bar serving drinks, sandwiches and fresh fruit. Serenity reigns throughout this adults-only refuge.

SOLAR DA PONTE

PRAÇA DAS MERCÊS S/N, TIRADENTES, MINAS GERAIS 36325-000
Tel: +55 32 33 55 12 55 **Fax:** +55 32 33 55 12 01
Web: www.johansens.com/solardaponte **E-mail:** reservas@solardaponte.com.br

Our inspector loved: *The comfort of the bedrooms, and enjoying the tasty breakfast while watching little monkeys playing in nearby trees.*

Price Guide: (including breakfast)
rooms U.S.$160-U.S.$260

18 8

This beautiful country mansion is set within peaceful shady gardens in the historical 18th-century mountain village of Tiradentes, with quaint winding streets and Baroque churches. The Colonial-style architecture creates a comfortable environment, and the spacious interiors feature light color schemes complemented by traditional décor and locally made furniture. Healthy, light meals are served in the bar and delicious breakfasts and afternoon teas are served in a spacious room with tree-top view. Take a stroll around the historic center of the town and admire the local, contemporary artworks on display and the variety of delightful handicrafts. The native tropical forests are breathtaking, and the imposing São José Mountain Range, now an ecological reserve, creates an awe-inspiring backdrop. Excursions to the countryside, visits to fazendas and preservation areas, on foot, horse-back, by jeep or bicycle can all be arranged by the hotel.

Attractions: Historic Center, close by; Historical Monuments, Shopping and Dining, 5-min walk; Steam Train, 15-min walk
Towns/Cities: São João del Rei, 15-min drive
Airports: São João del Rey Airport; 8 miles; Belo Horizonte (Confins) International Airport, 124 miles; Rio de Janeiro (Galeão) International Airport, 186 miles

Pousada Maravilha LIDA

RODOVIA BR-363, S/N, SUESTE, ILHA DE FERNANDO DE NORONHA, PERNAMBUCO 53990-000
Tel: +55 81 3619 0028 **Fax:** +55 81 3619 0162
Web: www.johansens.com/maravilha **E-mail:** reservas@pousadamaravilha.com.br

Our inspector loved: *The magnificent view of "Baía do Sueste" from all rooms, bungalows and the main building.*

Price Guide: (including breakfast and airport transfers)
rooms U.S.$615-U.S.$1,150
suites U.S.$720-U.S.$1,360

8 10 DVD WiFi

Attractions: Remédio's Village, 3 miles; Praia do Leão, 20-min walk
Towns/Cities: Natal, 224 miles; Recife, 336 miles
Airports: Local Airport, 0.6 miles

The sole tourist destination in a rugged, beautiful archipelago surrounded by dolphin-filled azure waters, Pousada Maravilha offers clean, minimalist luxury in harmony with its stunning natural setting. Rich Brazilian woods and comfortable, stylish furniture characterize the pousada's relaxed, but luxurious interior ambience. Bamboo hammocks, an elegant infinity pool, and an emphasis on large, open verandas create the perfect environment for outdoor contemplation and enjoyment of the breathtaking scenery. Candle-lit poolside meals are served at the restaurant, which specializes in inventive Brazilian and Italian-influenced cuisine. With a special emphasis on environmental preservation, no doubt inspired by its stunning surroundings, Pousada Maravilha is as eco-friendly as it is posh, making it an ideal location for the environmentally conscious traveler.

Nannai Beach Resort

RODOVIA PE-09, ACESSO À MURO ALTO, KM 3, IPOJUCA, PERNAMBUCO 55590-000
Tel: +55 81 3552 0100 **Fax:** +55 81 3552 1474
Web: www.johansens.com/nannaibeach **E-mail:** reservas@nannai.com.br

This Bali-style beach resort is tucked along the Atlantic coast of Pernambuco with private bungalows and terraced apartments nestled among beautiful tropical gardens and pools. Beautiful hardwood, bright colors and light linens create a fresh, cheerful atmosphere, and the personalized service enhances this oasis of relaxation. Enjoy live music while dining on regional and international cuisine in the ocean-facing restaurant or opt for the more casual atmosphere of the lounge, cyber café or beach bar. The plethora of activities available include pitch and putt golf, beach soccer, volleyball, water volleyball, hydro-gymnastics and dance classes, while free water sports such as snorkeling, kayaking, laser and jangada (a Brazilian raft) and sailing can be organized; motorized water sports are available for an additional fee. A dedicated children's area, babysitting services and children's programs are also offered, and massages, beauty services and excursions can all be arranged.

Our inspector loved: *The charming premium bungalows with private swimming pools, located right in front of Muro Alto beach.*

Price Guide: (including breakfast and dinner without beverages, excluding 10% service charge)
rooms U.S.$370-U.S.$560
bungalows U.S.$650-U.S.$1,200

91

Attractions: Tide Pools and Offshore Reefs, close by
Towns/Cities: Porto de Galinhas Village, 6 miles
Airports: Recife's International Airport, 37 miles

VILLA RASA MARINA

AV. JOSÉ BENTO RIBEIRO DANTAS 299, ARMAÇÃO DOS BÚZIOS, RIO DE JANEIRO 28950-000
Tel: +55 21 2172 1000 **Fax:** +55 21 2172 1010
Web: www.johansens.com/villarasamarina **E-mail:** reservas@hoteismarina.com.br

Our inspector loved: *The delicious food at the beautiful outdoor Oyster & Ceviche Bar after a wonderful walk along the beach in front of the hotel.*

Price Guide: (including breakfast)
rooms U.S.$265-U.S.$1,200

35 24 M 60 DVD Wi Fi SPA

Attractions: Geriba Beach, 5-min drive; Búzios Main Street, 10-min drive
Towns/Cities: Cabo Frio, 30-min drive; Arraial do Cabo, 45-min drive
Airports: Búzios Airport, 1 mile; Rio de Janeiro International Airport, 112 miles

Steps from the beaches of Praia Rasa, this modern boutique hotel is ideally located in the most exclusive and peaceful area of Búzios. Each room is stylish and rustic in design with clean, contemporary lines, recycled wood and soothing white décor featuring vibrant accents of color. Suite da Villa is perfect for couples seeking extra privacy. Its rustic straw-lined roof, private Japanese-style Jacuzzi and spacious ocean-front terrace will delight honeymooners. Executive Chef Felipe Bronze uses his renowned methods of cooking with charcoal and firewood to create delicious Mediterranean-inspired cuisine. And the Oyster & Ceviche Bar offers stunning beach-front views in a unique atmosphere. The new full-service spa provides a fitness center, yoga instructor, personal trainer and swimming pool where you can renew your mind, body and soul.

Casas Brancas Boutique-Hotel & Spa

ALTO DO HUMAITÁ 10, ARMAÇÃO DOS BÚZIOS, RIO DE JANEIRO 28950-000
Tel: +55 22 2623 1458 **Fax:** +55 22 2623 2147
Web: www.johansens.com/casasbrancas **E-mail:** info@casasbrancas.com.br

The unspoiled fishing village of Búzios became the place to visit and to be seen following a visit by Brigitte Bardot in 1964. Situated on a peninsula protruding into the Atlantic Ocean, and surrounded by no less than 25 beaches, the area soon became known as a tropical St. Tropez, and like its equivalent in the south of France, the village has grown over the years but retains a certain charm that is emphasized by seafront vistas and a cobbled main street. Built in a cool, Mediterranean style, the hotel has an appealing, elegant, laid back atmosphere with guest rooms looking out to the sea or garden. The restaurant is a dining experience to cherish thanks to the talented kitchen staff who produce excellent, imaginative international cuisine and Brazilian delights.

Our inspector loved: *Eating the great food while admiring the view of the charming fishing village.*

Price Guide: (including breakfast)
rooms U.S.$220-U.S.$380

32 5 SPA

Attractions: Búzios Center, 5-min walk; Geriba's Beach, 10-min drive
Towns/Cities: Arraial do Cabo, 45-min drive
Airports: Rio de Janeiro International Airport, 112 miles

Insólito Boutique Hotel

RUA E1 - LOT 3 E 4 , CONDOMÍNIO ATLÂTICO, ARMAÇÃO DE BÚZIOS, RIO DE JANEIRO 28,950-000
Tel: +55 22 2623 2172 **Fax:** +55 22 2623 2172
Web: www.johansens.com/insolitos **E-mail:** reservas@insolitos.com.br

Our inspector loved: *Eating a delicious breakfast while appreciating the beautiful view of Ferradura Beach.*

Price Guide: (including breakfast)
rooms U.S.$419-U.S.$914

Attractions: Búzios Main Street, 5-min drive
Towns/Cities: Cabo Frio, 30-min drive; Arraial do Cabo, 45-min drive
Airports: Búzios Local Airport, 15-min drive; Rio de Janeiro International Airport, 112 miles

Located in the fashionable area of Búzios, Insólito Boutique Hotel offers a lovely base from which to explore all of the shopping, dining, and entertainment options. Each room has cozy robes and towels, a wet bar, and some rooms offer a Jacuzzi on the balcony, while all have gorgeous views of the sea. Enjoy a relaxing day by the fresh or sea water pools, take a picnic to one of Búzios' stunning beaches or experience a relaxing treatment at the wellness center. If excitement is more your taste, water ski or wakeboard at Ferradura Beach, or kite surf on Manguinho's Beach. In the evening, dine in the restaurant, which is located on the roof of the hotel, and which serves seasonal Brazilian cuisine.

Parador Santarém Marina

ESTRADA CORREIA DA VEIGA, 96, PETRÓPOLIS, RIO DE JANEIRO 25745-260
Tel: +55 24 2222 9933 **Fax:** +55 24 2222 9933
Web: www.johansens.com/paradorsantarem **E-mail:** reservas@paradorsantarem.com.br

Our inspector loved: *The variety of places to relax and enjoy a good book or a glass of wine at this beautiful property.*

Price Guide: (including breakfast, excluding taxes) suites U.S.$240-U.S.$560

14 80 DVD WiFi

This boutique resort is surrounded by beautiful green mountain scenery of forests and waterfalls. Suites are designed for privacy and equipped with modern amenities. In addition, Orquídeas Suites feature granite or marble bathrooms and private verandas or covered patios. Hortênsias Suites have garden views, and several of the Bromélias Suites include sofa beds ideal for small families. Facilities include a swimming pool and bar, dry and steam saunas, Jacuzzi, volleyball and basketball courts and beaten sand tennis courts. In summer, breakfast can be enjoyed by the swimming pool overlooking a small lake, and the renowned good weather lends itself to the full enjoyment of these outdoor on-site activities including the 9-hole golf course and nearby horse stables.

Attractions: Itaipava District and Shops, 15-min drive; Serra dos Órgãos National Park, 30-min drive
Towns/Cities: Itaipava, 15-min drive; Petrópolis, 40-min drive
Airports: Rio de Janeiro International Airport, 90-min drive

SOLAR DO IMPÉRIO

KOELER AVENUE, 376 - CENTRO, PETRÓPOLIS, RIO DE JANEIRO
Tel: +55 24 2103 3000 **Fax:** +55 24 2242 0034
Web: www.johansens.com/solardoimperio **E-mail:** atendimento@solardoimperio.com.br

Our inspector loved: *The careful restoration of this 1875 mansion that creates a feeling of absolute peace.*

Price Guide: (including breakfast)
imperial suites U.S.$215-U.S.$245
real suite U.S.$280-U.S.$310
master suite U.S.$320-U.S.$425

16 80 DVD WiFi

Attractions: Historical Center, 5-min walk; Imperial Museum, 10-min walk; Cathedral and Crystal Palace, 10-min walk
Towns/Cities: Teresópolis, 31 miles; Friburgo, 37 miles; Rio de Janeiro, 50 miles
Airports: Rio de Janeiro International Airport, 1-hour drive

Located on a beautiful street in Petrópolis, Solar do Império is a 16-room hotel that offers a comfortable retreat in Rio de Janeiro's mountain region. Built within a mansion, the hotel is decorated in a neoclassical style with modern amenities such a dry and wet sauna, spa and massage area. Leopoldina restaurant offers breakfast each morning, and lunch and dinner menus are created by Executive Chef Claudia Mascarenhas who serves contemporary, international and Brazilian dishes. The restored and modernized former stables can be turned into 3 adjoining large halls for events, business meetings and parties. For an unusual experience take a ride on Vitorias: horse-drawn wagons that will pick you up from the hotel's gardens for tours through the nearby historical center and Imperial Museum.

Tankamana EcoResort

ESTRADA JÚLIO CÁPUA, S/N VALE DO CUIABÁ, ITAIPAVA - PETRÓPOLIS, RIO DE JANEIRO 25745-050
Tel: +55 24 2222 9181 **Fax:** +55 24 2242 0034
Web: www.johansens.com/tankamana **E-mail:** atendimento@pousadatankamana.com.br

The freshest, cleanest of air and the densest of greenery envelop this rustic mountain retreat. Surrounds are lush rainforests, almost impenetrable vegetation, sparkling waterfalls and the majestic heights of the Serra dos Órgãos Range. Sprawling over 880,000m^2 of parkland, the resort offers a unique vacation experience and the opportunity to shake off the stresses of busy, modern life thanks to facilities such as the saunas and natural stone pools. The 15 exclusive, well-spaced log cabins are the ultimate in relaxation and country-style luxury; built from eucalyptus trunks, each boasts 21st-century amenities and has delightful décor and furnishings. Very romantic as well as private, they also have hydromassage tubs and/or an ofurô facility (Japanese-style tub). Mouth-watering combinations of regional specialties and international cuisine are enjoyed in the transparent, glass-floored restaurant built over trout breeding tanks.

Our inspector loved: *The comfort of the cabins and the overwhelming beauty of the forest that surrounds the property.*

Price Guide: (including breakfast)
cabins U.S.$250-U.S.$510

15

Attractions: Rainforest Reserve, 5-min walk; Itaipava District and Shops, 20-min drive; Serra dos Órgãos National Park, 30-min drive
Towns/Cities: Petrópolis, 40-min drive; Teresópolis, 1-hour drive
Airports: Rio de Janeiro International Airport, 90-min drive

Hotel Marina All Suites

AV. DELFIM MOREIRA, 696, PRAIA DO LEBLON, RIO DE JANEIRO 22441-000
Tel: +55 21 2172 1001 **Fax:** +55 21 2172 1110
Web: www.johansens.com/marinaallsuites **E-mail:** reservas@hotelmarina.com.br

Our inspector loved: *The comfort, the unique décor and beautiful ocean view from some of the designer suites.*

Price Guide: (excluding tax)
suites U.S.$479-U.S.$1,553

38 10

Awards/Ratings: Condé Nast Johansens Most Excellent Boutique Hotel 2006

Attractions: Ipanema Beach, 10-min walk; Botanical Garden, 5-min drive
Towns/Cities: Petrópolis - Imperial City, 90-min drive; Búzios, 150-min drive
Airports: Rio de Janeiro Domestic Airport, 20-min drive; Rio de Janeiro International Airport, 40-min drive

With its prime location directly on Leblon Beach, this fashionable and sophisticated hotel will truly make you feel at home. This is the only deluxe boutique hotel in the city, and everything here is immensely stylish and aesthetically pleasing. All of the 38 individually decorated suites have ocean views and include generous living areas, and some have mini-kitchens. For a very special experience, choose one of the 8 designer suites, which have been created by some of the most talented Brazilian architects and interior designers. Delicious modern French cuisine is served in the Bar d'Hôtel restaurant, which attracts great numbers of "the beautiful people" of Rio. Movie lovers will be delighted with the charming air-conditioned home theater, which allows total privacy for up to 8 guests.

Toca da Coruja

AV. BAIA DOS GOLFINHOS, 464, PRAIA DA PIPA, TIBAU DO SUL, RIO GRANDE DO NORTE 59178-000
Tel: +55 84 3246 2226 **Fax:** +55 84 3246 2225
Web: www.johansens.com/tocadacoruja **E-mail:** tocadacoruja@tocadacoruja.com.br

Located 100 meters from the unspoiled Pipa Beach, within 25,000m² of lush gardens, Toca da Coruja is a tropical hideaway for nature lovers desiring a break from the pressures of every-day life. The hammock-adorned grounds include plenty of fruit trees, exotic birds and other fauna, a semi-Olympic size swimming pool, a sauna, hydro-massage and 23 colorful, well-appointed chalets and apartments, each with their own veranda. The hotel's interiors feature bright colors, bamboo furniture, ceramics by sculptor Francisco Brennard, and a distinctly Brazilian ambience. Brazilian-fusion and local dishes are served in the atmospheric restaurant and a poolside bar provides personalized service during the day. Hand-woven crafts can be purchased in the gift shop of this charming and stylish retreat.

***Our inspector loved:** Relaxing in the charming and beautifully designed gardens, which surround all rooms and bungalows.*

Price Guide: (including breakfast, excluding tax, double occupancy, 30% extra for additional person)
small suites U.S.$195
bungalows U.S.$315
deluxe bungalow U.S.$574

23 12 DVD WiFi

Attractions: Pipa's Main Street, 1-min walk; "Praia do Amor," 10-min drive; "Praia do Madeiro," 10-min drive; Ecological Sanctuary, 10-min drive
Towns/Cities: Goianinha, 16 miles; Natal, 53 miles
Airports: Natal Airport, 40 miles; Recife International Airport, 165 miles

ESTALAGEM ST. HUBERTUS

RUA CARRIERI, 974, GRAMADO, RIO GRANDE DO SUL 95670-000
Tel: +55 54 3286 1273 **Fax:** +55 54 3286 1273
Web: www.johansens.com/sthubertus **E-mail:** sthubertus@sthubertus.com

Our inspector loved: *Having a delicious breakfast overlooking the beautiful "Black Lake."*

Price Guide: (including breakfast)
rooms U.S.$190-U.S.$1,090

29

Attractions: Black Lake; Caracol's Waterfall, 15-min drive; Itaimbezinho's Canyons, 2-hour drive; Vineyard, 2-hour drive
Towns/Cities: Canela, 10-min drive; Nova Petrópolis, 30-min drive; Caxias do Sul, 1-hour drive; Porto Alegre, 2-hour drive
Airports: Porto Alegre International Airport, 83 miles

Situated above peaceful Lake Negro, Estalagem St. Hubertus offers cozy charm in an idyllic setting. Each room is individually decorated with floral print, wood furniture and a color-theme. The romantic, super luxury themed rooms come with names such as Tulip, Provence and Lake, and the unique Suite Real covers 92 sq. m. of space complete with luxurious marble bathrooms featuring hydromassage tubs and beautiful valley views. The charming ambience extends beyond the guest rooms to the reading room with mini-library and antlers set above its cozy fireplace. Sunlit dining areas overlook the lake. Pamper yourself with a massage, de-stress in the steam sauna or take a dip in the heated swimming pool at this bucolic yet upscale hotel.

KUROTEL

RUA NACÕES UNIDAS 533, P.O. BOX 65, GRAMADO, RIO GRANDE DO SUL 95670-000
Tel: +55 54 3295 9393 **Fax:** +55 54 3286 1203
Web: www.johansens.com/kurotel **E-mail:** reservas@kurotel.com.br

Our inspector loved: *The first-class service at the spa and the restaurant.*

Price Guide: (all inclusive, including nutritional guidance, select number of treatments, exercise classes, medical, psychological and beauty assessments)
apartments and suites U.S.$1,793-U.S.$3,833

35 60 12 SPA

Awards/Ratings: Condé Nast Johansens Most Excellent Spa Hotel, South America 2007 and 2008

Attractions: Waterfall Cable Car, 10-min drive; Rafting, 10-min drive; Canyons, 90-min drive; Vineyard, 90-min drive
Towns/Cities: Canela,10-min drive; Nova Petrópolis, 30-min drive; Caxias do Sul, 1-hour drive; Porto Alegre, 100-min drive
Airports: Porto Alegre International Airport, 100-min drive

With an international reputation for helping people achieve better health through predictive, preventive medicine, Kurotel Longevity Center and Spa offers over 27 years of family-guided experience. Kurotel's European-Colonial exterior is complemented by classic, richly appointed rooms and suites and is part pampering spa, part state-of-the-art medical center. There are many innovative programs including executive health, smoke cessation, stress control, weight control, and lifestyle focused on optimum health, as well as Kinder Kur, designed exclusively for mothers and their newborn babies. On the cutting-edge, the Cellular Revitalization Treatment assists in the organic functions and immunologic responses quality. With more than 2 staff members to attend to each client, the center provides truly personalized service by addressing all aspects of human behavior and makes each guest feel at home.

Pousada do Engenho

RUA ODON CAVALCANTE, 330, SÃO FRANCISCO DE PAULA 95400-000, RIO GRANDE DO SUL
Tel: +55 54 3244 1270
Web: www.johansens.com/pousadadoengenho **E-mail:** pousadadoengenho@pousadadoengenho.com.br

***Our inspector loved:** The exuberance evoked by the comfortable cabanas.*

Price Guide: (including breakfast)
cabanas U.S.$200-U.S.$330

Awards/Ratings: Condé Nast Johansens Most Excellent Lodge, South America 2008

Attractions: São Bernardo Lake, 0.4 miles; Passeio a Cavalo (Horse Riding) and Passo Alegre Farm, 14 miles; Buddhist Temple, 15 miles; Canions, 56 miles
Towns/Cities: Gramado, 25 miles
Airports: Porto Alegre International Airport, 2-hour drive

This small eco-friendly lodge is nestled in the forests of southern Brazil on the border between subtropical and temperate climate zones. The result is a beautiful and unique environment abundant with diverse flora and fauna. The Pousada consists of 10 individual cabanas tucked away in the forest for complete privacy whose rustic appearance blends into the surroundings and belies the modern comforts within such as Jacuzzis and wireless Internet access. Cabanas also feature skylights and verandas with hammocks. The cozy Casa de Babette restaurant, managed by the owners, offers a variety of fare from traditional Brazilian to Indian cuisine. Enjoy games in the lounge or venture out to try nearby trekking, rafting and horseback riding that can all be arranged for you.

BRAZIL - SANTA CATARINA (GOVERNADOR CELSO RAMOS)

PONTA DOS GANCHOS

RUA EUPÍDIO ALVES DO NASCIMENTO, 104, GOVERNADOR CELSO RAMOS, SANTA CATARINA 88190-000
Tel: +55 48 3262 5000 **Fax:** +55 48 3262 5046
Web: www.johansens.com/pontadosganchos **E-mail:** reservas@pontadosganchos.com.br

Clear blue water and lush green fauna surround this adults-only resort. All meals are included in the rates, and the restaurant closes after the last guest has retired for the evening. The gourmet kitchen serves regional Catarinese cuisine at lunch and international fare for dinner, while the well-stocked bars offer over 200 wines, fine liquors and various Cuban cigars. For a truly memorable evening, savor an evening meal on a private island served by your very own waiter. Scuba diving in the Marine Reserve and diving lessons with instructors, qualified by the P.A.D.I., can be arranged but for those who simply wish to kick back, there is a wide selection of D.V.D.s that can be viewed in the resort's cinema or in your very own bungalow. Alternately, spend some time in the Dior Spa.

Our inspector loved: *The sophisticated service and the food after a day at the exclusive beach.*

Price Guide: (all inclusive)
bungalows R$1,190-R$4,200

25 M 40 SPA

Awards/Ratings: Condé Nast Johansens Most Excellent Hotel, South America 2007 and 2008

Attractions: Dolphins Bay, 20-min boat ride; Ilha do Arvoredo, 25-min boat ride
Towns/Cities: Florianópolis, 19 miles; Balneário Camboriú, 34 miles
Airports: Florianópolis International Airport, 50-min drive

Affiliations: Relais & Châteaux

Ilha do Papagaio

ILHA DO PAPAGAIO, PALHOÇA, SANTA CATARINA 88131-970
Tel: +55 48 3286 1242 **Fax:** +55 48 3286 1342
Web: www.johansens.com/ilhadopapagaio **E-mail:** papagaio@papagaio.com.br

Our inspector loved: *The exclusivity of the comfortable ocean-front chalets.*

Price Guide: (including breakfast, per couple)
rooms U.S.$304-U.S.$520

20 23

Attractions: Whale-Watching; Marine Farm Raising Oysters and Mussels; Serra do Tabuleiro State Park
Towns/Cities: Florianópolis, 19 miles
Airports: Florianópolis International Airport, 24 miles

Surrounded by more than 100,000m² of naturally preserved vegetation, Ilha do Papagaio, or "Parrot Island," is perfect for nature lovers dreaming of a luxury eco-resort experience. This family-run resort is the only establishment on the island providing its guests with an escape from civilization that sacrifices none of its luxuries. The resort's 20 colorfully-decorated chalets, often featuring canopy beds, fireplaces, and balconies with exquisite views, are well-equipped with every modern amenity, and in the resort's grounds you will find a gym and games room. Relax by sitting under the thatched roof of the bar sipping a delicious island cocktail, or receive a complimentary massage. The restaurant, at which chef serves a wide variety of beautifully-presented and delicious dishes, comes highly recommended.

Pousada Solar Mirador

ESTRADA GERAL DO ROSA S/N, PRAIA DO ROSA, IMBITUBA, SANTA CATARINA 88780-000
Tel: +55 48 3355 6144 **Fax:** +55 48 3355 6697
Web: www.johansens.com/solarmirador **E-mail:** reserva@solarmirador.com.br

Perched high over Rosa Lake with privileged views of the beautiful Praia do Rosa, Pousada Solar Mirador is an intimate hotel immersed in natural beauty. Rooms are bright and airy and offer panoramic views of the beach, and public spaces decorated with stucco, stone and local art evoke a rustic elegance. The Pousada offers a lavish breakfast each morning, featuring home-made jams, quiches and cakes among other things, and Urucum restaurant serves Brazilian cuisine with an innovative fusion of native, African and Portuguese influences. During the day, lounge by the pool on the spacious deck that overlooks Rosa Bay or take a walk to the beautiful lake through the lush native vegetation.

Our inspector loved: *Eating the famous local seafood dish ("moqueca") while looking out to the wonderfull Praia do Rosa.*

Price Guide: (including breakfast)
rooms U.S.$145-U.S.$290

12 DVD SPA

Attractions: Whale-Watching, close by; Beach, 2-min walk; Surfing, Windsurfing and Horse Riding, 5-min walk; Praia Vermelha Trail, 40-min walk
Towns/Cities: Garopaba, 11 miles; Imbituba, 11 miles; Florianópolis, 40 miles
Airports: Florianópolis International Airport, 44 miles

HOTEL FRONTENAC

AV. DR. PAULO RIBAS, 295 CAPIVARI, CAMPOS DO JORDÃO - SP 12460-000
Tel: +55 12 3669 1000 **Fax:** +55 12 3669 1009
Web: www.johansens.com/frontenac **E-mail:** reservas@frontenac.com.br

Our inspector loved: *The atmosphere of the Brahm's Bar.*

Price Guide: (including breakfast, excluding tax)
rooms U.S.$178-U.S.$695

47 M 30 DVD

Attractions: Capivari's Touristic Center, 219 yards
Towns/Cities: Santo Antonio dos Pinhais, 15-min drive
Airports: São Paulo International Airport, 112 miles; Rio de Janeiro International Airport, 220 miles

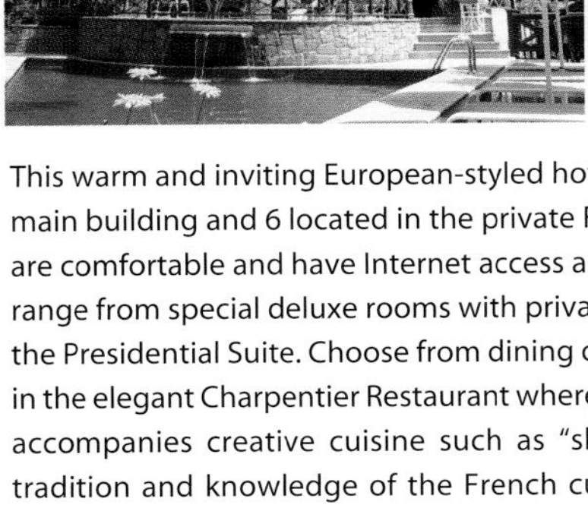

This warm and inviting European-styled hotel has 41 guest rooms within the main building and 6 located in the private Frontenac Chalet. Superior rooms are comfortable and have Internet access and L.C.D. televisions, while others range from special deluxe rooms with private balconies or indoor terraces to the Presidential Suite. Choose from dining on the relaxed, informal terrace or in the elegant Charpentier Restaurant where an extensive worldwide wine list accompanies creative cuisine such as "shrimp in papaya" based on the tradition and knowledge of the French culinary revival. Brahm's Bar is an authentic British pub; the ideal place to meet friends and play songs on the jukebox. There is also a library, a home theater and a fitness center.

DPNY Beach Hotel

AV. JOSÉ PACHECO DO NASCIMENTO, 7668, PRAIA DO CURRAL, ILHABELA, SÃO PAULO 11630-000
Tel: +55 12 3894 2121 **Fax:** +55 12 3894 2060
Web: www.johansens.com/dpnybeach **E-mail:** reservas@dpnybeach.com.br

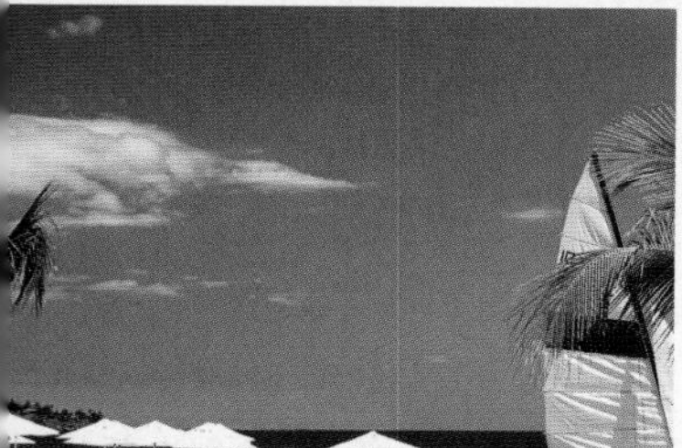

Located directly on the Ilhabela's north shore beach-front, this hotel is fashionable, luxurious, and undeniably Brazilian. Bright interiors decorated with hand-made clay figures and other local art, colorful tiled walls, animal-print furniture and an array of indoor vegetation, create a warm, tropical atmosphere. Rooms are sumptuous and well decorated, with touches such as shell detailing on the headboards of the king-sized canopied beds, muraled cabinets, bamboo furniture and native art creating an eclectic, stylish atmosphere. In addition to L.C.D. televisions, each room includes an iPod, Internet access and in some rooms a cordless phone reaching out to the beach. Enjoy Mediterranean-influenced Brazilian cuisine at Tróia, and spend the sunset and nights at the Hippie Chic Beach Club, where D.J.s spin fine Lounge and House music regularly.

Our inspector loved: *The hippie chic decór and mosaics.*

Price Guide: (including breakfast)
rooms U.S.$120-U.S.$600

70 8 WiFi

Attractions: 40 Beaches, nearby; Shipwrecks, Rivers and Streams, nearby; Cachoeira dos Três Tombos and Cachoeira do Gato Waterfalls, 30 and 45-min walk; Isolated Community of Surfing Bonete, 4-hour walk through rainforest
Airports: São Paulo International Airport, 124 miles; Rio de Janeiro International Airport, 218 miles

HOTEL EMILIANO

RUA OSCAR FREIRE 384, SÃO PAULO, SÃO PAULO 01426-000
Tel: +55 11 3068 4393 **Fax:** +55 11 3068 4394
Web: www.johansens.com/emiliano **E-mail:** reservas@emiliano.com.br

Our inspector loved: *The sophistication of the comfortable bedrooms as well as the perfect location of the hotel.*

Price Guide: (including breakfast)
rooms from $450
suites from $810

Attractions: First-Class Boutiques and Restaurants, 1-min walk
Airports: São Paulo Domestic Airport, 30-min drive; São Paulo International Airport, 1-hour drive

Affiliations: The Leading Small Hotels of the World

Located on Oscar Freire Street, São Paulo's most fashionable boulevard, the Emiliano is a chic and elegant hotel, perfect for the most discerning traveler. The eye-catching setting has a high-end modern flair, and each suite and deluxe room boasts incredibly high-tech features, the finest in Egyptian linens and impressive bathrooms made from blocks of Italian Carrara marble. State-of-the-art, large L.C.D. T.V.s, a home theater and Charles Eammes chairs will ensure that you have the perfect ambience. The restaurant serves contemporary Italian cuisine where you will enjoy the creativity of Chef José Baratino. Visit the Emiliano Spa located on the rooftop, and enjoy exclusive services of Decléor, its 2 Japanese bathtubs and beautiful chaises loungues perfect for relaxing and admiring the city views.

HOTEL UNIQUE

AV. BRIGADEIRO LUIS ANTONIO, 4.700, SÃO PAULO, SÃO PAULO 01402-002
Tel: +55 11 3055 4710 **Fax:** +55 11 3889 8100
Web: www.johansens.com/hotelunique **E-mail:** reservas@hotelunique.com.br

Our inspector loved: *Having a drink at the great lobby bar or at the hip rooftop restaurant with its unique view of São Paulo.*

Price Guide: (excluding taxes, small pets welcome at an additional charge)
rooms U.S.$395-U.S.$7,000

95 2000

Living up to its name, this hotel boasts a bold and modern design with its curved copper façade and sleek, modern interior. Choose from a variety of rooms designed to stimulate your senses with their innovative use of geometric shapes and color. Or experience a blend of glamour and art in a lavishly-appointed suite, which offers spacious accommodations and every technological amenity. The Body & Soul Fitness Center, as well as surrounding São Paulo, provide guests with opportunities to relax and explore. The hotel's main attraction however, consists of its trendy rooftop pool and bar area, featuring Skye restaurant. This fashionable venue offers stunning views of the São Paulo skyline as well as an exciting social scene, to be enjoyed either on the open-air deck or from the restaurant's floor-to-ceiling glass windows.

Attractions: Ibirapuera Park, 1 mile; Iguatemi Shopping Mall, 10-min drive
Airports: São Paulo Domestic Airport, 15-min drive; São Paulo International Airport, 40-min drive

Spa Unique Garden

ESTRADA LARAMARA, 3500, SERRA DA CANTAREIRA, SÃO PAULO 07600-970
Tel: +55 11 4486 8700 **Fax:** +55 11 4486 4420
Web: www.johansens.com/uniquegarden **E-mail:** uniquegarden@uniquegarden.com.br

Our inspector loved: *The wide range of options in terms of outdoor spiritual activities and spa treatments.*

Price Guide: (including breakfast)
rooms U.S.$440-U.S.$1,500

26 200 16 SPA

Attractions: The Last Natural Rainforest Reserve Park, on-site; Extreme Sports Area, 656 yards; Pedra Grande, 20-min drive
Towns/Cities: Campinas, 45-min drive; São Paulo, 50-min drive
Airports: São Paulo International Airport, 40-min drive; São Paulo Domestic Airport, 1-hour drive; Campinas International Airport, 75-min drive

With a philosophy aimed at body and soul rejuvenation, Spa Unique Garden is an oasis of well-being and relaxation. Its 26 apartments, spa, tennis courts and restaurants are situated within 300,000m^2 of aromatic gardens, a lake and woodlands full of exotic plants and birds. The spa is the highlight of the resort, with an array of innovative treatments ranging from Vinetherapy to Dead Sea baths and everything in between. The resort boasts 3 restaurants, one for each meal of the day. Chez Victor, the upscale dinner restaurant, features rich hues and votive candles and a menu of beautifully presented dishes, each adhering to the tenets of the Mediterranean diet. The well-appointed rooms range from light and airy to ultra-modern.

Chile

Ilo
PERU
Arica
Iquique
Tocopilla
Calama
336
Antofagasta
Uncia
SUCRE
BOLIVIA
Camiri
Tupiza
Mariscal Estigarribia
Corumbá
Miranda
BRAZIL
PARAGUAY
Concepción
Orán
San Pedro
ASUNCIÓN
Cor. Oviedo
Tres Isletas
Pilar
San Miguel de Tucumán
Resistencia
Posadas
Copiapó
Goya
Uruguaiana
La Rioja
La Serena
Coquimbo
Ovalle
Chimbas
Córdoba
Santa Fé
Salto
Rosario
ARGENTINA
URUGUAY
Quilpué
339
340
Valparaíso
SANTIAGO
Rancagua
San Rafael
BUENOS AIRES
MONTEVIDEO
Curicó
Talca
Linares
Santa Rosa
Olavarría
Talcahuano
Chillán
Concepción
Los Angeles
Mar del Plata
Bahía Blanca
PACIFIC OCEAN
Cipolletti
Temuco
335
Valdivia
Osorno
San Carlos de Bariloche
Puerto Montt
341
Rawson
Patagonia represented by shaded area
ATLANTIC OCEAN
Coihaique
Comodoro Rivadavia
337
Stanley
Río Gallegos
338
Punta Arenas
Ushuaia

Villarrica Park Lake Hotel

CAMINO A VILLARRICA KM.13, VILLARRICA, REGIÓN DE ARAUCANÍA
Tel: +56 2 207 7070 **Fax:** +56 2 207 7020
Web: www.johansens.com/villarrica **E-mail:** reservas@vplh.cl

Our inspector loved: *The immense lake, the pine woods and the Villarrica volcano.*

Price Guide: (including breakfast)
rooms U.S.$355-U.S.$385
suites U.S.$425-U.S.$2300

70 170 WiFi SPA

Attractions: Canopi Tour, 13 miles; Volcanic Cave Tour, 19 miles; Skiing, 19 miles
Towns/Cities: Pucon, 5 miles; Villarrica, 5 miles; Temuco, 56 miles
Airports: Temuco Airport, 56 miles

Located in the Northern Patagonia Lake District, set against the stunning backdrop of a magnificent snow-capped volcano, Villarrica Park Lake Hotel is surrounded by beautiful gardens and perched at the edge of a vast, deep blue lake. Combining sophisticated comfort with a location as dramatic as it is peaceful, the private guest room balconies, large floor-to-ceiling windows and terraces found liberally throughout the main areas of the hotel, highlight the privileged views of the resort's unique location in the Villarrica region. A sense of serenity fills the hotel and Aquarius Spa where you can treat yourself to a massage. Enjoy a local specialty in the Aguas Verdes restaurant and taste Chilean wines in the fifth floor Vertigo Bar to round off a well-spent day of relaxation or exploration.

Alto Atacama

CAMINO PUCARÀ S/N, SECTOR SUCHOR, AYLLÙ DE QUITOR, SAN PEDRO DE ATACAMA, REGIÓN DE ATACAMA
Tel: +562 436 0265 **Fax:** +562 436 0266
Web: www.johansens.com/altoatacama **E-mail:** reservas@altoatacama.com

Built in the traditional style of an adobe settlement, complete with llamas and crops traditional to the area, Alto Atacama seamlessly combines nature with luxury to recreate the look of an Altiplanic village. The location is ideal for exploring the surrounding terrain, from the Salt Mountains to the Katarpe Valley. Bilingual guides come armed with extensive knowledge for any type of excursion imaginable, by car, foot or bicycle. Each suite has a private terrace and is designed in an open-plan for a more relaxing stay. After a long day, relax in the extensive spa, in one of the 6 pools, 2 saunas, or with a massage treatment. Enjoy lunch and dinner at the restaurant, which serves a modern Chilean menu, or get a drink from the bar to enjoy on the terrace or by the roaring fire in the living room.

Our inspector loved: *The spectacular landscape surrounded by desert mountains, and the great outdoor activities.*

Price Guide: (all inclusive, double occupancy)
3-night stay U.S.$1,350
4-night stay U.S.$1,750

32 · 50 · SPA

Attractions: Laguna Cèjar, 15 miles; Salar de Atacama, 20 miles; Valle de La Luna, 20 miles; Tatio Geysers, 52 miles
Towns/Cities: Calama, 60 miles
Airports: Calama El Loa Airport, 65 miles

CHILE - REGION DE AYSEN (PATAGONIA - PUERTO GUADAL)

Hacienda Tres Lagos

CARRETERA AUSTRAL SUR KM 274, LOCALIDAD LAGO NEGRO, PUERTO GUADAL, REGION DE AYSEN, PATAGONIA

Tel: +56 2 333 4122 **Fax:** +56 2 334 5294

Web: www.johansens.com/treslagos **E-mail:** ventas@haciendatreslagos.cl

Our inspector loved: *The incredible menu of outdoor activities and the tranquility, privacy and relaxation guests can have at the hotel and spa.*

Price Guide: (including breakfast, per person)
rooms U.S.$269-U.S.$370

Attractions: 1-hour Tour of Marble Caves; Glacier Trekking, 8 miles; The Valley of Explorers, 32 miles
Towns/Cities: Puerto Guadal, 7 miles; Puerto Tranquilo, 32 miles; Chile Chico, 68 miles; Coyhaique, 170 miles
Airports: Balmaceda Airport, 140 miles

This beautifully designed hotel, consisting of individual bungalows and suites, is located in the heart of Patagonia, and overlooks the spectacular Negro Lake. "Tres Lagos" means Three Lakes and that is exactly what surrounds the property, which also has a private beach. The 2 restaurants, Don Domingo and Quincho mi querido Tio Pancho, serve a wide variety of traditional Patagonian food including barbecue, and there is a lovely bar in which to relax. This is a unique eco-tourism area where the adventurous can explore the natural habitat but return to comfort and privacy at the end of each day. Activities arranged by the hotel include canopy lining, boat trips, 4x4 adventure tours, fly fishing, trekking, horseriding and rafting. There is also a games room, bar, spa, sauna, Jacuzzi and massages available.

CHILE - REGIÓN DE MAGALLANES (PATAGONIA - PUERTO NATALES)

INDIGO PATAGONIA HOTEL & SPA

LADRILLEROS 105, PUERTO NATALES, REGIÓN DE MAGALLANES
Tel: +566 141 3609 **Fax:** +566 161 3453
Web: www.johansens.com/indigopatagonia **E-mail:** info@indigopatagonia.com

Amidst the spectacular and breathtaking scenery of southern Patagonia is Indigo Patagonia, a luxury hotel designed to complement the environment in which it is located. Each room offers incredible views and provides a unique experience thanks to special features such as hand-woven wool sheets and blankets. Pezglacier restaurant serves local products, such as freshly caught seafood and organic local vegetables, all cooked to enhance the experience of Patagonia. After a day full of excitement and emotion, relax at the rooftop spa in one of the Jacuzzis or have a cappuccino in the Pisco Sour Café, which turns into a lively bar during the evenings. Most importantly, take advantage of the once-in-a-lifetime activities, such as visiting the Glacier Serrano, riding horseback through the landscape or kayaking to the fjord, where you can see all types of wildlife in their natural habitat.

Our inspector loved: *The spectacular design and architecture mixed together with the excellent location and great views.*

Price Guide: (including breakfast)
rooms U.S.$208-U.S.$260
suites U.S.$273-U.S.$350

29 DVD WiFi
SPA

Attractions: "Ultima Esperanza Fjord" Boat Cruises to Serrano and Balmaceda Glaciers; Cueva del Milodòn, 20 miles; Torres del Paine, 90 miles
Towns/Cities: Punta Arenas, 170 miles
Airports: Puerto Natales Airport (During the Summer Only), 10 miles; Punta Arenas Airport, 180 miles

Hotel Manoir Atkinson

PASEO ATKINSON 165, CERRO CONCEPCION, VALPARAÍSO, REGIÓN DE VALPARAÍSO
Tel: +563 2235 1313 **Fax:** +563 2235 1313
Web: www.johansens.com/hotelatkinson **E-mail:** info@hotelatkinson.cl

Our inspector loved: *The spectacular view of Valparaiso seen from the terrace.*

Price Guide: (including breakfast)
rooms U.S.$160-U.S.$250

7

Attractions: Viña del Mar, 15 miles; Reñaca, 20 miles
Towns/Cities: Santiago, 90 miles
Airports: Arturo Merino Benitez Airport, Santiago, 70 miles

A charming French boutique-style hotel, Hotel Manoir Atkinson is located in the heart of the historic district of Valparaíso. Emanating a warm and hospitable atmosphere, the décor is classic while combining modern comfort with history. Each room is individually decorated and offers a serene atmosphere where you can enjoy a gourmet breakfast. The rooftop terrace looks out to superb panoramic views of the city, the coast and the bay, and is furnished with hammocks in which to relax and feel the cooling breeze. Steeped in history, the surrounding area is filled with intriguing architecture and a winding configuration throughout the hills. The hills are the reason for the multitude of funiculars, many of which are still in operation today, and have become a symbol of the city.

Hotel Del Mar - Enjoy Hotels

AV. PERÚ ESQUINA AV. LOS HÉROES, VIÑA DEL MAR, REGIÓN DE VALPARAÍSO
Tel: +56 2 770 5190 **Fax:** +56 2 770 5103
Web: www.johansens.com/hoteldelmarcl **E-mail:** reservas@enjoy.cl

Our inspector loved: *The amplitude of the luxurious rooms.*

Price Guide:
standard luxe U.S.$216-U.S.$534
suites U.S.$345-U.S.$855

60 2274 SPA

Attractions: Valparaíso, 10 miles; Reñaca Beaches, 10 miles; Valle de Casablanca, Vineyards, 40 miles
Towns/Cities: Valparaíso, 10 miles; Santiago, 85 miles
Airports: Arturo Merino Benitez Airport, Santiago, 75 miles

Considered one of the best 5-star hotels in Chile, Hotel Del Mar is an urban-beach hotel located directly across from the ocean and within walking distance of Viña del Mar's historic downtown. The spacious rooms all offer spectacular views of the ocean or the extensive gardens. The cuisine is modern and intriguing, combining Chilean tastes with international specialties. Also take time to experience the 3 fun bars, all serving a variety of cocktails and drinks. The Spa aims to harmonize the mind and body with massages, steam baths and hydro-massages, as well as a state-of-the-art fitness center. Head out to explore the port city of Valparaíso, which is a UNESCO World Heritage site, with its historic buildings and beautiful antique gardens. The hotel will organize a tour guide to show you all the city has to offer, and at night, have fun at the hotel's elegant casino, where hundreds of slot machines and various table games await you.

Nomads of the Seas

PUERTO MONTT, REGIÓN DE LOS LAGOS
Tel: +562 414 4600 **Fax:** +562 206 1450
Web: www.johansens.com/nomadsoftheseas **E-mail:** contacts@nomadsoftheseas.com

Our inspector loved: *The unique and luxurious experience of exploring and traveling by air, land and sea through amazing Patagonia.*

Price Guide: (all inclusive cruise, per person based on double occupancy per cabin, including taxes)
deluxe U.S.$10,115-U.S.$24,098
premium U.S.$12,138-U.S.$28,917

14 DVD WiFi SPA

Attractions: Fly-fishing, Heliski, Whale-watching, Birdwatching, Trekking and Hiking, Photographic Safaris, Helicopter Flights, Boating, Spa and Thalassotherapy and Various Adventures
Towns/Cities: Puerto Montt, Port of Departure, 600 miles south of Santiago
Airports: Puerto Montt "El Tepual" Airport, 10 miles from port of departure

Nomads of the Seas offers a unique and exciting way to explore the remote southern corner of the world: Patagonia. The Atmosphere, the base ship, cruises by night and during the day anchors off the coast for a full day of adventure. Choose from fly-fishing for trout and salmon excursions, trekking and hiking unexplored areas, kayaking in both the river and fjords, horse-back riding, rafting, jet-boating or airborne sightseeing in the ship's helicopter. Also partake in expertly guided bird or whale-watching tours. After a day of activities, relax with a spa treatment, soak in a thalassotherapy hot tub, listen to a fascinating lecture or indulge in the fresh gourmet cuisine prepared on board, which is also enjoyed in all of the day-long adventures. The service aboard the Atmosphere will make you feel at home, with the wilderness right outside your door.

Ecuador

Pacific Ocean
COLOMBIA
PERU
Florencia
Tumaco
Pasto
Mocoa
Túquerres
Ipiales
Tulcán
Puerto Asís
San Miguel
Esmeraldas
Ibarra
346
345
QUITO
344
Latacunga
Tena
Quevedo
Manta
Portoviejo
Ambato
Puyo
Guaranda
Riobamba
Babahoyo
Macas
Guayaquil
Milagro
Andoas
Cañar
Azogues
Mendez
Cuenca
343
Machala
Pasaje
Santa Rosa
Tumbes
Arenillas
Zamora
Loja
Macará
Ayabaca
Talara
Sullana
Chulucanas
San Ignacio

Mansión Alcázar Boutique Hotel

CALLE BOLÍVAR 12-55 Y TARQUI, CUENCA, AZUAY
Tel: +593 72823 918 **Fax:** +593 72823 554
Web: www.johansens.com/mansionalcazar **E-mail:** info@mansionalcazar.com

Our inspector loved: *Its luxurious, tasteful design and tranquil, romantic atmosphere.*

Price Guide: (including buffet breakfast, excluding 12% tax and 10% service charge)
rooms U.S.$80-U.S.$130
suites U.S.$180

14 M30 DVD WiFi

Attractions: Cathedral of the Immaculate Conception and Abdón Calderón Central Park, 3-min walk; "El Barranco," 5-min walk; Cajas National Park, 19 miles; Ruins of Cojitambo, 30 miles
Towns/Cities: Gualaceo and Chordeleg, 22 miles; Guayaquil, 30-min flight; Loja, 35-min flight from Quito; Valle de Yunguilla, 90-min drive
Airports: Cuenca, 10-min drive; Guayaquil International Airport, 30-min flight; Quito International Airport, 35-min flight

Mansión Alcázar Boutique Hotel is a sample of Ecuadorian Republican luxury style, fully restored to its original splendor and designed to make guests feel right at home. Relax in the sumptuous garden or taste champagne in the aptly named "Champagne Lounge," filled with lovely art and crystal chandeliers reminiscent of the old days of Colonial living. And enjoy drinks in "Le Bar," before dining at Casa Alonso, which serves local cuisine as well as international specialties, before retiring to your comfortable guest room. Each room is dedicated to a theme reflecting an aspect of Ecuadorian culture and climate. Take time to explore Cuenca, a UNESCO World Heritage Site, with its 4 rivers, breathtaking mountains and 14th and 15th-century architecture. Enjoy the centuries-old churches and plazas as well as the modern art museums, showcasing the breadth of the city's culture.

HACIENDA SAN AGUSTIN DE CALLO

77KM SOUTH OF QUITO ON THE PANAMERICAN HIGHWAY, LASSO, COTOPAXI
Quito Office: +593 2 2906157/8 **Hacienda:** +593 3 2719160
Web: www.johansens.com/haciendasanagustin **E-mail:** info@incahacienda.com

Built on the site of an Inca palace, later turned into an Augustinian Convent, and was also temporary home of the French Geodesic Mission (during 1742) whose scientific work determined the true shape of the earth, Hacienda San Agustin de Callo could not be more steeped in history. Purchased by a former President of Ecuador, this landmark has been fully restored and offers guests a unique look into the past. Guest rooms showcase vibrant colors and traditional art and furniture. The perfectly carved volcanic stone walls from the 15th century welcome guests to dinner, with authentic Andean cuisine prepared with ingredients fresh from the farm. Take time to trek by car up the side of the famous Cotopaxi volcano, go for a horseback ride on traditional Inca trails with a picnic or visit one of the many exciting native Indian markets.

Our inspector loved: *Taking a very warm bath in front of the open fireplace.*

Price Guide: (including meals, treks, fishing, 2-hour bicycle ride and visit to a rose plantation. 3-night stays include a visit to Saquisili Local Market on Thursdays. Longer stays include trips and excursions.)
rooms U.S.$228- U.S.$348
suites U.S.$398

11 10

Attractions: Horseback Riding With Picnic; Cotopaxi National Park, 45-min drive; Latacunga and Pujilí Market, 30-min drive; Volcanic Crater Lagoon of Quilotoa, 2-hour drive
Towns/Cities: Quito, 43 miles; Latacunga, 30-min drive; Salcedo, 1-hour drive; Ambato, 80-min drive
Airports: Quito International Airport, 90-min drive

Hacienda Zuleta

ANGOCHAGUA, IMBABURA
Tel: +593 6 266 2182 **Fax:** +593 6 266 2032
Web: www.johansens.com/zuleta **E-mail:** info@zuleta.com

Our inspector loved: *The delicious home-made food, and of course, the morning horseback ride to the Condor Huasi Project.*

Price Guide: (all inclusive, excluding alcoholic beverages, tours and activities)
rooms U.S.$275
junior suites U.S.$329

14 M 40 WiFi

Attractions: "El Taller" Embroidery Shop run by the Galo Plaza Lasso Foundation, on-site; Cheese Factory, Organic Garden and Milking Sheds, 5-min walk; Caranqui Pyramids, 15-min walk; Condor Huasi Rehabilitation Project, 40-min walk
Towns/Cities: Zuleta, 5-min walk; Ibarra, 30-min drive; Olmedo, 30-min drive; Otavalo, 1-hour drive
Airports: Quito International Airport, 90-min drive

Surrounded by the beauty of the Andes Mountains, Hacienda Zuleta sits on 4,446 private acres of land which completely support the inhabitants and guests of the hacienda. This private home was opened to guests only 10 years ago and each guest room is exquisitely decorated with antiques and hand-embroidered linen. The personalized service aims to make you feel like one of the family, inviting you to relax in the living and reading rooms, and offers superb cuisine prepared from fresh milk and cream made on-site, trout caught moments before serving and organic fruits and vegetables picked straight from the garden. Enjoy archeological tours of the Caranqui Pyramids, visit the different aspects of the farm, hike and bike through the extensive trails, or take guided horseback adventures throughout the property. Take time to visit some of the sustainable tourism activities such as the women's embroidery project and the condor rehabilitation project.

La Mirage Garden Hotel and Spa

COTACACHI, IMBABURA
Tel: +593 6 291 5237 **Fax:** +593 6 291 5065 **U.S./Canada Toll Free:** 1 800 327 3573
Web: www.johansens.com/mirage **E-mail:** mirage1@mirage.com.ec

Our inspector loved: *The superb food and the 90-minute Cofan Spiritual Spa Treatment.*

Price Guide: (including breakfast and dinner, excluding 12% tax and 10% service charge)
rooms U.S.$300
suites U.S.$350-U.S.$800

23 M 25 SPA

Perched on an Andean hillside, less than 3 hours north of Quito, is the hidden gem La Mirage Garden Hotel and Spa. Experience 5-star luxury accommodations mixed with the native flavor of the Andes. Each room, decorated with local and European art, fireplaces and sitting areas, has a beautiful view of the extensive gardens. The garden itself is stunning, with an array of flowers from dahlias to hibiscus, and is the perfect spot for a relaxing afternoon. If the garden is not enough, the spa offers many treatments, including the healing powers of a traditional shaman. Dining is also enjoyed in the garden for breakfast and lunch, with a gourmet 4-course dinner served in the Main Dining Room. Make sure to explore the surrounding natural sites such as Cuicocha Crater Lake or San Pablo Lake and make time for a visit to the traditional Indian market at Otavalo.

Attractions: Cuicocha Crater Lake, 11 miles; Otavalo Indian Market, 20-min drive; Condor Park, 30-min drive; San Pablo Lake, 30-min drive
Towns/Cities: Cotacachi, 5-min walk; Otavalo, 20-min drive; San Antonio, 30-min drive; City of Ibarra, 40-min drive
Airports: Quito International Airport, 2-hour drive; Esmeraldas Airport, 30-min flight from Quito; Guayaquil International Airport, 35-min flight from Quito

Affiliations: Relais & Châteaux

Peru

Túquerres
Esmeraldas
QUITO
Puerto Leguizamo
COLOMBIA
El Encanto
Quevedo
Manta
ECUADOR
Macas
Salinas
Santo An
do Içá
São Paulo de Olivença
Iquitos
Atalaia do Norte
Machala
Tumbes
Loja
Jutaí
Macará
Talara
Sullana
Chulucanas
Paita
Piura
San Ignacio
Yurimaguas
Moyobamba
Chachapoyas
Tarapolo
BRAZIL
Chiclayo
Cajamarca
Chepén
San Pedro de Lloc
Cruzeiro do Sul
Tarauacá
Bôca do A
Pucallpa
Puerto Chicama
Trujillo
Santa Rosa
Rio Branco
Progresso
Tingo María
Chimbote
Huaráz
Huánuco
Cobija
Cerro de Pasco
Barranca
Huacho
Tarma
Huaral
Chosica
La Oroya
Huancayo
Puerto Maldonado
349
LIMA
Huancavelica
Mala
Ayacucho
San Vicente de Cañete
Cuzco
Cangallo
Abancay
Huancapi
Chincha Alta
Pisco
Sicuani
Apolo
Ica
Ayaviri
BOLI
PACIFIC OCEAN
Palpa
Nazca
Juliaca
Marcona
Puno
Ilave
Copacaban
Arequipa
LA
Camana
Moquegua
Mollendo
Tacna
CHILE

Refugios Del Peru - Viñak Reichraming

SANTIAGO DE VIÑAK, YAUYOS, LIMA
Tel: +511 421 7777 **Fax:** +511 421 8476
Web: www.johansens.com/refugiosdelperu **E-mail:** info@refugiosdelperu.com

Our inspector loved: *The breathtaking scenery and vivid culture surrounding the lodge.*

Price Guide: (all inclusive, including unlimited mountain bike hire and hiking with guide) rooms U.S.$75-U.S.$99

Attractions: 50 Miles of Trekking Routes; Canoeing, 50 miles; Inca Archeological Ruins of Inkawasi, 62 miles
Towns/Cities: Lunahuana, 50 miles; Lima, 124 miles
Airports: Lima International Airport, 124 miles

Refugios del Peru is a cozy, intimate hotel situated high in unforgettably beautiful scenery. With extremely comfortable accommodations, you will be spoiled by the personal service and quiet charm, perfect for unwinding and leaving the pressures of modern life behind. Warm wood and stone buildings bathe in sunlight and effortlessly blend into the surrounding rural landscapes. There are over 44 miles of walking paths and mountain bike trails in the area and many diverse outdoor activities to choose from. Rooms are spacious and light with natural wood furniture and subtle color schemes; all benefit from a breathtaking outlook as well as independent water and heating control. The stunning panoramic restaurant has views that stretch as far as the eye can see over rolling hillsides, and serves a delicious fusion of Andean and European cuisine.

Uruguay

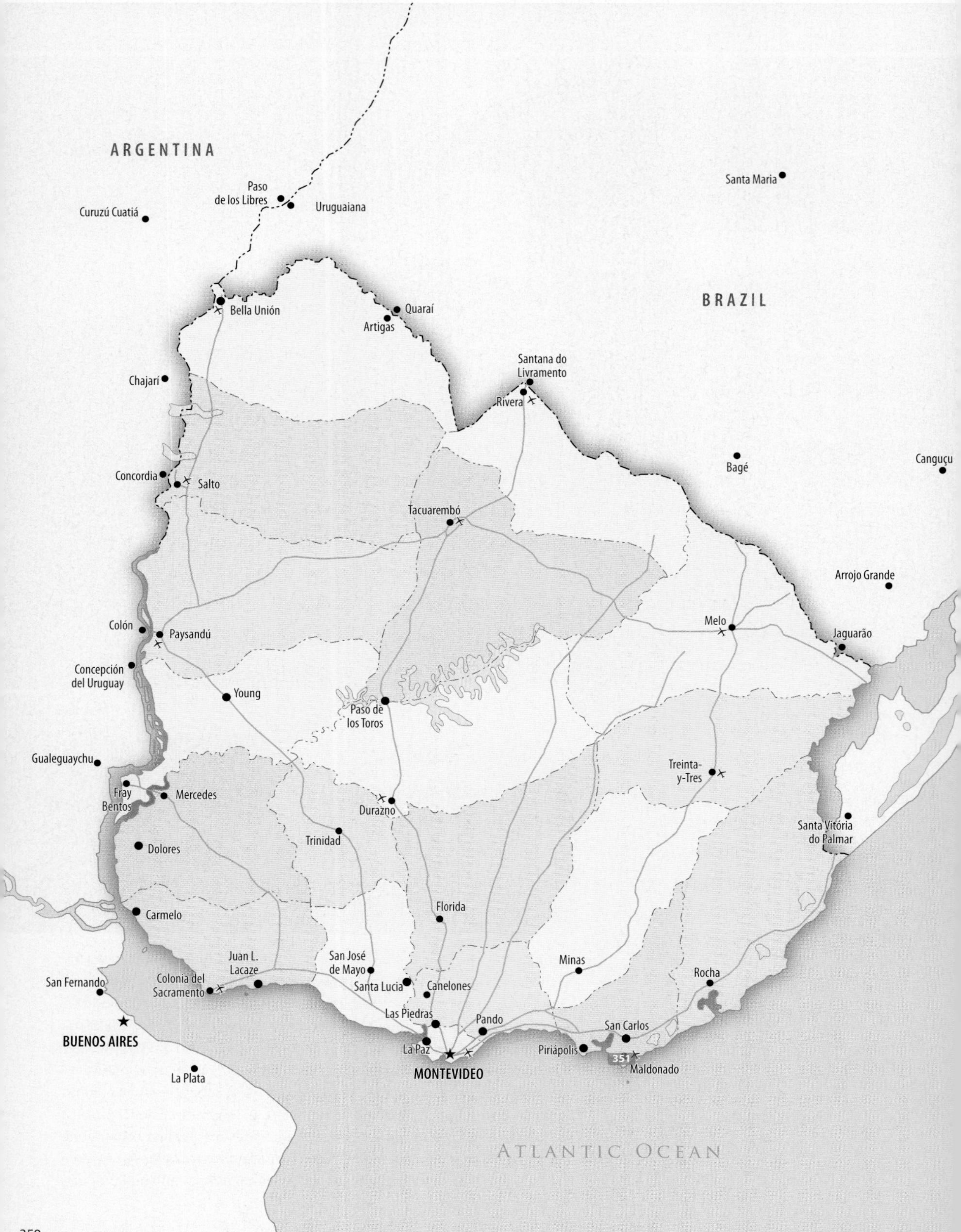
ARGENTINA
BRAZIL
Santa Maria
Paso de los Libres
Uruguaiana
Curuzú Cuatiá
Bella Unión
Quaraí
Artigas
Santana do Livramento
Rivera
Chajarí
Bagé
Canguçu
Concordia
Salto
Tacuarembó
Arrojo Grande
Melo
Colón
Paysandú
Jaguarão
Concepción del Uruguay
Young
Paso de los Toros
Gualeguaychu
Treinta-y-Tres
Fray Bentos
Mercedes
Durazno
Santa Vitória do Palmar
Trinidad
Dolores
Florida
Carmelo
Minas
Juan L. Lacaze
San José de Mayo
Rocha
San Fernando
Colonia del Sacramento
Santa Lucia
Canelones
Las Piedras
Pando
San Carlos
BUENOS AIRES
La Paz
Piriápolis
351
Maldonado
MONTEVIDEO
La Plata
ATLANTIC OCEAN

L'AUBERGE

CARNOUSTIE Y AV. DEL AGUA, BARRIO PARQUE DE GOLF, PUNTA DEL ESTE CP20100
Tel: +598 42 48 2601 **Fax:** +598 42 48 3408
Web: www.johansens.com/laubergeuruguay **E-mail:** lauberge@laubergehotel.com

Our inspector loved: *The luxury European atmosphere.*

Price Guide: (including breakfast)
single/double U.S.$130-U.S.$360
junior suite/suite U.S.$250-U.S.$960

22

Attractions: Isla Gorriti, 15-min drive; Josè Ignacio, 20-min drive; Isla de Lobos, 45-min drive
Towns/Cities: Maldonado, 5 miles; Montevideo, 85 miles; Colonia, 180 miles
Airports: Punta del Este Airport, 14 miles; Carrasco - Montevideo Airport, 85 miles

Located in an upscale neighborhood of Punta del Este, L'Auberge is well known for its old water tower that has been renovated into luxury guest rooms, and has stunning views of the entire city. The hotel aims to combine a first-class European-style lodging with a Uruguayan feel, offering rooms designed with every modern comfort. Spend an afternoon in the gardens or relax by the swimming pool, and finish your afternoon by enjoying traditional tea and Belgian waffles in the hotel's Tea Room. The cuisine is all fresh meat and fish or exquisitely prepared pasta paired with expertly chosen wines. While in Punta del Este, make sure to visit the lovely beaches, high-end shopping and dining, as well as museums and galleries showcasing Uruguay's interesting past, all while rubbing shoulders with the South American elite.

Bahamas

UNITED STATES
Fort Lauderdale
Miami
Bimini Islands
West End
353
Freeport
Grand Bahama
Little Abaco
Marsh Harbour
Sandy Point
Great Abaco
Berry I.
STRAIT OF FLORIDA
Morgan's Bluff
Andros
NASSAU
New Providence
Spanish Wells
Harbour Island
ATLANTIC OCEAN
Governors Harbour
Andros Town
Eleuthera
Moxey Town
Arthurs Town
Cat Island
Red Shank Cay
Mars Bay
Devils Point
Great Exuma
San Salvador
Seymour's
George Town
OLD BAHAMA CHANNEL
Rum Cay
Long Island
Clarence Town
Ciego de Ávila
Colonel Hill
Florida
Spring Point
Mayaguana
Acklins Islands
Betsy Bay
CUBA
TURKS
CAICO
Holguín
Little Inagua
Manzanillo
Great Inagua
Matthew Town
Guantánamo
Santiago de Cuba
CARIBBEAN SEA

OLD BAHAMA BAY BY GINN SUR MER

WEST END, GRAND BAHAMA ISLAND
Tel: +1 242 350 6500 **Fax:** +1 242 346 6546 **U.S./Canada Toll Free:** 1 800 444 9469
Web: www.johansens.com/oldbahamabay **E-mail:** info@oldbahamabay.com

Our inspector loved: *The marina where one's yacht can be moored.*

Price Guide: (excluding 12% tax and 8% service charge per night)
junior suites U.S.$235-U.S.$620
2-bedroom suites U.S.$769-U.S.1,509

Attractions: Eight Mile Rock, 15 miles; Port Lucaya Marketplace, 35 miles
Towns/Cities: Freeport, 25 miles; Lucaya, 35 miles
Airports: Grand Bahama Island International Airport, 25 miles

Affiliations: Preferred Boutique

Situated within 228 acres on the western-most tip of Grand Bahama Island, just 56 miles from the Florida coast, stands the tranquil and luxurious Old Bahama Bay by Ginn Sur Mer. A family-friendly destination, it comprises 73 spacious ocean view and ocean-front junior suites and 2-bedroom suites, an ocean-front pool, restaurants, massage pavilion, a 72-slip port of entry marina and a waterfront residential community. Each of the junior suites and 1 and 2-bedroom suites include custom-designed furnishings, a fiber-optic cable for phone, ocean-front terraces and much more. The luxurious bathrooms feature Kohler fixtures, either 6-ft. soaking tubs or whirlpool tubs. Relax in the 4,000 sq. ft. heated pool with infinity-edge lounging area and massage jets, overlooking the ocean before adjourning to one of the 3 restaurants. The Bonefish Folley's Bar & Grille overlooks the marina, the Straw Bar is an ocean-side café and bar, and Aqua offers Bahamian fusion cuisine.

Bermuda

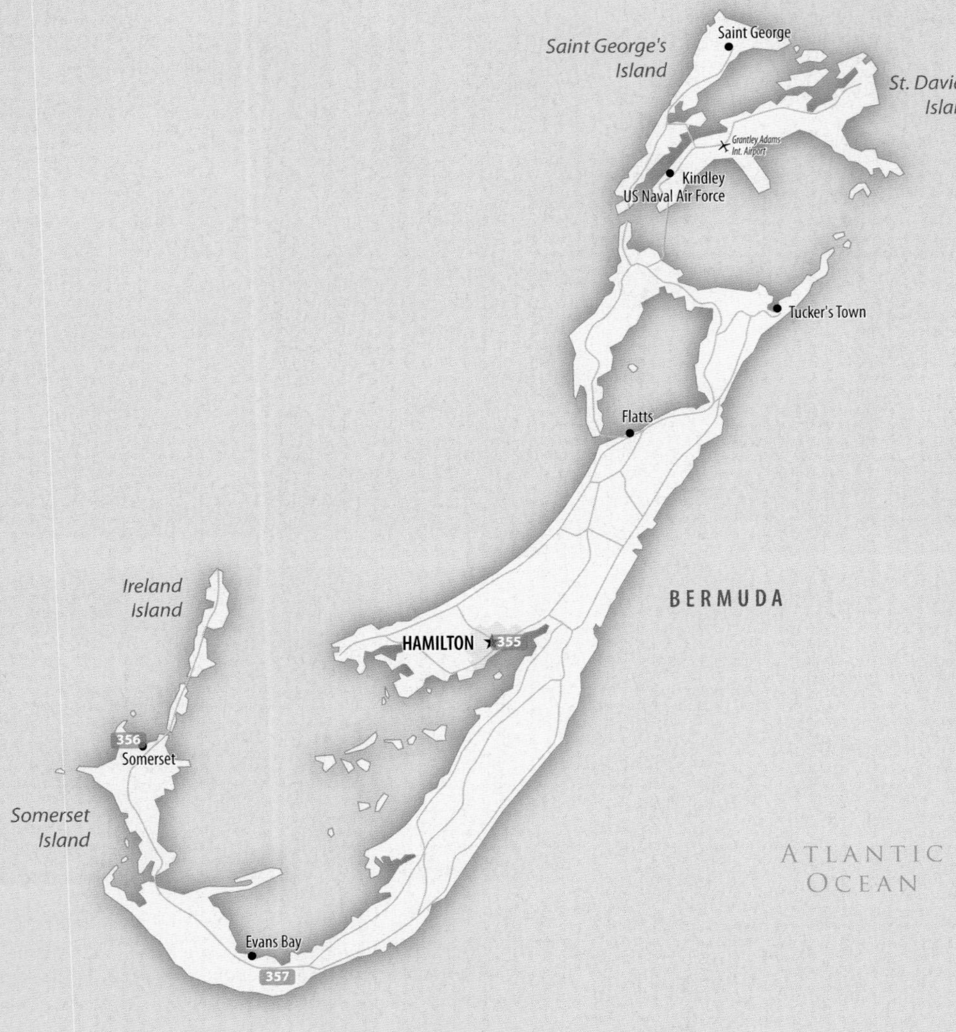

Saint George
Saint George's Island
St. David's Island
Grantley Adams Int. Airport
Kindley
US Naval Air Force
Tucker's Town
Flatts
BERMUDA
Ireland Island
HAMILTON
355
356
Somerset
Somerset Island
Evans Bay
357
ATLANTIC OCEAN

Rosedon Hotel

P.O. BOX HM 290, HAMILTON HMAX
Tel: +1 441 295 1640 **Fax:** +1 441 295 5904 **U.S./Canada Toll Free:** 1 800 742 5008
Web: www.johansens.com/rosedonhotel **E-mail:** info@rosedon.com

Our inspector loved: *The new "honor larder" where you can help yourself to a snack.*

Price Guide: (including breakfast)
rooms U.S.$224-U.S.$442

44

Attractions: Front Street Hamilton, 1 mile; Harbor, 1 mile; South Shore Beach, 2 miles
Airports: Bermuda Airport, 9 miles

Originally built in 1903 by an expatriate English family, this stunningly refurbished Colonial hotel provides a quiet, friendly and relaxed atmosphere in sensational surroundings. Enclosed by natural tropical gardens, this is a tranquil sanctuary only minutes from the bustling town of Hamilton. Suffused with the atmosphere of Colonial splendor, the main house is decorated in a traditional style and is festooned with antique furniture. The Bermudian-style rooms are all spacious and have balconies overlooking the swimming pool. Breakfast and lunch are served at the poolside patio and light dinners are available on request. Introductions to the island's championship golf courses can be organized, and transportation to a South Shore Beach and tennis club is available.

CAMBRIDGE BEACHES RESORT & SPA

SANDYS, SOMERSET
Tel: +1 441 234 0331 **Fax:** +1 441 234 3352 **U.S./Canada Toll Free:** 1 800 468 7300
Web: www.johansens.com/cambeaches **E-mail:** cambeach@ibl.bm

Set on a private 30-acre peninsula, Cambridge Beaches enjoys spectacular sea views, charming cottage accommodations, beautiful private beaches and award-winning cuisine. Incredible water-front pool suites (the only ones in Bermuda) offer complete privacy and panoramic views, and the gourmet cuisine at the international Tamarisk Room remains among Bermuda's best. Dinner may also be taken by candlelight at Shutters, around the infinity pool overlooking Mangrove Bay or on Long Bay Beach at the trendy beach-front bistro, Breezes. For the ultimate romantic experience couples can enjoy private beach dinners or exclusive evenings on a nearby private island. There are endless activities with extensive leisure facilities including a world-class spa and wellness center, a putting green and private marina. Enquire about year-round family and reunion packages.

***Our inspector loved:** The Sothy of Paris facial at the Ocean Spa.*

Price Guide: (including afternoon tea)
rooms U.S.$335-U.S.$850
suites U.S.$550-U.S.$985
pool suites U.S.$1,285-U.S.$1,870

94 M 40 5 SPA

Awards/Ratings: Condé Nast Johansens Most Excellent Spa Hotel 2006

Attractions: Naval Dockyard & Dolphin Quest, 10-min drive; Hamilton Front Street, 30-min drive
Towns/Cities: Hamilton, 30-min drive; St. Georges, 40-min by ferry
Airports: Bermuda's L.F. Wade International Airport, 40-min drive

THE REEFS

56 SOUTH SHORE ROAD, SOUTHAMPTON
Tel: +1 441 238 0222 **Fax:** +1 441 238 8372 **U.S./Canada Toll Free:** 1 800 742 2008
Web: www.johansens.com/thereefs **E-mail:** irr@worldnet.att.net

Our inspector loved: *The "dining on the beach" option - very romantic.*

Price Guide: (per person)
rooms U.S.$294-U.S.$544

65 SPA

Attractions: Bermuda Aquarium, 35-min drive; Crystal Caves, 35-min drive; Bermuda Maritime Museum, 40-min drive
Towns/Cities: Hamilton, 20-min drive
Airports: Bermuda International Airport, 40-min drive

Nestled along high coral cliffs and overlooking its own private beach, this intimate 65-room resort provides a relaxing atmosphere where you will feel perfectly at ease. With great rooms, exquisite cuisine and impeccable service, every room and suite in the main resort commands sweeping ocean and sunset vistas. There are also 1, 2, and 3-bedroom Bermudian cottages popular with small groups of friends and families, and each has its own private Jacuzzi. There are 3 different dining options that open on a rotational basis. Ocean Echo is perched on the cliff-side and offers spectacular views of South Shore, while Royston's offers a traditional superb club feel. Coconuts is an ocean-front restaurant where you can dine with your toes in the sand. For an after-dinner drink head to the Lounge, a favorite rendezvous where traditional English Tea and live entertainment are enjoyed daily. For an indulgent break, stop by the highly-acclaimed day spa.

Anguilla

Atlantic Ocean
Scrub Island
ANGUILLA
Island Harbour
The Fountain
Seal Island
Dog Island
East End Village
Prickly Pear Cays
THE VALLEY
Wallblake Airport
Sandy Island
Sandy Ground
Blowing Point Village
Long Bay Village
359
360
West End
Anguillita Islands
Tintamarre
Caribbean Sea
SAINT-MARTIN
MARIGOT
PHILIPSBURG

CuisinArt Resort & Spa

P.O. BOX 2000, RENDEZVOUS BAY
Tel: +1 264 498 2000 **Fax:** +1 264 498 2010 **U.S./Canada Toll Free:** 1 800 943 3210
Web: www.johansens.com/cuisinartresort **E-mail:** reservations@cuisinart.ai

Our inspector loved: *The Anguillan Coconut Pineapple Scrub at the first-class Venus Spa.*

Price Guide: (including Continental breakfast)
rooms U.S.$400-U.S.$3,400
suites U.S.$1,700-U.S.$5,800

93 M 120 SPA

Awards/Ratings: Condé Nast Traveler Gold List '07-'08; Wine Spectator Award of Excellence '07-'08

Attractions: 18-Hole Greg Norman Signature Golf Course, close by; Catamaran Sails, from the beach; Blowing Point Ferry, 8 miles
Towns/Cities: The Valley, 5 miles; Shoal Bay, 8 miles
Airports: Blowing Point Ferry, 3 miles; Wallblake Airport, 5 miles; Princess Juliana Airport, Saint Maarten, 20-min high-speed boat shuttle

Affiliations: The Leading Small Hotels of the World

The jewel of Anguilla's Rendezvous Bay, CuisinArt will give you the ultimate Caribbean experience thanks to its stunning ocean-front location, remarkable cuisine and the 27,000 sq. ft., world-class Venus Spa. Overlooking miles of powdery white sand and crystal blue waters, its gorgeous Greek-style architecture is breathtaking. After a day in the sun, retreat to your luxurious accommodations and take a soak in your marble bath or sip a fruit-infused rum on your private balcony overlooking the Caribbean Sea. The Resort offers an epicurean journey with its restaurants that feature the freshest of ingredients from the Hydroponic Farm and organic gardens. Indulge at either award-winning Santorini, serving exquisite contemporary French-Caribbean cuisine, the more casual Mediterraneo, with a brasserie flair, or experience the exclusive Chef's Table for a culinary indulgence, including wine pairings selected from the award-winning Wine Cellar.

SHERIVA VILLA HOTEL

MAUNDAYS BAY ROAD, WEST END AI-2640
Tel: +1 264 498 9898 **Fax:** +1 264 498 9595
Web: www.johansens.com/sheriva **E-mail:** info@sheriva.com

Our inspector loved: *The delicious cuisine prepared by the villa's private chef.*

Price Guide: (including full breakfast)
pool suites U.S.$1,100-U.S.$3,800
villas U.S.$2,800-U.S.$10,200

20

Attractions: Maundays Bay Beach, 2-min golf cart ride; Kids' Water Slide, 3-min drive; Temenos Golf Course, 5-min drive
Towns/Cities: The Valley, 15-min drive; Shoal Bay East, 20-min drive
Airports: Anguilla Wallblake Airport (AXA), 15-min drive; Princess Juliana International Airport (SXM), 7-min flight or 20-min boat ride; V. C. Bird International Airport (ANU), 45-min flight

Sheriva is an ideal escape for those seeking the privacy of a villa with all the amenities of a luxury hotel. Located on the West End of Anguilla with gorgeous views of St. Martin, Cove Bay and the Caribbean Sea, each beautifully designed villa offers understated elegance and a contemporary flair. Couples will enjoy the 1-bedroom private pool suite or if bringing friends and/or family, indulge in the grand 7-bedroom villa. Each is lavish in size with an expansive terrace surrounded by lush gardens and a total of 7 pools accented with fine marble, granite and exotic hardwoods. Your own private chef will tempt your palate with gourmet Caribbean cuisine, daily afternoon canapés and island cocktails. The Concierge Privé will cater to your every need.

Goat Island
Atlantic Ocean
The Caves
Codrington
Codrington Airport
Dulcina
BARBUDA
Coco Point
Caribbean Sea
ANTIGUA
365
Crosbies
Cedar Grove
Long Island
Friars Hill
Barnes Hill
VC Bird Airport
ST. JOHN'S
Osbourn
Guiana Island
362
Five Islands
Grays Hill
Gunthorpes
Parham
364
Seatons
Creekside
Mount Joy
Willikies
363
Glanvilles
Jennings
Emanuel
Green Island
All Saints
Elmes
Swetes
Willocks
St. Philips
Freetown
York Island
John Hugues
Bethesda
Crab Hill
Urlings
Claremont
Falmouth
Barters
366
367
Old Road
English Harbour Town
Atlantic Ocean

Galley Bay Resort & Spa

FIVE ISLANDS, ST. JOHN'S
Tel: +1 954 481 8787 **Fax:** +1 954 481 1661 **U.S./Canada Toll Free:** 1 800 858 4618
Web: www.johansens.com/galleybay **E-mail:** res@eliteislandresorts.com

This adults-only Tahitian-style resort is situated on a pristine stretch of white sandy beach. A romantic Caribbean hideaway, the endless sunshine and unspoiled beauty of Antigua make this an ideal laid-back vacation destination. Thatch-roofed bungalows and ocean-front rooms are set amidst 40 acres of lush gardens filled with majestic coconut palms, a lagoon and a bird sanctuary. The décor is simple yet stylish with rattan and bamboo furniture filling each of the spacious rooms. Creole and Euro-Caribbean dishes are available in the Sea Grape Restaurant, while traditional grilled fare is served at the beach-side Gauguin Restaurant where an idyllic evening can be spent sipping sundowners at sunset. Cascading waterfalls are a feature of the freeform swimming pool, and the fitness center overlooks the lagoon. Enjoy a relaxing massage at the new Indulge Spa.

Our inspector loved: *The aromatherapy massage at the new Indulge Spa.*

Price Guide: (including all meals, beverages, non-motorized water sports, taxes and service charges)
rooms U.S.$665-U.S.$990
suites U.S.$690-U.S.$1,350

98 SPA

Awards/Ratings: Condé Nast Traveler Gold List 2007

Attractions: St. John's, 10-min drive; Shirley Heights, 45-min drive; Devil's Bridge, 45-min drive; English Harbour, 50-min drive
Towns/Cities: St John's, 10-min drive
Airports: V.C. Bird International Airport, 25-min drive

HERMITAGE BAY HOTEL

ST. JOHN'S
Tel: +1 268 562 5500 **Fax:** +1 268 562 8080
Web: www.johansens.com/hermitagebay **E-mail:** info@hermitagebay.com

Our inspector loved: *The incredible feeling of privacy and seclusion.*

Price Guide: (all inclusive)
suites U.S.$700-U.S.$1,750

SPA

Attractions: Jolly Harbour Marina Complex, 10-min drive; Nelson's Dockyard, 45-min drive
Towns/Cities: Jolly Harbour, 10-min drive; St. John's, 30-min drive
Airports: V.C. Bird International Airport, 35-min drive

Set in a secluded bay on a beautifully landscaped hillside overlooking the turquoise Caribbean waters on western Antigua, this boutique hotel is the perfect place for a relaxing vacation. Well-appointed and spacious Cottage Suites exude an old Caribbean-colonial feel but with modern contemporary style. Many of the Beach Suites have panoramic views of the ocean, or for the most spectacular views, choose one of the Hillside Cottage Suites, each with their own private plunge pool and sundeck. Personal Housekeepers will take care of your every need including appointments at the Spa such as a romantic Togetherness Massage for couples. Dining at Hermitage Bay is a treat with a menu of Caribbean and European cuisine that places an emphasis on fresh, local ingredients. Dine alfresco or opt for a private dinner in your suite.

The Verandah Resort & Spa

INDIAN TOWN ROAD, ST. JOHN'S
Tel: +1 954 481 8787 **U.S./Canada Toll Free:** 1 800 858 4618
Web: www.johansens.com/verandah **E-mail:** Reservations@eliteislandresorts.com

Our inspector loved: *The family-friendly Kidz Club, giving parents a chance to relax and unwind.*

Price Guide: (all inclusive)
suites U.S.$420-U.S.$1,350

200 · 100 · DVD · WiFi · SPA

Attractions: Devil's Bridge, 10-min walk; Green Island and Bird Island, 15-min boat ride; Shirley Heights, 40-min drive; Nelson's Dockyard, 40-min drive
Towns/Cities: St. John's, 30-min drive
Airports: V.C. Bird International Airport, 30-min drive

Located on 30 spectacular waterfront acres, The Verandah is a new luxury eco-friendly retreat hidden away on the beautiful north-east coast of Antigua. Lush landscapes and classic Caribbean décor make the resort feel like a tropical home-away-from-home, and the spacious verandahs are perfect for taking in views of the turquoise waters of this reef-protected bay. Spend the afternoon walking the nature trails at the adjacent national park or snorkeling off the white sand beach. In the evenings enjoy drinks at one of 5 bars with live entertainment. There are 3 restaurants: the gourmet Nicole's; Seabreeze, which serves Caribbean specialties and international favorites; and Bucaneers, a family-themed restaurant. Children will enjoy their own dedicated restaurant and activities.

Blue Waters

P.O. BOX 257, ST. JOHN'S
Tel: +44 870 360 1245 **Fax:** +44 870 360 1246 **U.S./Canada Toll Free:** 1 800 557 6536
Web: www.johansens.com/bluewaters **E-mail:** bluewaters@threesixtyhotels.com

Our inspector loved: *Staying in the private Rock Cottage Villa built into the rocks with incredible ocean views.*

Price Guide: (including breakfast and afternoon tea)
rooms U.S.$349-U.S.$875
suites U.S.$526-U.S.$1,775

118 SPA

Attractions: Jolly Harbour Golf Course, 6 miles; Nelson's Dockyard, 9 miles; Shirley Heights, 9 miles
Towns/Cities: English Harbour, 9 miles
Airports: Antigua International Airport, 6 miles

This intimate, family-owned luxury hotel is nestled among 17 acres of cascading bougainvillea, flowering hibiscus and shady palm trees, surrounded by 2 white sandy beaches. The warm and friendly atmosphere and exceptional service ensures a relaxing stay where each of the beautiful guest rooms has cool terracotta tile flooring and sea or garden views. For the ultimate in luxury accommodations, stay in the newly developed Rock Cottage Villa with a private plunge pool, Jacuzzi, landing stage, exceptional furnishings, kitchen, lounge and dining room. Equally special are the new Cove Suites with private pools overlooking fabulous cliff-top sea vistas. Before the day's end, visit one of 3 bars for a refreshing "afternoon cooler" and don't miss Vyviens Restaurant for excellent gourmet cuisine. Alternately, enjoy outdoor dining at the Palm Restaurant, which has regular evening entertainment, and fine dining at the new Cove Restaurant with its breathtaking sunset views.

CURTAIN BLUFF

P.O. BOX 288, ST. JOHN'S
Tel: +1 268 462 8400 **Fax:** +1 268 462 8409 **U.S./Canada Toll Free:** 1 888 289 9898
Web: www.johansens.com/curtainbluff **E-mail:** curtainbluff@curtainbluff.com

Our inspector loved: *Relaxing at the new spa located on the bluff with its beautiful ocean views.*

Price Guide: (all inclusive)
rooms U.S.$645-U.S.$1,445
suites U.S.$775-U.S.$3,900

72 24 12 SPA

Awards/Ratings: Condé Nast Traveler Gold List 2007

Attractions: Rainforest Canopy Tour, 2 miles; Sting Ray City, 4 miles; Nelson's Dockyard, 5 miles; Shirley Heights, 5 miles
Towns/Cities: St. John's, 8 miles
Airports: V.C. Bird International Airport, 10 miles

With a smooth, lagoon-fed beach on one side and windward surf on the other, Curtain Bluff is truly idyllic. Meticulous attention to detail is evident throughout, from the immaculate tropical gardens to the spacious rattan-styled bedrooms. Culinary excellence is in the capable hands of French-born Chef Christophe Blatz, and the impressive wine cellar consists of 25,000 bottles. Fine dining is available in the garden pavilion, while a more casual setting is found at the beach bar. For total privacy, dinner may be taken on your balcony. Facilities include a 5,000 sq. ft. spa, 5-star tennis facilities, squash and a putting green. With its private peninsula, the water-sport activities are unrivaled. There is even the opportunity to sail on Sentio, Curtain Bluff's 49-ft. Wellington ketch.

CARLISLE BAY

OLD ROAD, ST. MARY'S
Tel: +1 268 484 0000 **Fax:** +1 268 484 0001 **U.S./Canada Toll Free:** +1 866 502 2855
Web: www.johansens.com/carlislebay **E-mail:** info@carlisle-bay.com

Our inspector loved: *Relaxing in the the inspiring and peaceful setting of the Blue Spa.*

Price Guide: (including full breakfast and afternoon tea)
suites U.S.$555-U.S.$4,000

82 40 SPA

Awards/Ratings: Condé Nast Traveler Gold List 2006 and 2007

Attractions: Fig Tree Drive, 0.5 miles; Antigua Rainforest Canopy Tour, 15-min drive; Nelson's Dockyard, 20-min drive; Betty Hope's Sugar Plantation, 45-min drive
Towns/Cities: English Harbour, 20-min drive; St. John's, 30-min drive
Airports: V.C. Bird Intl. Airport, 30-min drive

Affiliations: The Leading Small Hotels of the World

This contemporary luxury resort is set against a dramatic backdrop of rolling hills and rainforest on the magnificent south coast of Antigua. Each spacious suite has cool, calm interiors and a private balcony or terrace from which to take in the breathtaking ocean views. Carlisle Bay's philosophy of well-being and feeling great is enhanced by the exceptional spa services, yoga and Pilates Pavilion, 9 tennis courts and an array of complimentary water sports. There are 2 excellent restaurants: East, with its pan-Asian menu in a contemporary setting and the more informal Indigo on the Beach offering delicious healthy grills, seafood and salads. The Cool Kids Club for children aged 6 months to 12 years, the library and a screening room ensure a good time is had by all.

Barbados

Atlantic Ocean
Greenidge
Hope
Cave Hill
Nesfield
Boscobel
Road Fustic
Rose Hill
Mont Brevitor
Belleplaine
Speightstown
Sion Hill
Mose Bottom
Bathsheba
370
371
Chimborazo
Holetown
Rock Hall
Pothouse
Ashbury
Holders Hill
Steward Hill
Eden Lodge
Robinsons
Black Rock
Turnpike
Six Cross Roads
The Crane
Edey
St. Patrick
Belleville
BRIDGETOWN
Gemswick
Bartletts
Newton Terrace
Charnocks
Grantley Adams Int. Airport
Hastings
Worthing
Oistins
369
Caribbean Sea

Little Arches

ENTERPRISE BEACH ROAD, CHRIST CHURCH
Tel: +1 246 420 4689 **Fax:** +1 246 418 0207 **U.S./Canada Toll Free:** 1 800 764 1000
Web: www.johansens.com/littlearches **E-mail:** paradise@littlearches.com

Our inspector loved: *The vivid blue of the Caribbean Sea from the magnificent Café Luna restaurant.*

Price Guide: (excluding 7.5% tax and 10% gratuity)
rooms U.S.$192-U.S.$399
suites U.S.$336-U.S.$552

Attractions: Oistins' Fish Market, 5-min drive; Bridgetown, 20-min drive
Towns/Cities: Oistins, 5-min drive; Bridgetown, 20-min drive
Airports: Grantley Adams Airport, 10-min drive

This charming boutique hotel is situated in the parish of Christ Church on the southern edge of the island, steps from a pristine white sand beach. With only 10 rooms and suites, this privately owned hotel lends an ambience of informality and intimacy. Each of the rooms is carefully appointed with cool, crisp linens, terrazzo flooring, oversized beds and looks out to dramatic ocean views. In addition, 2 of the suites have private Jacuzzis or plunge pools. The acclaimed alfresco restaurant, Café Luna, is the perfect spot to watch the sun set while enjoying international cuisine. Little Arches' villa-charm continues with yachting fun aboard a 44-ft. luxury catamaran, available for private charters and memorable small weddings.

Coral Reef Club

ST. JAMES
Tel: +1 246 422 2372 **Fax:** +1 246 422 1776 **U.S./Canada Toll Free:** 1 800 223 1108
Web: www.johansens.com/coralreefclub **E-mail:** coral@caribsurf.com

Quietly nestled in 12 acres of lush tropical gardens and white sand beach on Barbados's famed west coast, this is a wonderful family-owned and managed property. For the past 50 years, the O'Hara family has been dedicated to providing the most excellent and comfortable getaway possible. A quiet stroll along the coast is a great way to explore the surroundings before sampling fresh seafood at the elegant ocean-front restaurant. You will notice that each of the rooms is cleverly named after the flowers, fruit and trees found within the grounds. Choose to stay in a luxury cottage with your own private plunge pool or for the utmost luxury, unwind in one of the 5 Plantation Suites; the epitome of 21st-century style. After a full day of activity, relax with one of the many treatments at the resort's brand new spa.

Our inspector loved: *The cocktail party for guests, hosted at the owners' family home on the property.*

Price Guide: (including breakfast)
rooms U.S.$245-U.S.$865
suites U.S.$475-U.S.$2,600

88 SPA

Attractions: Wildlife Reserve, 5 miles; Plantation Houses, 7 miles; Barbados Museum, 10 miles
Towns/Cities: Holetown, 1 mile; Bridgetown, 9 miles
Airports: Grantley Adams Airport, 18 miles

Affiliations: Small Luxury Hotels of the World

THE SANDPIPER

HOLETOWN, ST. JAMES
Tel: +1 246 422 2251 **Fax:** +1 246 422 0900 **U.S./Canada Toll Free:** 1 800 223 1108
Web: www.johansens.com/sandpiper **E-mail:** coral@caribsurf.com

Our inspector loved: *The "South Seas" atmosphere of the hotel at night, with the flaming torches subtly lighting up the waterfalls.*

Price Guide: (including breakfast)
rooms U.S.$310-U.S.$865
suites U.S.$450-U.S.$2,600

47

Attractions: Limestone Caves, 5 miles; Wildlife Reserve, 5 miles; Atlantis Submarine, 8 miles; Historic Houses, 8 miles
Towns/Cities: Holetown, 0.5 miles
Airports: Grantley Adams Airport, 18 miles

Affiliations: Small Luxury Hotels of the World

This gem of a hotel is located on the desirable west coast of Barbados and has quickly become a favorite spot for discerning guests looking for intimacy, relaxation and privacy. Lush tropical gardens lead to the white sand beach in the middle of a large bay sloping down to the clear Caribbean Sea. Each of the bedrooms and suites has its own private terrace with spacious and airy décor and touches of the Caribbean. 2 premier Tree Top Suites benefit from beach-front locations and have private plunge pools, sun decks and chic furnishings, adding further luxury to this family-owned hotel. The restaurant, set in a blossoming garden and surrounded by tranquil koi ponds, offers an international menu with a Caribbean flair.

British Virgin Islands

Biras Creek Resort

NORTH SOUND, VIRGIN GORDA

Tel: +1 248 364 2421 **Fax:** +1 248 364 2477 **U.S./Canada Toll Free:** 1 877 883 0756

Web: www.johansens.com/birascreek **E-mail:** biras@biras.com

Our inspector loved: *The panoramic ocean views from the hilltop restaurant where you can watch the sun rise and set over the sea.*

Price Guide: (including breakfast, lunch, afternoon tea, dinner and airport transfers with minimum 4-night stay, excluding tax)
suites U.S.$675-U.S.$1,950

SPA

Awards/Ratings: Condé Nast Johansens Most Excellent Hotel, Atlantic, Caribbean & Pacific Islands 2008

Attractions: Snorkeling at Oil Nut Bay, 15-min boat ride; The Baths Day Trip, 40-min boat ride; Anegada Day Trip, 1.5-hour boat ride

Airports: Beef Island Airport, Tortola, 40-min boat ride

Affiliations: Relais & Châteaux

This elegant and rustic hideaway, located on a 140-acre nature reserve, is accessible only by boat or helicopter. The 31 luxury suites are set amidst 3 distinct bodies of water: the North Sound; Atlantic Ocean; and Caribbean Bay. All feature a comfortable, stylish décor capitalizing on the outdoor beauty. Each suite has a lovely garden view or vista of Bercher's Bay on the Atlantic shore. Central to the property is a hilltop stone castle, which accommodates the reception, main dining room and a lovely terrace bar. The private white sand beach is a paradise for swimming, sailing, and snorkeling. Guests receive complimentary usage of Boston Whalers, Hobi sailboats, snorkel gear and windsurfing equipment. Sip afternoon tea in the Arawak Room overlooking the North Sound, enjoy the many hiking trails, or visit the Biras Spa, which uses signature Decléor aromatherapy treatments. The restaurant has an extensive wine menu and offers European and Caribbean dishes.

Peter Island Resort

PETER ISLAND
Tel: +770 476 9988 **Fax:** +770 476 4979 **U.S./Canada Toll Free:** 1 800 346 4451
Web: www.johansens.com/peterislandresort **E-mail:** reservations@peterisland.com

Located on its own pristine private island in the heart of the British Virgin Islands, Peter Island Resort offers unspoiled white sand beaches, turquoise waters, lush vegetation and an unforgettable Resort experience. Both the Ocean View Rooms and Beach Front Junior Suites offer stunning views of colorful gardens, the Sir Francis Drake Channel and the shimmering sea from hammock-slung palms. The Resort's grounds include tennis courts, a swimming pool, elegant beach-front Spa and fitness center, and delicious dining opportunities abound. The Tradewinds Restaurant serves international cuisine with a selection of local Caribbean flavors. Guests may reserve a spot at the Vintner Dinner held in the Restaurant's Wine Room for a more sophisticated dining experience. Culinary events such as the weekly West Indian night and the magnificent Seafood Buffet ensure that you are well-fed, comfortable and happy at this Caribbean gem.

***Our inspector loved:** The serene ocean-front setting of the elegant spa.*

Price Guide: (including breakfast, lunch and dinner, excluding 18% tax and service charges)
ocean view rooms U.S.$340-U.S.$1,200
beach-front junior suites U.S.$650-U.S.$1,875

52 SPA

Awards/Ratings: Wine Spectator Award of Excellence, 2007 and 2008; Condé Nast Traveler Gold List 2007 and 2008

Attractions: Rhone Marine Park, 10-min boat ride; Sunset at The Loop, 20-min drive; The Baths, Virgin Gorda, 40-min boat ride
Towns/Cities: Road Town, Tortola, 20-min boat ride; Charlotte Amalie, St. Thomas, 90-min boat ride
Airports: Beef Island, Tortola, 45-min boat ride

Affiliations: Preferred Boutique

THE VILLAS AT PETER ISLAND

PETER ISLAND

Tel: +770 476 9988 **Fax:** +770 476 4979 **U.S./Canada Toll Free:** 1 800 346 4451
Web: www.johansens.com/villaspeterisland **E-mail:** reservations@peterisland.com

Our inspector loved: *The unsurpassed privacy, luxury and views offered by these villas perched on hilltops.*

Price Guide: (including breakfast, lunch, afternoon refreshments and dinner, excluding 18% tax and service charges)
3-6-bedroom villas U.S.$3,500-U.S.$23,500

13 SPA

Attractions: Rhone Marine Park, 10-min boat ride; Sunset at The Loop, 20-min drive; The Baths, Virgin Gorda, 40-min boat ride
Towns/Cities: Road Town, Tortola, 20-min boat ride; Charlotte Amalie, St. Thomas, 90-min boat ride
Airports: Beef Island Airport, Tortola, 45-min boat ride

Affiliations: Preferred Boutique

For those seeking the ultimate privacy a private island can offer, The Peter Island Resort offers The Villas at Peter Island: 3 elegantly furnished Villa Estates as luxurious as they are exclusive. Each Villa, nestled into the hillside overlooking the Caribbean Sea and surrounded by lush tropical vegetation, is customized according to guests' preferences so that when you arrive it is stocked with your preferred beverages, music and bedding, and ready to serve. Villas are individually designed although private plunge pools and wraparound sundecks are custom fittings, and a full private staff dedicated to most. Falcon's Nest, the most recent addition, offers 6 sumptuous master bedrooms and evokes an Old World Caribbean atmosphere with a modern perspective. It includes an infinity pool, cascading waterfall, swim-up pool bar, 2 kitchens and a custom couples Spa room.

Curaçao

Westpunt
Lagún
Barber
Soto
Caribbean Sea
San Willebrordus
Tera Kora
Grote Berg
Hato Airport
Sint Michiel
Buena Vista
Emmastad
Sinta Catharina
Santa Rosa
Willemstad
Salina
377
New Port

AVILA HOTEL ON THE BEACH

PENSTRAAT 130, WILLEMSTAD
Tel: +599 9 461 4377 **Fax:** +599 9 461 1493 **U.S./Canada Toll Free:** 1 800 747 8162
Web: www.johansens.com/avilabeach **E-mail:** info@avilahotel.com

Our inspector loved: *The spectacular ocean views.*

Price Guide: (excluding 12% service charge and 7% tax, breakfast $15)
rooms U.S.$200-U.S.$420
suites U.S.$290-U.S.$1,500

150 150
SPA

Attractions: Seaquarium, 3-min drive; Dive Center, 3-min drive
Towns/Cities: Willemstad, 10-min walk
Airports: Curaçao Hato Airport, 30-min drive

Originally the governor's residence, this hotel is a stunning testament to classic and contemporary Dutch-Caribbean-style architecture. The interiors are simply breathtaking: the "Blues Wing" consists of rooms on a pier, with vaulted ceilings in white and soft pastel colors and features Caribbean wicker and cane furniture. These rooms look out to a panoramic vista across the ocean and have a private balcony or terrace. The luxurious Octagon Wing has spacious rooms decorated in pastels with splashes of Caribbean colors, and there is also the amazing top-floor Bolivar Suite; an absolute indulgence! Renowned for its fine outdoor dining, you are truly spoiled for choice with the convivial Avila Café, the casual elegant Belle Terrace and the cool Blues Bar and Seafood Restaurant. The Avila Spa & Wellness offers a wide range of body and beauty treatments for men and women and state-of-the art TechnoGYM equipment.

Dominican Republic

Maxim Bungalows Resort and Spa

1 PARADISE DRIVE, COFRESI BEACH, PUERTO PLATA
Tel: +1 866 970 3364 **Fax:** +1 809 970 3156 **U.S./Canada Toll Free:** 1 877 858 2422
Web: www.johansens.com/maximbungalows **E-mail:** info@maximbungalows.com

Our inspector loved: *The caviar facial and private cabanas at the luxury spa.*

Price Guide: (per person, based on double occupancy)
studios U.S.$378
doubles U.S.$391
kings U.S.$403

108 SPA

Attractions: Ocean World Adventure Park, 5-min drive
Towns/Cities: Puerta Plata, 15-min drive
Airports: Puerto Plata "Gregorio Luperon" International Airport, 30-min drive; Santiago International Airport, 1-hour drive

An active resort for the sophisticated traveler, Maxim Bungalows is the newest all inclusive, adults only, luxury hotel on the northern coast of Cofresi Beach. The Bungalows are sleekly designed with spacious terraces and chaises longue beds where you can enjoy the Caribbean breeze and the picturesque Dominican mountains. Your private concierge will cater to your every whim. Spend the day relaxing at the private beach club, kite surfing or sailing to Castaway Beach for a private barbecue aboard the 54 ft. yacht, Independence. The evenings are set aside for savoring gourmet cuisine at the Social Restaurant or cocktails and Cuban cigars at the ultra-stylish Social Lounge. Renew yourself at the impressive 17,000 sq. ft. spa, which offers a bamboo shower, private pools and 2 outdoor cabanas, and spa cuisine in the Asian-inspired garden.

Casa Colonial Beach & Spa

P.O. BOX 22, PUERTO PLATA
Tel: +1 809 320 3232 **Fax:** +1 809 320 3131
Web: www.johansens.com/casacolonial **E-mail:** reservascc@vhhr.com

This AAA 4 Diamond property and Virtuoso member, known for its stately Victorian houses and views of the Atlantic Ocean, feels like a private estate and offers European elegance in the warmth of a Caribbean island. Many of the suites reflect the style of great plantations, while others reveal a contemporary flair. The sands of Playa Dorada suggest a swim before breakfast, while the infinity pool and 4 temperature controlled Jacuzzi whirlpools on the rooftop, provide hours of relaxation. Vibrant sunsets can be viewed from the beach or from the bars offering panoramic "vistas." A gazebo on the beach is perfect for parties and unique wedding or anniversary celebrations. Lucia restaurant serves international gourmet food, and Bagua Spa uses natural resources to create treatments rooted in the ancient healing arts as well as classic therapies. Local activities include sport fishing and a round at Playa Dorada's golf course designed by Robert Trent Jones Sr.

Our inspector loved: *The gourmet Asian fusion cuisine, beautifully prepared at Lucia restaurant.*

Price Guide:
suites U.S.$350-U.S.$1,400

50 M50 SPA

Attractions: Playa Dorada Golf Course, 3-min walk; Playa Dorada Mall, 5-min walk; Ocean World, 20-min drive; Imbert Waterfall, 45-min drive
Towns/Cities: Puerto Plata, 5 miles; Sosua 16 miles; Cabarete, 25 miles; Santiago, 47 miles
Airports: Puerto Plata Airport, 15-min drive

Affiliations: Small Luxury Hotels of the World

Agua Resort & Spa

UVERO ALTO, PUNTA CANA
Tel: +1 809 468 0000 **Fax:** +1 809 468 0001 **U.S./Canada Toll Free:** 1 866 757 AGUA (2482)
Web: www.johansens.com/aguaresort **E-mail:** agua@aguaresort.com

Our inspector loved: *The intimate size and away-from-it-all feel of the resort.*

Price Guide: (excluding 26% taxes)
suites U.S.$350-U.S.$1,050
villas U.S.$870-U.S.$2,400

51 M 120 DVD WiFi SPA

Attractions: Punta Cana Golf Club, 10-min drive; Altos de Chavon, 35 miles; La Aleta, 35 miles
Towns/Cities: La Romana, 37 miles; Santo Domingo, 86 miles
Airports: Punta Cana International Airport, 25 miles; La Romana International Airport, 42 miles

This luxury boutique hotel features on the Condé Nast Traveler Hotel List 2008 and is a relaxing oasis situated on 25 square miles of reserve land on the north-eastern part of the island. Designed in typical Caribbean style alongside modern touches, the architecture features natural wood, stone and traditional thatched roofs throughout. 18 quiet villas are home to 53 deluxe suites, some facing the hotel's very own private beach overlooking the turquoise sea. Some of the suites boast private mini pools, rich hardwood floors, deep soaking tubs, attractive high ceilings and incredible views. The resort's 2 gourmet restaurants or the informal Caribbean beach grille will tempt your palate with their delectable Caribbean menus. The relaxing Yarari Spa offers you an expansive choice of treatments, specializing in the Phytomar experience.

CARIBBEAN - DOMINICAN REPUBLIC (PUNTA CANA)

SIVORY PUNTA CANA

PLAYA SIVORY, UVERO ALTO/PUNTA CANA
Tel: +1 809 333 0500 **Fax:** +1 809 334 0500
Web: www.johansens.com/sivory **E-mail:** reservations@sivorypuntacana.com

This welcoming Caribbean retreat is high on style and comfort. East Asian influences are seen throughout combining the natural beauty of the eastern Caribbean with the style of a traditional Polynesian paradise. Each of the beautifully designed rooms features the finest furnishings and has a private balcony or patio. There are 3 unique restaurants, a cigar lounge and an extensive wine library housing an impressive 8,000 bottles of the world's finest wine to enjoy. And the Aquarea Spa & Wellness Center, situated within 4,300 sq. ft. of lush tropical gardens, will help you achieve the maximum level of relaxation during your stay. Whether walking the pristine beach, lounging by the infinity pool or experiencing Caribbean-infused cuisine, you are guaranteed personalized service and exceptional luxury.

Our inspector loved: *Enjoying a gourmet breakfast on the suite's balcony overlooking the sea.*

Price Guide: (excluding taxes)
suites from U.S.$290

55 · 24 · M 150 · DVD · WiFi · SPA

Attractions: Golf Courses, 30-min drive; Bavaro, 30-min drive; Higuey, 45-min drive
Towns/Cities: Punta Cana, 1-hour drive; La Romana, 90-min drive; Santo Domingo, 3.5-hour drive
Airports: International Punta Cana Airport, 1-hour drive; International La Romana Airport, 90-min drive

Affiliations: Small Luxury Hotels of the World

Tortuga Bay, Puntacana Resort & Club

PUNTA CANA, DOMINICAN REPUBLIC
Tel: +1 809 959 2262 **U.S./Canada Toll Free:** 1 888 442 2262
Web: www.johansens.com/puntacana **E-mail:** reservationstb@puntacana.com

Our inspector loved: *The very convenient V.I.P. airport service.*

Price Guide: (including breakfast)
suites U.S.$500-U.S.$1650
villas U.S.$1560-U.S.$3260

13 SPA

Attractions: Marina, 5-min golf cart ride; Ecological Park, 5-min golf cart ride; Puntacana Village, 5-min drive; Ocean-front Golf Course, on-site
Towns/Cities: Higuey, 45-min drive; Bavaro, 30-min drive; Romana, 90-min drive; Santo Domingo, 3-hour drive
Airports: Punta Cana International Airport, 5-min drive

Affiliations: The Leading Small Hotels of the World

Located on 5 miles of white sandy beach, in a private gated community alongside the homes of Oscar de la Renta and Julio Iglesias, Tortuga Bay serves as an ideal getaway for those seeking a vacation spot both exclusive and relaxing. Its 30 suites, located in 13 spacious luxury villas, designed by de la Renta, offer an understated, airy elegance characterized by neutral tones, wicker furniture, rich woods and plenty of natural light. Each comes equipped with a plasma television and D.V.D. player, a golf cart for convenient navigation of the resort's grounds, and a butler offering warm, personal service. Guests at Tortuga Bay are given full access to the Puntacana Resort & Club with its many restaurants and bars, shopping mall, spa and ecological reserve.

Grenada

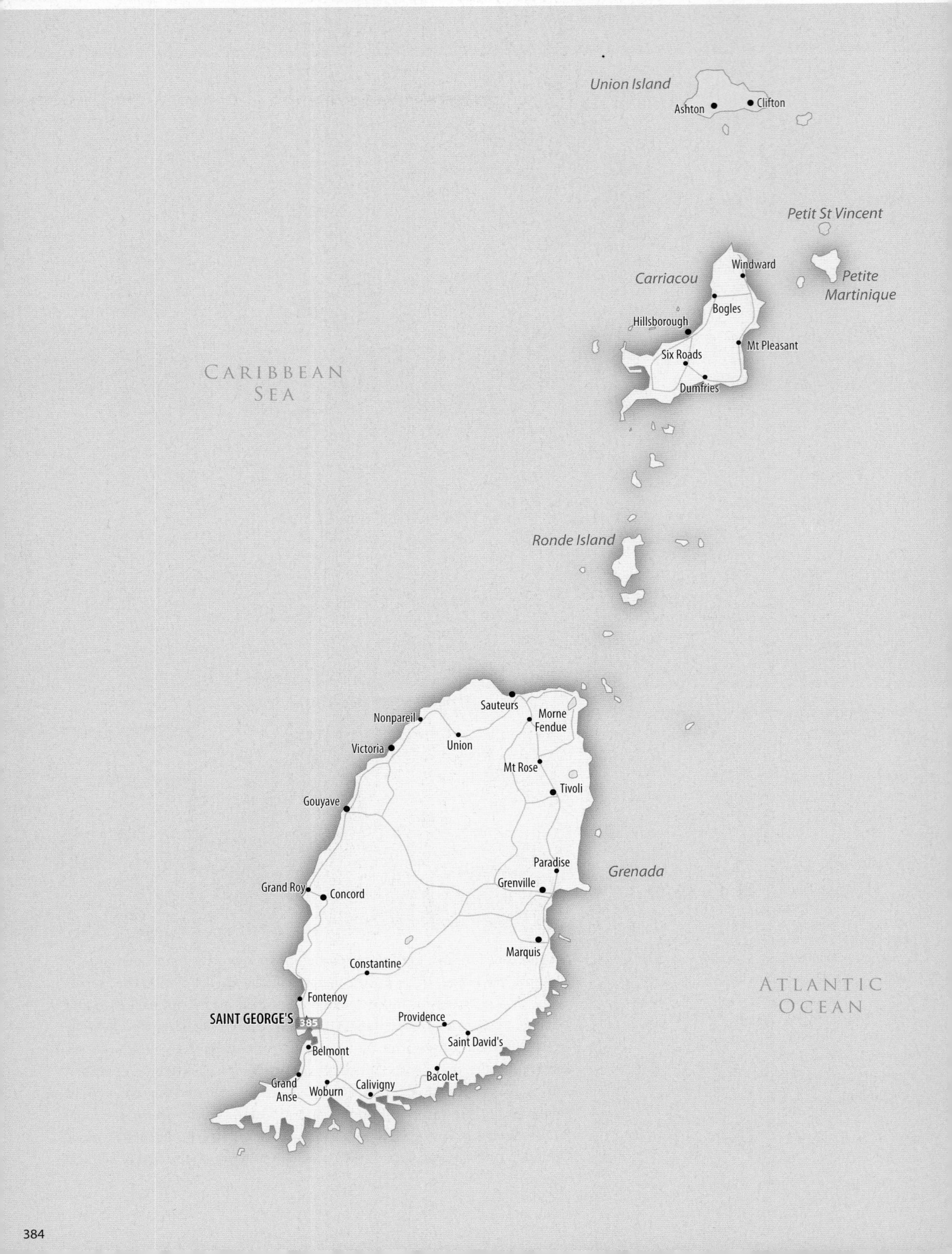
Union Island
Ashton
Clifton
Petit St Vincent
Carriacou
Windward
Petite Martinique
Bogles
Hillsborough
Mt Pleasant
Six Roads
Dumfries
CARIBBEAN SEA
Ronde Island
Sauteurs
Nonpareil
Morne Fendue
Union
Victoria
Mt Rose
Tivoli
Gouyave
Paradise
Grenada
Grenville
Grand Roy
Concord
Marquis
Constantine
ATLANTIC OCEAN
Fontenoy
SAINT GEORGE'S
385
Providence
Saint David's
Belmont
Grand Anse
Woburn
Calivigny
Bacolet

Spice Island Beach Resort

GRAND ANSE BEACH, ST. GEORGE'S
Tel: +1 473 444 4423/4258 **Fax:** +1 473 444 4807
Web: www.johansens.com/spiceisland **E-mail:** spiceisl@spiceisle.com

Our inspector loved: *The palatial 1-bedroom beach suites.*

Price Guide: (all inclusive)
singles U.S.$535-U.S.$1,220
doubles U.S.$635-U.S.$1,625
suites U.S.$935-U.S.$2,475

64 50 SPA

Awards/Ratings: Condé Nast Johansens Most Excellent Business Partner, The Americas, Atlantic, Caribbean & Pacific Islands 2007

Attractions: Annadale Falls, 20-min drive; Grand Etang Rainforest and Lake, 35-min drive
Towns/Cities: St. George's, 15-min drive
Airports: Point Salines International Airport, 10-min drive

Affiliations: Small Luxury Hotels of the World

Powdery white sands, the crystal clear waters of the Caribbean Sea and the shade of palm trees create the backdrop for this relaxing paradise. Courtyards and terraces are filled with tropical flora and fauna while bedrooms have breathtaking views of the sea or gardens. For the ultimate in luxury, experience the 1,440 sq. ft. 1-bedroom Cinnamon and Saffron Suites set on the beach with wet bars, 6-person dining rooms, lounges and living rooms. The ocean-front restaurant serves an excellent menu, a Caribbean buffet on Friday nights and a barbecue lunch buffet on Sundays. In the evenings, international cuisine with local and Creole infusions, can be enjoyed with local entertainment 3-6 times a week. Janissa's Spa boasts indoor and outdoor treatment rooms, a sauna and Jacuzzi.

Jamaica

CARIBBEAN SEA
Montego Bay
387
Lucea
388
Falmouth
Rio Bueno
St. Ann's Bay
389
Ocho Rios
Port Maria
Montpelier
Negril
Savanna la Mar
Newmarket
Balaclava
Ewarton
Buff Bay
Port Antonio
Chapelton
Black River
Mandeville
Spanish Town
KINGSTON
May Pen
Alligator Pond
Portland Cave
Morant Bay
Bowden
CARIBBEAN SEA

HALF MOON

ROSE HALL

Tel: +1 876 953 2211 **Fax:** +1 876 953 2731 **U.S./Canada Toll Free:** 1 888 830 5969
Web: www.johansens.com/halfmoon **E-mail:** reservations@halfmoon.com

Our inspector loved: *The Fern Tree Spa.*

Price Guide: (room only, excluding tax and service charge)
rooms U.S.$250-U.S.$470
suites U.S.$380-U.S.$1,800

398 1100 SPA

Attractions: Dunn's River Falls, 60 miles
Towns/Cities: Montego Bay, 6 miles
Airports: Sangster International Airport, 5 miles

Set in 400 acres of tropical gardens edged by a crescent-shaped bay and a 2-mile white sandy beach, this elegant, luxurious resort offers a wide variety of accommodations comprising 398 rooms including suites, cottages and 32 Royal Villas with private porch and pool, butler service, a cook and maid. For sheer indulgence stay in one of the 11 truly opulent Imperial Suites. Half Moon has no less than 6 restaurants ranging from the open-air Seagrape Terrace to the romantic Il Giardino and enchanting gourmet Sugar Mill. Enjoy your surroundings and swim with the dolphins, play on one of the 13 tennis courts, 4 squash courts or the 18-hole championship golf course, with pro-shop and the Half Moon Golf Academy.

TRYALL CLUB

P.O. BOX 1206, MONTEGO BAY
Tel: +1 876 956 5660 **Fax:** +1 876 956 5673 **U.S./Canada Toll Free:** 1 800 238 5290
Web: www.johansens.com/tryallclub **E-mail:** reservation@tryallclub.com

Our inspector loved: *The stylish individuality of the villas, their privacy and stunning views.*

Price Guide: (per week)
villas U.S.$2,750-U.S.$30,000

73

Attractions: Chukka Blue, 5-min drive; Mountain Valley Rafting, 40-min drive; Mayfield Falls, 45-min drive; Negril Beach, 45-min drive
Towns/Cities: Montego Bay, 12 miles; Lucea, 15 miles; Negril, 35 miles
Airports: Montego Bay Jamaica, Sangster International Airport, 12 miles; Norman Manley International Airport, Kingston, 220 miles

Along an avenue of tall, elegant coconut palms, is the imposing 18th-century "Georgian Great House" and Restaurant. A home-from-home on a grand estate of 2,200 acres, the individually designed and furnished, privately owned villas include the intriguingly named "No Problem" and "Satisfy my Soul". They offer from 1 to 7 bedrooms, private pools and full-time staff including a cook, maid, laundress and butler. The 18-hole, 72 par golf course, designed by Ralph Plummer, has hosted the Johnnie Walker World Championship, the Jamaica Classic and Mazda Championship. This challenging course enjoys a panorama of forest green hills, coconut palms, fruit trees, lily ponds and a full half-mile along the Caribbean shore. Facilities also include 9 "Nova-Cushion" night illuminated tennis courts.

CARIBBEAN - JAMAICA (OCHO RIOS)

ROYAL PLANTATION

MAIN STREET , P.O. BOX 2, OCHO RIOS
U.K. Tel: +44 (0) 20 7590 262 **Local:** +1 876 974 5601 **U.S./Canada Toll Free:** 1 888 48 ROYAL
Web: www.johansens.com/royalplantation **E-mail:** info@royalplantation.com

Our inspector loved: *Afternoon tea on The Terrace.*

Price Guide:
premium ocean-front junior suites U.S.$645
luxury ocean-front junior suites U.S.$680
honeymoon grande luxe ocean-front suites U.S.$790

74 215 SPA

Attractions: Glass Bottom Boat Tours, close by; Swimming with Dolphins, 15-min drive; Dunn's River Falls, 15-min drive
Towns/Cities: Ocho Rios, 10-min drive; Montego Bay, 90-min drive; Kingston, 2-hour drive
Airports: Montego Bay Airport, 90-min drive; Kingston Airport, 2-hour drive

Affiliations: The Leading Small Hotels of the World

Whether soaking up the sun sipping ice cold "mangosas" delivered by your unobtrusive beach butler, taking afternoon tea on The Terrace, or indulging in a glass or two of champagne in the C-Bar, Royal Plantation knows exactly how to give you the perfect experience! Built in the glamorous 1950s, this serene sanctuary maintains a stellar reputation as one of Jamaica's most exquisite beach boutique resorts. Romantically nestled on a breezy bluff 25ft. above the shimmering Caribbean Sea, each of its 74 sumptuous suites has heart-stopping views of the ocean. Bask on the spectacular private twin beaches in the sunshine or enjoy the complete privacy of Villa Plantana with its own garden, 3 bedrooms, private pool and butler. A superb choice of Mediterranean or French cuisine, alongside excellent wines, can be savored in the elegant surroundings of The Terrace and Le Papillon. A visit to Red Lane® Spa is a must; try the "Lover's Lane" package, perfect for couples!

Puerto Rico

ATLANTIC OCEAN
Puerto Rico
Isabela
Arecibo
Vega Baja
391
SAN JUAN
Isla desecheo
Aguadilla
Manatí
Bayamon
Carolina
Rio Grande
Luquillo
Isla de Culebra
Rincon
392
San Sebastián
Fajardo
Añasco
Utuado
Comerio
Caguas
Naguabo
Mayagüez
Maricao
Baranquitas
Adjuntas
Isabel Segunda
Humacao
Cayey
Esperanza
Isla de Mona
San Germán
Coamo
Yubucoa
Isla de Vieques
Boquerón
Yauco
Ponce
Guayama
Santa Isabel
Salinas
Guanica
Isla Caja de Muertos
CARIBBEAN SEA

CHATEAU CERVANTES

RECINTO SUR 329, OLD SAN JUAN
Tel: +787 724 7722 **Fax:** +787 289 8909
Web: www.johansens.com/cervantes **E-mail:** reservations@cervantespr.com

Our inspector loved: *The excellent dining experience at Panza.*

Price Guide: (including Continental breakfast)
superior rooms U.S.$225-U.S.$300
penthouse suites U.S.$1,500-U.S.$2,700

12 M 50 DVD SPA

Attractions: El Morro Castle, San Cristobal Fortress, La Fortaleza, close by; Cathedral of San Juan, 5-min walk; Puerto Rico Art Museum, 10 miles; El Yunque Rainforest and Luquillo Beach, 25 miles
Towns/Cities: Old San Juan, on-site; Metropolitan San Juan/Condado, 3 miles; Isla Verde Beach, 10 miles
Airports: Luis Munoz Marin International Airport, 9 miles

Named for the author of Don Quixote, Chateau Cervantes is characterized by a combination of modern elegance, classic sophistication and a warm, personal ambience, brought to you in the heart of old San Juan. The spacious accommodations inside this restored 16th-century building, with their tall, gracefully arched doorways and striking contemporary art by famous local artists, offer a custom-line of natural body care products in marble-tiled bathrooms and private balconies with views of the city. Larger suites offer a personalized butler service. Panza, the boutique hotel's aptly named restaurant, serves innovative, flavorful international cuisine presented with elegance in its high-ceilinged, mirrored dining room. Ask the knowledgeable wait staff for advice on choosing a vintage from the restaurant's extensive wine list.

HORNED DORSET PRIMAVERA

APARTADO 1132, RINCÓN 00677
Tel: +1 787 823 4030 **Fax:** +1 787 823 5580 **U.S./Canada Toll Free:** 1 800 633 1857
Web: www.johansens.com/horneddorset **E-mail:** info@horneddorset.com

Our inspector loved: *The new ocean-front Horned Dorset Residences with private plunge pools and Moroccan-style interiors.*

Price Guide: (per couple, including breakfast and dinner)
suites U.S.$690-U.S.$1,800

55 30 SPA

Awards/Ratings: Condé Nast Johansens Most Excellent Hotel, Atlantic, Caribbean & Pacific Islands '07; Condé Nast Traveler Gold List '02-'07

Attractions: The Point Lighthouse, 5-min drive; Surfing at Spanish Wall, Pools and Sandy Beach, 5-min drive; Golf Course, 35-min drive
Towns/Cities: Aguadilla, 10 miles; Mayaguez, 12 miles; San Juan, 95 miles
Airports: Aguadilla Airport (BQN), 45-min drive; San Juan Intl. Airport (SJU), 2.5-hour drive

Affiliations: Relais & Châteaux

This exclusive 8-acre hillside property overlooks the Caribbean Sea and offers a luxurious, romantic setting with an interior featuring antiques, exotic woods and marble baths. The Primavera Suites are 1,400 sq. ft., 2-story, king-bedded town house suites with private terraces and plunge pools facing the endless horizon of the Straits of Mona. The furnishings are Spanish, Dutch, and Caribbean mahogany and teak, and look out to the 17th-century Spanish Empire of Carlos I. 17 luxurious beach-front villas have private dipping pools, teak mahogany furnishings, imported rugs and lamps in the Spanish Mozarabic. Gourmet cuisine at Restaurant Aaron offers a selection of creative and delectable menus, and each morning breakfast is served alfresco in The Verandah, on the terrace of the Blue Room or in the privacy of your suite.

Caribbean Sea
Ile Chevreau
Ile Frégate
Ile Toc Vers
La Tortue
Colombier
Point Milou
Anse de Cayes
Corossol
395
Lorient
Vitet
St. Jean
Toiny
La Petitie Saline
Pain de Sucre
Les Gros Islets
GUSTAVIA
394
Les Petits Saints
Gouverneur
La Grande Saline
Atlantic Ocean
Ile Coco

HÔTEL LE TOINY

ANSE DE TOINY
Tel: +590 590 27 88 88 **Fax:** +590 590 27 89 30
Web: www.johansens.com/letoiny **E-mail:** reservations@letoiny.com

Hôtel Le Toiny is nestled on a hillside, overlooking the Caribbean Sea, on the southeastern tip of St. Barths. Privacy and serenity are key themes here, where over 38 acres include a sandy beach, walking trails and a palm grove. Each of the 15 Villa Suites, completely renovated in 2008 in a vibrant French Colonial style, features a large terrace, heated pool and kitchenette. Enjoy the cozy cocktail bar or renowned Restaurant Le Gaïac with a view of the Caribbean Sea, indulge in a massage or beauty treatment in the new Serenity Spa Cottage, on the terrace, or in a beach-side cabana and visit the recently opened gym and infinity pool.

Our inspector loved: *The newly renovated rooms complete with iPod stations and music library.*

Price Guide:
junior suites €520-€1,840
1-bedroom villas €710-€1,840
2/3-bedroom villas €1,210-€3,310

15 SPA

Awards/Ratings: Condé Nast Traveler Gold List 2006

Attractions: Shell Museum, 15-min drive
Towns/Cities: Gustavia, 15-min drive
Airports: Gustaf III Airport, 5 miles

Affiliations: Relais & Châteaux

Hotel Guanahani & Spa

GRAND CUL DE SAC
Tel: +590 590 27 66 60 **Fax:** +590 590 27 70 70 **U.S./Canada Toll Free:** 1 800 216 3774
Web: www.johansens.com/guanahani **E-mail:** guanahani@wanadoo.fr

Our inspector loved: *The relaxing massage at the sophisticated and serene Guanahani Spa.*

Price Guide: (including Continental or American breakfast, non-motorized water sports and airport/port transfers)
rooms €360-€1,360
suites €600-€3,300
la villa €1,000-€5,700

68 30 SPA

Awards/Ratings: Condé Nast Traveler Gold List 2006 and 2008

Attractions: Beach, on-site; Shops, 10-min drive
Towns/Cities: St. Jean, 10-min drive; Gustavia, 20-min drive
Airports: Gustaf III Airport, 15-min drive

Affiliations: The Leading Small Hotels of the World

This delightful luxury resort is set in a beautiful location overlooking 2 private bays on a private 16-acre peninsula. Its pastel interiors with bright furnishings, rich mahogany floors and tropical woods in each of the bungalow-styled suites creates an ideal romantic honeymoon getaway. Gourmet cuisine is central to Guanahani: Executive Chef Philippe Masseglia creates international cuisine with a French flair in Bartolomeo, and Indigo is a casual poolside restaurant overlooking the beach. The exquisite menu at Bartolomeo is complemented by nightly music, while the Lounge Bar'Tô bar is a pleasant setting for pre-dinner cocktails. The open-air Spa by Clarins offers 11 treatment rooms, hammam ritual bath, beauty salon, herbal tea room and Frederic Fekkai hairdressing salon. Private boat, plane and helicopter charters can be arranged, and complimentary children's programs are available.

St. Kitts & Nevis

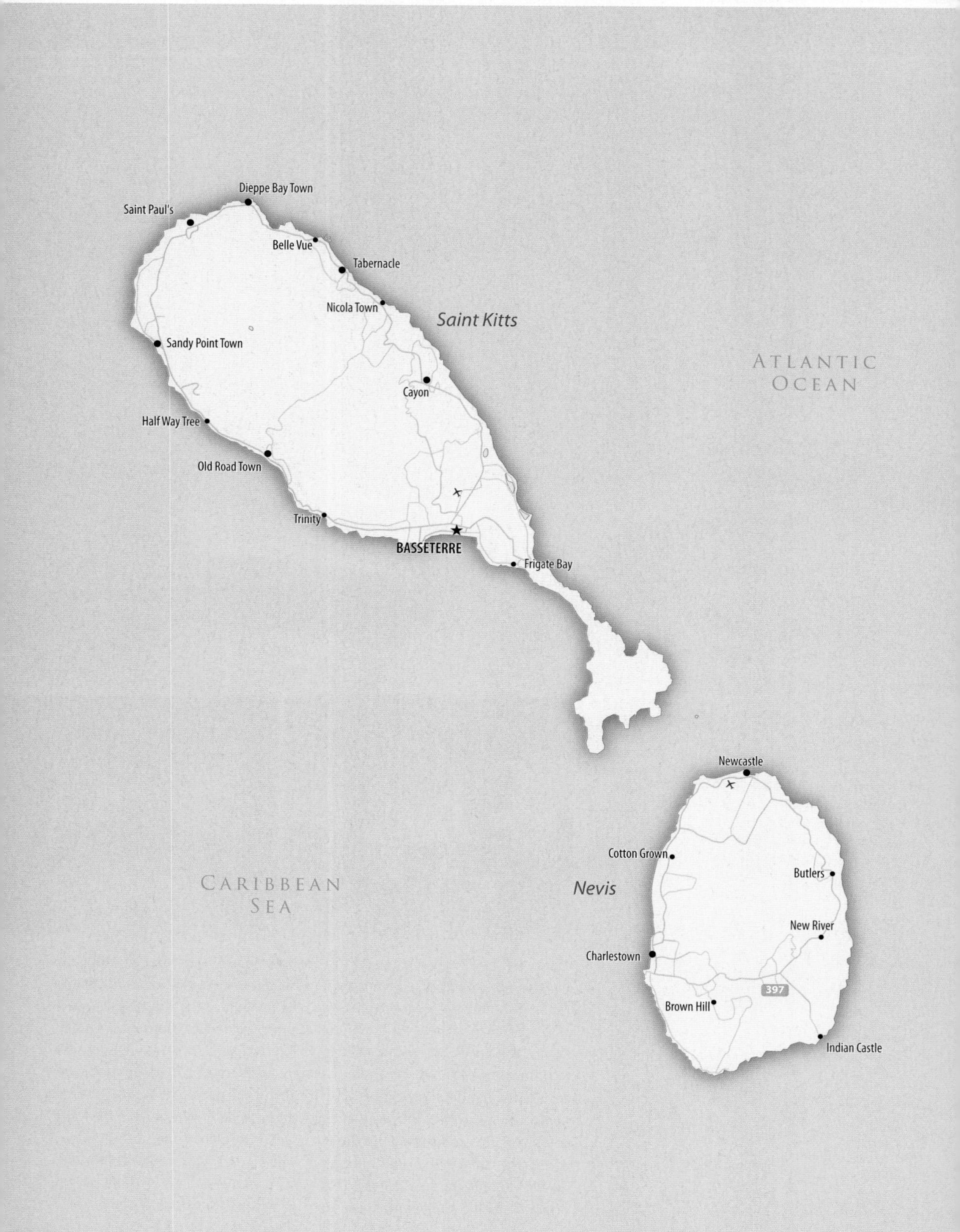

MONTPELIER PLANTATION

P.O. BOX 474, NEVIS
Tel: +1 869 469 3462 **Fax:** +1 869 469 2932
Web: www.johansens.com/montpelierplantation **E-mail:** info@montpeliernevis.com

Our inspector loved: *The warm hospitality shown by the Hoffman family and staff.*

Price Guide: (including full English breakfast, afternoon tea and private beach access with transfers)
premier U.S.$300-U.S.$500
plantation U.S.$360-U.S.$560
suite U.S.$560-U.S.$1,200

18 8

Attractions: The Botanical Gardens, 5-min walk; Horatio Nelson Museum, 3 miles; 18th-Century Thermal Baths, 3 miles
Towns/Cities: Charlestown, 4 miles
Airports: Nevis Airport, 25-min drive

Affiliations: Relais & Châteaux

Located 750 feet above the sea on the slopes of Mount Nevis, this completely refurbished property was once a sugar estate and in 1787 the venue for Horatio Nelson and Fanny Nisbet's wedding. Today, the Hoffman family has created a "country house" hotel ambience with an informal style and unspoiled tranquility. Each of the rooms is designed to catch the breeze and has a private veranda offering stunning views of the sea, mountains and the lights of Nevis and St. Kitts at night. The Plantation rooms are recently refurbished and the new Villa Suite has a private pool and 2 bedrooms. A large freshwater pool is found in the tropical gardens and during the day a complimentary bus service travels to a private 2-acre Caribbean beach. The restaurant's Nevisian and international chefs create classic cuisine with a Caribbean contemporary twist using fresh local produce, and after cocktails in The Great Room, dinner is served outside on The Terrace or inside The Mill.

St. Lucia

Atlantic Ocean
Gros Islet
399
Marisule Estate
Grande Rivière
Marquis
CASTRIES
Grande Anse
Cicéron
Forestière
La Croix Maingot
Dernière Rivière
Anse la Raye
Dennery
Canaries
Millet
Praslin
400
401
402
Soufrière
Fond St. Jacques
Micoud
Desruisseaux
La Pointe
Morne Vert
Choiseul
Saint-Urbain
Laborie
Caribbean Sea
Vieux Fort

Windjammer Landing Villa Beach Resort & Spa

P.O. BOX 1504, CASTRIES, ST. LUCIA
Tel: +1 758 456 9000 **Fax:** +1 758 452 9454 **U.S./Canada Toll Free:** 1 800 958 7376
Web: www.johansens.com/windjammerlanding **E-mail:** reservations@windjammer-landing.com

Our inspector loved: *The new hillside villas with private pools and incredible views.*

Price Guide: (all inclusive packages are available)
suites U.S.$250-U.S.$950
villas U.S.$350-U.S.$1,760

237 SPA

Attractions: Bonne Terra Tropical Gardens, 15-min drive; Indies Nightclub (Rodney Bay), 15-min drive; Pigeon Island National Landmark, 25-min drive; Lesleen M. Shipwreck (Diving), 35-min drive
Towns/Cities: Castries, 10-min drive; Gros Islet, 10-min drive; Rodney Bay, 15-min drive; Choc Bay, 20-min drive
Airports: S.L.U. George F. Charles Airport, 15-min drive; U.V.F. Hewannora Airport, 1-hour drive

This tropical 56-acre resort, on the northwest tip of St. Lucia, is idyllic for Caribbean weddings, romantic escapes and enjoyable family holidays. Private luxury suites and villas exude tropical elegance, each with breathtaking views of the stunning sapphire Caribbean Sea. The new Anthurium Lily Suites and Hibiscus Jacuzzi Suites are highly recommended in addition to the new Estate Villas, each with 3 or 4 bedrooms, private pools and spacious terraces with gorgeous panoramic views. For your culinary pleasure, a personal chef will prepare a gourmet feast in the privacy of your villa. Venture down to the beach-front or to the hillside for restaurants where you can sample international fare followed by evening island entertainment. With a myriad of treatments, the Serenity Spa, a hillside oasis, is a relaxing and sublime experience.

ANSE CHASTANET

SOUFRIÈRE
Tel: +1 758 459 7000 **Fax:** +1 758 459 7700 **U.S./Canada Toll Free:** 1 800 223 1108
Web: www.johansens.com/ansechastanet **E-mail:** ansechastanet@candw.lc

This romantic hideaway is situated on a 600-acre estate with 2 stunning natural beaches and 2 natural valleys, capped off by spectacular mountains. Each of the bedrooms incorporates locally crafted furniture and features art from local and international artists. Scattered over the flower-decked hillside, many of the bedrooms benefit from views of the Piton Mountains and Caribbean Sea; 12 are found at beach level and are just a few steps from the water's edge. Piton Restaurant serves tropical world cuisine while the more informal beach-side restaurant offers Creole and traditional favorites. The resort operates its own P.A.D.I. 5-star Gold Palm/S.S.I. scuba center and there is also mountain biking, the resort's 42-ft. yacht, a library and art gallery to browse around. Kai Belte offers traditional and Ayurvedic treatments from professional therapists.

***Our inspector loved:** The beach-front location with pristine coral reefs right off shore, and the Piton Mountains views from open-air rooms.*

Price Guide: (double occupancy, excluding tax, winter rates include breakfast and dinner)
standard U.S.$300-U.S.$610
superior U.S.$380-U.S.$720
beach/hillside U.S.$450-U.S.$810

49 M 50 10 SPA

Awards/Ratings: Condé Nast Traveler Gold List 2008

Attractions: Marine Park, close by; Botanical Gardens, 15-min drive; Volcano and Sulphur Springs, 25-min drive; Rainforest, 35-min drive
Towns/Cities: Soufrière, 1.5 miles; Castries, 27 miles
Airports: Hewanorra International Airport, 1-hour drive

JADE MOUNTAIN AT ANSE CHASTANET

SOUFRIÈRE

Tel: +1 758 459 4000 **Fax:** +1 758 459 4002 **U.S./Canada Toll Free:** 1 800 223 1108
Web: www.johansens.com/jademountain **E-mail:** jademountain@ansechastanet.com

***Our inspector loved:** Each sanctuary's private infinity pool, surfaced in glass tiles and illuminated at night with colored fiber-optic lights.*

Price Guide: (room only, double occupancy, excluding tax)
sky jacuzzi suites U.S.$950-U.S.$1,100
star sanctuaries U.S.$1,250-U.S.$1,450
moon sanctuaries U.S.$1,450-U.S.$1,650
sun sanctuaries U.S.$1,750-U.S.$1,950

24 M 50 15 SPA

Attractions: Marine Park, close by; Botanical Gardens, 15-min drive; Volcano and Sulphur Springs, 25-min drive; Rainforest, 35-min drive
Towns/Cities: Soufrière, 1.5 miles; Castries, 27 miles
Airports: Hewanorra International Airport, 1-hour drive

Rising majestically above the 600-acre beach-front estate of Anse Chastanet, Jade Mountain, with its organic architecture, celebrates and complements St. Lucia's stunning scenic beauty. Your spacious open-plan bedroom glides easily into your living area and oversized private infinity pool. With the forth wall missing entirely in each of the guest room sanctuaries, architect owner Nick Troubetzkoy, has created a setting from which to embrace St. Lucia's World Heritage Pitons Mountains and enjoy one of the most unforgettable views of the shimmering Caribbean Sea. Integral to the sanctuaries is the Jade Mountain Club where you can enjoy drinks and "Jade cuisine" created by James Beard award-winner Allen Susser. Above the Jade Mountain Club is the Celestial Terrace, a wonderful location from which to stargaze.

LADERA RESORT

SOUFRIÈRE
Tel: +1 758 459 7323 **Fax:** +1 758 459 5156 **U.S./Canada Toll Free:** 1 800 738 4752
Web: www.johansens.com/ladera **E-mail:** ladera@candw.lc

This hilltop resort is nestled in mango groves and takes full advantage of its natural surroundings. All of the secluded suites and villas are designed with an "open wall" that faces west, affording breathtaking views of the 2 volcanic Piton peaks and the ocean, and feature private plunge or swimming pools. Dasheene serves an eclectic, stylish interpretation of St. Lucian cuisine and offers a menu of fresh fish caught by the island's fishermen and fruits and vegetables that are grown locally. Cooking classes are available every Saturday morning. Enjoy cocktails at the Tcholit Bar or by the infinity pool, a relaxing treatment at the Ti Kai Posé Spa and the entertainment performed each evening. Staff will organize activities such as hiking and rainforest walks, sailing excursions and island tours.

Our inspector loved: *The new mineral soaking tubs in the Ti Kai Posé spa gardens.*

Price Guide: (including breakfast, afternoon tea, resort facilities, beach shuttle and snorkeling equipment)
rooms U.S.$380-U.S.$815
suites U.S.$535-U.S.$810
villas U.S.$430-U.S.$1,330

27 15 SPA

Awards/Ratings: Condé Nast Traveler Gold List 2006-2008; Condé Nast Johansens Most Excellent Resort 2006

Attractions: Piton Mountains, 10-min drive; Diamond Waterfalls, 15-min drive; Botanical Gardens, 15-min drive; Rainforest Tours, 40-min drive
Towns/Cities: Soufrière, 2 miles
Airports: Hewanorra International Airport, 40-min drive

Caribbean Sea
Saint-Martin
Grand Case
French Cul de Sac
Orleans
MARIGOT
Columbier
Terres Basses
Mornes Rouge
405
South Reward
St. Peter
Lowlands
Cul de Sac
Almond Grove
Sucker Garden
Billy Folly
PHILIPSBURG
Point Blanche
Sint Maarten

La Samanna

P.O. BOX 4077, 97064 CEDEX
Tel: +590 590 87 64 00 **Fax:** +590 590 87 87 86 **U.S./Canada Toll Free:** 1 800 854 2252
Web: www.johansens.com/lasamanna **E-mail:** reservations@lasamanna.com

Our inspector loved: *The specially designed spa treatments at the fantastic Elysées Spa.*

Price Guide: (including buffet breakfast, snorkeling and wind surfing activities)
rooms from U.S.$995
suites U.S.$3,000-U.S.$5,275

81 M 90 DVD SPA

Awards/Ratings: Condé Nast Traveler Gold List 2007

Attractions: Cupecoy Beach, 1 mile; Marigot Market, 6 miles; Loterie Farm, 7 miles; Butterfly Farm, 10 miles
Towns/Cities: Marigot, 6 miles; Grand Case, 12 miles; Orient, 15 miles; Phillipsburg, 15 miles
Airports: Princess Juliana Airport, 4 miles

Surrounded by lush foliage with colorful splashes of flowers, this chic resort appeals to discriminating, international travelers looking for seclusion, relaxation, fine dining and personalized service. Exuding a French spirit with a Caribbean soul, the resort comprises 81 suites on 55 acres of breathtaking beach-front. The comfortable suites range from 1 to 3 bedrooms with private terraces and rich amenities; there are 5 specialty suites. The Baie Longue Suite is an exclusive 3-bedroom Presidential Suite; often a celebrity hideaway. And the new La Samanna Villas offer the ultimate in luxury and privacy while enjoying full use of all the main resort amenities. Savor French-Caribbean cuisine at the Grill or in the elegant restaurant. Bar de Champagne and the Beach Bar are popular gathering spots. Wine enthusiasts will love the award-winning wine cellar with over 10,000 bottles. Take a Pilates class at the only studio in the Caribbean or have a treatment at the world-class Elysées Spa.

St. Vincent & The Grenadines

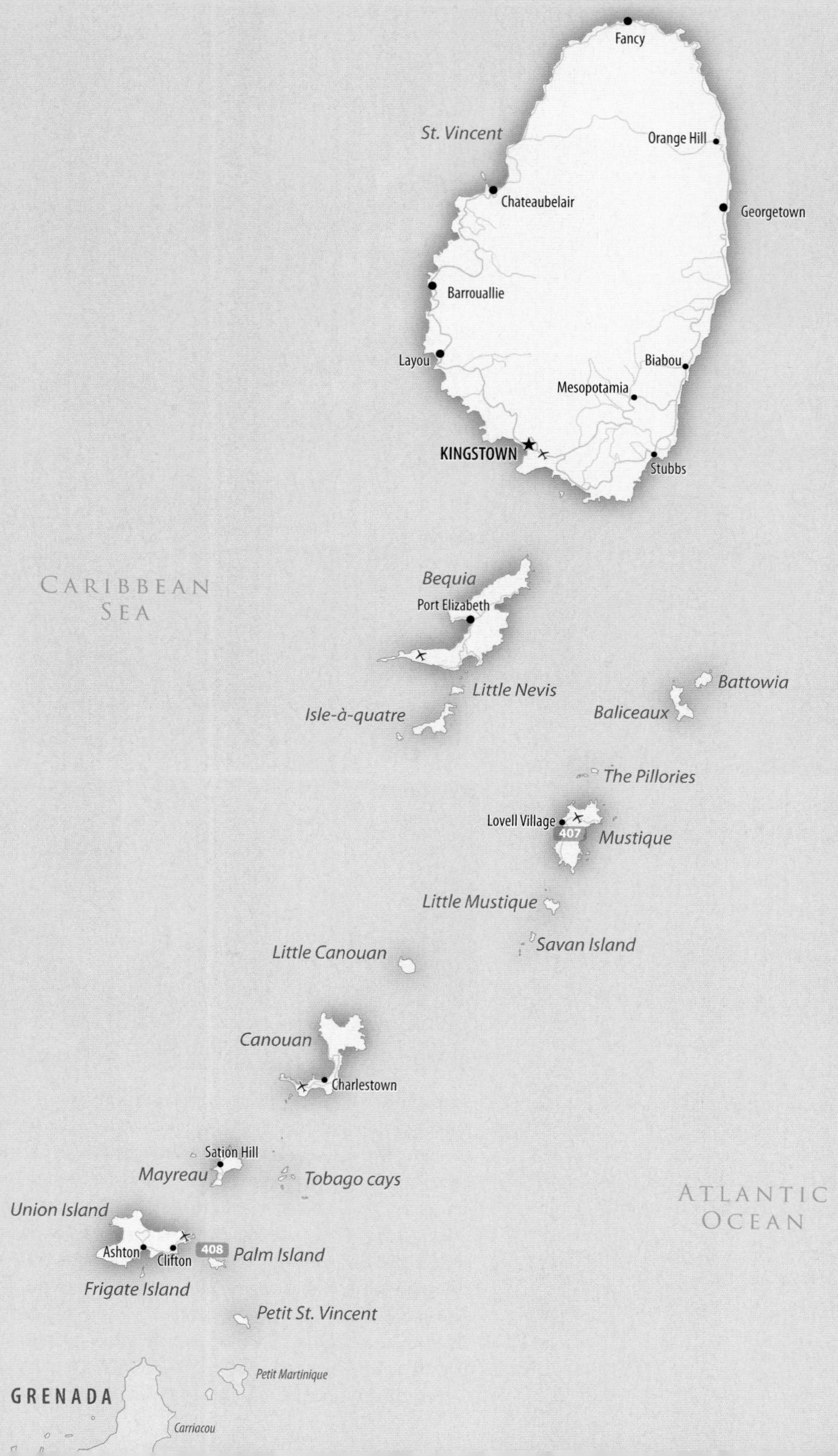

FIREFLY

MUSTIQUE ISLAND
Tel: +1 784 488 8414 **Fax:** +1 784 488 8514
Web: www.johansens.com/firefly **E-mail:** enquiries@fireflymustique.com

Our inspector loved: *Firefly's bar lounge, a lively place during the evening, with its grand piano and impromptu perfomances by the occasional star guest!*

Price Guide: (including breakfast, lunch, afternoon tea and dinner and an electric car)
rooms U.S.$950-U.S.$1,200

Attractions: Firefly Bequia, 8 miles; Tobago Keys, 8 miles
Airports: Mustique Airport, 5-min drive

Exquisitely perched on a hillside with amazing views of the Caribbean Sea, this boutique hotel offers 5 light and airy individually designed bedrooms. All rooms feature fully loaded iPods, four-poster beds, and mesmerizing views of the sea; some come with "tropical plunge pools." Lush tropical gardens criss-crossed by paths, surround the hotel. A pagoda has comfortable lounge chairs looking out at the garden and sea and hammocks are idyllically placed by the pool and Jacuzzi. Dining on the covered terrace affords beautiful sunset views and the frequently changing menu features fresh seafood in a Caribbean style alongside an excellent choice of international wines. Each guest has the use of an electric car to explore this unspoiled island.

PALM ISLAND

PALM ISLAND
Tel: +1 954 481 8787 **Fax:** +1 954 481 1661 **U.S./Canada Toll Free:** 1 800 858 4618
Web: www.johansens.com/palmisland **E-mail:** reservations@eliteislandresorts.com

One of Condé Nast Traveler's Top 25 Caribbean Resorts, Readers' Choice Awards 2007, this is a tranquil paradise of dazzling white sand beaches fringed with palms, breathtaking seascapes and tropical landscapes. There are 5 beaches, a swimming pool with cascading waterfalls, 2 bars, 2 restaurants, a vast range of activities and, at an additional charge, snorkel, boat trips to the nearby Tobago Cays. Accommodation is simple but stylish; all guest rooms have air conditioning, rattan and bamboo furniture, original artwork and a balcony or patio. The Palm View and Beachfront bungalows are nestled among shady palm trees and colorful gardens, just a few yards from the sand and with views of distant islands, and the stilted Island Lofts - individual wooden cottages - have private terraces, deep-soaking tubs and a separate shower. Gourmet meals are enjoyed in the Royal Palm, while casual, grill-type fare is served in the Sunset Beach Restaurant.

Our inspector loved: *The romantic setting of this private island escape.*

Price Guide: (including all meals, beverages, non-motorized water sports, Internet access, tax, service charge and transfer from Union Island)
rooms/suites U.S.$755-U.S.$1,640
villas U.S.$895-U.S.$1,425
lofts U.S.$1,015-U.S.$1,445

44

Attractions: Tobago Cays, 30-min boat ride
Towns/Cities: Union Island, 5-min boat ride; St. Vincent, 15-min flight
Airports: Union Island Airport, 10-min flight

Turks & Caicos Islands

THE ESTATE AT GRACE BAY CLUB

P.O. BOX 128, PROVIDENCIALES
Tel: +649 946 8323 **Fax:** +649 946 5758 **U.S./Canada Toll Free:** 1 800 946 5757
Web: www.johansens.com/estateatgracebay **E-mail:** info@gracebayclub.com

Setting the standard for luxury accommodations, The Estate at Grace Bay Club is an innovative development of 22 custom-designed residences and penthouses that combine the service and amenities of a lavish hotel with all the comforts of home. Perched on 11 acres of the famous white sand Grace Bay Beach, each ultra-elegant residence features breathtaking, unobstructed ocean views, expansive indoor and outdoor living spaces, stylishly designed bedrooms and bathrooms, a library/media room and open wraparound terrace. In addition, each residence boasts a private outdoor shower or private plunge pool, oversized ocean view showers, and the finest amenities and details. Relax by the eye-catching infinity pool or rejuvenate with a spa treatment inside your very own cabana. The Personal Concierge program will cater to your every whim.

Our inspector loved: *The private plunge pools at the beach-level residences and the ultra-cool cabanas around the black granite infinity pool.*

Price Guide:
residences U.S.$800-U.S.$7,300
penthouse U.S.$5,500-U.S.$11,500

Attractions: Turtle Cove Marina, 3 miles; Provo Golf Club, 3 miles; Conch Farm, 4 miles
Towns/Cities: Leeward Marina, 3 miles
Airports: Providenciales International Airport, 7 miles

Affiliations: The Leading Small Hotels of the World

GRACE BAY CLUB

P.O. BOX 128, PROVIDENCIALES
Tel: +1 649 946 5050 **Fax:** +1 649 946 5758 **U.S./Canada Toll Free:** 1 800 946 5757
Web: www.johansens.com/gracebayclub **E-mail:** info@gracebayclub.com

Our inspector loved: The stylish new Infiniti Bar, the longest bar in the Caribbean.

Price Guide: (including breakfast)
rooms U.S.$501-U.S.$3,482
suites U.S.$550-U.S.$11,500

59 30 SPA

Awards/Ratings: Condé Nast Johansens Most Excellent Resort Award, Atlantic, Caribbean & Pacific Islands 2007 and 2008; Condé Nast Traveler Gold List 1997-2007

Attractions: Provo Golf Club, 0.25 miles; Turtle Cove Marina, 3 miles; Conch Farm, 4 miles
Towns/Cities: Leeward Marina, 2 miles
Airports: Providenciales Intl. Airport, 7 miles

Affiliations: The Leading Small Hotels of the World

Located on 11 acres of white sand beach, this luxury all-suite hotel offers the ultimate in pampered relaxation. The Resort, divided into 3 separate sections for discerning travelers of all tastes include: the adults-only Hotel area with private restaurant, bar and swimming pool, the family friendly Villas with their own restaurant bar and pool, in addition to the uber-luxe Estate with a complete set of exclusive amenities. The lavishly designed penthouse suites, with stunning turquoise ocean views, are a celebrity favorite with an outdoor Jacuzzi, infinity-edge balcony and personal concierge services. Indulge at the Anani Spa while the little ones partake in Kidstown Eco-Activity Program. Savor Caribbean-infused tapas and tropical cocktails in the chic lounge or at the Infiniti Bar, the Caribbean's longest bar, before dinner by the sea at the gourmet Anacaona. The ultra-luxurious Estate at Grace Bay Club is the newest addition to their award-winning portfolio.

Turks & Caicos Club

WEST GRACE BAY BEACH, P.O. BOX 687, PROVIDENCIALES
Tel: +1 649 946 5800 **Fax:** +1 649 946 5858
Web: www.johansens.com/turksandcaicos **E-mail:** info@turksandcaicosclub.com

Our inspector loved: *Snorkeling in the warm turquoise water off the hotel's pristine white sand beach.*

Price Guide: (including full American breakfast, closed September 1st-30th)
1-bedroom suites U.S.$325-U.S.$695
2-bedroom suites U.S.$525-U.S.$1,295

21 50

Attractions: Turtle Cove Marina, 1 mile; Bight Reef, 2-min walk; Provo Golf Club, 2 miles; Conch Farm, 4 miles
Airports: Providenciales International Airport, 3 miles

Located on a stunning stretch of the Grace Bay Beach's white sands, steps from the island's best snorkeling reef, this elegant Colonial-style mansion is the epitome of intimate island luxury. There are just 21 suites with 1 or 2 bedrooms featuring all the amenities of a private home-away-from-home. Ideal for romantic getaways or family vacations, each suite is beautifully designed with custom rattan furnishings, maple cabinetry, fully-fitted kitchens, four-poster beds and subtle safari prints. Large private balconies provide cool seclusion for a rejuvenating seaside massage. The discreet and friendly service ensures a relaxing stay. The popular Simba Restaurant & Bar offers Caribbean lobster and native conch. Simply relax on the beach with a tropical drink or go windsurfing, sea-kayaking, HobieCat sailing or snorkeling.

THE SOMERSET ON GRACE BAY

PRINCESS DRIVE, PROVIDENCIALES
Tel: +1 649 946 5900 **Fax:** +1 649 946 5944
Web: www.johansens.com/somersetgracebay **E-mail:** reservations@thesomerset.com

Our inspector loved: *The exquisite setting and gourmet cuisine of O'Soleil restaurant.*

Price Guide: (including Continental breakfast)
suites U.S.$570-U.S.$3,000
1-5-bedroom suites U.S.$1,080-U.S.$7,200

54 200

Attractions: Provo Golf Club, 2.5 miles; Smith's Reef, 3 miles; Conch Farm, 4 miles
Airports: Providenciales International Airport, 7 miles

Affiliations: Small Luxury Hotels of the World

On the water's edge of Grace Bay Beach, this luxury resort comprises several accommodations: Estate Suites, Stirling House and English Cottages. The spectacular Estate Suites range from 1 to 5-bedroom suites with panoramic ocean views, marble baths, private outdoor Jacuzzis, gourmet kitchens, wired audio systems and spacious terraces. The Stirling House also offers ocean views, a master suite and many of the exquisite amenities of the Estate Suites. The charming English Cottages have lovely garden views. Central to the resort is the beautiful infinity pool with underwater surround stereo system and lap current for swimming. Enjoy a tropical drink or casual fare at the poolside bar before sampling gourmet cuisine at O'Soleil. Rejuvenate and pamper yourself with a spa treatment in the comfort of your very own suite, go diving, parasailing or take a tour of the local conch farm.

Parrot Cay & COMO Shambhala Retreat

P.O. BOX 164, PROVIDENCIALES
Tel: +1 649 946 7788 **Fax:** +1 649 946 7789 **U.S./Canada Toll Free:** 1 877 754 0726
Web: www.johansens.com/parrotcay **E-mail:** res@parrotcay.como.bz

Parrot Cay is a 1,000-acre private island surrounded by over 3 miles of unspoiled white sand and clear turquoise water. There is a combination of rooms, suites and villas from garden and ocean-facing rooms with four-poster beds to ocean-front beach houses, 30 meters from the beach. The larger villas, Parrot Cay Estates, come complete with a private butler. The interiors are sleek with whitewashed walls accentuated by clean-lined teak furniture, expansive bathrooms and soft linens. In the main building of the hotel the Terrace Restaurant & Bar serves a Mediterranean influenced menu, while Lotus, the poolside restaurant, offers light meals at lunchtime and Asian and Caribbean cuisine at dinner. COMO Shambhala Retreat has extensive facilities including specialized therapists who administer Asian-inspired holistic treatments.

Our inspector loved: *The daily yoga sessions at the COMO Shambhala Retreat.*

Price Guide: (incl. breakfast and transfer to/from airport, excl. service charge and 10% tax)
rooms U.S.$400-U.S.$975
suites U.S.$1,000-U.S.$1,650
villas US.$2,050-U.S.$11,000

65 SPA

Awards/Ratings: Condé Nast Johansens Most Excellent Spa Hotel, Atlantic, Caribbean & Pacific Islands 2007 and 2008

Attractions: Iguana Island, 20-min boat ride; Bottom Reef Fishing; 20-min boat ride; Provo Golf & Country Club, 30-min boat ride; Sand Dollar Island, 30-min boat ride
Towns/Cities: Providenciales, 10 miles
Airports: Providenciales Intl. Airport, 10 miles

Affiliations: Leading Small Hotels of the World

POINT GRACE

P.O. BOX 700, PROVIDENCIALES
Tel: +1 649 946 5096 **Fax:** +1 649 946 5097 **U.S./Canada Toll Free:** 1 866 924 7223
Web: www.johansens.com/pointgrace **E-mail:** reservations@pointgrace.com

Our inspector loved: *The romantic fine dining at Grace's Cottage.*

Price Guide:
suites U.S.$475-U.S.$2,867
penthouse U.S.$4,000-U.S.$7,500

29 SPA

Awards/Ratings: Condé Nast Traveler Gold List 2008

Attractions: Provo Golf Club, 2 miles; Conch Farm, 2 miles
Airports: Providenciales International Airport, 6 miles

This exceptional hideaway is beautifully designed and overlooks spectacular views of the pristine 12-mile beach of Grace Bay. The attention to detail is inspiring with its cool colors, stylish fabrics and tastefully decorated suites. Each suite is filled with exquisite Indonesian teak furniture and has an expansive living area and luxurious bathroom. Grace's Cottage, the elegant gourmet restaurant, is open for dinner, while breakfast and lunch are served at Hutchings. Bar service is available throughout the day and complimentary bottled water and mister service is available at the pool and beach. Outdoor pursuits include diving and sailing in the clear waters and coral reefs, and the marine parks and wildlife reserves in the area are exciting to explore.

The Regent Palms, Turks & Caicos

P.O. BOX 681, GRACE BAY, PROVIDENCIALES
Tel: +649 946 8666 **Fax:** +649 946 5188 **U.S./Canada Toll Free:** 1 866 877 7756
Web: www.johansens.com/regentpalms **E-mail:** reservationstc@regentexperience.com

Beautifully situated on 12 acres of landscaped gardens on the world-famous Grace Bay Beach is The Regent Palms, voted one of the Top 100 Resorts in the World 2008 by The Robb Report and included on the Condé Nast Traveler Hot List for New Spas 2008. This stunning property has whitewashed exteriors and the turquoise sea as its backdrop with marble floors, impressive vaulted ceilings and custom-made mahogany furnishings inside offering a residential feel. Luxury rooms and suites, some with ocean views, are elegantly appointed in cool Caribbean colors and feature hand-tufted king bedding. Daily butler service is available in the penthouses for that little extra pampering. Parallel23 serves tropical fusion cuisine alongside an impressive wine list in a casually elegant setting. And for more casual fare you can enjoy the poolside Plunge restaurant. Indulge yourself with a world-class treatment at the 25,000 sq. ft. spa, while the kids are entertained at the Conch Kritters Club.

Our inspector loved: *The family-friendly ethos. Younger guests are entertained at the Conch Kritters Club.*

Price Guide: (including breakfast, excluding tax and service charges)
rooms U.S.$325-U.S.$1,400
suites U.S.$625-U.S.$4,700
3-bedroom penthouses U.S.$2,100-U.S.$6,500

72 M 100 DVD WiFi
SPA

Attractions: Provo Golf Club, 5-min drive; Princess Alexandra Marine Park, 5-min drive; Turtle Cove Marina, 10-min drive; Conch Farm, 15-min drive
Airports: Providenciales International Airport, 15-min drive

Pacific Ocean
418
Labasa
Buca
Vanua Levu
421
422
420
Yadua
Nabouwalu
Taveuni
427
426
425
Yasawa Islands
Koro
Mamanuca Islands
Vatukoula
Ba
419
Lautoka
Ovalau
Wakaya Island
Levuka
Viti Levu
Nadi
Nairai
Nausori
Toberua Island
Suva
Gau
Sigatoka
423
Moala
Beqa
424
Royal Davui
Vatulele
Totoya
Kadavu
Matuku

NUKUBATI ISLAND, GREAT SEA REEF, FIJI

P.O. BOX 1928, LABASA
Tel: +61 2 93888 196 **Fax:** +61 2 93888 204 **U.S./Canada Toll Free:** 1 800 224 0220
Web: www.johansens.com/nukubati **E-mail:** info@nukubati.com

Upon arrival by sea plane step onto the white sands and instantly feel free from working-day stresses and the concept of time. Alternately, arrive via Labasa Airport and drive through lush farmland past sugar cane and rice crops, and stop to pick fresh guava and other seasonal fruit. The airy pavilion is a stunning place to relax and sip an evening cocktail while watching the sunset, although it is a hard choice to make between this and the intimate privacy of your own veranda. The open-plan layout is beautifully appointed with comfortable lounges and quiet writing tables, while the bathrooms are luxuriously large. The extremely fresh food is all taken from Chef's island garden or the local waters, and the fruit from the "Fijian Garden" is unrivaled.

Our inspector loved: *The intimacy of this exclusive 5-star island retreat with pristine reefs and pure white sand all to yourself.*

Price Guide: (including all meals, alcoholic and non-alcoholic beverages, non-motorized sporting activities, daily laundry service, return transfers and taxes, per couple)
beach-front bures U.S.$820.05
honeymoon bures U.S.$993.30

7 12

Attractions: Day Trips to Savusavu and Labasa Villages; Pearl Farm, 4 miles; Great Sea Reef, 20-min boat ride
Towns/Cities: Labasa, 30 miles
Airports: Labasa Airport, 30 miles

Blue Lagoon Cruises

183 VITOGO PARADE, LAUTOKA
Tel: +679 6661 622 **Fax:** +679 6664 098 **U.S./Canada Toll Free:** 1 818 424 7550
Web: www.johansens.com/bluelagooncruises **E-mail:** reservations@blc.com.fj

Our inspector loved: *The true Fijian experience - it is a MUST for your "to do" list! This is small luxury boat cruising at its best and the only way to access these pristine waters and reefs.*

Price Guide: (all inclusive)
4-day cruise U.S.$1,000-U.S.$1,500
7-day cruise U.S.$1,350-U.S.$1,650

70 120 SPA

Attractions: Yasawa Islands
Towns/Cities: Lautoka, 2 miles; Nadi, 16 miles
Airports: Nadi International Airport, 12 miles

The magnificent Blue Lagoon Cruises provides a choice of 2 stunning vessels that will take you on a breathtaking 4 or 7-day cruise around the beautiful and untouched Yasawa Islands. The M.V. Fiji Princess is an awe-inspiring 60-meter catamaran. Its 34 deluxe air-conditioned cabins are spacious and luxuriously appointed with large panoramic windows and every modern convenience imaginable. Built with the utmost in comfort and extravagance in mind, the Mystique Princess is truly a millionaire's yacht for you to enjoy. The friendly crew create an atmosphere perfect for you to feel pampered and let any worries drift away. Take an early morning swim in warm azure waters followed by a stroll along white sandy beaches before sampling the delicious fresh local cuisine.

Qamea Resort & Spa

P.A. MATEI, TAVEUNI
Tel: +649 360 0858 **Fax:** +649 360 0859 **U.S./Canada Toll Free:** 1 866 867 2632
Web: www.johansens.com/qamea **E-mail:** reservations@qamea.com

On a mile-long pristine white sandy beach, this intimate luxury property consists of 17 spacious ocean-front bures and villas nestled in 100 acres of landscaped gardens and bushland, with a stunning backdrop of jagged South Pacific mountains. Strategically positioned for maximum privacy and unobstructed views of the sunset, each thatched roof bure and villa has been designed in traditional Fijian style. A split-level honeymoon villa and 2 honeymoon bures have Jacuzzis and the 2 premium villas have private pools. 4 Fijian chefs and visiting chefs from Australia and New Zealand create gourmet Fijian and Continental Pacific Rim dining in the Bure Kalau. Some of the world's best diving and snorkeling sites can be found on the doorstep, while excursions to the neighboring islands can be arranged. Alternately, head to the recently opened Jungle Spa, comprising 5 treatment bures and offering over 50 body and facial treatments.

***Our inspector loved:** The way this award-winning resort gets better and better each year with its wonderful 5-star service and facilities all at a 4-star rate.*

Price Guide: (including all meals and non-motorized activities, excluding tax)
rooms U.S.$600-U.S.$950

17 16
SPA

Attractions: World Renowned Scuba Diving, close by; Pearl Farm, 6 miles; Bouma Waterfall, 10 miles
Airports: Matei Airport, Taveuni Island, 10 miles

Jean-Michel Cousteau Fiji Islands Resort

LESIACEVA POINT, SAVUSAVU
Tel: +1 415 788 5794 **Tel Australia:** +61 3 98 15 03 79 **U.S./Canada Toll Free:** 1 800 246 3454
Web: www.johansens.com/jean-michelcousteau **E-mail:** jmcfir@alphalink.com.au

Our inspector loved: *The complimentary welcome foot massage upon arrival.*

Price Guide: (all inclusive, per couple, excluding alcoholic and specialty beverages and tax)
bures U.S.$669-U.S.$1,178
villa U.S.$2,400

25 60 SPA

Awards/Ratings: Condé Nast Traveler Gold List 2006; Condé Nast Johansens Most Excellent Resort 2006

Attractions: Marine Sanctuary, on-site; Private Island Escapes, 10-min boat ride; Black Pearl Farm and Savusavu Farmers' Market, 15-min drive; Fijian Village Visit, 30-min drive
Towns/Cities: Savusavu, 5 miles
Airports: Savusavu Airport, 8 miles

This multi-award winning luxury eco-friendly resort is situated on 17 acres of the unspoiled island of Vanua Levu overlooking the peaceful clear waters of Savusavu Bay. Reminiscent of an authentic Fijian village, it is surrounded by world-renowned pristine coral reefs, secluded coastline, tropical gardens and stunning sunset ocean views. The 24 spacious individual bures exude tropical elegance, and the magnificent villa features a four-poster bedroom suite, sunken bathroom with Jacuzzi, pool and daybed pavilion. Guests dine by lantern light on mouth-watering fusions of local and international cuisine. The resort is the perfect combination of relaxation and discovery for discerning travelers of all ages. The variety of complimentary activities is exceptional and includes an excursion to a waterfall and the rainforest, world-class snorkeling with resident marine biologist, yoga classes, diving, sailing and much more.

NAMALE - FIJI ISLANDS RESORT & SPA

P.O. BOX 244, SAVUSAVU
Tel: +679 8850 435 **Fax:** +679 8850 400 **U.S./Canada Toll Free:** 1 800 727 FIJI (3454)
Web: www.johansens.com/namale **E-mail:** reservations@namaleresort.com

Our inspector loved: *The memory of Namale's exotic location that will stay in your heart forever.*

Price Guide: (all inclusive)
rooms U.S.$925-U.S.$1,275
suites U.S.$1,625

37 M 40 WiFi
SPA

Set majestically on the edge of the Koro Sea, Namale is an oasis of seclusion and luxury. Begin the day when the Lali drum signals breakfast, then choose from the array of activities offered by the resort, from horseback riding to water sports, or just relax in the sun on the beach, by the pool or on your private deck. The friendly Fijian staff, or "family," will make you feel at home. After an action packed day, relax at the 10,000 sq. ft. Namale Spa and Sanctuary where you can experience a range of soothing treatments. For the evening, enjoy Fijian and South Pacific cuisine in the Vale Levu main bure, or have one of the friendly staff bring a cocktail to you anywhere within the resort grounds.

Attractions: Kava Bowl 1-min walk; Hiking and Mountain Biking, 1-min walk; Diving and Snorkeling, 1-min walk
Towns/Cities: Savusavu, 4 miles
Airports: Savusavu Airport, 3 miles

MYOLA PLANTATION

P.O. BOX 638, SIGATOKA
Tel: +679 652 1084 **Fax:** +679 652 0899
Web: www.johansens.com/myola **E-mail:** myola@connect.com.fj

Our inspector loved: *The exclusivity and seclusion of this most exquisite and serene place.*

Price Guide: (all inclusive)
2-suite villas U.S.$2,100-U.S.$2,400

2 16 SPA

Awards/Ratings: AAA 5 Diamond

Attractions: Sigatoka Sand Dunes, 5-min drive; Sigatoka Shopping, 20-min train ride; Kula Eco Bird Park, 20-min drive; Natadola Beach, 25-min drive
Towns/Cities: Sigatoka, 10-min drive; Nadi, 45-min drive; Suva, 2-hour drive
Airports: Nadi International Airport, 45-min drive

Atop a cliff on 10 acres of Viti Levu, just west of Sigatoka, this secluded private villa of landscaped tropical gardens and citrus groves offers unrivaled Pacific views across a pristine turquoise coral reef where you will be the only guests with every facility and member of staff available to cater for your every whim. 10 personal staff, a personal chef, maid service and extras such as in-room massages make for a truly indulgent stay. Each of the 2 Master Suites has its own spa, outdoor shower and plunge pool. A large open-plan lounge, entertainment area, dining area, fully-equipped kitchen and office complete the facilities, and sweeping balconies, luxury amenities and objets d'art complete the ambience. Discover the exotic flavours of Fijian and Western cuisine, expertly prepared by the Plantation's chef with only the freshest of ingredients harvested from the nearby lush Sigatoka Valley and local seafood is plentiful. This is a perfect place to host a wedding and honeymoon.

ROYAL DAVUI ISLAND RESORT - FIJI

P.O. BOX 3171, LAMI
Tel: +679 336 1624 **Fax:** +679 336 1253
Web: www.johansens.com/royaldavui **E-mail:** res@royaldavui.com

Idyllic, romantic and exclusive, Royal Davui offers true island seclusion in total luxury and style. This remote and lush green hideaway stands above a colorful barrier reef fringed by soft, pristine white sandy beaches and clear sapphire waters. 16 spacious vales (villas) nestle in the cliffs' tropical vegetation with dramatic views over Beqa Lagoon. Each is cool with mahogany floors, thatched roof, sea-grass ceiling and an open-plan layout featuring extensive glass areas and bi-folding doors that take full advantage of the stunning views. They also feature king-size beds, Jacuzzis, indoor and outdoor showers, 2 decks and plunge pools. Delicious à la carte breakfasts, lunches and dinners are beautifully presented in the sumptuous Banyan Restaurant, and the menu is Pacific rim inspired with the emphasis on fruit, vegetables and seafood. Picnic hampers can be delivered to your room or to a special location.

Our inspector loved: *This ultimate getaway offering the 3 "r's": Rest, Relaxation and Rejuvenation.*

Price Guide: (including breakfast, lunch and dinner in the Banyan Restaurant or by the pool. Tea, coffee and purified water are also included.)
deluxe vales U.S.$1,165
premium vales U.S.$1,350
Royal Davui suites U.S.$1,515

16 16

Awards/Ratings: Condé Nast Johansens Most Romantic Hideaway, Atlantic, Caribbean & Pacific Islands 2007 and 2008

Attractions: Diving, Snorkeling and Fishing, 2-min walk; Fiji Village Visit, Nacewa, 4 miles; Picnic on a Sand Island, 4 miles
Towns/Cities: Pacific Harbour, 16 miles; Suva, 50 miles
Airports: Nausori Airport, 50 miles; Suva Airport, 50 miles; Nadi International Airport, 180 miles

NAVUTU STARS RESORT

P.O. BOX 1838, LAUTOKA
Tel: +679 664 0553/4 **Fax:** +679 666 0807
Web: www.johansens.com/navutustars **E-mail:** reservations@navutustarsfiji.com

Our inspector loved: *The natural beauty and Fijian/Italian chic. This is a barefoot paradise, a resort for the sophisticated castaway.*

Price Guide: (all inclusive, per couple)
grand bures U.S.$590-U.S.$850

9 18 SPA

Attractions: Blue Lagoon, 1 mile; Traditional Fijian Village, 1 mile; Underwater Relic, 2 miles; Underwater Caves, 5 miles
Airports: Nadi International Airport, 60 miles

Tucked away on a peaceful turquoise bay, each of the 9 spacious, open-plan bures is decorated in a fusion of Asian-Mediterranean-Fijian styles, with South-east Asian art pieces and fabrics. Bures also feature double stone vanities, open-plan living rooms, wet bars and an outdoor daybed. Cook up your catch in a local cuisine demonstration, take part in a yoga workshop - only available in season - or attend a Lovo night with local singing and a South Pacific Kava ceremony. Italian cuisine, with a tropical twist, featuring local seafood and produce, is served on the main veranda under the stars. You may choose to enjoy your meal at a table on the beach or on your very own private terrace. Relax in the spa with a menu of treatments based on local ingredients such as algae, coconut oil and clay.

TURTLE ISLAND

P.O. BOX 9317, NADI, YASAWA ISLAND
Tel: +1 360 256 4347 **Fax:** +1 360 253 3934 **U.S./Canada Toll Free:** 1 800 255 4347
Web: www.johansens.com/turtleisland **E-mail:** request@turtlefiji.com

The site of the movie, "The Blue Lagoon," Turtle Island is everything you could want in an exclusive luxury retreat. Dedicated to couples' escapes, you can experience the ultimate romantic getaway. Choose from a romantic picnic for two on one of the private beaches, a moonlit dinner by the water, adventuring on horseback along the beach or a relaxing couples' massage. Also enjoy swimming, snorkeling and windsurfing off the shores of the island. Finish your day with a sunset cruise where you will be entertained with traditional songs and dances. Then retire to your bure, a traditional 2-room cottage with 21-ft. ceilings, king-size bed, walk-in shower, and stocked bar with fresh tropical fruit. Built to preserve the natural beauty and biodiversity, Turtle Island works with the community to develop sustainable tourism projects such as local schools and reintroduction of native plant life.

Our inspector loved: *Everything about this blissful place.*

Price Guide: (all inclusive)
deluxe bure U.S.$1,765
tu ga bure U.S.$2,136
vonu point U.S.$2,585

14

Attractions: The Famous Blue Lagoon, on-site
Airports: Nadi International Airport, 30-min seaplane ride; Turtle Island Sea Planes, 1-min walk

Yasawa Island Resort & Spa

P.O. BOX 10128, NADI AIRPORT, NADI
Tel: +679 672 2266 **Fax:** +679 672 4456
Web: www.johansens.com/yasawaisland **E-mail:** reservations@yasawa.com.fj

Our inspector loved: *The Honeymoon Suite. "Lomalagi" means heaven in Fijian and this private, secluded suite is just that.*

Price Guide: (all inclusive)
rooms U.S.$900-U.S.$1,300
honeymoon suite U.S.$1,800

SPA

Awards/Ratings: Condé Nast Johansens Most Excellent Romantic Hideaway 2006

Attractions: Deep Sea Fishing, 4 meters; Fijian Village Visits, 20-min walk; Blue Lagoon Caves, 2 miles
Airports: Yasawa Island Airport, 4-min drive; Nadi International Airport, 50 miles

Secluded and exclusive, this exceptional resort nestles on 1km of white sandy beach with a backdrop of palm trees and grass hut villages. Combining beauty and tranquility with the modern and romantic, the ultimate in luxury and pampering is found here where each of the en-suite bures is beautifully decorated and includes a separate living area. The ultra-secluded Lomalagi is recognized as the most exclusive bure in Fiji and has a private infinity lap pool and beach. The beach-front Bavari Spa is housed beneath a thatched roof with a 180° view of the ocean and offers 4 different massages as well as many other treatments. Fresh seafood is caught and served daily, and some real treasures are found on the wine list, considered the best in the Pacific.

Hotels, Great Britain & Ireland

All the properties listed below can be found in our Recommended Hotels & Spas, Great Britain & Ireland 2009 Guide and our Recommended Small Hotels, inns & Restaurants, Great Britain & Ireland 2009 Guide. More information on our portfolio of guides can be found on page 463

Channel Islands

The Atlantic Hotel	Jersey	+44 (0)1534 744101
The Club Hotel & Spa	Jersey	+44 (0)1534 876500
Fermain Valley Hotel	Guernsey	+44 (0)1481 235 666
Longueville Manor	Guernsey	+44 (0)1534 725501
The Old Government House Hotel	Guernsey	+44 (0)1481 724 921
The Royal Yacht Hotel	Guernsey	+44 (0)1534 720 511

England

The Bath Priory Hotel, Restaurant & Spa	B & NE Somerset	+44 (0)1225 331922
Dukes Hotel	B & NE Somerset	+44 (0)1225 787960
Homewood Park	B & NE Somerset	+44 (0)1225 723731
Hunstrete House	B & NE Somerset	+44 (0)1761 490490
The Park	B & NE Somerset	+44 (0)1179 371800
The Royal Crescent Hotel	B & NE Somerset	+44 (0)1225 823333
Luton Hoo Hotel, Golf & Spa	Bedfordshire	+44 (0)1582 734437
Cliveden & The Pavilion Spa	Berkshire	+44 (0)1628 668561
Donnington Valley Hotel and Spa	Berkshire	+44 (0)1635 551199
Fredrick's – Hotel Restaurant Spa	Berkshire	+44 (0)1628 581000
The French Horn	Berkshire	+44 (0)1189 692204
Harte & Garter Hotel & Spa	Berkshire	+44 (0)1753 863426
The Vineyard At Stockcross	Berkshire	+44 (0)1635 528770
Danesfield House Hotel and Spa	Buckinghamshire	+44 (0)1628 891010
Hartwell House Hotel, Restaurant & Spa	Buckinghamshire	+44 (0)1296 747444
Stoke Park	Buckinghamshire	+44 (0)1753 717171
Stoke Place	Buckinghamshire	+44 (0)1753 534790
Green Bough Hotel	Cheshire	+44 (0)1244 326241
Rowton Hall Hotel, Health Club & Spa	Cheshire	+44 (0)1244 335262
Budock Vean - The Hotel on the River	Cornwall	+44 (0)1326 252100
Fowey Hall & Aquae Sulis Retreat	Cornwall	+44 (0)1726 833866
The Garrack Hotel & Restaurant	Cornwall	+44 (0)1736 796199
Hell Bay	Cornwall	+44 (0)1720 422947
The Lugger Hotel	Cornwall	+44 (0)1872 501322
Meudon Hotel	Cornwall	+44 (0)1326 250541
The Nare Hotel	Cornwall	+44 (0)1872 501111
The Polurrian Hotel	Cornwall	+44 (0)1326 240421
St Michael's Hotel & Spa	Cornwall	+44 (0)1326 312707
Talland Bay Hotel	Cornwall	+44 (0)1503 272667
Armathwaite Hall Country House	Cumbria	+44 (0)17687 76551
Dale Head Hall Lakeside Hotel	Cumbria	+44 (0)17687 72478
Holbeck Ghyll Country House Hotel	Cumbria	+44 (0)15394 32375
The Inn on the Lake	Cumbria	+44 (0)17684 82444
Lakeside Hotel on Lake Windermere	Cumbria	+44 (0)15395 30001
Linthwaite House Hotel	Cumbria	+44 (0)15394 88600
The Lodore Falls Hotel	Cumbria	+44 (0)17687 77285
Lovelady Shield Country House Hotel	Cumbria	+44 (0)1434 381203
Netherwood Hotel	Cumbria	+44 (0)15395 32552
Rothay Manor	Cumbria	+44 (0)15394 33605
The Samling	Cumbria	+44 (0)1539 431 922
Sharrow Bay Country House Hotel	Cumbria	+44 (0)1768 486 301
Tufton Arms Hotel	Cumbria	+44 (0)17683 51593
Callow Hall	Derbyshire	+44 (0)1335 300900
Cathedral Quarter Hotel	Derbyshire	+44 (0)1332 546080
The Izaak Walton Hotel	Derbyshire	+44 (0)1335 350555
Riber Hall	Derbyshire	+44 (0)1629 582795
Risley Hall Hotel and Spa	Derbyshire	+44 (0)115 939 9000
The Arundell Arms	Devon	+44 (0)1566 784666
Buckland-Tout-Saints	Devon	+44 (0)1548 853055
Combe House	Devon	+44 (0)1404 540400
Gidleigh Park	Devon	+44 (0)1647 432367
Hotel Riviera	Devon	+44 (0)1395 515201
Ilsington Country House Hotel	Devon	+44 (0)1364 661452
Langdon Court Country House Hotel	Devon	+44 (0)1752 862358
Lewtrenchard Manor	Devon	+44 (0)1566 783222
Northcote Manor Country House Hotel	Devon	+44 (0)1769 560501
Orestone Manor	Devon	+44 (0)1803 328098
Soar Mill Cove Hotel	Devon	+44 (0)1548 561566
The Tides Reach Hotel	Devon	+44 (0)1548 843466
Watersmeet Hotel	Devon	+44 (0)1271 870333
The Woolacombe Bay Hotel	Devon	+44 (0)1271 870388
Moonfleet Manor	Dorset	+44 (0)1305 786948
The Priory Hotel	Dorset	+44 (0)1929 551666
Stock Hill Country House Hotel	Dorset	+44 (0)1747 823626
Summer Lodge Country House Hotel	Dorset	+44 (0)1935 482000
Seaham Hall Hotel & Serenity Spa	Durham	+44 (0)1915 161 400
Maison Talbooth	Essex	+44 (0)1206 322367
Burleigh Court	Gloucestershire	+44 (0)1453 883804
Calcot Manor Hotel & Spa	Gloucestershire	+44 (0)1666 890391
Charingworth Manor	Gloucestershire	+44 (0)1386 593555
Corse Lawn House Hotel	Gloucestershire	+44 (0)1452 780479
The Greenway	Gloucestershire	+44 (0)1242 862352
Lower Slaughter Manor	Gloucestershire	+44 (0)1451 820456
Stonehouse Court Hotel	Gloucestershire	+44 (0)1453 794950
Washbourne Court	Gloucestershire	+44 (0)1451 822143
Thornbury Castle	S Gloucestershire	+44 (0)1454 281182
Chewton Glen	Hampshire	+44 (0)1425 275341
Chilworth Manor	Hampshire	+44 (0)23 8076 7333
Esseborne Manor	Hampshire	+44 (0)1264 736444
New Park Manor and Bath House Spa	Hampshire	+44 (0)1590 623467
Oakley Hall	Hampshire	+44 (0)1256 783 350
Tylney Hall	Hampshire	+44 (0)1256 764881
Westover Hall	Hampshire	+44 (0)1590 643044
Castle House	Herefordshire	+44 (0)1432 356321
Down Hall Country House Hotel	Hertfordshire	+44 (0)1279 731441
Great Hallingbury Manor Hotel	Hertfordshire	+44 (0)1279 506475
St Michael's Manor	Hertfordshire	+44 (0)1727 864444
Eastwell Manor	Kent	+44 (0)1233 213000
The Gibbon Bridge Hotel	Lancashire	+44 (0)1995 61456
Stapleford Park Country House Hotel	Leicestershire	+44 (0)1572 787 000
The George Of Stamford	Lincolnshire	+44 (0)1780 750750
41	London	+44 (0)20 7300 0041
51 Buckingham Gate	London	+44 (0)20 7769 7766
Beaufort House	London	+44 (0)20 7584 2600
The Capital Hotel & Restaurant	London	+44 (0)20 7589 5171
The Egerton House Hotel	London	+44 (0)20 7589 2412
Jumeirah Carlton Tower	London	+44 (0)20 7235 1234
Jumeirah Lowndes Hotel	London	+44 (0)20 7823 1234
Kensington House Hotel	London	+44 (0)20 7937 2345
The Mandeville Hotel	London	+44 (0)20 7935 5599
The Mayflower Hotel	London	+44 (0)20 7370 0991
Milestone Hotel	London	+44 (0)20 7917 1000
The New Linden Hotel	London	+44 (0)20 7221 4321
No.11 London	London	+44 (0)20 7730 7000
The Parkcity Hotel	London	+44 (0)20 7341 7091
Sofitel London St James	London	+44 (0)20 7747 2200
Twenty Nevern Square	London	+44 (0)20 7565 9555
Westbury Hotel	London	+44 (0)20 7629 7755
The Wyndham Grand London Chelsea Harbour	London	+44 (0)20 7823 3000
Congham Hall	Norfolk	+44 (0)1485 600250
The Hoste Arms	Norfolk	+44 (0)1328 738777
Rushton Hall Hotel & Spa	Northamptonshire	+44 (0)1536 713001
Whittlebury Hall	Northamptonshire	+44 (0)1327 857857
Hart's Hotel	Northamptonshire	+44 (0)1159 881900
Lace Market Hotel	Northamptonshire	+44 (0)1158 523232
Ye Olde Bell Hotel & Restaurant	Northamptonshire	+44 (0)1777 705121
Le Manoir Aux Quat' Saisons	Oxfordshire	+44 (0)1844 278881
Old Bank Hotel	Oxfordshire	+44 (0)1865 799599
The Old Parsonage Hotel	Oxfordshire	+44 (0)1865 310210
The Springs Hotel & Golf Club	Oxfordshire	+44 (0)1491 836687
Hambleton Hall	Rutland	+44 (0)1572 756991
The Castle at Taunton	Somerset	+44 (0)1823 272671
Charlton House Hotel	Somerset	+44 (0)1749 342008
Mount Somerset Country House Hotel	Somerset	+44 (0)1823 442500
Ston Easton Park	Somerset	+44 (0)1761 241631
Hoar Cross Hall Spa Resort	Staffordshire	+44 (0)1283 575671
Bedford Lodge Hotel	Suffolk	+44 (0)1638 663175
The Dower House Apartments	Suffolk	+44 (0)1284 735350
Hintlesham Hall	Suffolk	+44 (0)1473 652334
The Ickworth Hotel	Suffolk	+44 (0)1284 735350
Kesgrave Hall	Suffolk	+44 (0)1473 333741
Seckford Hall	Suffolk	+44 (0)1394 385678
Great Fosters	Surrey	+44 (0)1784 433822
Lythe Hill Hotel & Spa	Surrey	+44 (0)1428 651251
The Richmond Gate Hotel	Surrey	+44 (0)20 8940 0061
Ashdown Park Hotel and Country Club	East Sussex	+44 (0)1342 824988
Dale Hill	East Sussex	+44 (0)1580 200112
Deans Place Hotel	East Sussex	+44 (0)1323 870248

Hotels, Great Britain & Ireland

All the properties listed below can be found in our Recommended Hotels & Spas, Great Britain & Ireland 2009 Guide and our Recommended Small Hotels, inns & Restaurants, Great Britain & Ireland 2009 Guide. More information on our portfolio of guides can be found on page 463

The Grand Hotel	East Sussex	+44 (0)1323 412345
Horsted Place Country House Hotel	East Sussex	+44 (0)1825 750581
Lansdowne Place, Boutique Hotel & Spa	East Sussex	+44 (0)1273 736266
Newick Park	East Sussex	+44 (0)1825 723633
Pelham House	East Sussex	+44 (0)1273 488 600
The PowderMills	East Sussex	+44 (0)1424 775511
Royal York Hotel	East Sussex	+44 (0)1273 766 700
Amberley Castle	West Sussex	+44 (0)1798 831992
Bailiffscourt Hotel & Spa	West Sussex	+44 (0)1903 723511
The Goodwood Park Hotel	West Sussex	+44 (0)1243 775537
Ockenden Manor	West Sussex	+44 (0)1444 416111
The Spread Eagle Hotel & Spa	West Sussex	+44 (0)1730 816911
The Vermont Hotel	Tyne & Wear	+44 (0)191 233 1010
Ardencote Manor Hotel	Warwickshire	+44 (0)1926 843111
Mallory Court	Warwickshire	+44 (0)1926 330214
Nailcote Hall	Warwickshire	+44 (0)2476 466174
Wroxall Abbey Estate	Warwickshire	+44 (0)1926 484470
Bishopstrow House & Spa	Wiltshire	+44 (0)1985 212312
Howard's House	Wiltshire	+44 (0)1722 716392
Lucknam Park, Bath	Wiltshire	+44 (0)1225 742777
The Pear Tree At Purton	Wiltshire	+44 (0)1793 772100
Whatley Manor	Wiltshire	+44 (0)1666 822888
Woolley Grange	Wiltshire	+44 (0)1225 864705
Brockencote Hall	Worcestershire	+44 (0)1562 777876
Buckland Manor	Worcestershire	+44 (0)1386 852626
The Cottage in the Wood	Worcestershire	+44 (0)1684 588860
The Elms Hotel & Aquae Sulis Spa	Worcestershire	+44 (0)1299 896666
The Evesham Hotel	Worcestershire	+44 (0)1386 765566
Black Swan Hotel	North Yorkshire	+44 (0)1439 770466
Burythorpe House	North Yorkshire	+44 (0)1653 658 200
The Devonshire Arms Country House	North Yorkshire	+44 (0)1756 718111
The Grange Hotel	North Yorkshire	+44 (0)1904 644744
Judges Country House Hotel	North Yorkshire	+44 (0)1642 789000
Middlethorpe Hall Hotel	North Yorkshire	+44 (0)1904 641241
The Pheasant	North Yorkshire	+44 (0)1439 771241
Simonstone Hall	North Yorkshire	+44 (0)1969 667255

Ireland

Mount Wolseley Hotel	Carlow	+353 599 180100
Longueville House	Cork	+353 22 47156
Harvey's Point	Donegal	+353 74 972 2208
Fitzpatrick Castle Hotel	Dublin	+353 1 230 5400
Abbeyglen Castle	Galway	+353 95 21201
Ballynahinch Castle Hotel	Galway	+353 953 1006
Cashel House	Galway	+353 95 31001
The Brehon	Kerry	+353 64 30700
Cahernane House Hotel	Kerry	+353 64 31895
The Europe Hotel & Resort	Kerry	+353 64 71300
Hotel Dunloe Castle	Kerry	+353 64 44111
Park Hotel Kenmare & Sámas	Kerry	+353 64 41200
Ashford Castle	Mayo	+353 94 95 46003
The Harlequin	Mayo	+353 949 286 200
Knockranny House Hotel & Spa	Mayo	+353 98 28600
Mount Falcon Country House Hotel	Mayo	+353 967 4472
Nuremore Hotel and Country Club	Monaghan	+353 42 9661438
The Horse and Jockey Hotel	Tipperary	+353 504 44192
Dunbrody Country House	Wexford	+353 51 389 600
Kelly's Resort Hotel & Spa	Wexford	+353 53 91 32114
Marlfield House	Wexford	+353 53 94 21124
The Ritz-Carlton, Powerscourt	Wicklow	+353 1 274 8888

N Ireland

Ten Square	Antrim	+44 (0)28 90 241 001

Scotland

Craigellachie Hotel of Speyside	Aberdeenshire	+44 (0)1340 881204
Ardanaiseig	Argyll & Bute	+44 (0)1866 833333
Stonefield Castle	Argyll & Bute	+44 (0)1880 820836
Auchen Castle	Dumfries & Galloway	+44 (0)1683 300407
Kirroughtree House	Dumfries & Galloway	+44 (0)1671 402141
Old Course Hotel Golf Resort & Spa	Fife	+44 (0)1334 474371
Mar Hall Hotel & Spa	Glasgow	+44 (0)141 812 9999
Bunchrew House Hotel	Highland	+44 (0)1463 234917
Cuillin Hills Hotel	Highland	+44 (0)1478 612003
Inverlochy Castle	Highland	+44 (0)1397 702177
Rocpool Reserve	Highland	+44 (0)1463 240089
Royal Highland Hotel	Highland	+44 (0)1463 231926
The Torridon	Highland	+44 (0)1445 791242
Tulloch Castle Hotel	Highland	+44 (0)1349 861325
Dalhousie Castle and Spa	Midlothian	+44 (0)1875 820153
Glenskirlie House & Castle	Stirling	+44 (0)1324 840201

Wales

Miskin Manor Country House Hotel	Cardiff	+44 (0)1443 224204
Falcondale Mansion Hotel	Ceredigion	+44 (0)1570 422910
Ynyshir Hall	Ceredigion	+44 (0)1654 781209
Bodysgallen Hall & Spa	Conwy	+44 (0)1492 584466
St Tudno Hotel & Restaurant	Conwy	+44 (0)1492 874411
Palé Hall	Gwynedd	+44 (0)1678 530285
Penmaenuchaf Hall	Gwynedd	+44 (0)1341 422129
Celtic Manor Resort	Newport	+44 (0)1633 413000
Lamphey Court Hotel & Spa	Pembrokeshire	+44 (0)1646-672273
St Brides Spa Hotel	Pembrokeshire	+44 (0)1834 812 304
Warpool Court Hotel	Pembrokeshire	+44 (0)1437 720300
The Lake Country House and Spa	Powys	+44 (0)1591 620202
Lake Vyrnwy Hotel	Powys	+44 (0)1691 870 692
Llangoed Hall	Powys	+44 (0)1874 754525
Holm House	Vale of Glamorgan	+44 (0)2920 701572

Properties from our Recommended Small Hotels, Inns & Restaurants, Great Britain & Ireland 2009 Guide

Channel Islands

Château La Chaire	Jersey	+44 (0)1534 863354
The Farmhouse	Guernsey	+44 (0)1481 264 181
La Sablonnerie	Guernsey	+44 (0)1481 832061
The White House	Guernsey	+44 (0)1481 722159

England

Saco House, Bath	B & NE Somerset	+44 (0)1225 486540
Cornfields Restaurant & Hotel	Bedfordshire	+44 (0)1234 378990
Cantley House Hotel	Berkshire	+44 (0)118 978 9912
The Christopher Hotel Bar & Grill	Berkshire	+44 (0)1753 852359
The Inn on the Green	Berkshire	+44 (0)1628 482638
The Olde Bell Coaching Inn	Berkshire	+44 (0)1628 825881
Stirrups Country House Hotel	Berkshire	+44 (0)1344 882284
The Crown Hotel	Buckinghamshire	+44 (0)1494 721541
Fox Country Inn	Buckinghamshire	+44 (0)1491 639333
The Anchor Inn at Sutton Gault	Cambridgeshire	+44 (0)1353 778537
The Tickell Arms, Restaurant	Cambridgeshire	+44 (0)1223 833128
The Cormorant Hotel and Restaurant	Cornwall	+44 (0)1726 833426
The Old Coastguard Hotel	Cornwall	+44 (0)1736 731222
Rose-In-Vale Country House Hotel	Cornwall	+44 (0)1872 552202
The Rosevine	Cornwall	+44 (0)1872 580206
Talland Bay Hotel	Cornwall	+44 (0)1503 272667
Trevalsa Court Country House Hotel	Cornwall	+44 (0)1726 842468
Broadoaks Country House	Cumbria	+44 (0)1539 445566
Crosby Lodge Country House Hotel	Cumbria	+44 (0)1228 573618
Fayrer Garden House Hotel	Cumbria	+44 (0)15394 88195
Hipping Hall	Cumbria	+44 (0)15242 71187
The Pheasant	Cumbria	+44 (0)17687 76234
West Vale Country House & Restaurant	Cumbria	+44 (0)1539 442 817
The Wheatsheaf @ Brigsteer	Cumbria	+44 (0)15395 68254
The Crown Inn	Derbyshire	+44 (0)1889 590 541
Dannah Farm Country House	Derbyshire	+44 (0)1773 550273
Donington Manor Hotel	Derbyshire	+44 (0)1332 810 253
East Lodge Country House Hotel	Derbyshire	+44 (0)1629 734474

Small Hotels, Great Britain & Ireland

All the properties listed below can be found in our Recommended Hotels & Spas, Great Britain & Ireland 2009 Guide and our Recommended Small Hotels, inns & Restaurants, Great Britain & Ireland 2009 Guide. More information on our portfolio of guides can be found on page 463

The Plough Inn	Derbyshire	+44 (0)1433 650319
The Edgemoor	Devon	+44 (0)1626 832466
Kingston House	Devon	+44 (0)1803 762 235
Mill End	Devon	+44 (0)1647 432282
The Turtley Corn Mill	Devon	+44 (0)1364 646100
The White House	Devon	+44 (0)1548 580505
BridgeHouse Beaminster	Dorset	+44 (0)1308 862200
The Grange at Oborne	Dorset	+44 (0)1935 813463
Channels Lodge	Essex	+44 (0)1245 441547
Beaumont House	Gloucestershire	+44 (0)1242 223311
Bibury Court	Gloucestershire	+44 (0)1285 740337
The Dial House	Gloucestershire	+44 (0)1451 822244
Lower Brook House	Gloucestershire	+44 (0)1386 700286
Lypiatt House	Gloucestershire	+44 (0)1242 224994
New Inn At Coln	Gloucestershire	+44 (0)1285 750651
The Redesdale Arms	Gloucestershire	+44 (0)1608 650308
Langrish House	Hampshire	+44 (0)1730 266941
The Mill At Gordleton	Hampshire	+44 (0)1590 682219
The Nurse's Cottage	Hampshire	+44 (0)1590 683402
The Old House Hotel	Hampshire	+44 (0)1329 833049
Aylestone Court	Herefordshire	+44 (0)1432 341891
The Chase Hotel	Herefordshire	+44 (0)1989 763161
Glewstone Court	Herefordshire	+44 (0)1989 770367
Moccas Court	Herefordshire	+44 (0)1981 500 019
Wilton Court Hotel	Herefordshire	+44 (0)1989 562569
Auberge du Lac	Hertfordshire	+44 (0)1707 368888
Kick & Dicky	Hertfordshire	+44 (0)1920 821424
The White House and Lion & Lamb Bar & Restaurant	Hertfordshire	+44 (0)1279 870257
The Hambrough	Isle of Wight	+44 (0)1983 856333
The Priory Bay Hotel	Isle of Wight	+44 (0)1983 613146
Rylstone Manor	Isle of Wight	+44 (0)1983 862806
Winterbourne Country House	Isle of Wight	+44 (0)1983 852 535
Little Silver Country Hotel	Kent	+44 (0)1233 850321
Romney Bay House Hotel	Kent	+44 (0)1797 364747
The Royal Harbour Hotel	Kent	+44 (0)1843 591514
Wallett's Court Hotel & Spa	Kent	+44 (0)1304 852424
The White Cliffs Hotel	Kent	+44 (0)1304 852229
Brooklands Country Retreat	Lancashire	+44 (0)1995 605162
Ferrari's Restaurant & Hotel	Lancashire	+44 (0)1772 783148
Number One South Beach	Lancashire	+44 (0)1253 343900
The Crown Hotel	Lincolnshire	+44 (0)1780 763136
Tree Tops Country House Hotel	Merseyside	+44 (0)1704 572430
Broad House	Norfolk	+44 (0)1603 783567
Felbrigg Lodge	Norfolk	+44 (0)1263 837588
The Kings Head Hotel	Norfolk	+44 (0)1485 578 265
The Old Rectory	Norfolk	+44 (0)1603 700772
Titchwell Manor Hotel	Norfolk	+44 (0)1485 210221
Braunston Manor	Northamptonshire	+44 (0)1788 890267
The Orchard House	Northumberland	+44 (0)1669 620 684
The Otterburn Tower	Northumberland	+44 (0)1830 520620
Waren House Hotel	Northumberland	+44 (0)1668 214581
Cockliffe Country House Hotel	Nottinghamshire	+44 (0)115 968 0179
Greenwood Lodge	Nottinghamshire	+44 (0)115 962 1206
Langar Hall	Nottinghamshire	+44 (0)1949 860559
Burford House	Oxfordshire	+44 (0)1993 823151
Burford Lodge Hotel & Restaurant	Oxfordshire	+44 (0)1993 823354
Duke Of Marlborough Country Inn	Oxfordshire	+44 (0)1993 811460
The Goose	Oxfordshire	+44 (0)1491 612304
The Lamb Inn	Oxfordshire	+44 (0)1993 823155
The Nut Tree Inn	Oxfordshire	+44 (0)1865 331253
Weston Manor	Oxfordshire	+44 (0)1869 350621
Barnsdale Lodge	Rutland	+44 (0)1572 724678
The Lake Isle Hotel & Restaurant	Rutland	+44 (0)1572 822951
Nick's Restaurant	Rutland	+44 (0)1572 723199
The Inn at Grinshill	Shropshire	+44 (0)1939 220410
Pen-Y-Dyffryn Country Hotel	Shropshire	+44 (0)1691 653700
Soulton Hall	Shropshire	+44 (0)1939 232786
Bellplot House Hotel	Somerset	+44 (0)1460 62600
Beryl	Somerset	+44 (0)1749 678738
Bindon Country House Hotel	Somerset	+44 (0)1823 400070
Binham Grange	Somerset	+44 (0)1984 640024
Compton House	Somerset	+44 (0)1934 733944
Farthings Country House Hotel	Somerset	+44 (0)1823 480664
Karslake Country House and Cottage	Somerset	+44 (0)1643 851242
Three Acres Country House	Somerset	+44 (0)1398 323730
Woodlands Country House Hotel	Somerset	+44 (0)1278 760232
Dunsley Hall Hotel	Staffordshire	+44 (0)1384 877077
The Manor at Hanchurch	Staffordshire	+44 (0)1782 643 030
The Angel Hotel	Suffolk	+44 (0)1787 247388
Clarice House	Suffolk	+44 (0)1284 705550
The Cornwallis Country Hotel	Suffolk	+44 (0)1379 870326
The Westleton Crown	Suffolk	+44 (0)1728 648777
The Crown Inn	Surrey	+44 (0)1428 682255
Pride of the Valley	Surrey	+44 (0)1428 605799
The Mill House Hotel	West Sussex	+44 (0)1903 892426
Episode Hotel	Warwickshire	+44 (0)1926 883777
The George Hotel	Warwickshire	+44 (0)1608 661453
Beechfield House	Wiltshire	+44 (0)1225 703700
The Castle Inn	Wiltshire	+44 (0)1249 783030
The Lamb at Hindon	Wiltshire	+44 (0)1747 820 573
The Pear Tree Inn	Wiltshire	+44 (0)1225 709131
Stanton Manor Hotel	Wiltshire	+44 (0)1666 837552
Widbrook Grange	Wiltshire	+44 (0)1225 864750
The Old Rectory	Worcestershire	+44 (0)1527 523000
Riverside Hotel and Restaurant	Worcestershire	+44 (0)1386 446200
Royal Forester Country Inn	Worcestershire	+44 (0)1299 266286
The White Lion Hotel	Worcestershire	+44 (0)1684 592551
Kilham Hall	E Riding of Yorkshire	+44 (0)1262 420466
The Austwick Traddock	North Yorkshire	+44 (0)15242 51224
The Devonshire Fell	North Yorkshire	+44 (0)1756 718111
Dunsley Hall	North Yorkshire	+44 (0)1947 893437
George and Dragon Inn	North Yorkshire	+44 (0)1969 663358
Marmadukes Hotel	North Yorkshire	+44 (0)1904 640101
The Worsley Arms Hotel	North Yorkshire	+44 (0)1653 628234
The Dusty Miller & Coiners Restaurant	West Yorkshire	+44 (0)1422 885959
Hey Green Country House Hotel	West Yorkshire	+44 (0)1484 848000
The Shibden Mill Inn	West Yorkshire	+44 (0)1422 365 840

Ireland

Ard Na Sidhe	Kerry	+353 66 976 9105

Scotland

Darroch Learg	Aberdeenshire	+44 (0)13397 55443
Balcary Bay Hotel	Dumfries & Galloway	+44 (0)1556 640217
Corsewall Lighthouse Hotel	Dumfries & Galloway	+44 (0)1776 853220
The Hudson Hotel	Edinburgh	+44 (0)131 247 7000
Dunain Park Hotel & Restaurant	Highland	+44 (0)1463 230512
Forss House Hotel	Highland	+44 (0)1847 861201
Greshornish House	Highland	+44 (0)1470 582266
Loch Ness Lodge	Highland	+44 (0)1456 459469
Royal Marine Hotel, Restaurant & Spa	Highland	+44 (0)1408 621252
Ruddyglow Park	Highland	+44 (0)1571 822216
Skeabost Country House	Highland	+44 (0)1470 532202
The Steadings at The Grouse & Trout	Highland	+44 (0)1808 521314
Toravaig House	Highland	+44 (0)1471 833231
Knockomie Hotel	Moray	+44 (0)1309 673146
Castle Venlaw	Scottish Borders	+44 (0)1721 720384
Fauhope Country House	Scottish Borders	+44 (0)1896 823184
Culzean Castle – The Eisenhower Apartment	South Ayrshire	+44 (0)1655 884455

Wales

Ty Mawr Country Hotel	Carmarthenshire	+44 (0)1267 202332
Tan-Y-Foel Country House	Conwy	+44 (0)1690 710507
Pentre Mawr Country House	Denbighshire	+44 (0)1824 790732
Bae Abermaw	Gwynedd	+44 (0)1341 280550
Llwyndu Farmhouse	Gwynedd	+44 (0)1341 280144
Porth Tocyn Country House Hotel	Gwynedd	+44 (0)1758 713303
The Bell At Skenfrith	Monmouthshire	+44 (0)1600 750235
The Crown At Whitebrook	Monmouthshire	+44 (0)1600 860254
Penally Abbey	Pembrokeshire	+44 (0)1834 843033
Wolfscastle Country Hotel & Restaurant	Pembrokeshire	+44 (0)1437 741225
Egerton Grey	Vale of Glamorgan	+44 (0)1446 711666

Hotels - Europe & The Mediterranean

Properties listed below can be found in our Recommended Hotels & Spas - Europe & The Mediterranean 2009 Guide.
More information on our portfolio of guides can be found on page 463.

ANDORRA (GRAU ROIG)

Hotel Grau Roig

Grandvalira Ski Resort, AD 200 Grau Roig, Andorra

Tel: +376 75 55 56
Web: www.johansens.com/hotelgrauroig

ANDORRA (SOLDEU)

Sport Hotel Hermitage & Spa

Ctra. General S/N, AD100 Soldeu, Andorra

Tel: +376 870 670
Web: www.johansens.com/sporthotelhermitage

AUSTRIA (VIENNA)

Palais Coburg Residenz

Coburgbastei 4, 1010 Vienna, Austria

Tel: +43 1 518 180
Web: www.johansens.com/palaiscoburg

BELGIUM (KORTRIJK)

Grand Hotel Damier

Grote Markt 41, 8500 Kortrijk, Belgium

Tel: +32 56 22 15 47
Web: www.johansens.com/damier

BELGIUM (MALMÉDY)

Hostellerie Trôs~Marets

Route des Trôs~Marets 2, 4960 Malmédy, Belgium

Tel: +32 80 33 79 17
Web: www.johansens.com/trosmarets

BELGIUM (TURNHOUT)

Hostellerie Ter Driezen

18 Herentalsstraat, 2300 Turnhout, Belgium

Tel: +32 14 41 87 57
Web: www.johansens.com/terdriezen

CZECH REPUBLIC (PRAGUE)

Aria Hotel Prague

Trziste 9, 118 00 Prague 1, Czech Republic

Tel: +420 225 334 111
Web: www.johansens.com/aria

CZECH REPUBLIC (PRAGUE)

Bellagio Hotel Prague

U Milosrdnych 2, 110 00 Prague 1, Czech Republic

Tel: +420 221 778 999
Web: www.johansens.com/bellagio

CZECH REPUBLIC (PRAGUE)

Golden Well Hotel

U Zlaté studne 166/4, 118 00 Prague 1, Czech Republic

Tel: +420 257 011 213
Web: www.johansens.com/goldenwell

CZECH REPUBLIC (PRAGUE)

MaMaison Pachtuv Palace

Karolíny Svetlé 34, Staré Mesto, 110 00 Prague, Czech Republic

Tel: +420 234 705 111
Web: www.johansens.com/pachtuvpalace

CZECH REPUBLIC (PRAGUE)

MaMaison Riverside Hotel

Janáckovo Nábreží 15, 150 00 Prague 5, Czech Republic

Tel: +420 225 994 611
Web: www.johansens.com/riversideprague

CZECH REPUBLIC (TÁBOR)

Hotel Nautilus

Žižkovo námestí 20, 39002 Tábor, Czech Republic

Tel: +420 380 900 900
Web: www.johansens.com/nautilus

ESTONIA (PÄRNU)

Ammende Villa

Mere Pst 7, 80010 Pärnu, Estonia

Tel: +372 44 73 888
Web: www.johansens.com/ammende

FRANCE / ALSACE~LORRAINE (COLMAR)

Hôtel Les Têtes

19 Rue des Têtes, BP 69, 68000 Colmar, France

Tel: +33 3 89 24 43 43
Web: www.johansens.com/lestetes

FRANCE / ALSACE~LORRAINE (COLMAR)

Romantik Hôtel le Maréchal

4 Place Six Montagnes Noires, Petite Venise, 68000 Colmar, France

Tel: +33 3 89 41 60 32
Web: www.johansens.com/marechal

FRANCE / ALSACE~LORRAINE (CONDÉ NORTHEN)

Domaine de la Grange de Condé

41 rue des Deux Nieds, 57220 Condé Northen, France

Tel: +33 3 87 79 30 50
Web: www.johansens.com/grangedeconde

Hotels - Europe & The Mediterranean

Properties listed below can be found in our Recommended Hotels & Spas - Europe & The Mediterranean 2009 Guide.
More information on our portfolio of guides can be found on page 463.

FRANCE / ALSACE~LORRAINE (GÉRARDMER)

Hostellerie Les Bas Rupts Le Chalet Fleuri

181 Route de la Bresse, 88400 Gérardmer, Vosges, France

Tel: +33 3 29 63 09 25
Web: www.johansens.com/lesbasrupts

FRANCE / ALSACE~LORRAINE (OBERNAI)

Hôtel à la Cour d'Alsace

3 Rue de Gail, 67210 Obernai, France

Tel: +33 3 88 95 07 00
Web: www.johansens.com/couralsace

FRANCE / BRITTANY (BILLIERS)

Domaine de Rochevilaine

Pointe de Pen Lan, BP 69, 56190 Billiers, France

Tel: +33 2 97 41 61 61
Web: www.johansens.com/domainerochevilaine

FRANCE / BRITTANY (PERROS~GUIREC)

Hôtel l'Agapa & Spa

12, Rue des Bons Enfants, 22700 Perros~Guirec, France

Tel: +33 2 96 49 01 10
Web: www.johansens.com/lagapa

FRANCE / BRITTANY (ST~MALO - LA GOUESNIÈRE)

Château de Bonaban

35350 La Gouesnière, France

Tel: +33 2 99 58 24 50
Web: www.johansens.com/chateaudebonaban

FRANCE / BRITTANY (TREBEURDEN)

Ti al Lannec

14 Allée de Mezo~Guen, 22560 Trebeurden, France

Tel: +33 2 96 15 01 01
Web: www.johansens.com/tiallannec

FRANCE / BURGUNDY - FRANCHE~COMTE (BEAUNE / CHAMBOLLE MUSIGNY)

Château Hôtel André Ziltener

Rue de la Fontaine, 21220 Chambolle - Musigny, France

Tel: +33 3 80 62 41 62
Web: www.johansens.com/ziltener

FRANCE / BURGUNDY - FRANCHE~COMTÉ (LA BUSSIÈRE~SUR~OUCHE)

Abbaye de la Bussière

21360 La Bussière~sur~Ouche, Côte d'Or, France

Tel: +33 3 80 49 02 29
Web: www.johansens.com/abbayedelabussiere

FRANCE / BURGUNDY - FRANCHE~COMTÉ (POLIGNY)

Hostellerie des Monts de Vaux

Les Monts de Vaux, 39800 Poligny, France

Tel: +33 3 84 37 12 50
Web: www.johansens.com/montsdevaux

FRANCE / BURGUNDY - FRANCHE~COMTÉ (VAULT DE LUGNY)

Château de Vault de Lugny

11 Rue du Château, 89200 Vault de Lugny, France

Tel: +33 3 86 34 07 86
Web: www.johansens.com/vaultdelugny

FRANCE / CHAMPAGNE~ARDENNES (ETOGES~EN~CHAMPAGNE)

Château d'Etoges

51270 Etoges~en~Champagne, France

Tel: +33 3 26 59 30 08
Web: www.johansens.com/etoges

FRANCE / CHAMPAGNE~ARDENNES (FÈRE~EN~TARDENOIS)

Château de Fère

02130 Fère~en~Tardenois, France

Tel: +33 3 23 82 21 13
Web: www.johansens.com/chateaufere

FRANCE / CHAMPAGNE~ARDENNES (STE~PREUVE - LAON)

Domaine du Château de Barive

02350 Sainte~Preuve, France

Tel: +33 3 23 22 15 15
Web: www.johansens.com/barive

FRANCE / CÔTE D'AZUR (ÈZE VILLAGE)

Château Eza

Rue de la Pise, 06360 Èze Village, France

Tel: +33 4 93 41 12 24
Web: www.johansens.com/eza

FRANCE / CÔTE D'AZUR (LE RAYOL - CANADEL~SUR~MER)

Le Bailli de Suffren

Avenue des Américains, Golfe de Saint~Tropez, 83820 Le Rayol – Canadel~Sur~Mer, France

Tel: +33 4 98 04 47 00
Web: www.johansens.com/lebaillidesuffren

FRANCE / CÔTE D'AZUR (MOUGINS)

Le Moulin de Mougins

Quartier Notre~Dame~de~Vie, 06250 Mougins, France

Tel: +33 4 93 75 78 24
Web: www.johansens.com/moulindemougins

Hotels - Europe & The Mediterranean

Properties listed below can be found in our Recommended Hotels & Spas - Europe & The Mediterranean 2009 Guide.
More information on our portfolio of guides can be found on page 463.

FRANCE / CÔTE D'AZUR (NICE)

Hôtel La Pérouse

11 Quai Rauba~Capeu, 06300 Nice, France

Tel: + 33 4 93 62 34 63
Web: www.johansens.com/hotellaperouse

FRANCE / LOIRE VALLEY (ST~CALAIS)

Château de la Barre

72120 Conflans~sur~Anille, France

Tel: +33 2 43 35 00 17
Web: www.johansens.com/delabarre

FRANCE / CÔTE D'AZUR (RAMATUELLE - ST~TROPEZ)

La Ferme d'Augustin

Plage de Tahiti, 83350 Ramatuelle, near Saint~Tropez, France

Tel: +33 4 94 55 97 00
Web: www.johansens.com/fermeaugustin

FRANCE / LOIRE VALLEY (STE~MAURE~DE~TOURAINE)

Hostellerie des Hauts de Sainte~Maure

2-4 avenue du Général~de~Gaulle, 37800 Sainte~Maure~de~Touraine, France

Tel: +33 2 47 65 50 65
Web: www.johansens.com/saintemaure

FRANCE / CÔTE D'AZUR (ST~RAPHAËL)

La Villa Mauresque

1792 route de la Corniche, 83700 Saint~Raphaël, France

Tel: +33 494 83 02 42
Web: www.johansens.com/mauresque

FRANCE / MIDI~PYRÉNÉES (CARCASSONNE - FLOURE)

Château de Floure

1, Allée Gaston Bonheur, 11800 Floure, France

Tel: +33 4 68 79 11 29
Web: www.johansens.com/floure

FRANCE / LOIRE VALLEY (AMBOISE)

Château de Pray

Route de Chargé, 37400 Amboise, France

Tel: +33 247 57 23 67
Web: www.johansens.com/chateaudepray

FRANCE / MIDI~PYRÉNÉES (MARSOLAN - GERS)

Hôtel Lous Grits

Le Village, 32700 Marsolan - Gers, France

Tel: +33 562 283 710
Web: www.johansens.com/lousgrits

FRANCE / LOIRE VALLEY (AMBOISE)

Le Manoir les Minimes

34 Quai Charles Guinot, 37400 Amboise, France

Tel: +33 2 47 30 40 40
Web: www.johansens.com/lemanoirlesminimes

FRANCE / NORMANDY (ARROMANCHES)

Manoir de Mathan

14480 Crépon, France

Tel: +33 2 31 22 21 73
Web: www.johansens.com/mathan

FRANCE / LOIRE VALLEY (AMBOISE)

Le Manoir Saint Thomas

1 Mail Saint Thomas, 37400 Amboise, France

Tel: +33 2 47 23 21 82
Web: www.johansens.com/saintthomas

FRANCE / NORMANDY (BAYEUX / PORT~EN~BESSIN)

Château la Chenevière

Escures-Commes, 14520 Port~en~Bessin, France

Tel: +33 2 31 51 25 25
Web: www.johansens.com/cheneviere

FRANCE / LOIRE VALLEY (CHAMPIGNÉ)

Château des Briottières

49330 Champigné, France

Tel: +33 2 41 42 00 02
Web: www.johansens.com/chateaudesbriottieres

FRANCE / NORMANDY (DEAUVILLE - CAMBREMER)

Château les Bruyères

Route du Cadran, 14340 Cambremer, France

Tel: +33 2 31 32 22 45
Web: www.johansens.com/lesbruyeres

FRANCE / LOIRE VALLEY (SAUMUR)

Château de Verrières

53, Rue d'Alsace, 49400 Saumur, Loire Valley, France

Tel: +33 2 41 38 05 15
Web: www.johansens.com/verrieres

FRANCE / NORMANDY (HONFLEUR - CRICQUEBOEUF)

Manoir de la Poterie, Spa "Les Thermes"

Chemin Paul Ruel, 14113 Honfleur (Cricqueboeuf), France

Tel: +33 2 31 88 10 40
Web: www.johansens.com/manoirdelapoterie

Hotels - Europe & The Mediterranean

Properties listed below can be found in our Recommended Hotels & Spas - Europe & The Mediterranean 2009 Guide.
More information on our portfolio of guides can be found on page 463.

FRANCE / NORTH - PICARDY (COURCELLES~SUR~VESLES)

Château de Courcelles

8, Rue de Château, 02220 Courcelles~sur~Vesle (Aisne), France

Tel: +33 3 23 74 13 53
Web: www.johansens.com/courcelles

FRANCE / PARIS (ETOILE - PORTE MAILLOT)

Hôtel Duret

30 rue Duret, 75116 Paris, France

Tel: +33 1 45 00 42 60
Web: www.johansens.com/duret

FRANCE / NORTH - PICARDY (LILLE)

Carlton Hôtel

3 Rue de Paris, 59000 Lille, France

Tel: +33 3 20 13 33 13
Web: www.johansens.com/carltonlille

FRANCE / PARIS (INVALIDES)

Hôtel le Tourville

16 Avenue de Tourville, 75007 Paris, France

Tel: +33 1 47 05 62 62
Web: www.johansens.com/tourville

FRANCE / NORTH - PICARDY (RECQUES~SUR~HEM - CALAIS)

Château de Cocove

Avenue de Cocove, 62890 Recques~sur~Hem, France

Tel: +33 3 21 82 68 29
Web: www.johansens.com/chateaudecocove

FRANCE / PARIS (JARDIN DU LUXEMBOURG)

Hôtel des Académies et des Arts

15, Rue de la Grande Chaumière, 75006 Paris, France

Tel: +33 1 43 26 66 44
Web: www.johansens.com/hoteldesacademies

FRANCE / PARIS (CHAMPS~ELYSÉES)

Hospes Lancaster

7, Rue de Berri, 75008 Paris, France

Tel: +33 1 40 76 40 76
Web: www.johansens.com/hospeslancaster

FRANCE / PARIS (JARDIN DU LUXEMBOURG)

Le Sainte~Beuve

9 Rue Sainte~Beuve, 75006 Paris, France

Tel: +33 1 45 48 20 07
Web: www.johansens.com/saintebeuve

FRANCE / PARIS (CHAMPS~ELYSÉES)

Hôtel Balzac

6, Rue Balzac, 75008 Paris, France

Tel: +33 1 44 35 18 00
Web: www.johansens.com/balzac

FRANCE / PARIS (MARAIS)

Hôtel du Petit Moulin

29-31 Rue de Poitou, 75003 Paris, France

Tel: +33 1 42 74 10 10
Web: www.johansens.com/petitmoulin

FRANCE / PARIS (CHAMPS~ELYSÉES)

Hôtel de Sers

41, Avenue Pierre 1er de Serbie, 75008 Paris, France

Tel: +33 1 53 23 75 75
Web: www.johansens.com/hoteldesers

FRANCE / PARIS (ST~GERMAIN~DES~PRÉS)

Hôtel Duc de Saint~Simon

14 rue de Saint~Simon, 75007 Paris, France

Tel: +33 1 44 39 20 20
Web: www.johansens.com/saintsimon

FRANCE / PARIS (CHAMPS~ELYSÉES)

Hôtel San Régis

12 Rue Jean Goujon, 75008 Paris, France

Tel: +33 1 44 95 16 16
Web: www.johansens.com/sanregis

FRANCE / PARIS (ST~GERMAIN~DES~PRÉS)

Le Bellechasse

8 rue de Bellechasse, 75007 Paris, France

Tel: +33 1 45 50 22 31
Web: www.johansens.com/lebellechasse

FRANCE / PARIS (CHAMPS~ELYSÉES)

La Trémoille

14 Rue de la Trémoille, 75008 Paris, France

Tel: +33 1 56 52 14 00
Web: www.johansens.com/tremoille

FRANCE / POITOU~CHARENTES (CHÂTEAUBERNARD - COGNAC)

Château de l'Yeuse

65 Rue de Bellevue, Quartier de L'Echassier, 16100 Châteaubernard, France

Tel: +33 5 45 36 82 60
Web: www.johansens.com/yeuse

Hotels - Europe & The Mediterranean

Properties listed below can be found in our Recommended Hotels & Spas - Europe & The Mediterranean 2009 Guide.
More information on our portfolio of guides can be found on page 463.

FRANCE / POITOU~CHARENTES (LA ROCHELLE)

Hôtel "Résidence de France"

43 Rue Minage, 17000 La Rochelle, France

Tel: +33 5 46 28 06 00
Web: www.johansens.com/residencedefrance

FRANCE / PROVENCE (GRIGNAN)

Manoir de la Roseraie

Route de Valréas, 26230 Grignan, France

Tel: +33 4 75 46 58 15
Web: www.johansens.com/manoirdelaroseraie

FRANCE / PROVENCE (LE PARADOU - LES BAUX~DE~PROVENCE)

Domaine le Hameau des Baux

Chemin de Bourgeac, 13520 Le Paradou, France

Tel: +33 4 90 54 10 30
Web: www.johansens.com/hameaudesbaux

FRANCE / PROVENCE (LE THOR)

La Bastide Rose

99 Chemin des Croupières, 84250 Le Thor, Provence, France

Tel: + 33 4 90 02 14 33
Web: www.johansens.com/bastiderose

FRANCE / PROVENCE (LES STES~MARIES~DE~LA~MER)

L'Estelle en Camargue

Route du Petit Rhône,
13460 Les Saintes~Maries~de~la~Mer, France

Tel: +33 4 90 97 89 01
Web: www.johansens.com/lestelle

FRANCE / PROVENCE (ORGON - EYGALIÈRES)

Le Mas de la Rose

Route d'Eygalières, 13660 Orgon, France

Tel: +33 4 90 73 08 91
Web: www.johansens.com/masdelarose

FRANCE / PROVENCE (PORT CAMARGUE)

Le Spinaker

Pointe de la Presqu'île, Port Camargue,
30240 Le Grau~du~Roi, France

Tel: +33 4 66 53 36 37
Web: www.johansens.com/spinaker

FRANCE / PROVENCE (SABRAN - BAGNOLS~SUR~CÈZE)

Château de Montcaud

Combe, Bagnols~sur~Cèze, 30200 Sabran,
near Avignon, France

Tel: +33 4 66 89 60 60
Web: www.johansens.com/montcaud

FRANCE / PROVENCE (UCHAUX)

Château de Massillan

Chemin Hauteville, 84100 Uchaux, France

Tel: +33 4 90 40 64 51
Web: www.johansens.com/massillan

FRANCE / RHÔNE~ALPES (BAGNOLS~EN~BEAUJOLAIS)

Château de Bagnols

69620 Bagnols, France

Tel: +33 4 74 71 40 00
Web: www.johansens.com/bagnols

FRANCE / RHÔNE~ALPES (CONDRIEU)

Le Beau Rivage

2 rue du Beau-Rivage, 69420 Condrieu, France

Tel: +33 4 74 56 82 82
Web: www.johansens.com/beaurivage

FRANCE / RHÔNE~ALPES (LES GÊTS)

Chalet Hôtel La Marmotte

61 Rue du Chêne, 74260 Les Gêts, France

Tel: +33 4 50 75 80 33
Web: www.johansens.com/marmotte

FRANCE / RHÔNE~ALPES (LES MENUIRES)

Chalet Hôtel Kaya

Village de Reberty, Les Menuires, 73440
Saint~Martin~de~Belleville, France

Tel: +33 4 79 41 42 00
Web: www.johansens.com/hotelkaya

FRANCE / RHÔNE~ALPES (MEGÈVE)

Le Fer à Cheval

36 route du Crêt d'Arbois, 74120 Megève, France

Tel: +33 4 50 21 30 39
Web: www.johansens.com/cheval

FRANCE / RHÔNE~ALPES (SCIEZ~SUR~LÉMAN)

Château de Coudrée

Domaine de Coudrée, Bonnatrait, 74140
Sciez~sur~Léman, France

Tel: +33 4 50 72 62 33
Web: www.johansens.com/coudree

FRANCE / RHÔNE~ALPES (VALS~LES~BAINS)

Hôtel Helvie

Avenue Claude Expilly, 07600 Vals~les~Bains,
Rhône~Alpes, France

Tel: +33 4 75 94 65 85
Web: www.johansens.com/hotelhelvie

Hotels - Europe & The Mediterranean

Properties listed below can be found in our Recommended Hotels & Spas - Europe & The Mediterranean 2009 Guide.
More information on our portfolio of guides can be found on page 463.

FRANCE / SOUTH WEST (BERGERAC - DORDOGNE)

Château les Merles

Tuilières, 24520 Mouleydier, Dordogne, Near Bergerac, France

Tel: +33 5 53 63 13 42
Web: www.johansens.com/lesmerles

FRANCE / SOUTH WEST (BIARRITZ)

Hôtel du Palais

1 Avenue de L'Impératrice, 64200 Biarritz, France

Tel: +33 5 59 41 64 00
Web: www.johansens.com/palais

FRANCE / SOUTH WEST (ST~EMILION)

Le Relais du Château Franc Mayne

Château Franc Mayne, 33330 Saint~Emilion, France

Tel: +33 5 57 24 62 61
Web: www.johansens.com/francmayne

FRANCE / SOUTH WEST (STE~RADEGONDE)

Château de Sanse

33350 Sainte~Radegonde, France

Tel: +33 5 57 56 41 10
Web: www.johansens.com/chateaudesanse

GREAT BRITAIN / ENGLAND (BEDFORDSHIRE)

Luton Hoo Hotel, Golf & Spa

The Mansion House, Luton Hoo, Luton, Bedfordshire, LU1 3TQ, England

Tel: +44 1582 734437
Web: www.johansens.com/lutonhoo

GREAT BRITAIN / ENGLAND (BERKSHIRE)

The French Horn

Sonning~on~Thames, Berkshire, RG4 6TN, England

Tel: +44 1189 692 204
Web: www.johansens.com/frenchhorneuro

GREAT BRITAIN / ENGLAND (EAST SUSSEX)

Ashdown Park Hotel

Wych Cross, Forest Row, East Sussex RH18 5JR, England

Tel: +44 1342 824 988
Web: www.johansens.com/ashdownparkeuro

GREAT BRITAIN / ENGLAND (EAST SUSSEX)

The Grand Hotel

King Edward's Parade, Eastbourne, East Sussex, BN21 4EQ, England

Tel: +44 1323 412345
Web: www.johansens.com/grandeastbourneeuro

GREAT BRITAIN / ENGLAND (HAMPSHIRE)

Tylney Hall

Rotherwick, Hook, Hampshire, RG27 9AZ, England

Tel: +44 1256 764881
Web: www.johansens.com/tylneyhalleuro

GREAT BRITAIN / ENGLAND (LONDON)

Jumeirah Carlton Tower

On Cadogan Place, London SW1X 9PY, England

Tel: +44 20 7235 1234
Web: www.johansens.com/carltontowereuro

GREAT BRITAIN / ENGLAND (LONDON)

Jumeirah Lowndes Hotel

21 Lowndes Street, Knightsbridge, London SW1X 9ES, England

Tel: +44 20 7823 1234
Web: www.johansens.com/lowndeseuro

GREAT BRITAIN / ENGLAND (LONDON)

The Mayflower Hotel

26-28 Trebovir Road, London SW5 9NJ, England

Tel: +44 20 7370 0991
Web: www.johansens.com/mayflowereuro

GREAT BRITAIN / ENGLAND (LONDON)

The New Linden Hotel

58-60 Leinster Square, Notting Hill, London W2 4PS, England

Tel: +44 20 7221 4321
Web: www.johansens.com/newlindeneuro

GREAT BRITAIN / ENGLAND (LONDON)

Twenty Nevern Square

20 Nevern Square, London SW5 9PD, England

Tel: +44 20 7565 9555
Web:
www.johansens.com/twentynevernsquareeuro

GREECE (ATHENS)

O&B Athens Boutique Hotel

7 Leokoriou Str, Psiri, 10554 Athens, Greece

Tel: +30 210 331 2940
Web: www.johansens.com/ochreandbrown

GREECE (CHIOS)

Argentikon Luxury Suites

Kambos, 82100 Chios, Greece

Tel: +30 227 10 33 111
Web: www.johansens.com/argentikon

Hotels - Europe & The Mediterranean

Properties listed below can be found in our Recommended Hotels & Spas - Europe & The Mediterranean 2009 Guide.
More information on our portfolio of guides can be found on page 463.

GREECE (CRETE)

OUT OF THE BLUE, Capsis Elite Resort

Aghia Pelaghia, Heraklion, 71500 Crete, Greece

Tel: +30 210 6149563
Web: www.johansens.com/outoftheblue

GREECE (CRETE)

Paradise Island Villas

Aristophani Street, Anissaras Hersonissos, 70014 Crete, Greece

Tel: +30 289 702 2893
Web: www.johansens.com/paradiseisland

GREECE (CRETE)

Pleiades Luxurious Villas

Plakes, 72100 Aghios Nikolaos, Crete, Greece

Tel: +30 28410 90450
Web: www.johansens.com/pleiades

GREECE (CRETE)

St Nicolas Bay Resort Hotel & Villas

PO Box 47, 72100 Aghios Nikolaos, Crete, Greece

Tel: +30 2841 025041
Web: www.johansens.com/stnicolasbay

GREECE (CRETE)

Villas Hotel Domes of Elounda

Elounda, 72053 Crete, Greece

Tel: +30 28410 41924
Web: www.johansens.com/domesofelounda

GREECE (LEFKADA)

Pavezzo Country Retreat

Katouna, Lefkada, Greece

Tel: +30 26450 71782
Web: www.johansens.com/pavezzo

GREECE (MYKONOS)

Apanema

Tagoo, Mykonos, Greece

Tel: +30 22890 28590
Web: www.johansens.com/apanema

GREECE (MYKONOS)

Mykonos Theoxenia Hotel

84600 Kato Mili, Mykonos, Greece

Tel: +30 22890 22230
Web: www.johansens.com/mykonostheoxenia

GREECE (MYKONOS)

Tharroe of Mykonos

Mykonos Town, Angelica, 84600 Mykonos, Greece

Tel: +30 22890 27370
Web: www.johansens.com/tharroe

GREECE (PATMOS ISLAND)

Petra Hotel

Grikos, 85500 Patmos Island, Greece

Tel: +30 22470 34020
Web: www.johansens.com/petrahotel

GREECE (SANTORINI)

Canaves Oia

Oia, 87402 Santorini, Greece

Tel: +30 22860 71453/71128
Web: www.johansens.com/canavesoia

GREECE (SANTORINI)

Ikies Traditional Houses

Oia, 84702 Santorini, Greece

Tel: +30 22860 71311
Web: www.johansens.com/ikies

HUNGARY (TIHANY - LAKE BALATON)

Allegro Hotel - Tihany Centrum

H-8237 Tihany, Batthyány u. 6, Hungary

Tel: +36 87 448 456
Web: www.johansens.com/hoteltihany

ITALY / CAMPANIA (FURORE, AMALFI COAST)

Furore Inn Resort & Spa

Via dell'Amore, 84010 Furore, Amalfi Coast, Italy

Tel: +39 089 830 4711
Web: www.johansens.com/furoreinn

ITALY / CAMPANIA (RAVELLO, AMALFI COAST)

Hotel Villa Maria

Via S. Chiara 2, 84010 Ravello (SA), Amalfi Coast, Italy

Tel: +39 089 857255
Web: www.johansens.com/villamaria

ITALY / EMILIA ROMAGNA (PARMA)

Palazzo Dalla Rosa Prati

Strada al Duomo 7, 43100 Parma, Italy

Tel: +39 0521 386 429
Web: www.johansens.com/palazzodallarosaprati

Hotels - Europe & The Mediterranean

Properties listed below can be found in our Recommended Hotels & Spas - Europe & The Mediterranean 2009 Guide. More information on our portfolio of guides can be found on page 463.

ITALY / EMILIA ROMAGNA (PIACENZA - BORGO DI RIVALTA)

Torre di San Martino - Historical Residence

Loc. Borgo di Rivalta, 29010 Gazzola, Piacenza, Italy

Tel: +39 0523 972002
Web: www.johansens.com/torredisanmartino

ITALY / EMILIA ROMAGNA (RAVENNA - RUSSI)

Hotel Villa Roncuzzi

Via M. Silvestroni, 6/10, 48026 Russi - Fraz. San Pancrazio, Ravenna, Italy

Tel: +39 0544 534776
Web: www.johansens.com/villaroncuzzi

ITALY / EMILIA ROMAGNA (REGGIO EMILIA)

Hotel Posta (Historical Residence)

Piazza del Monte, 2, 42100 Reggio Emilia, Italy

Tel: +39 05 22 43 29 44
Web: www.johansens.com/posta

ITALY / LAZIO (PALO LAZIALE)

La Posta Vecchia

Palo Laziale, 00055 Ladispoli, Rome, Italy

Tel: +39 0699 49501
Web: www.johansens.com/postavecchia

ITALY / LAZIO (ROME)

Buonanotte Garibaldi

Via Garibaldi 83, 00153 Rome, Italy

Tel: +39 06 58 330 733
Web: www.johansens.com/garibaldi

ITALY / LAZIO (ROME)

Casa Howard Guest Houses - Rome & Florence

Via Capo le Case 18, 00186 Rome, Lazio, Italy

Tel: +39 06 69924555
Web: www.johansens.com/casahowardrome

ITALY / LAZIO (ROME)

Casa Montani - Luxury Town House

Piazzale Flaminio 9, 00196 Rome, Italy

Tel: +39 06 3260 0421
Web: www.johansens.com/casamontani

ITALY / LAZIO (ROME)

Hotel dei Borgognoni

Via del Bufalo 126 (Piazza di Spagna), 00187 Rome, Italy

Tel: +39 06 6994 1505
Web: www.johansens.com/borgognoni

ITALY / LAZIO (ROME)

Hotel dei Consoli

Via Varrone 2/d, 00193 Rome, Italy

Tel: +39 0668 892 972
Web: www.johansens.com/deiconsoli

ITALY / LAZIO (ROME)

Hotel Fenix

Viale Gorizia 5/7, 00198 Rome, Italy

Tel: +39 06 8540 741
Web: www.johansens.com/fenix

ITALY / LAZIO (ROME)

Villa Spalletti Trivelli

Via Piacenza 4, 00184 Rome, Italy

Tel: +39 06 48907934
Web: www.johansens.com/villaspallettitrivelli

ITALY / LAZIO (VITERBO - ALTO LAZIO)

Villa La Cerretana

Strada Ortana 40, Bagnaia, 01100 Viterbo, Lazio, Italy

Tel: +39 0761 1762565
Web: www.johansens.com/villalacerretana

ITALY / LIGURIA (FINALE LIGURE)

Hotel Punta Est

Via Aurelia 1, 17024 Finale Ligure (SV), Italy

Tel: +39 019 600611
Web: www.johansens.com/puntaest

ITALY / LIGURIA (MONEGLIA - CINQUE TERRE)

Abbadia San Giorgio - Historical Residence

Piazzale San Giorgio, 16030 Moneglia (GE), Italy

Tel: +39 0185 491119
Web: www.johansens.com/abbadiasangiorgio

ITALY / LIGURIA (PORTOFINO)

Hotel San Giorgio - Portofino House

Via del Fondaco, 11, 16034 Portofino (Genova), Italy

Tel: +39 0185 26991
Web: www.johansens.com/portofinohouse

ITALY / LIGURIA (SANREMO COAST - DIANO MARINA)

Grand Hotel Diana Majestic

Via Oleandri 15, 18013 Diano Marina (IM), Italy

Tel: +39 0183 402 727
Web: www.johansens.com/dianamajestic

Hotels - Europe & The Mediterranean

Properties listed below can be found in our Recommended Hotels & Spas - Europe & The Mediterranean 2009 Guide.
More information on our portfolio of guides can be found on page 463.

ITALY / LIGURIA (SANTA MARGHERITA LIGURE - PORTOFINO COAST)

Grand Hotel Miramare

Via Milite Ignoto, 30, 16038 Santa Margherita Ligure - Genova, Liguria, Italy

Tel: +39 0185 287013
Web: www.johansens.com/grandmiramare

ITALY / LIGURIA (SESTRI LEVANTE)

Hotel Vis à Vis

Via della Chiusa 28, 16039 Sestri Levante (GE), Italy

Tel: +39 0185 42661
Web: www.johansens.com/visavis

ITALY / LOMBARDY (BORMIO - BAGNI NUOVI - VALTELLINA)

Bagni di Bormio Spa Resort

Località Bagni Nuovi, 23038 Valdidentro (Sondrio), Italy

Tel: +39 0342 910131
Web: www.johansens.com/bagnidibormio

ITALY / LOMBARDY (ERBUSCO)

L'Albereta

Via Vittorio Emanuele II, no 23, 25030 Erbusco (BS), Italy

Tel: +39 030 7760 550
Web: www.johansens.com/albereta

ITALY / LOMBARDY (LAKE GARDA - GARDONE RIVIERA)

Grand Hotel Gardone Riviera

Via Zanardelli 84, 25083 Gardone Riviera (BS), Lake Garda, Italy

Tel: +39 0365 20261
Web: www.johansens.com/gardoneriviera

ITALY / LOMBARDY (LAKE GARDA - SALÒ)

Hotel Bellerive

Via Pietro da Salò 11, 25087 Salò (BS), Italy

Tel: +39 0365 520 410
Web: www.johansens.com/bellerive

ITALY / LOMBARDY (LAKE LUGANO & COMO - PORLEZZA)

Hotel Parco San Marco Beach Resort, Golf & SPA

Viale Privato San Marco 1, 22010 Cima di Porlezza (CO), Italy

Tel: +39 0344 629111
Web: www.johansens.com/parcosanmarco

ITALY / LOMBARDY (MILAN)

Petit Palais Maison de Charme

Via Molino delle Armi 1, 20123 Milan, Italy

Tel: +39 02 584 891
Web: www.johansens.com/petitpalais

ITALY / LOMBARDY (MILAN)

THE PLACE - Luxury serviced apartments

Via Romagnosi 4, 20121 Milan, Italy

Tel: +39 02 76026633
Web: www.johansens.com/theplace

ITALY / LOMBARDY (MONZA, NR MILAN)

Hotel de la Ville

Viale Regina Margherita di Savoia 15, 20052 Monza (MI), Italy

Tel: +39 039 39421
Web: www.johansens.com/hoteldelaville

ITALY / PIEMONTE (ALAGNA - MONTE ROSA)

Hotel Cristallo

Piazza degli Alberghi, 13021 Alagna (VC), Italy

Tel: +39 0163 922 822/23
Web: www.johansens.com/cristallo

ITALY / PIEMONTE (DOGLIANI - BAROLO WINE REGION)

Foresteria dei Poderi Einaudi

Borgata Gombe, 31, 12063 Dogliani (CN), Italy

Tel: +39 0173 70414
Web: www.johansens.com/poderieinaudi

ITALY / PIEMONTE (GAVI)

Albergo L'Ostelliere

Frazione Monterotondo 56, 15065 Gavi (AL), Piemonte, Italy

Tel: +39 0143 607 801
Web: www.johansens.com/ostelliere

ITALY / PIEMONTE (LAKE MAGGIORE - BELGIRATE)

Villa dal Pozzo d'Annone

Strada Statale del Sempione 5, 28832 Belgirate (VB), Lake Maggiore, Italy

Tel: +39 0322 7255
Web: www.johansens.com/dalpozzodannone

ITALY / PIEMONTE (LAKE MAGGIORE - CANNOBIO)

Hotel Pironi

Via Marconi 35, 28822 Cannobio, Lake Maggiore (VB), Italy

Tel: +39 0323 70624
Web: www.johansens.com/pironihotel

ITALY / PIEMONTE (LAKE MAGGIORE - STRESA)

Villa e Palazzo Aminta

Via Sempione Nord 123, 28838 Stresa (VB), Italy

Tel: +39 0323 933 818
Web: www.johansens.com/aminta

Hotels - Europe & The Mediterranean

Properties listed below can be found in our Recommended Hotels & Spas - Europe & The Mediterranean 2009 Guide.
More information on our portfolio of guides can be found on page 463.

ITALY / PIEMONTE (LANGHE - SANTO STEFANO BELBO)

Relais San Maurizio

Località San Maurizio 39, 12058 Santo Stefano Belbo (CN), Italy

Tel: +39 0141 841900
Web: www.johansens.com/relaissanmaurizio

ITALY / PIEMONTE (LANGHE - TREZZO TINELLA)

Cascina Langa

Via Cappelletto 36, 12050 Trezzo Tinella (Cuneo), Italy

Tel: +39 0173 630289
Web: www.johansens.com/cascinalanga

ITALY / PIEMONTE (TURIN)

Hotel Principi di Piemonte

Via Gobetti, 15, 10123 Turin, Italy

Tel: +39 011 55151
Web: www.johansens.com/principidipiemonte

ITALY / PUGLIA (CANOSA)

Country House Cefalicchio

Contrada Cefalicchio, Canosa di Puglia (Bari), Italy

Tel: +39 0883 642123
Web: www.johansens.com/cefalicchio

ITALY / PUGLIA (POLIGNANO A MARE)

Borgobianco Resort & SPA

Contrada Casello Cavuzzi , 70044 Polignano a Mare (BA), Italy

Tel: +39 080 8870001
Web: www.johansens.com/borgobianco

ITALY / SAN MARINO REPUBLIC (SAN MARINO)

Hotel Titano

Contrada del Collegio 31, 47890 San Marino (RSM), San Marino Republic

Tel: +378 0549 991007
Web: www.johansens.com/hoteltitano

ITALY / SARDINIA (ALGHERO)

Villa Las Tronas

Lungomare Valencia 1, 07041 Alghero (SS), Italy

Tel: +39 079 981 818
Web: www.johansens.com/lastronas

ITALY / SARDINIA (COSTA SMERALDA - SAN PANTALEO)

Petra Segreta Resort & SPA

Strada Buddeu, CP 130, 07026 San Pantaleo, Olbia, Italy

Tel: +39 0789 183 1365
Web: www.johansens.com/petrasegretaresort

ITALY / SARDINIA (PORTO CERVO - COSTA SMERALDA)

Grand Hotel in Porto Cervo

Località Cala Granu, 07020 Porto Cervo (OT), Italy

Tel: +39 0789 91533
Web: www.johansens.com/portocervo

ITALY / SICILY (AEOLIAN ISLANDS - LIPARI)

Grand Hotel Arciduca

Via G Franza, 98055 Lipari (ME), Isole Eolie, Italy

Tel: +39 090 9812136
Web: www.johansens.com/arciduca

ITALY / SICILY (AEOLIAN ISLANDS - SALINA)

Hotel Signum

Via Scalo 15, 98050 Salina~Malfa, Italy

Tel: +39 090 9844222
Web: www.johansens.com/signum

ITALY / SICILY (MODICA)

Palazzo Failla Hotel

Via Blandini 5, 97010 Modica (RG), Italy

Tel: +39 0932 941059
Web: www.johansens.com/palazzopfailla

ITALY / SICILY (RAGUSA)

Locanda Don Serafino

Via XI Febbraio, 15 Ragusa Ibla, Italy

Tel: +39 0932 220065
Web: www.johansens.com/serafino

ITALY / SICILY (RAGUSA)

Poggio del Sole Resort

S.P. Ragusa/Marina di Ragusa, km 57, 97100 Ragusa, Sicily, Italy

Tel: +39 0932 666 452
Web: www.johansens.com/poggiodelsole

ITALY / SICILY (TAORMINA RIVIERA - GIARDINI NAXOS)

Grand Hotel Atlantis Bay

Via Nazionale 161, Taormina Mare (ME), Italy

Tel: +39 0942 618011
Web: www.johansens.com/atlantis

ITALY / SICILY (TAORMINA RIVIERA - GIARDINI NAXOS)

Grand Hotel Mazzarò Sea Palace

Via Nazionale 147, 98030 Taormina (ME), Sicily, Italy

Tel: +39 0942 612111
Web: www.johansens.com/mazzaroseapalace

Hotels - Europe & The Mediterranean

Properties listed below can be found in our Recommended Hotels & Spas - Europe & The Mediterranean 2009 Guide.
More information on our portfolio of guides can be found on page 463.

ITALY / SICILY (TAORMINA RIVIERA - MARINA D'AGRO)

Baia Taormina Grand Palace Hotels & Spa

Via Nazionale, km 39, 98030 Marina d'Agro, Taormina Riviera (ME), Italy

Tel: +39 0942 756292
Web: www.johansens.com/baiataormina

ITALY / SICILY (TAORMINA RIVIERA - TAORMINA)

Hotel Villa Carlotta

Via Pirandello 81, 98039 Taormina (ME), Italy

Tel: +39 0942 626058
Web: www.johansens.com/villacarlotta

ITALY / SICILY (TAORMINA RIVIERA - TAORMINA)

Hotel Villa Ducale

Via Leonardo da Vinci 60, 98039 Taormina (ME), Sicily, Italy

Tel: +39 0942 28153
Web: www.johansens.com/villaducale

ITALY / TRENTINO - ALTO ADIGE / DOLOMITES (AVELENGO/HAFLING - MERANO/MERAN)

GranPanorama Hotel Miramonti

St. Kathreinstr, Santa Catharina 14, 39010 Avelengo/Hafling - Merano/Meran, Italy

Tel: +39 0473 27 93 35
Web: www.johansens.com/hotelmiramonti

ITALY / TRENTINO - ALTO ADIGE / DOLOMITES (COLFOSCO - CORVARA)

Romantik Hotel Cappella

Str. Pecei 17, Alta Badia - Dolomites, 39030 Colfosco - Corvara (BZ), Italy

Tel: +39 0471 836183
Web: www.johansens.com/cappella

ITALY / TRENTINO - ALTO ADIGE / DOLOMITES (MERANO - BOLZANO)

Castel Fragsburg

Via Fragsburg 3, 39012 Merano, Italy

Tel: +39 0473 244071
Web: www.johansens.com/fragsburg

ITALY / TRENTINO - ALTO ADIGE / DOLOMITES (NOVA LEVANTE)

Romantik Hotel Post Cavallino Bianco

Via Carezza 30, 39056 Nova Levante (Bz), Dolomites, Italy

Tel: +39 0471 613113
Web: www.johansens.com/postcavallino

ITALY / TRENTINO - ALTO ADIGE / DOLOMITES (ORTISEI - VAL GARDENA)

Hotel Gardena Grödnerhof

Str. Vidalong 3, 39046 Ortisei, Italy

Tel: +39 0471 796 315
Web: www.johansens.com/gardena

ITALY / TRENTINO - ALTO ADIGE / DOLOMITES (RIVA DEL GARDA)

Du Lac et Du Parc Grand Resort

Viale Rovereto 44, 38066 Riva del Garda (TN), Italy

Tel: +39 0464 566600
Web: www.johansens.com/dulacetduparc

ITALY / TRENTINO - ALTO ADIGE / DOLOMITES (SAN GIOVANNI IN VALLE AURINA)

Alpenpalace Deluxe Hotel & Spa Resort

I-39030 St. Johann im Ahrntal, San Giovanni in Valle Aurina, South Tyrol, Italy

Tel: +39 0474 670230
Web: www.johansens.com/alpenpalace

ITALY / TUSCANY (AREZZO - LORO CIUFFENNA)

Relais Villa Belpoggio (Historical House)

Via Setteponti Ponente 40, 52024 Loro Ciuffenna, Arezzo, Italy

Tel: +39 055 9694411
Web: www.johansens.com/villabelpoggio

ITALY / TUSCANY (CASTAGNETO CARDUCCI - MARINA)

Tombolo Talasso Resort

Via del Corallo 3, 57022 Marina di Castagneto Carducci (LI), Italy

Tel: +39 0565 74530
Web: www.johansens.com/tombolo

ITALY / TUSCANY (CASTELNUOVO BERARDENGA - SIENA)

Borgo San Felice

Località San Felice, 53019 Castelnuovo Berardenga (SI), Tuscany, Italy

Tel: +39 0577 3964
Web: www.johansens.com/borgosanfelice

ITALY / TUSCANY (CASTIGLIONE DELLA PESCAIA - MAREMMA)

L'Andana

Tenuta La Badiola, Localitá Badiola, 58043 Castiglione della Pescaia (Grosseto), Italy

Tel: +39 0564 944 800
Web: www.johansens.com/andana

ITALY / TUSCANY (ELBA ISLAND - PORTOFERRAIO)

Hotel Villa Ottone

Loc. Ottone, 57037 Portoferraio (LI), Isola d'Elba, Italy

Tel: +39 0565 933 042
Web: www.johansens.com/ottone

ITALY / TUSCANY (FLORENCE)

Casa Howard Guest Houses - Rome and Florence

Via della Scala 18, Piazza Santa Maria Novella, Florence, Italy

Tel: +39 066 992 4555
Web: www.johansens.com/casahoward

Hotels - Europe & The Mediterranean

Properties listed below can be found in our Recommended Hotels & Spas - Europe & The Mediterranean 2009 Guide. More information on our portfolio of guides can be found on page 463.

ITALY / TUSCANY (FLORENCE)

Marignolle Relais & Charme

Via di S Quirichino a Marignolle 16, 50124 Florence, Italy

Tel: +39 055 228 6910
Web: www.johansens.com/marignolle

ITALY / TUSCANY (FLORENCE)

Palazzo Magnani Feroni - all-suites florence

Borgo San Frediano 5, 50124 Florence, Italy

Tel: +39 055 2399544
Web: www.johansens.com/florencepalace

ITALY / TUSCANY (FLORENCE)

Relais Piazza Signoria

Via Vacchereccia 3, 50122 Florence, Italy

Tel: +39 055 3987239
Web: www.johansens.com/piazzasignoria

ITALY / TUSCANY (FLORENCE)

Relais Santa Croce

Via Ghibellina 87, 50122 Florence, Italy

Tel: +39 055 234 2230
Web: www.johansens.com/santacroce

ITALY / TUSCANY (FLORENCE)

Relais Villa Antea

Via Puccinotti 46, 50129 Florence, Italy

Tel: +39 055 484106
Web: www.johansens.com/villaantea

ITALY / TUSCANY (FLORENCE)

Residenza del Moro

Via del Moro 15, 50123 Florence, Italy

Tel: +39 055 290884
Web: www.johansens.com/delmoro

ITALY / TUSCANY (FLORENCE)

Villa le Piazzole

Via Suor Maria Celeste, 28, 50125 Florence, Italy

Tel: +39 055 223520
Web: www.johansens.com/villalepiazzole

ITALY / TUSCANY (FLORENCE - BORGO SAN LORENZO)

Monsignor Della Casa Country Resort

Via di Mucciano 16, 50032 Borgo San Lorenzo, Florence, Italy

Tel: +39 055 840 821
Web: www.johansens.com/monsignor

ITALY / TUSCANY (FORTE DEI MARMI)

Hotel Byron

Viale A Morin 46, 55042 Forte dei Marmi (LU), Italy

Tel: +39 0584 787 052
Web: www.johansens.com/byron

ITALY / TUSCANY (LUCCA - PIETRASANTA)

Albergo Pietrasanta - Palazzo Barsanti Bonetti

Via Garibaldi 35, 55045 Pietrasanta (Lucca), Italy

Tel: +39 0584 793 727
Web: www.johansens.com/pietrasanta

ITALY / TUSCANY (MONTALCINO)

Castello Banfi - Il Borgo

Castello di Poggio alle Mura, 53024 Montalcino (SI), Italy

Tel: +39 0577 877 700
Web: www.johansens.com/castellobanfi

ITALY / TUSCANY (MONTEBENICHI - CHIANTI REGION)

Country House Casa Cornacchi

Loc. Montebenichi, 52021 Arezzo, Tuscany, Italy

Tel: +39 055 998229
Web: www.johansens.com/cornacchi

ITALY / TUSCANY (MONTEPULCIANO - SIENA)

Villa Poggiano

Via di Poggiano 7, 53045 Montepulciano (Siena), Tuscany, Italy

Tel: +39 0578 758292
Web: www.johansens.com/villapoggiano

ITALY / TUSCANY (PORTO ERCOLE - ARGENTARIO)

Il Pellicano Hotel

Loc. Sbarcatello, 58018 Porto Ercole (Gr), Tuscany, Italy

Tel: +39 0564 858111
Web: www.johansens.com/ilpellicano

ITALY / TUSCANY (SAN VINCENZO - COSTA DEGLI ETRUSCHI)

Relais Poggio ai Santi

Via San Bartolo 100, 57027 San Vincenzo - Livorno, Italy

Tel: +39 0565 798032
Web: www.johansens.com/poggioaisanti

ITALY / TUSCANY (SIENA - BAGNAIA)

Borgo La Bagnaia Resort, Spa and Events Venue

Strada Statale 223, Km 56,
53016 Localita Bagnaia - Siena, Italy

Tel: +39 0577 813000
Web: www.johansens.com/labagnaia

Hotels - Europe & The Mediterranean

Properties listed below can be found in our Recommended Hotels & Spas - Europe & The Mediterranean 2009 Guide.
More information on our portfolio of guides can be found on page 463.

ITALY / TUSCANY (SIENA - LUCIGNANO D'ASSO)

Lucignanello Bandini (Borgo Storico)

Loc. Lucignano d'Asso, 53020 San Giovanni d'Asso (SI), Italy

Tel: +39 0577 803 068
Web: www.johansens.com/lucignanello

ITALY / TUSCANY (SIENA - PIEVESCOLA)

Relais la Suvera (Dimora Storica)

53030 Pievescola – Siena, Italy

Tel: +39 0577 960 300
Web: www.johansens.com/relaislasuvera

ITALY / TUSCANY (TERME DI PETRIOLO - MAREMMA)

Petriolo Spa & Resort

Loc. Grand Hotel Terme - (S.S. 223 SI > GR, Km 40,600) 58045 Pari, Civitella Paganico (GR), Italy

Tel: +39 0564 9091
Web: www.johansens.com/petriolo

ITALY / TUSCANY (VIAREGGIO)

Hotel Plaza e de Russie

Piazza d'Azeglio 1, 55049 Viareggio (LU), Italy

Tel: +39 0584 44449
Web: www.johansens.com/russie

ITALY / UMBRIA (ASSISI - ARMENZANO)

Romantik Hotel le Silve di Armenzano

06081 Loc. Armenzano, Assisi (PG), Italy

Tel: +39 075 801 9000
Web: www.johansens.com/lesilve

ITALY / UMBRIA (GUBBIO)

Castello di Petroia

Località Scritto di Gubbio, Petroia, 06020 Gubbio (Pg), Italy

Tel: +39 075 92 02 87
Web: www.johansens.com/castellodipetroia

ITALY / UMBRIA (ORVIETO - ALLERONA)

I Casali di Monticchio

Vocabolo Monticchio 34, 05011 Allerona, Orvieto (TR), Italy

Tel: +39 0763 62 83 65
Web: www.johansens.com/monticchio

ITALY / UMBRIA (PERUGIA - DERUTA)

L'Antico Forziere

Via della Rocca 2, 06051 Casalina Deruta (PG), Italy

Tel: +39 075 972 4314
Web: www.johansens.com/anticoforziere

ITALY / UMBRIA (PERUGIA - PIEVE SAN QUIRICO)

Le Torri di Bagnara (Mediaeval Historical Residences)

Strada della Bruna 8, 06134 Pieve San Quirico, Perugia, Italy

Tel: +39 075 579 2001 and +39 335 6408 549
Web: www.johansens.com/bagnara

ITALY / UMBRIA (UMBERTIDE - SAN FAUSTINO)

Abbazia San Faustino - Luxury Country House

Località San Faustino di Bagnolo, 06026 Pietralunga (PG), Italy

Tel: +39 339 720 1717
Web: www.johansens.com/sanfaustino

ITALY / VALLE D'AOSTA (COURMAYEUR - MONT BLANC)

Mont Blanc Hotel Village

Localita La Croisette 36, 11015 La Salle (AO), Valle d'Aosta, Italy

Tel: +39 0165 864 111
Web: www.johansens.com/montblanc

ITALY / VALLE D'AOSTA (GRESSONEY~LA~TRINITÉ)

Hotel Jolanda Sport

Loc. Edelboden 31, Gressoney~La~Trinité, 11020 Gressoney~La~Trinité (Aosta), Italy

Tel: +39 0125 366 140
Web: www.johansens.com/jolandasport

ITALY / VENETO (BARDOLINO - VERONA)

Color Hotel

Via Santa Cristina 5, 37011 Bardolino (VR), Italy

Tel: +39 045 621 0857
Web: www.johansens.com/color

ITALY / VENETO (COSTERMANO)

Locanda San Verolo

Località San Verolo, 37010 Costermano (VR), Italy

Tel: +39 045 720 09 30
Web: www.johansens.com/sanverolo

ITALY / VENETO (GARDA)

Locanda San Vigilio

Località San Vigilio, 37016 Garda (VR), Italy

Tel: +39 045 725 66 88
Web: www.johansens.com/sanvigilio

ITALY / VENETO (LIDO DI JESOLO)

Park Hotel Brasilia

Via Levantina, 2o acc al mare 3, 30016 Lido di Jesolo, Italy

Tel: +39 0421 380851
Web: www.johansens.com/parkhotelbrasilia

Hotels - Europe & The Mediterranean

Properties listed below can be found in our Recommended Hotels & Spas - Europe & The Mediterranean 2009 Guide.
More information on our portfolio of guides can be found on page 463.

ITALY / VENETO (NEGRAR - VERONA)

Relais la Magioca

Via Moron 3, 37024 Negrar - Valpolicella (VR), Italy

Tel: +39 045 600 0167
Web: www.johansens.com/lamagioca

ITALY / VENETO (PADOVA)

Methis Hotel

Riviera Paleocapa 70, 35141 Padova, Italy

Tel: +39 049 872 5555
Web: www.johansens.com/methis

ITALY / VENETO (ROLLE DI CISON DI VALMARINO)

Relais Duca di Dolle

Via Piai Orientale 5, 31030 Rolle di Cison di Valmarino (TV), Italy

Tel: +39 0438 975 809
Web: www.johansens.com/foresteriabisol

ITALY / VENETO (VENICE)

Ca Maria Adele

Dorsoduro 111, 30123 Venice, Italy

Tel: +39 041 52 03 078
Web: www.johansens.com/camariaadele

ITALY / VENETO (VENICE)

Ca' Nigra Lagoon Resort

Santa Croce 927, Venice, Italy

Tel: +39 041 2750047
Web: www.johansens.com/canigra

ITALY / VENETO (VENICE)

Ca' Sagredo Hotel

Campo Santa Sofia 4198/99, 30121 Venice, Italy

Tel: +39 041 2413111
Web: www.johansens.com/casagredo

ITALY / VENETO (VENICE)

Charming House DD724

Dorsoduro 724, 30123 Venice, Italy

Tel: +39 041 277 0262
Web: www.johansens.com/dd724

ITALY / VENETO (VENICE)

Hotel Flora

San Marco 2283/A, 30124 Venice, Italy

Tel: +39 041 52 05 844
Web: www.johansens.com/hotelflora

ITALY / VENETO (VENICE)

Hotel Giorgione

SS Apostoli 4587, 30131 Venice, Italy

Tel: +39 041 522 5810
Web: www.johansens.com/giorgione

ITALY / VENETO (VENICE)

Hotel Sant' Elena Venezia

Calle Buccari 10, Sant' Elena, 30132 Venice, Italy

Tel: +39 041 27 17 811
Web: www.johansens.com/santelena

ITALY / VENETO (VENICE)

Londra Palace

Riva degli Schiavoni, 4171, 30122 Venice, Italy

Tel: +39 041 5200533
Web: www.johansens.com/londra

ITALY / VENETO (VENICE)

Novecento Boutique Hotel

San Marco 2684, 30124 Venice, Italy

Tel: +39 041 24 13 765
Web: www.johansens.com/novecento

ITALY / VENETO (VENICE - LIDO)

Albergo Quattro Fontane - Residenza d'Epoca

Via Quattro Fontane 16, 30126 Lido di Venezia, Venice, Italy

Tel: +39 041 526 0227
Web: www.johansens.com/quattrofontane

LATVIA (JŪRMALA)

TB Palace Hotel & Spa

8 Pilsonu Street, Jūrmala, LV-2015, Latvia

Tel: +371 6 7147094
Web: www.johansens.com/tbpalace

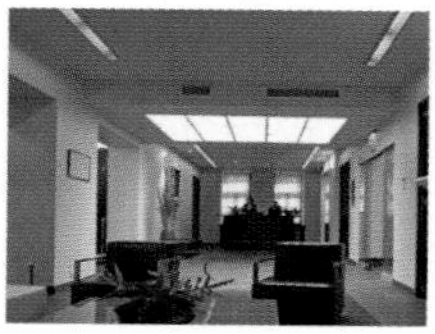

LATVIA (RIGA)

Hotel Bergs

Bergs Bazaar, Elizabetes Street 83/85, LV-1050, Riga, Latvia

Tel: +371 6777 0900
Web: www.johansens.com/bergs

LUXEMBOURG (REMICH)

Hotel Saint~Nicolas & Spa

31 Esplanade, 5533 Remich, Luxembourg

Tel: +35 226 663
Web: www.johansens.com/saintnicolas

Hotels - Europe & The Mediterranean

Properties listed below can be found in our Recommended Hotels & Spas - Europe & The Mediterranean 2009 Guide.
More information on our portfolio of guides can be found on page 463.

THE NETHERLANDS (AMSTERDAM)

Ambassade Hotel

Herengracht 341, 1016 Amsterdam, The Netherlands

Tel: +31 20 5550 222
Web: www.johansens.com/ambassade

THE NETHERLANDS (VEERE)

Auberge de Campveerse Toren

Kaai 2, 4351 AA Veere, The Netherlands

Tel: +31 0118 501 291
Web: www.johansens.com/campveersetoren

POLAND (WARSAW)

MaMaison Le Régina Hotel

Koscielna 12, 00-218 Warsaw, Poland

Tel: +48 22531 6000
Web: www.johansens.com/leregina

PORTUGAL / ALENTEJO (BEJA)

Quinta da Malhadinha Nova

7800-601 Albernoa, Beja, Alentejo, Portugal

Tel: +351 284 965 432
Web: www.johansens.com/malhadinhanova

PORTUGAL / ALENTEJO (EVORA)

Convento do Espinheiro, Heritage Hotel & Spa

Canaviais, 7005-839 Évora, Portugal

Tel: +351 266 788 200
Web: www.johansens.com/espinheiro

PORTUGAL / ALENTEJO (REDONDO)

Convento de São Paulo

Aldeia da Serra, 7170-120 Redondo, Portugal

Tel: +351 266 989 160
Web: www.johansens.com/conventodesaopaulo

PORTUGAL / ALGARVE (ALMANCIL)

Quinta Jacintina - my secret garden hotel

Garrâo de Cima, 8135 - 025 Almancil, Portugal

Tel: +351 289 350 090
Web: www.johansens.com/jacintina

PORTUGAL / ALGARVE (ALMANCIL)

Ria Park Hotel & Spa

Vale do Lobo, 8135-951 Almancil, Algarve, Portugal

Tel: +351 289 359 800
Web: www.johansens.com/riapark

PORTUGAL / ALGARVE (LAGOS)

Casa da Moura

Rua Cardeal Neto, 10, 8600 Lagos, Portugal

Tel: +351 282 770730
Web: www.johansens.com/casadamoura

PORTUGAL / ALGARVE (QUINTA DO LAGO - ALMANCIL)

Hotel Quinta do Lago

8135-024 Almancil, Algarve, Portugal

Tel: +351 289 350 350
Web: www.johansens.com/quintadolago

PORTUGAL / ALGARVE (VILAMOURA)

As Cascatas Hotel Apartamentos

Rua do Brasil 4.11.1b, 8125 Vilamoura, Portugal

Tel: +351 289 304 900
Web: www.johansens.com/ascascatas

PORTUGAL / ALGARVE (VILAMOURA)

Hilton Vilamoura As Cascatas Golf Resort & Spa

Rua da Torre d'Agua Lote 4.11.1B, 8125615 Vilamoura, Portugal

Tel: +351 289 304 000
Web: www.johansens.com/hiltonvilamoura

PORTUGAL / ALGARVE (VILAMOURA)

Tivoli Marina Vilamoura

8125-901 Vilamoura, Portugal

Tel: +351 289 303 303
Web: www.johansens.com/tivolimarina

PORTUGAL / LISBON & TAGUS VALLEY (CASCAIS)

Hotel Albatroz

Rua Frederico Arouca 100, 2750-353 Cascais, Lisbon, Portugal

Tel: +351 21 484 73 80
Web: www.johansens.com/albatroz

PORTUGAL / LISBON & TAGUS VALLEY (CASCAIS)

Hotel Cascais Mirage

Av. Marginal, No 8554, 2754-536 Cascais, Portugal

Tel: +351 210 060 600
Web: www.johansens.com/cascaismirage

PORTUGAL / LISBON & TAGUS VALLEY (ESTORIL)

Palacio Estoril, Hotel & Golf

Rua Particular, 2769-504 Estoril, Portugal

Tel: +351 21 464 80 00
Web: www.johansens.com/estoril

Hotels - Europe & The Mediterranean

Properties listed below can be found in our Recommended Hotels & Spas - Europe & The Mediterranean 2009 Guide.
More information on our portfolio of guides can be found on page 463.

PORTUGAL / LISBON & TAGUS VALLEY (LISBON)

As Janelas Verdes

Rua das Janelas Verdes 47, 1200-690 Lisbon, Portugal

Tel: +351 21 39 68 143
Web: www.johansens.com/janelasverdes

PORTUGAL / LISBON & TAGUS VALLEY (LISBON)

Heritage Av Liberdade

Avenida da Liberdade 28, 1250-145 Lisbon, Portugal

Tel: +351 213 404 040
Web: www.johansens.com/liberdade

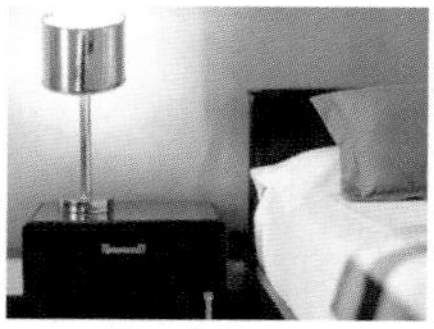

PORTUGAL / LISBON & TAGUS VALLEY (LISBON)

Hotel Britania

Rua Rodrigues Sampaio 17, 1150-278 Lisbon, Portugal

Tel: +351 21 31 55 016
Web: www.johansens.com/britania

PORTUGAL / LISBON & TAGUS VALLEY (LISBON)

Lisboa Plaza Hotel

TV. Salitre / Av. Liberdade, 1269-066 Lisbon, Portugal

Tel: +351 213 218 218
Web: www.johansens.com/lisboa

PORTUGAL / LISBON & TAGUS VALLEY (LISBON)

Solar do Castelo

Rua das Cozinhas 2, 1100-181 Lisbon, Portugal

Tel: +351 218 806 050
Web: www.johansens.com/solardocastelo

PORTUGAL / LISBON & TAGUS VALLEY (LISBON)

Tivoli Lisboa

Av. da Liberdade 185, 1269-050 Lisbon, Portugal

Tel: + 351 21 319 89 00
Web: www.johansens.com/tivolilisboa

PORTUGAL / LISBON & TAGUS VALLEY (TURCIFAL, TORRES VEDRAS)

The Westin CampoReal Golf Resort & Spa

Rua do Campo, 2565-779 Turcifal, Torres Vedras, Portugal

Tel: +351 261 960 900
Web: www.johansens.com/camporeal

PORTUGAL / MADEIRA (FUNCHAL)

CS Madeira Atlantic Resort & Sea Spa

Estrada Monumental 175-177, 9000-100 Funchal, Portugal

Tel: +351 291 717 600
Web: www.johansens.com/csmadeira

PORTUGAL / MADEIRA (FUNCHAL)

Quinta da Bela Vista

Caminho do Avista Navios 4, 9000 Funchal, Madeira, Portugal

Tel: +351 291 706 400
Web: www.johansens.com/quintadabelavista

PORTUGAL / MADEIRA (FUNCHAL)

Quinta das Vistas Palace Gardens

Caminho de Santo Antonio 52, 9000-187 Funchal, Madeira, Portugal

Tel: +351 291 750 000
Web: www.johansens.com/quintadasvistas

PORTUGAL / MADEIRA (FUNCHAL)

Quinta do Monte

Caminho do Monte 192, 9050-288 Funchal, Madeira, Portugal

Tel: +351 291 780 100
Web: www.johansens.com/quintadomonte

PORTUGAL / OPORTO & NORTHERN PORTUGAL (ERVEDOSA DO DOURO)

Quinta de San José

5130-123 Ervedosa do Douro, Portugal

Tel: +351 254 422017
Web: www.johansens.com/quintasanjose

PORTUGAL / OPORTO & NORTHERN PORTUGAL (PINHÃO)

CS Vintage House Hotel

Lugar da Ponte, 5085-034 Pinhão, Portugal

Tel: +351 254 730 230
Web: www.johansens.com/vintagehouse

RUSSIA (MOSCOW)

MaMaison-Pokrovka Suite Hotel

Pokrovka Street 40, Building 2, 103062 Moscow, Russia

Tel: +7 495 229 5757
Web: www.johansens.com/pokrovamoscow

SLOVENIA (BLED)

Hotel Golf Bled

Cankarjeva 4, 4260 Bled, Slovenia

Tel: +386 4579 1700
Web: www.johansens.com/hotelgolfsi

SPAIN (FUERTEVENTURA)

Gran Hotel Atlantis Bahía Real

Avenida Grandes Playas s/n, 35660 Corralejo, Fuerteventura, Canary Islands

Tel: +34 928 53 64 44
Web: www.johansens.com/bahiareal

Hotels - Europe & The Mediterranean

Properties listed below can be found in our Recommended Hotels & Spas - Europe & The Mediterranean 2009 Guide.
More information on our portfolio of guides can be found on page 463.

SPAIN / ANDALUCÍA (AGUA AMARGA - ALMERÍA)

Mikasa Suites Resort

Ctra. de Carboneras, s/n, 04149 Agua Amarga - Almería, Spain

Tel: +34 950 138 073
Web: www.johansens.com/mikasa

SPAIN / ANDALUCÍA (ALCALÁ DE GUADAIRA - SEVILLA)

Hacienda La Boticaria

Ctra. Alcalá - Utrera Km 12, 41500 Alcalá de Guadaira (Sevilla), Spain

Tel: +34 955 69 88 20
Web: www.johansens.com/haciendalaboticaria

SPAIN / ANDALUCÍA (BENALUP~CASAS VIEJAS)

Fairplay Golf Hotel & Spa

C/La Torre s/n , 11190 Benalup~Casas Viejas (Cádiz), Spain

Tel: +34 956 429100
Web: www.johansens.com/fairplaygolf

SPAIN / ANDALUCÍA (CÓRDOBA)

Hospes Palacio del Bailío

Ramirez de las Casas Deza 10-12, 14001 Córdoba, Spain

Tel: +34 957 498 993
Web: www.johansens.com/hospesbailio

SPAIN / ANDALUCÍA (ÉCIJA - SEVILLA)

Hotel Palacio de Los Granados

Emilio Castelar 42, 41400 Écija, Sevilla, Spain

Tel: +34 955 905 344
Web: www.johansens.com/granados

SPAIN / ANDALUCÍA (ESTEPONA)

Gran Hotel Elba Estepona & Thalasso Spa

Urb. Arena Beach, Ctra. Estepona-Cádiz 151, 29680 Estepona, Spain

Tel: +34 952 809 200
Web: www.johansens.com/elbaestepona

SPAIN / ANDALUCÍA (GRANADA)

El Ladrón de Agua

Carrera del Darro 13, 18010 Granada, Spain

Tel: +34 958 21 50 40
Web: www.johansens.com/ladrondeagua

SPAIN / ANDALUCÍA (GRANADA)

Hospes Palacio de los Patos

C/ Solarillo de Gracia 1, 18002 Granada, Andalucía, Spain

Tel: +34 958 535 790
Web: www.johansens.com/lospatos

SPAIN / ANDALUCÍA (GRANADA)

Hotel Casa Morisca

Cuesta de la Victoria 9, 18010 Granada, Spain

Tel: +34 958 221 100
Web: www.johansens.com/morisca

SPAIN / ANDALUCÍA (GRANADA)

Hotel Palacio de Santa Inés

Cuesta de Santa Inés 9, 18010 Granada, Spain

Tel: +34 958 22 23 62
Web: www.johansens.com/sanaines

SPAIN / ANDALUCÍA (GRANADA)

Palacio de los Navas

Calle Navas 1, 18009 Granada, Spain

Tel: +34 958 21 57 60
Web: www.johansens.com/palaciodelosnavas

SPAIN / ANDALUCÍA (GRANADA)

Santa Isabel la Real

C/Santa Isabel La Real 19, 18010 Granada, Spain

Tel: +34 958 294 658
Web: www.johansens.com/santaisabel

SPAIN / ANDALUCÍA (GRANADA - LOJA)

Barceló la Bobadilla

Finca La Bobadilla, Ctra. Salinas - Villanueva de Tapias, Km 65.5, 18300 Loja, Granada, Spain

Tel: +34 958 32 18 61
Web: www.johansens.com/bobadilla

SPAIN / ANDALUCÍA (JEREZ DE LA FRONTERA)

Casa Viña de Alcantara

Ctra. de Arcos Km 7.8, Jerez (Cádiz), Spain

Tel: +34 956 393 010
Web: www.johansens.com/vinadealcantara

SPAIN / ANDALUCÍA (LA JOYA - ANTEQUERA)

Hotel La Fuente del Sol

Paraje Rosas Bajas, 29260 La Joya, Antequera, Spain

Tel: +34 951 700 770
Web: www.johansens.com/fuentedelsol

SPAIN / ANDALUCÍA (MARBELLA)

Hotel Incosol

Urb. Golf Río Real, 29600 Marbella, Spain

Tel: +34 952 860909
Web: www.johansens.com/incosolhotel

Hotels - Europe & The Mediterranean

Properties listed below can be found in our Recommended Hotels & Spas - Europe & The Mediterranean 2009 Guide.
More information on our portfolio of guides can be found on page 463.

SPAIN / ANDALUCÍA (MONTORO)

Hacienda La Colorá

Ctra. Adamuz-Montoro Km 9, 14600 Montoro (Cordoba), Spain

Tel: +34 957 336077
Web: www.johansens.com/lacolora

SPAIN / ANDALUCÍA (MOTRIL - GRANADA)

Casa de los Bates

Carretera Nacional 340 Málaga - Almeria, Km 329, 5 Salobreña - Motril, Provincia de Granada, Spain

Tel: +34 958 349 495
Web: www.johansens.com/casadelosbates

SPAIN / ANDALUCÍA (RINCÓN DE LA VICTORIA - MÁLAGA)

El Molino de Santillán

Ctra. de Macharaviaya, Km 3, 29730 Rincón de la Victoria, Málaga, Spain

Tel: +34 952 40 09 49
Web: www.johansens.com/molinodesantillan

SPAIN / ANDALUCÍA (SANLÚCAR DE BARRAMEDA - CÁDIZ)

Posada de Palacio

C/ Caballeros, 11, 11540 Sanlúcar de Barrameda (Cádiz), Spain

Tel: +34 956 36 4840
Web: www.johansens.com/posadadepalacio

SPAIN / ANDALUCÍA (SANLÚCAR LA MAYOR - SEVILLA)

Hacienda Benazuza el Bulli Hotel

C/Virgen de las Nieves S/N, 41800 Sanlúcar La Mayor, Seville, Spain

Tel: +34 955 70 33 44
Web: www.johansens.com/haciendabenazuza

SPAIN / ANDALUCÍA (SEVILLA)

Casa No 7

Calle Virgenes No 7, 41004 Sevilla, Spain

Tel: +34 954 221 581
Web: www.johansens.com/casanumero7

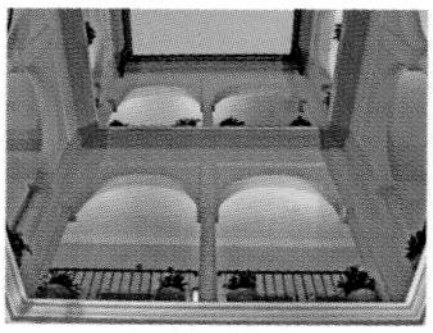

SPAIN / ANDALUCÍA (SEVILLA)

Casa Romana Hotel Boutique

Calle Trajano 15, 41002 Sevilla, Spain

Tel: +34 954 915 170
Web: www.johansens.com/casaromana

SPAIN / ANDALUCÍA (SEVILLA)

Hospes las Casas del Rey de Baeza

C/Santiago, Plaza Jesús de la Redención 2, 41003 Sevilla, Spain

Tel: +34 954 561 496
Web: www.johansens.com/reydebaeza

SPAIN / ANDALUCÍA (VEJER DE LA FRONTERA)

V...

Calle Rosario 11-13, Vejer de la Frontera, 11150 Cádiz, Spain

Tel: +34 956 451 757
Web: www.johansens.com/hotelvvejer

SPAIN / ASTURIAS (CANGAS DE ONÍS)

Hotel La Cepada

Avenida Contranquil s/n, 33550 Cangas de Onís, Spain

Tel: +34 985 84 94 45
Web: www.johansens.com/cepada

SPAIN / ASTURIAS (VILLAMAYOR)

Palacio de Cutre

La Goleta S/N, Villamayor, 33583 Infiesto, Asturias, Spain

Tel: +34 985 70 80 72
Web: www.johansens.com/palaciodecutre

SPAIN / BALEARIC ISLANDS (IBIZA)

Atzaró Agroturismo

Ctra. San Juan, Km 15, 07840 Santa Eulalia, Ibiza, Balearic Islands

Tel: +34 971 33 88 38
Web: www.johansens.com/atzaroagroturismo

SPAIN / BALEARIC ISLANDS (IBIZA)

Can Lluc

Crta. Santa Inés, km 2, 07816 San Rafael, Ibiza, Balearic Islands

Tel: +34 971 198 673
Web: www.johansens.com/canlluc

SPAIN / BALEARIC ISLANDS (IBIZA)

Cas Gasi

Camino Viejo de Sant Mateu s/n, PO Box 117, 07814 Santa Gertrudis, Ibiza, Balearic Islands

Tel: +34 971 197 700
Web: www.johansens.com/casgasi

SPAIN / BALEARIC ISLANDS (IBIZA)

Hotel Mirador de Dalt Vila

Plaza de España, 4, Dalt Vila, 07800 Ibiza, Balearic Islands, Spain

Tel: +34 971 30 30 45
Web: www.johansens.com/hotelmiradoribiza

SPAIN / BALEARIC ISLANDS (MALLORCA)

Blau Porto Petro Beach Resort & Spa

Avenida des Far 12, 07691 Porto Petro (Santanyi), Mallorca, Balearic Islands

Tel: +34 971 648 282
Web: www.johansens.com/portopetro

Hotels - Europe & The Mediterranean

Properties listed below can be found in our Recommended Hotels & Spas - Europe & The Mediterranean 2009 Guide.
More information on our portfolio of guides can be found on page 463.

SPAIN / BALEARIC ISLANDS (MALLORCA)

Hospes Maricel

Carretera d'Andratx 11, 07181 Cas Català, (Calvià)
Mallorca, Balearic Islands

Tel: +34 971 707 744
Web: www.johansens.com/maricel

SPAIN / BALEARIC ISLANDS (MALLORCA)

Hotel Aimia

Santa Maria del Camí, 1 07108 Port de Sóller,
Mallorca, Balearic Islands

Tel: +34 971 631 200
Web: www.johansens.com/aimia

SPAIN / BALEARIC ISLANDS (MALLORCA)

Hotel Cala Sant Vicenç

c/Maressers 2, Cala Sant Vicenç, 07469 Pollença,
Mallorca, Balearic Islands

Tel: +34 971 53 02 50
Web: www.johansens.com/hotelcala

SPAIN / BALEARIC ISLANDS (MALLORCA)

Hotel La Moraleja

Urbanización Los Encinares s/n, 07469 Cala San
Vicenç, Mallorca, Balearic Islands

Tel: +34 971 534 010
Web: www.johansens.com/lamoraleja

SPAIN / BALEARIC ISLANDS (MALLORCA)

Hotel Tres

C/ Apuntadores 3, 07012 Palma de Mallorca,
Balearic Islands

Tel: +34 971 717 333
Web: www.johansens.com/hoteltres

SPAIN / BALEARIC ISLANDS (MALLORCA)

Palacio Ca Sa Galesa

Carrer de Miramar 8, 07001 Palma de Mallorca,
Balearic Islands

Tel: +34 971 715 400
Web: www.johansens.com/casagalesa

SPAIN / BALEARIC ISLANDS (MALLORCA)

Read's Hotel & Vespasian Spa

Carretera Vieja de Alaro S/n, Santa María 07320,
Mallorca, Balearic Islands

Tel: +34 971 14 02 61
Web: www.johansens.com/reads

SPAIN / BALEARIC ISLANDS (MALLORCA)

Son Brull Hotel & Spa

Ctra. Palma - Pollença, MA 2200 - Km 49.8, 07460
Pollença, Mallorca, Balearic Islands

Tel: +34 971 53 53 53
Web: www.johansens.com/sonbrull

SPAIN / BALEARIC ISLANDS (MALLORCA)

Valldemossa Hotel & Restaurant

Ctra. Vieja de Valldemossa s/n, 07170
Valldemossa, Mallorca, Balearic Islands

Tel: +34 971 61 26 26
Web: www.johansens.com/valldemossa

SPAIN / BALEARIC ISLANDS (MENORCA)

Son Granot

Ctra. de Sant Felip s/n, 07720 Es Castell, Menorca,
Balearic Islands

Tel: +34 971 355 555
Web: www.johansens.com/songranot

SPAIN / CANARY ISLANDS (LANZAROTE)

Gran Melía Salinas

Avda. Islas Canarias s/n, Playa De Las Cucharas,
35509 Costa Teguise, Lanzarote, Canary Islands

Tel: +34 928 59 00 40
Web: www.johansens.com/salinas

SPAIN / CANARY ISLANDS (LANZAROTE)

Princesa Yaiza Suite Hotel Resort

Avenida Papagayo 6, 35580 Playa Blanca, Yaiza,
Lanzarote, Canary Islands

Tel: +34 928 519 222
Web: www.johansens.com/yaiza

SPAIN / CANARY ISLANDS (TENERIFE)

Abama

Carretera General TF-47, Km 9, 38687 Guía de
Isora, Tenerife, Canary Islands

Tel: +34 902 105 600
Web: www.johansens.com/abama

SPAIN / CANTABRIA (BARCENILLA)

Posada Los Nogales

Barrio la Partilla 7, Piélagos, 39477 Barcenilla,
Spain

Tel: +34 942 589 222
Web: www.johansens.com/losnogales

SPAIN / CANTABRIA (CAMALEÑO)

La Casona de Cosgaya

Barrio Areños, 39582 Cosgaya, Cantabria, Spain

Tel: +34 942 733 077
Web: www.johansens.com/casonadecosgaya

SPAIN / CASTILLA Y LEÓN (AMPUDIA - PALENCIA)

Posada de la Casa del Abad de Ampudia

Plaza Francisco Martín Gromaz, No 2, 34191
Ampudia (Palencia), Spain

Tel: +34 979 768 008
Web: www.johansens.com/abaddeampudia

Hotels - Europe & The Mediterranean

Properties listed below can be found in our Recommended Hotels & Spas - Europe & The Mediterranean 2009 Guide.
More information on our portfolio of guides can be found on page 463.

SPAIN / CASTILLA Y LEÓN (SALAMANCA)

Hotel Rector

c/Rector Esperabé 10-Apartado 399, 37008 Salamanca, Spain

Tel: +34 923 21 84 82
Web: www.johansens.com/rector

SPAIN / CASTILLA~LA MANCHA (BELVÍS DE LA JARA - TALAVERA DE LA REINA)

Finca Canturias

Ctra. Alcaudete - Calera, Km 12, 45660 Belvís de la Jara, Toledo, Spain

Tel: +34 925 59 41 08
Web: www.johansens.com/canturias

SPAIN / CASTILLA~LA MANCHA (CIUDAD REAL)

Hotel Palacio de la Serna

Calle Cervantes No 18, Ballesteros de Calatrava, 13432 Ciudad Real, Castilla~La Mancha, Spain

Tel: +34 926 84 2208/2413
Web: www.johansens.com/palaciodelaserna

SPAIN / CASTILLA~LA MANCHA (OROPESA)

Valdepalacios Hotel

Ctra de Oropesa a Puente del Arzobispo, Km 9, 45572 Torrico, Oropesa - Toledo Province, Spain

Tel: +34 925 457 534
Web: www.johansens.com/valdepalacios

SPAIN / CATALUÑA (BARCELONA)

Abac Barcelona

Avenida Tibidabo 1, 08022 Barcelona, Spain

Tel: +34 93 319 6600
Web: www.johansens.com/abacbarcelona

SPAIN / CATALUÑA (BARCELONA)

Hotel Barcelona Catedral

C/ Dels Capellans, 4, 08002 Barcelona, Spain

Tel: +34 93 304 22 55
Web: www.johansens.com/barcelonacatedral

SPAIN / CATALUÑA (BARCELONA)

Hotel Casa Fuster

Passeig de Gràcia 132, 08008 Barcelona, Spain

Tel: +34 93 255 30 00
Web: www.johansens.com/fuster

SPAIN / CATALUÑA (BARCELONA)

Hotel Claris

Pau Claris 150, 08009 Barcelona, Spain

Tel: +34 93 487 62 62
Web: www.johansens.com/claris

SPAIN / CATALUÑA (BARCELONA)

Hotel Cram

C/ Aribau 54, 8011 Barcelona, Spain

Tel: +34 93 216 77 00
Web: www.johansens.com/hotelcram

SPAIN / CATALUÑA (BARCELONA)

Hotel Duquesa de Cardona

Paseo Colon 12, 08002 Barcelona, Spain

Tel: +34 93 268 90 90
Web: www.johansens.com/duquesadecardona

SPAIN / CATALUÑA (BARCELONA)

Hotel Gran Derby

Calle Loreto 28, 08029 Barcelona, Spain

Tel: +34 93 445 2544
Web: www.johansens.com/granderby

SPAIN / CATALUÑA (BARCELONA)

Hotel Granados 83

C/ Enric Granados 83, 08008 Barcelona, Spain

Tel: +34 93 492 96 70
Web: www.johansens.com/granados83

SPAIN / CATALUÑA (BARCELONA)

Hotel Omm

Rosselló 265, 08008 Barcelona, Spain

Tel: +34 93 445 40 00
Web: www.johansens.com/hotelomm

SPAIN / CATALUÑA (COSTA BRAVA)

Hotel Rigat Park & Spa Beach Hotel

Av. America 1, Playa de Fenals, 17310 Lloret de Mar, Costa Brava, Gerona, Spain

Tel: +34 972 36 52 00
Web: www.johansens.com/rigat

SPAIN / CATALUÑA (COSTA BRAVA)

Hotel Santa Marta

Playa de Santa Cristina, 17310 Lloret de Mar, Costa Brava, Spain

Tel: +34 972 364 904
Web: www.johansens.com/santamarta

SPAIN / CATALUÑA (LA SELVA DEL CAMP)

Mas Passamaner

Camí de la Serra 52, 43470 La Selva del Camp (Tarragona), Spain

Tel: +34 977 766 333
Web: www.johansens.com/passamaner

Hotels - Europe & The Mediterranean

Properties listed below can be found in our Recommended Hotels & Spas - Europe & The Mediterranean 2009 Guide.
More information on our portfolio of guides can be found on page 463.

SPAIN / CATALUÑA (MASQUEFA)

Can Bonastre Wine Resort

Ctra. B224 km 13, 2 08783 - Masquefa, near Barcelona, Spain

Tel: +34 93 772 87 67
Web: www.johansens.com/canbonastre

SPAIN / CATALUÑA (PUIGCERDÀ)

Hospes Villa Paulita

Av. Pons i Gash, 15, 17520 Puigcerdà (Gerona), Spain

Tel: +34 972 884 662
Web: www.johansens.com/villapaulita

SPAIN / CATALUÑA (ROSES)

Romantic Villa - Hotel Vistabella

Cala Canyelles Petites, PO Box 3, 17480 Roses (Gerona), Spain

Tel: +34 972 25 62 00
Web: www.johansens.com/vistabella

SPAIN / CATALUÑA (SITGES)

Dolce Sitges Hotel

Av. Cami de Miralpeix 12, Sitges 08870, Spain

Tel: +34 938 109 000
Web: www.johansens.com/dolcesitges

SPAIN / CATALUÑA (SITGES)

San Sebastian Playa Hotel

Calle Port Alegre 53, 08870 Sitges (Barcelona), Spain

Tel: +34 93 894 86 76
Web: www.johansens.com/sebastian

SPAIN / EXTREMADURA (ZAFRA)

Casa Palacio Conde de la Corte

Plaza Pilar Redondo 2, 06300 Zafra (Badajoz), Spain

Tel: +34 924 563 311
Web: www.johansens.com/condedelacorte

SPAIN / GALICIA (SANXENXO)

Augusta Spa Resort

Lugar de Padriñan 25 s/n, 36960 Sanxenxo, Galicia, Spain

Tel: +34 986 72 78 78
Web: www.johansens.com/augustasparesort

SPAIN / MADRID (MADRID)

AC Hotel Santo Mauro

C/Zurbano 36, 28010 Madrid, Spain

Tel: +34 91 319 69 00
Web: www.johansens.com/santomauro

SPAIN / MADRID (MADRID)

Gran Meliá Fénix

Hermosilla 2, 28001 Madrid, Spain

Tel: +34 91 431 67 00
Web: www.johansens.com/granmeliafenix

SPAIN / MADRID (MADRID)

Hospes Madrid

Plaza de la Independencia, 3, 28001 Madrid, Spain

Tel: +34 914 322 911
Web: www.johansens.com/hospesmadrid

SPAIN / MADRID (MADRID)

Hotel Orfila

C/Orfila, No 6, 28010 Madrid, Spain

Tel: +34 91 702 77 70
Web: www.johansens.com/orfila

SPAIN / MADRID (MADRID)

Hotel Urban

Carrera de San Jerónimo 34, 28014 Madrid, Spain

Tel: +34 91 787 77 70
Web: www.johansens.com/urban

SPAIN / MADRID (MADRID)

Hotel Villa Real

Plaza de las Cortes 10, 28014 Madrid, Spain

Tel: +34 914 20 37 67
Web: www.johansens.com/villareal

SPAIN / MADRID (MADRID - BOADILLA DEL MONTE)

Antiguo Convento

C/ de Las Monjas, s/n Boadilla del Monte, 28660 Madrid, Spain

Tel: +34 91 632 22 20
Web: www.johansens.com/elconvento

SPAIN / PAÍS VASCO (HONDARRIBIA)

Hotel Pampinot

Nagusi Kalea 5, 20280 Hondarribia - Fuenterrabía, Guipúzcoa, Spain

Tel: +34 943 640 600
Web: www.johansens.com/hotelpampinot

SPAIN / PAÍS VASCO (ZEANURI)

Hotel Etxegana

Ipiñaburu 38, Zeanuri, 48144 Bizkaia, Spain

Tel: +34 946 338 448
Web: www.johansens.com/etxegana

Hotels - Europe & The Mediterranean

Properties listed below can be found in our Recommended Hotels & Spas - Europe & The Mediterranean 2009 Guide.
More information on our portfolio of guides can be found on page 463.

SPAIN / VALENCIA (ALICANTE)

Hospes Amérigo

C/ Rafael Altamira 7, 03002 Alicante, Spain

Tel: +34 965 14 65 70
Web: www.johansens.com/amerigo

SPAIN / VALENCIA (ALICANTE)

Hotel Sidi San Juan & Spa

C/ La Doblada, 8 - Playa de San Juan, 03540 Alicante, Spain

Tel: +34 96 516 13 00
Web: www.johansens.com/sanjuan

SPAIN / VALENCIA (ALICANTE - BENISSA)

La Madrugada

Partida Benimarraig, 61 b, 03720 Benissa, Spain

Tel: +34 965 733 156
Web: www.johansens.com/lamadrugada

SPAIN / VALENCIA (BENICÀSSIM)

Hotel Termas Marinas el Palasiet

Partida Cantallops s/n, 12560 Benicàssim, Castellón, Costa del Azahar, Spain

Tel: +34 964 300 250
Web: www.johansens.com/termasmarinas

SPAIN / VALENCIA (BOCAIRENT)

Hotel Ferrero

Ctra. Ontinyent-Villena, Km 16 46880, Bocairent, Valencia, Spain

Tel: +34 962 35 51 75
Web: www.johansens.com/hotelferrero

SPAIN / VALENCIA (CALPE - ALICANTE)

Villa Marisol

Urb. Marisol Park 1-A, 03710 Calpe, Alicante, Spain

Tel: +34 96 587 57 00
Web: www.johansens.com/marisol

SPAIN / VALENCIA (JÁTIVA - XÀTIVA)

Hotel Mont Sant

Subida Al Castillo, s/n Játiva - Xàtiva, 46800 Valencia, Spain

Tel: +34 962 27 50 81
Web: www.johansens.com/montsant

SPAIN / VALENCIA (VALENCIA)

Hospes Palau de la Mar

Navarro Reverter 14, 46004 Valencia, Spain

Tel: +34 96 316 2884
Web: www.johansens.com/palaudelamar

SPAIN / VALENCIA (VALENCIA)

Hotel Neptuno

Paseo de Neptuno, 2, Playa de Las Arenas, 46011 Valencia, Spain

Tel: +34 963 567 777
Web: www.johansens.com/neptuno

SPAIN / VALENCIA (VALENCIA)

Hotel Sidi Saler & Spa

C/ Gola del Puchol, s/n - Playa El Saler, 46012 Valencia, Spain

Tel: +34 961 61 04 11
Web: www.johansens.com/saler

SPAIN / VALENCIA (VILAMARXANT)

Mas de Canicattí

Ctra. de Pedralba, Km 2.9, 46191 Vilamarxant, Valencia, Spain

Tel: +34 96 165 05 34
Web: www.johansens.com/canicatti

SWITZERLAND (WEGGIS)

Park Hotel Weggis

Hertensteinstrasse 34, 6353 Weggis, Switzerland

Tel: +41 41 392 05 05
Web: www.johansens.com/weggis

SWITZERLAND (WENGEN)

Hotel Caprice

3823 Wengen, Switzerland

Tel: +41 33 856 06 06
Web: www.johansens.com/caprice

TURKEY (ANTALYA)

The Marmara Antalya

Eski Lara Yolu No 136, Sirinyali, Antalya, Turkey

Tel: +90 242 249 36 00
Web: www.johansens.com/marmaraantalya

TURKEY (ANTALYA)

Tuvana Residence

Tuzcular Mahallesi, Karanlik Sokak 7, 07100 Kaleiçi - Antalya, Turkey

Tel: +90 242 247 60 15
Web: www.johansens.com/tuvanaresidence

TURKEY (ANTALYA - KEMER)

Sungate Port Royal Deluxe Resort Hotel

Ciftecesmeler Mevkii 1, 1 Beldibi - Kemer, Antalya, Turkey

Tel: +90 242 824 00 00
Web: www.johansens.com/sungateport

Hotels - Europe & The Mediterranean

Properties listed below can be found in our Recommended Hotels & Spas - Europe & The Mediterranean 2009 Guide. More information on our portfolio of guides can be found on page 463.

TURKEY (BODRUM)

Ada Hotel

Bagarasi Mahallesi, PK 350, Göl - Türkbükü, Bodrum, Turkey

Tel: +90 252 377 59 15
Web: www.johansens.com/adahotel

TURKEY (BODRUM)

Divan Bodrum Palmira

Kelesharim Caddesi 6, Göltürkbükü, Mugla, 48483 Bodrum, Turkey

Tel: +90 252 377 5601
Web: www.johansens.com/divanpalmira

TURKEY (BODRUM)

Kempinski Hotel Barbaros Bay

Kizilagaç Köyu, Gerenkuyu Mevkii, Yaligiftlik, 48400 Bodrum, Turkey

Tel: +90 252 311 0303/11
Web: www.johansens.com/barbaros

TURKEY (BODRUM)

The Marmara Bodrum

Suluhasan Caddesi, Yokusbasi, Mahallesi No 18, PO Box 199, 48400 Bodrum, Turkey

Tel: +90 252 313 8130
Web: www.johansens.com/marmarabodrum

TURKEY (FETHIYE - ÖLÜDENIZ)

Oyster Residence

Belcekız Mevkii, 1.Sokak Ölüdeniz, Fethiye, Turkey

Tel: +90 252 617 0765
Web: www.johansens.com/oyster

TURKEY (ISTANBUL)

A'jia Hotel

Ahmet Rasim Pasa Yalisi, Çubuklu Caddesi, No 27, Kanlica, Istanbul, Turkey

Tel: +90 216 413 9300
Web: www.johansens.com/ajiahotel

TURKEY (ISTANBUL)

Bosphorus Palace Hotel

Yaliboyu Caddesi No 64, Beylerbeyi, 80210 Istanbul, Turkey

Tel: +90 216 422 00 03
Web: www.johansens.com/bosphoruspalace

TURKEY (ISTANBUL)

The Marmara Istanbul

Taksim Meydani, Taksim, 34437 Istanbul, Turkey

Tel: +90 212 251 4696
Web: www.johansens.com/maramaraistanbul

TURKEY (ISTANBUL)

The Marmara Pera

Mesrutiyet Caddesi, Tepebasi, 34430 Istanbul, Turkey

Tel: +90 212 251 4646
Web: www.johansens.com/marmarapera

TURKEY (ISTANBUL)

Sirkeci Konak

Taya Hatun Sokak, No 5, 34120 Sirkeci - Istanbul, Turkey

Tel: +90 212 528 4344
Web: www.johansens.com/sirkecikonak

TURKEY (ISTANBUL)

Sumahan On The Water

Kulelí Caddesi No 51, Çengelköy, 34684 Istanbul, Turkey

Tel: +90 216 422 8000
Web: www.johansens.com/sumahan

TURKEY (KALKAN)

Villa Mahal

PO Box 4 Kalkan, 07960 Antalya, Turkey

Tel: +90 242 844 32 68
Web: www.johansens.com/villamahal

TURKEY (MARMARIS)

Golden Key Bördübet

Bördübet Mevkii, Marmaris, Mugla, Turkey

Tel: +90 252 436 92 30
Web: www.johansens.com/goldenkey

TURKEY (SAPANCA - SAKARYA)

Richmond Nua Wellness - Spa

Sahilyolu, 54600 Sapanca, Sakarya, Turkey

Tel: +90 264 582 2100
Web: www.johansens.com/richmondnua

TURKEY (UCHISAR-CAPPADOCIA)

Cappadocia Cave Resorts & Spa

Tekelli Mahallesi, Göreme Caddesi 83, 50240 Uchisar-Cappadocia, Nevsehir, Turkey

Tel: +90 384 219 3194
Web: www.johansens.com/ccrhotels

TURKEY (ÜRGÜP)

Sacred House

Dutlu Cami Mahallesi, Barbaros Hayrettin Sokak, No 25, 50400 Ürgüp - Cappadocia, Turkey

Tel: +90 384 341 7102
Web: www.johansens.com/sacredhouse

Index by Property

0-9

A

B

C

D

E

Index by Property

Index by Property

K

L

M

N

O

P

Q

Index by Property

R

S

T

V

W

Y

Index by Location

Canada

Mexico

U.S.A.

Index by Location

Index by Location

Central America

South America

Index by Location

Atlantic

Caribbean

Pacific